ROMANCING
THE
SHADOW

ROMANCING THE SHADOW

ILLUMINATING THE DARK SIDE OF THE SOUL

CONNIE ZWEIG, PH.D.,
AND STEVE WOLF, PH.D.

BALLANTINE BOOKS
NEW YORK

Grateful acknowledgment is made to the following to reprint previously
published material:

Coleman Barks and Maypop: "The Guest House" by Jelaluddin Rumi from *Say I
Am You,* translated by John Moyne and Coleman Barks, published 1994 by
Maypop. Reprinted by permission of Coleman Barks and Maypop.

Doubleday and Faber and Faber Ltd: Excerpt from "In a Dark Time" from *The
Collected Poems of Theodore Roethke* by Theodore Roethke. Copyright © 1960 by
Beatrice Roethke, Administratrix of the Estate of Theodore Roethke. Reprinted
by permission of Doubleday, a division of Bantam Doubleday Dell Publishing
Group, Inc. and Faber and Faber Ltd.

HarperCollins Publishers, Inc.: Excerpt from "Sometimes a Man Stands Up . . ."
from *Selected Poems of Rainer Maria Rilke,* edited and translated by Robert Bly.
Copyright © 1981 by Robert Bly. "A Man and a Woman Sit Near Each Other"
from *Selected Poems* by Robert Bly. Copyright © 1986 by Robert Bly. Reprinted by
permission of HarperCollins Publishers, Inc.

Hardie St. Martin: "Throw Yourself Like Seed" by Miguel de Unamuno from *Roots
and Wings* by Miguel de Unamuno, translated by Robert Bly. Reprinted by permission of Hardie St. Martin.

Threshold Books: "The Minute I Heard" by Jelaluddin Rumi from *Essential Rumi,*
translated by Coleman Barks, originally published by and reprinted by permission
of Threshold Books, 139 Main Street, Brattleboro, VT 05301.

Viking Penguin and Laurence Pollinger Limited: "Healing" by D. H. Lawrence from
The Complete Poems of D. H. Lawrence by D. H. Lawrence, edited by V. de Sola
Pinto and F. W. Roberts. Copyright © 1964, 1971 by Angelo Ravagli and
C. M. Weekley, Executors of the Estate of Frieda Lawrence Ravagli. Reprinted by
permission of Viking Penguin, a division of Penguin Books USA Inc. and Lau-
rence Pollinger Limited for the Estate of Frieda Lawrence Ravagli.

http://www.randomhouse.com

Library of Congress Cataloging-in-Publication Data
Zweig, Connie.
Romancing the shadow : illuminating the dark side of the soul / Connie Zweig,
Steve Wolf.—1st ed.
p.   cm.
Includes bibliographical references and index.
ISBN 0-345-41739-9 (alk. paper)
1. Shadow (Psychoanalysis)   2. Good and evil—Psychological aspects.
3. Jungian psychology.   4. Psychoanalysis.   I. Wolf, Steve, 1945–   .   II. Title.
BF175.5.S55Z84   1997
155.2'64—dc21   97-19716

Text design by Holly Johnson

Manufactured in the United States of America

First Edition: September 1997

10   9   8   7   6   5   4   3   2   1

Contents

ACKNOWLEDGMENTS   ix

INTRODUCTION TO SHADOW-WORK   3

OUR STORIES   24
Connie's story: a tale of shadow-work   24
Steve's story: a tale of shadow-work   30

CHAPTER 1. ME AND MY SHADOW   36
Meeting the shadow: abusers, abandoners, addicts, critics,
    thieves   39
Romancing the shadow: King Arthur and the Knights of
    the Round Table   43
Tracing the roots of the shadow in personal psychology   45
Defending ourselves with shields: power, sex, money,
    addiction   48
Tracing the roots of the shadow in culture   52
The shadow as redeemer: finding gold in the dark side   55

CHAPTER 2. THE FAMILY SHADOW:
CRADLE OF THE BEST AND THE WORST   57
The missing ingredient: family soul   61
Sins of our fathers and mothers: shame, envy,
    depression, anxiety, addiction, and self-hate   63
Family secrets: the sacrifice of authenticity   69
Shadow sisters/shadow brothers   72

Sexual shadows: incest and initiation 75
Money shadows: inheritance, self-worth, and greediness 82
Leaving the family home: cultivating individual and
    family soul 86

Chapter 3. A Parent's Betrayal as Initiation into Shadow 88
The father's son: reclaiming feminine shadow 93
The mother's son (the *puer*): reclaiming masculine shadow 96
The mother's daughter: reclaiming masculine shadow 100
The father's daughter: reclaiming feminine shadow 102
Reclaiming masculine and feminine soul 107

Chapter 4. Looking for the Beloved:
Dating as Shadow-Work 110
Shame and the single person 113
Single women and the shadow 116
Single men and the shadow 119
An archetypal perspective on dating 121
Dating: the shadow's search for shelter 124
A story of dating as shadow-work 126
Sex, money, and power shadows 131
Sexual shadows: erotic intoxication and risky behavior 132
Money shadows: success objects and successful fathers 135
Power shadows: victims and victimizers 137
Introducing crises of commitment 139
Crisis of commitment: when to have sex 141

Chapter 5. Shadow-Boxing:
Wrestling with Romantic Partners 144
Meeting the Other: projections hit their targets 146
Compensating the Other: two parts make a whole 149
Partners as parents: the psychology of love 154
Partners as gods: the archetypes of love 159
The breakdown of projections:
    meeting the witch and the tyrant 164
Power shadows: shaming, deprivation, and entitlement 166
Sexual shadows: demanding and withholding intimacy 168
An archetypal perspective on romance 172
When relationships end: the shadow's moving target 173

Redefining successful relationship: From shadow-boxing
 to shadow-dancing 175

CHAPTER 6. SHADOW-DANCING TILL DEATH DO US PART 177
 The Third Body: the soul of the relationship 181
 Meeting the Beloved: taking projections home 184
 French and Turkish: the art of conscious communication 187
 Crisis of commitment: moving in, becoming engaged 191
 The ex-spouse complex 196
 Crisis of commitment: the shadow marriage 198
 Power shadows: anger and depression,
  withholding and witchiness 200
 Sexual shadows: compulsions, affairs, and demon lovers 203
 Money shadows: from dating to commitment 210
 Crisis of commitment: having a child 212
 Relationship as a vehicle for soul work 214

CHAPTER 7. SHADOWS AMONG FRIENDS:
ENVY, ANGER, AND BETRAYAL 215
 The loss of the loyal friend 217
 Soul friends/shadow friends 221
 Meeting the Other: friends as parents, friends as gods 225
 An archetypal perspective on friendship 231
 Women and men as friends: dangers and delights 233
 Sexual shadows: triangles and loyalty wars 235
 Power shadows: superiority and inferiority 237
 Money shadows: shame, class, and the myth of equality 240
 Racism and addiction between friends 242
 Redefining successful friendship: a vehicle for soul work 245

CHAPTER 8. THE SHADOW AT WORK:
THE SEARCH FOR SOUL ON THE JOB 247
 The loss of soulful work: the myth of Sisyphus 250
 The promises of shadow-work: nurturing soul on the job 252
 A portrait of the new employee: a Sufi tale 255
 Meeting the shadow of workaholism:
  overcoming the inner tyrant 258
 Meeting the Other in a company hierarchy:
  healing family patterns 261

Contents

Meeting the Other in a collaboration:
 taking projections home   266
An archetypal perspective on work   268
Power shadows: denying power, abusing power   271
Sexual shadows: corporate harassment and sex in therapy   275
Money shadows: the mistaken grail   277
Redefining successful work as soulful work   279

CHAPTER 9. MIDLIFE AS DESCENT TO THE UNDERWORLD AND
ASCENT OF THE LOST GODS   280
Meeting the shadow at midlife: the promise of renewal   282
Midlife as the emergence of new priorities: Steve's story   286
Midlife as descent to the underworld: Connie's story   289
The call of the Self: Inanna's story   292
The changing of the gods: reimagining midlife depression   295
Bodily symptoms as shadow speaking   296
Reclaiming the unlived life: the resurrection of lost gods   298

EPILOGUE   305

A SHADOW-WORK HANDBOOK   308

WHO'S WHO IN GREEK MYTH: FROM APHRODITE TO ZEUS   317

NOTES   321

BIBLIOGRAPHY   333

INDEX   341

Acknowledgments

This book is the fruit of a deep and abiding friendship. Our first meeting sixteen years ago was a meeting of souls. We recognized a kinship with one another and have been close friends ever since. We share both a keen interest in psychological development, especially in Jungian-oriented psychology, and a dedication to spiritual work. As a practicing psychologist, Steve has worked to integrate the Eastern vision of spirituality and mysticism into Western psychological models. The unique clinical approach in this book, an extension of Jung's original work on the shadow, is the result of his efforts.

As a meditation teacher, Connie shared his passion for this larger vision. Her professional history as a writer and as an editor in the publishing industry, coupled with her doctorate in Jungian and archetypal psychology, led her to edit a best-selling collected volume, *Meeting the Shadow: The Hidden Power of the Dark Side in Human Nature*. As a practicing therapist, she collaborated on cases with Steve.

Eventually we began to discuss a book that would express Steve's approach, Connie's love of myth, case vignettes from both of our practices, and a deepening of the ideas in the earlier anthology: from meeting the shadow to romancing the shadow—that is, living in relation to it in everyday life.

We met often in restaurants and coffeehouses for long hours of ecstatic conversation, which felt like what the Sufis call *sobet*, a communion of souls. We discovered a profound affinity and, at times, we wrestled with our differences. Slowly, the work began to take shape. Many incidents of synchronicity left us laughing and sometimes awed. We found that, as we worked through certain ideas in a given chapter, they appeared in our lives, either in our primary relationships or in our dreams. Or a patient walked through the door with a story that illustrated the very issue we wished to explore. And we felt gratitude for the magic that appeared throughout the life of this project.

So, we wish to acknowledge one another, first of all, for the opportunity and for the love. We wish to honor each other's authority in shadow-work in both our practices and our own lives. To my soul sister, Connie Zweig, for the openness of her heart, the lucidity of her mind, and the generosity of her spirit. To my *frater mystico* (soul brother), Steve Wolf, whose authenticity and capacity to hear the voice of the Self has inspired me all these years.

Steve Wolf's acknowledgments:

To my wife and soul mate, Paula Perlman Wolf, for your playful spirit. Without your love, support, and depth of feeling, this work would not have been possible.

To my loving son, Jed, for the constant challenge to be true to my highest principles and for my best laugh of the day.

To Mimi, Leo, Janice, Jack, Jacqueline, and Jason for the foundation of family and for the joy of sharing my blessings.

To Rich Katims, soul friend, old friend, for shared mountaintop moments and your wise commentary on the manuscript.

To Howard Wallman, Dennis Hicks, and John Anderson, my trusted compadres on the path.

To Joel and Ann Isaacs and Bill Barnum for reading sections of the manuscript.

To my men's groups, present and past, for providing a space to hear the voice of spirit and the music of soul.

To Nathan Schwart-Salant, Gilda Frantz, and Allen Koehn for guiding me through the labyrinth.

To Oscar Ichazo and the Arica School for the gift of the spirit's ascent.

To my clients, for the honor to serve their evolution.

Connie Zweig's acknowledgments:

To Dr. Neil Schuitevoerder, loved and loving partner and best friend, for embracing Kali, even loving her, and living to tell the tale. I have time to play now, Sweetie.

To my mother, Tina, for the quest of consciousness; to my dad, Mike, for the social conscience; to my sister, Jane, for the ongoing struggle of sisterhood.

To the community of Pacifica Graduate Institute, whose doctoral program helped me to weave together the fabric of my life.

To my friends who read the manuscript: Tom Rautenberg, Marion Woodman, Aaron Kipnis, Marian Rose, Michael Ortiz Hill, Naomi Lowinsky, Pami Bluehawk Ozaki. Thank you for precious time, thoughtful comments, and ongoing soulful conversations.

To my mentors: Carl Jung, who should have received the Nobel Peace Prize for his work on the shadow. Suzanne Wagner and Pat Katsky, who, like Ariadne, held the thread while I descended. Deena Metzger and Marilyn Ferguson, for the craft.

To soul friends: Jeremy Tarcher, for full-time authenticity and business acumen with heart; Belinda Berman Real, for more than twenty-five years of sisterhood; Shoneen Santesson, Lisa Rafel, and Gary Pearle, for sharing the journey with a full heart.

To my clients, whose stories grace these pages: blessings on you.

To Linda Wiedlinger, librarian extraordinaire, Lore Zeller, a store-house of wisdom, and Bobbie Yow, for the elegant monograph, at the C. G. Jung Institute in Los Angeles.

First and last, to Athena, who lives in me as I live in her.

Our joint acknowledgments:

To Candice Fuhrman, literary agent supreme, who, like Hermes, appeared at the moment of need, shepherded the work from the world of imagination into the world of commerce, and became a trusted friend. To Linda Michaels, our international agent, whose enthusiasm and expertise brought the work to a global audience.

To Clare Ferraro, visionary publisher and shadow-worker, who supported the soulfulness of the work, and to Liz Williams, brilliant publicist and gal pal. Thanks also to Kim Hovey, Jennifer Richards, Cheong Kim, Alice Kesterson, and Jim Geraghty.

To Tom Grady, editor extraordinaire, who demonstrated great faith in this project from the start.

To Mark Waldman, Ruth Strassberg, and Kathleen O'Connell for clerical and permissions support.

And, of course, to the giggle group: Janet Bachelor, Bruce Lang-horn, Maureen Nathan, Linda Novack, Rhoda Pregerson, Malcolm Schultz, and Riley Smith. For laughs even in tough times, for ruthless honesty, and for the spirit of community.

ROMANCING THE
THE
SHADOW

Introduction to
Shadow-Work

*Perhaps all the dragons of our lives are princesses who are only waiting to
see us once beautiful and brave. Perhaps everything terrible is in its deepest
being something helpless that wants help from us.*
—Rainer Maria Rilke

In Oscar Wilde's only novel, *The Picture of Dorian Gray*, the central
character, Dorian, a beautiful, vain young man in nineteenth-
century England, sees a painting of himself that is startlingly handsome and without a blemish. Suddenly, he desires to remain youthful
and perfect forever, with no sign of aging or imperfection. To this end,
he makes a pact with the devil: All signs of his aging and degenera-
tion, even evidence of his greed and cruelty, would from then on appear on the painting rather than on his own face. And the painting
gets hidden away, never to be seen by anyone. But from time to time
the young man's curiosity gnaws at him. He cautiously pulls the picture out of the darkness and takes a quick glance, only to see the
youthful face growing more and more hideous.

Each of us is like Dorian Gray. We seek to present a beautiful, innocent face to the world; a kind, courteous demeanor; a youthful, intelligent image. And so, unknowingly but inevitably, we push away
those qualities that do not fit the image, that do not enhance our self-
esteem and make us stand proud but, instead, bring us shame and make
us feel small. We shove into the dark cavern of the unconscious those

feelings that make us uneasy—hatred, rage, jealousy, greed, competition, lust, shame—and those behaviors that are deemed wrong by the culture—addiction, laziness, aggression, dependency—thereby creating what could be called shadow content. Like Dorian's painting, these qualities ultimately take on a life of their own, forming an invisible twin that lives just behind our life, or just beside it, but as distinct from the one we know as a stranger.

This stranger, known in psychology as the shadow, is us, yet is not us. Hidden from our awareness, the shadow is not a part of our conscious self-image. So it seems to appear abruptly, out of nowhere, in a range of behaviors from off-color jokes to devastating abuses. When it emerges, it feels like an unwanted visitor, leaving us ashamed, even mortified. For instance, when a man who views himself as a responsible husband and provider is suddenly taken over by a dream of freedom and independence, his shadow is speaking. When a woman with a health-conscious lifestyle craves ice cream and feels compelled to binge in the dark of night, her shadow is acting out. When a normally kind mother belittles her child, her shadow is showing. When a pious priest sneaks off to find a prostitute in a back alley, his shadow is erupting.

In each of these instances, the individual's persona, the mask shown to the world, is split off from the shadow, the face hidden from the world. The deeper this rift and the more unconscious the shadow, the more we experience it as a stranger, an Other, an alien invader. Therefore, we cannot face it in ourselves or tolerate it in others. Whether this invasion takes the form of such self-destructive behaviors as addiction • eating disorders • depression • anxiety disorders • psychosomatic disorders • severe guilt or shame • or whether it takes the form of such destructive behaviors toward others as verbal abuse • physical abuse • sexual abuse • marital affairs • lying • envy • blaming • stealing • or betrayal, it brings pain and crisis in its wake. It introduces us to the Other, the one within who feels as if it cannot be tamed, who seems as if it cannot be controlled. It shakes us out of complacency, making us feel unacceptable, anxious, irritable, disgusted, outraged at ourselves.

A woman may shake her head and say to herself, "I can't believe that I had unprotected sex with that man. I wasn't myself last night."

Or a man may hang his head and say, "I was drunk. It was the wine that made me say those mean things. It will never happen again." But the meeting with the shadow has occurred. Meeting the shadow in ourselves is disquieting because it tears holes in our masks. It causes us to act irrationally and feel ashamed, embarrassed, unacceptable, regretful—and to quickly deny responsibility for what we said or did.

THE CHALLENGE OF ROMANCING THE SHADOW

Denial is entrenched because the shadow does not want to come out of its hiding place. Its nature is to hide, to remain outside of awareness. So the shadow acts out indirectly, concealed in a sour mood or sarcastic remark. Or it sneaks out compulsively, camouflaged in an addictive behavior. Therefore, we need to learn how to catch a glimpse of it when it appears. We need to sharpen our senses to be awake enough when it erupts. Then we can learn to romance it, to coax it out, to seduce it into awareness. Like a coy lover, it will recede once more behind the curtain. And again, with patience, we can invite it out to dance. This slow process of bringing the shadow to consciousness, forgetting, and recognizing it again is the nature of shadow-work. Eventually, we can learn to create an ongoing conscious relationship to it, thereby reducing its power to unconsciously sabotage us.

Romancing the shadow is subversive: The culture teaches us to be extroverted, quick, ambitious, productive. Workaholism is lauded; contemplation is shunned. But shadow-work is slow, cautious; it moves like an animal in the night. It moves us against the collective mandate to think positively, be productive, focus outwardly, and protect our image.

The shadow is a demanding taskmaster: It requires endless patience, keen instinct, fine discrimination, the compassion of a Buddha. It requires one eye to be turned out toward the world of light, while the other eye is turned in toward the world of darkness.

To live with shadow awareness is to turn away from the peaks toward the valleys, away from the heights and the rarified air, toward the depths and the dark and the dense. It is to turn toward the unpleasant thoughts, hidden fantasies, marginal feelings that are so taboo. To live with shadow awareness is to move our eyes from up to down, to relinquish the clarity of blue-sky thinking for the uncertain murkiness of a foggy morning.

As psychotherapists, we have helped hundreds of clients catch a glimpse of their elusive shadows. Seeing it—meeting the shadow— is the important first step. Learning to live with it—romancing the shadow—is a lifelong challenge. But the rewards are profound: Shadow-work enables us to alter our self-sabotaging behavior so that we can achieve a more self-directed life. It expands our awareness to include a wider range of who we are so that we can attain more complete self-knowledge and eventually feel more genuine self-acceptance. It permits us to defuse the negative emotions that taint our loving relationships so that we can create a more authentic intimacy. And it opens the storehouse of creativity in which our talents remain hidden and out of reach. In each of these ways, shadow-work permits us to find gold in the dark side.

In this book we offer the fundamental skills of shadow-work that are needed to move from meeting the shadow to romancing the shadow as a way of life. Romancing the shadow means reading the messages encoded in the events of our daily lives in such a way that we gain consciousness, substance, soul. Romancing the shadow means meeting the shadow for a private rendezvous; eventually, it means taking it seriously enough to learn to embrace it in a long-term relationship.

Of course, some people find this shift distasteful, even abhorrent. Why not simply behave properly, they ask, shape our attitudes, cut and trim our feelings so that they fit moral, ethical, god-given outlines? Then white is white and black is black, and the struggle with grays can end.

The mind is dangerous, they say, like a tiger in a cage. Open the door and it will think cruel, inhuman thoughts. The body is wild, they say, like some unruly beast. Let it run loose and it will do terrible, perverted, aggressive things.

These people believe that we need more protection from the lures of the shadow—stricter morals, higher fences. They wish to bring back old fundamentalisms to shield us against forbidden feelings, ambiguous choices. They seek to widen the split between good and evil, between Jesus and his dark brother Satan, between the followers of Allah and the heathens, between the members of their religious cults and the rest of fallen humanity. Longing to remain on god's side, they refuse to engage the darkness in their own souls.

But this deep-seated denial of shadow, this pervasive resistance to looking in its eye is accompanied by a strange obsession with it. Just as we turn away from the gloomy facts of life, we also turn toward them again in curiosity, compelled in some strange way to try to understand the dark side of our nature. Millions of us read terrifying gothic novels with great appetite, regularly visiting domains of cruelty, lust, perversion, and crime. Or we sit for hours transfixed by films about cold, vengeful, bloody behavior that, in the outside world, would be deemed inhuman. The conventions of gothic horror even shape our daily newspaper reporting and broadcast news programs, which tell front-page tales of hero-villains who lead double lives. The shadow is both dangerous and familiar, repulsive and attractive, grotesque and alluring.

In truth, we can no longer afford these extreme attitudes toward the shadow: We cannot afford to look away from the beast in denial, pretending that a naive, trusting stance will protect us from it "out there." And we cannot afford to look too directly at the beast for too long, for we risk numbing our own souls. Instead, we need to cultivate an attitude of respect toward the shadow, to see it honestly without dismissing it or becoming overwhelmed by it.

In this way an encounter with the shadow might become an initiation, a call to remember the multifaceted complexity of human nature and the fertile depths of the human soul. We need to start by acknowledging the dark side—but we do not end there. Ideally, an encounter with the shadow might open debate about pressing social questions and even bring about change in social policy. For example, a wave of accusations of satanic cult abuse might lead to an inquiry into the growing fascination with demonic forces. Or a series of allegations of pedophilia among the clergy might result in a deeper examination of the role of celibacy in the lives of religious people. Or a rash of hate crimes based on racial prejudice might enhance efforts toward racial reconciliation.

This book suggests that for most people—that is, those without serious psychological problems—greater shadow awareness can lead to greater morality. In fact, Carl Jung, who coined the term "shadow," posed it as a moral problem. He suggested that we need a reorientation or fundamental change of attitude, a *metanoia*, to look it squarely in the eyes—that is, our own eyes:

> The individual who wishes to have an answer to the problem of evil has need, first and foremost, of self-knowledge, that is, the utmost possible knowledge of his own wholeness. He must know relentlessly how much good he can do, and what crimes he is capable of, and must beware of regarding the one as real and the other as illusion. Both are elements within his nature, and both are bound to come to light in him, should he wish— as he ought—to live without self-deception or self-delusion.

This idea—that to face the best and the worst in our own natures is to live an authentic life—is not new. Theologians and philosophers in many traditions have pointed to the hidden reality of our split nature, and its secret value. The great psychologist William James wrote: "There is no doubt that healthy-mindedness is inadequate as a philosophical doctrine, because the evil facts which it positively refuses to account for are a genuine portion of reality; and they may after all be the best key to life's significance, and possibly the only opener of our eyes to the deepest levels of truth." More recently, Russian writer Aleksandr Solzhenitsyn put it beautifully: "If only there were evil people somewhere insidiously committing evil deeds, and it were necessary only to separate them from the rest of us and destroy them. But the line dividing good and evil cuts through the heart of every human being. And who is willing to destroy a piece of his own heart?"

Thus, throughout human history, wise women and men, in their own ways, have understood the old Sufi parable of the person who looks for the key under the lamppost because that's where the light is, but it's not where the key was dropped, which is in the darkness.

Looking into the darkness or living with shadow awareness is not an easy path, a road on which the debris has been cleared and the direction lies straight ahead. Rather, to live with shadow awareness we follow the detours; we walk into the debris, groping our way through dark corridors and past dead ends. We look for the key where it is difficult to find. Shadow-work asks us to turn in that direction.

It asks us to stop blaming others.

It asks us to take responsibility.

It asks us to move slowly.

It asks us to deepen awareness.

It asks us to hold paradox.

It asks us to open our hearts.

Is asks us to sacrifice our ideals of perfection.

It asks us to live the mystery.

We suggest that you relate to the shadow as a mystery, rather than as a problem to be solved or an illness to be cured. When the Other arrives, honor that part of yourself as a guest. You may discover that it comes bearing gifts. You may discover that shadow-work is, indeed, soul work.

When shadow-work is neglected, the soul feels dry, brittle, like an empty vessel. Then, people suffer depression rather than embark on a fruitful descent. When shadow-work is denied, the soul feels banished, exiled from its habitats in the wilds of nature, in the soft nights of lovemaking, or in the sacred objects of art. Then, people suffer anxiety and loneliness, cut off from a sense of place, the mystery of the Beloved, or the beauty of things.

But when shadow-work is attended to, the soul feels round, full, sated. When shadow-work is invited into a life, the soul feels welcomed, alive in the gardens, aroused in passion, awake in sacred things.

SHADOW-WORK VS. OTHER THERAPIES

We hope that the voice of our book is the voice of the empathic therapist. We hope that you will feel held and that the book will act as a container, like the therapeutic relationship, so that you can move into unexplored territory, which may at times seem embarrassing, anxiety-provoking, or frightening.

That territory is vast. We will explore those topics—romantic love, creative work, family kinship, loyal friendship, midlife freedom, and the urge for power, sex, and money—that carry what we call the projection of soul: They shine with divine energies. We will examine them in personal, cultural, and archetypal contexts. But unlike other books on these same topics, we will view them in the unique context of the shadow and offer hope, via shadow-work, for a more authentic connection to the Self.

This book differs from other books that explore relationships and similar topics in another way: We view them in the context of personal development or the evolution of consciousness. We hope to show that, whatever the topic—dating, romance, marriage, friendship, work, midlife—evolution is at work. And the shadow, in seeking the light of consciousness, is the driver of this growth.

But without shadow awareness and the tools of shadow-work, evolution stalls, and the internal saboteur leads us to repeat old patterns again and again. We may adopt strategies of adaptation that permit us to survive terrible circumstances, but we do not heal; yesterday's adaptations become today's enemies. When the shadow erupts once more, we may then realize that our old patterns no longer serve. Like Sleeping Beauty in her glass coffin, we may awaken as if from a deep sleep and begin to gather the tools we need to stay awake for longer periods.

Let us clarify the distinctions, then, between the tools of shadow-work and the many other forms of psychotherapy now available. We draw here on the great tradition of depth psychology, whose founders, Freud and Jung, used myth to enlarge the frame of individual human life. Jung, especially, developed a psychotherapy that was oriented toward soul. Unlike Freud, who viewed the unconscious as a boiling cauldron of evil impulses, Jung uncovered our lost creative impulses lying there, as well as the lost gods or mythological images that he called archetypes.

- For us, healing is not merely the intellectual discovery of shadow content, which is like fool's gold. It may bring insight, but it will ring hollow if it does not touch the soul. Healing at the level of soul is a natural, regenerative process, like new skin that grows to close a wound. It is not a cure, but a deep sense of acceptance and a reorientation toward life and toward the gods.
- For us, healing is not simply about finding a single cause in the past, such as childhood abuse, that leads in a direct, linear way to a single effect in the present, such as low sexual desire, depression, or addiction. This view does not account for the complicated, nonlinear nature of the unconscious. It does not acknowledge the

power of a psychological complex to grip a person with multiple consequences. Instead, it reduces problems to personal psychology alone, rather than including cultural and archetypal issues.

- For us, healing is not simply about indiscriminately blaming perpetrators and blindly protecting victims. This viewpoint does not acknowledge the multifaceted personal histories of all people involved, including the intractability of family shadow patterns. And it tends to displace the adult victim's opportunity for personal responsibility while maintaining the split between evil and good, thereby obviating the need for inner work and the realization that each person contains both darkness and light.

We do not intend in any way to minimize the bloody pain of family wounds or dismiss the crippling effects of abuse and trauma. We wish to acknowledge, instead, that the healing model from the recovery movement has helped millions of people to gain access to childhood memories, find explanations for aberrant behaviors, express their anger at perpetrators, and feel a sense of forgiveness. However, its formulaic approach does not account for the power of the unconscious. And at times it becomes so oversimplified that its proponents risk reductionism and the peril of reification—the danger of believing that to name something is to fully understand it ("Oh, you were abused as a child, or you come from an alcoholic family. That explains why you feel like such a victim").

In addition, the medical model, which is championed by proponents of Alcoholics Anonymous (who eschew drugs) and psychiatrists (who rely on drugs to eliminate symptoms), also does not account for much of our unconscious process. Certainly, the AA method holds an honorable place in treating compulsions, such as addictions to alcohol, drugs, nicotine, caffeine, and sex, and it often leads people to uncover their individual and family shadow patterns. Yet the deeper needs of the shadow may remain camouflaged by this more behavioral approach.

For us, healing is not simply about curing symptoms or eliminating addictions. This view does not honor the gods or archetypal images that underlie our pathologies and inform their expression. For instance, one man may suffer from a Dionysian-style addiction to cocaine: Like the god of ecstasy, he seeks rapture at any cost. Another may suffer from a Hades-like alcoholism, which pulls him down into the stillness of the underworld, the home of Hades, lord of darkness. Or a woman may struggle with a Kali-style depression, striking out destructively at those around her much like the Indian goddess of birth, death, and transformation. But another woman's depression may feel like a Persephone-style melancholy, which stems from her marriage to an underworld god. When we can uncover the god hidden within our suffering, we can begin to detect its story and what it is seeking there.

Finally, although *psyche* means *soul*, many of the current trends in psychotherapy today are empty of soul. Focused on short-term treatment and behavioral change, they lack an orientation to depth. Focused on medication, they lack a permeability to the underworld. Focused on personal psychology alone, they fail to honor the gods. Focused on insight alone, they fail to include the body. In addition, most psychotherapy lacks an orientation to Self, the transpersonal voice within that can guide us through the darkness.

Shadow-work, however, can begin to compensate for these deficiencies. By learning how to identify shadow figures when they emerge in self-sabotaging, uncontrollable behaviors; by detecting their appearance with bodily and emotional cues; by tracing their roots in family patterns and in cultural edicts; by exploring their archetypal sources in myth and story; and eventually by uncovering their deeper needs—the gold in the dark side—we can begin to build a more conscious relationship with these unconscious forces. In this way, eventually we can accomplish directly what the shadow tries to accomplish indirectly.

As we begin to acknowledge hidden so-called negative traits— laziness, jealousy, impulsivity, self-centeredness—as well as undeveloped positive traits—creative talents, parenting skills, healing abilities—in our shadow figures, we expand the range of who we are. For example, our client Jordan, thirty-two, felt bored, emotionally wooden, and dependent on his new wife, Phyllis, to fill his emptiness. When she took a high-paying job, he felt adrift, cut off from his moorings. As we explored Jordan's bored, dependent shadow character, we uncovered a secret desire: to become a screenwriter. When he honored this dream and began to write for a few hours each week, his vitality returned. Soon, he was attending a writing course and working feverishly into the night. Gradually, his neediness of Phyllis decreased as his soul felt fed by his own creative muse.

Our client Jill faced her shadow at midlife: As a child, she was not encouraged to achieve academically or to think creatively. Jill had worked with some satisfaction as a landscape gardener. But when she turned thirty-five, she no longer felt content to be independent; she yearned to build a home with a husband and child. Working with a recurrent dream of a vicious dog, Jill uncovered her buried aggression and used drawing to express the anger, impatience, and intolerance that had been banished into her shadow as a young girl.

At around the same time, her mind awoke: Taking courses in philosophy at a local university, she found enjoyment in thinking about grand ideas and asserting herself in debates with others. Somehow her aggression and her thinking ability had been exiled into the shadow together. As she mined one from the darkness, the other emerged as well, presenting her with a surprising gift: the gold in her dark side. Apparently, Jill had to be willing to accept her aggression, the raw, unrefined aspect of her shadow, in order to uncover the pleasure of her newfound intellectual creativity, the more refined gold.

Beneath or behind these patterns of personal psychology lie the timeless archetypal or mythological patterns. In detecting them in our own lives, we deepen into our own story, as well as into mythological reality. When we come to recognize a particular myth as a connecting thread in our lives, we come to understand how certain moments that seemed accidental actually belong to the whole story. For instance, when Jill discovered that she had unknowingly lived out the myth of Artemis, a virgin goddess who lives alone in the wilderness, she felt stunned; she needed a new story if she were to build a life with a Beloved, which was her dream.

Approaching This Book with Soul

This book combines an archetypal approach, which uses mythic tales to lift you out of the pain of personal stories into the Larger Story, with case vignettes, which bring you back down into the immediacy of daily life with soul. Myths are universal tales that appear within particular cultural contexts. Unlike the singular Judeo-Christian image of God, the many gods and goddesses of Greek mythology cast dark shadows. They commit incest, parricide, theft, murder, and sexual violations. Buried in the foundations of Western civilization, they may hold clues to some of our invisible assumptions, the concealed, unconscious patterns that drive us unknowingly but no longer serve us in this time or place. In fact, the rejected stone, the god or goddess who has been banished into the shadow, may become the cornerstone of a new life.

These gods and goddesses do not represent a mere cluster of traits, a secret formula by which we can become an ideal Hera/wife, Aphrodite/lover, Zeus/king, or Ares/warrior. They are not fixed, archaic images to be acted out like theatrical roles. Rather, they represent dynamic, ever-reappearing aspects of human experience with the capacity to ignite our imaginations and free us from stereotyped prisons. As we uncover the archetypal patterns in our lives—the tales of the gods and goddesses—we discover that we are living a unique version of a universal theme. We are participating in a larger story, which connects us to something greater than ourselves. Used in this way, their psychological effects can be enlivening, their political effects liberating. (To familiarize yourself with the major mythological Greek figures, see the Who's Who at the back of the book.)

We also use the stories of individual clients to illustrate the personal dimension of these larger stories. Although disguised to protect the identities of clients and friends, these vignettes are not fictionalized accounts; they are based on the lives of people we have known, and we owe them a debt of gratitude. We hope that through their examples you will learn how to uncover shadow content, honor and respect it, and welcome it into your life.

As you read the stories, we ask that you take a self-reflective attitude, contemplate these ideas and images and observe your own internal response. At times, you may feel that you are looking into a mirror, seeing your own reflection and reliving a portion of your life. Stop and pay attention. You may feel provoked or agitated; you may feel grief or loss. In fact, it is our intention to activate shadowy feelings and images in you, to quicken your soul and beckon you to inner work. It is also our hope to open a window onto a larger dimension of your tale, enabling you to glance beyond your individual skin to the archetypal realm.

Take these moments of disquietude as an opportunity to slow down, gently nudge aside your denial, and begin an honest conversation with yourself. You may wish to use a journal to record your thoughts and feelings, draw your own images, or track your dreams. Throughout the book, you will find soulful writing by clients who used their journals to do shadow-work.

If, as you read, you feel startled or grow too uncomfortable, stop; put down the book. You are meeting your shadow. Be reassured that this material may be difficult for many people. It is slippery and evasive, charged and even frightening. But stay with it, moving at your own pace; eventually, as your self-knowledge grows, so will your compassion for yourself.

Take these moments as opportunities for self-reflection. In "A Shadow-Work Handbook," found in the back of the book, we offer a breathing exercise for centering, which can help you to gain a vantage point for self-observation while you read. With regular practice, this can enable you to witness your shadow characters, watching your emotions without identifying with them. You may wish at this time to turn to the Handbook and read that section, or you may wish to wait until you have read how our many clients used this practice throughout the book.

As you continue to read and begin to imagine your life more archetypally, you might ask yourself which god or goddess in you is reading the text. If it's Athena, then as the goddess of weaving she may be knitting together ideas from various aspects of your life, so that patterns emerge that you may not have seen before. If it's Hermes, then as the god who steals he may be taking ideas from here and there to be used elsewhere, appropriating them for his own ends. If it's Apollo, then as a rational and aloof figure he may be standing apart and examining the text for errors, so that you miss its immediate, emotional impact. If it's Demeter, then as a maternal goddess she may be exploring how to use shadow-work to nurture and heal her friends and loved ones.

In addition, as you read through the book you will want to know the meanings of the terms we use. The psychology/spirituality literature has become a Tower of Babel. Many terms, such as ego and self, are used vaguely and interchangeably, thus losing their clarity and potency. Others are used with such specificity that their applications are rare. In this section we will make our meanings explicit so you can share our assumptions. As a result, our larger framework will become clear as well, containing and clarifying our case anecdotes.

In the tradition of Jung, we view the shadow as an archetype or universal blueprint in the human soul. At the center of every psychological complex, or emotionally charged group of unconscious images and ideals, lies an archetype, which holds these personal patterns in a larger story. For example, at the center of the mother complex, which forms a miniature world of images and feelings about mother, lies the Great Mother archetype, which connects the complex to collective, timeless images of her. At the center of the *puer* complex, within the boy or girl who will not grow up, lies the archetype of Eternal Youth, which connects us to spiritual possibilities. At the heart of the seducer/lover sits Aphrodite, the archetype of beauty, passion, and seduction. And at the core of the tyrant/ruler stands Zeus, the archetypal king of Olympus.

Like Jung, we might ask which comes first: Do we live in the archetypes, or do they live in us? As you contemplate this question, you may uncover its truths from various points of view.

Following in the footsteps of Jung, for us the term "Self" denotes the "God within," the transpersonal realm within the personal life. The Self contains the potential for the totality of personality, including the shadow. An experience of the Self brings purpose and meaning to life, a connection to something larger than the individual ego. The goal of individuation, as Jung defined it, could be called reconciliation with the Self. When one can hear the voice of the Self and learn to obey it, one walks and talks with authenticity.

The Self also has an ethical dimension, which ties it to the shadow. Freud pointed out in his work on superego that collective morality, which stems from society, religion, and parents, results in feelings of guilt and conscience. This might be imagined as the eye of god that, after Cain killed his brother Abel, follows the murderer everywhere he goes. But Jung suggested that there exists a personal moral urge as well, which he sometimes called the two-million-year-old man within us. It is this voice of the Self that dictates right action with a certain conviction, even when it appears to conflict with collective codes, such as Krishna telling Arjuna in the *Bhagavad Gita* to kill his brothers, or God telling Abraham to sacrifice his son. In the spiritual literature, this reconciling with the Self has been called aligning with the Tao, living one's dharma, or being in the flow of life.

We use the term "ego" to signify the inauthentic "I" or self (with a small "s") that develops to survive in difficult environments and to become acceptable to the conventional world. We view ego as the result of many inevitable adaptations to forces that cannot tolerate the authentic expressions of the Self—helplessness in a small boy develops into overcompetence; rage in a pretty girl eventually becomes social demureness; sensuality in a young teen slowly turns into rigidity; and depression in one member of a so-called happy family emerges as an insidious addiction. In each case, the intolerable feeling is banished into the shadow, turning into its opposite in a persona mask, with which the ego quickly identifies. The proper role of this inauthentic ego, then, is to protect the authentic soul by attempting to ensure that the child will be loved and accepted while he or she learns to adapt and survive in social settings.

There are many aspects of this authentic Self that are unacceptable to the ego ideal. Like old family heirlooms, they are stuffed into a trunk in the cellar. The trunk is like the personal "shadow," a container that holds the dusty old heirlooms or lost and neglected shadow contents. The personal shadow is that portion of the whole unconscious that is closest to consciousness. It is shaped by a confluence of forces: the collective or cultural shadow, which forms the sea of moral and social values in which we swim; the family shadow, which forms the vessel in which we grow; and the parents' shadows, which form a legacy of abuse and betrayal.

The personal shadow can contain anything that is forbidden, shamed, or taboo, depending on the cultural, familial, and parental training. For example, while proponents of a culture at large may praise accumulating wealth and a particular family worships the idol of money, another family may scorn any display of greed. So, money comes to carry numinous value for some, immoral or shameful value for others. This difference has vast implications for how people invest their time, find work, seek partnership, and experience their own self-worth.

Similarly, in a family that frowns upon athletic ability, a natural athlete may feel forced to go to law school, thus banishing his giftedness into the shadow. In a family that disdains the arts as child's play, a gifted painter or poet may feel coerced to become a businessperson or scientist. In these ways, authentic feelings and behaviors, both positive and negative, are banished into the darkness, only to reappear later in distorted forms, such as rage, addiction, depression, abuse, or envy, which tear apart the fabric of our precious relationships. Consciously, of course, an addict does not know why he craves his drug; an abusive mother does not know why she beats her child. But unconsciously, the shadow knows its purpose: It seeks to make the unconscious conscious; it tries to tell its secret. Through repeated patterns of addictive or abusive behavior, through choosing the wrong person to love again and again, the shadow tells its tale. The aim of this book is to learn how to listen and to discover your shadow's purpose.

We are using the term "shadow" in three ways: First, the shadow is the darkroom in which our images and dreams lie dormant. Shadow-work is the process of development in which our images and dreams come back to life.

Second, it refers to the contents themselves, those archetypal images that are immediately, intuitively recognizable as a troubling part of us: a witch, sadist, saboteur, liar, victim, addict. In addition, we are calling those latent talents and positive impulses shadow content that were banished in childhood, such as musical, poetic, or athletic talents.

Finally, used as an adjective, the term refers to the shadow aspect or dark side of a person or archetype, such as the dark side of one's mother or the dark side of the Great Mother. Because most of us are trained as children to split off God from Satan and good from evil, we cannot hold the tension of these opposites: light side and dark side. Instead, we tend to seek out untarnished, idealized heroes in an attempt to remain optimistic and hopeful. Or another part of us, which is jaded and cynical, expects the worst of others.

As an alternative to this kind of splitting, romancing the shadow is a way of seeing that is simultaneously a way of knowing. When a shadow-worker directs the attention to a person or object, he or she sees both its light side and its dark side. To practice light side/dark side thinking is to practice holding opposites, a subversive act in our either/or culture. For Jung, this act is a developmental step, the end of a naive all-good view or a cynical all-bad view, which results in a more nuanced perception of reality and a capacity to tolerate paradox and ambiguity. This, too, is one of the promises of shadow-work.

We have extended an old Sufi story that portrays the development of human consciousness via shadow-work. The Master of a large household needs to go abroad for an indeterminate length of time. He decides to leave his trusted, capable Butler in charge of his affairs. After many years the Master returns, only to discover that the Butler no longer recognizes him; the Butler believes that it is Master of the house.

Early in our development, the Self goes dormant and the ego takes control of our conscious lives. It runs the house like an efficient servant and eventually forgets that the Master is gone. The Butler says: "I'm in charge. I have my own priorities. I have power over people. But the people don't know who I really am, so I have to hide." Eventually, the Butler hides so well that it forgets how it got the job in the first place. Its range of feeling narrows as it becomes nice, polite, unthreatening; its range of thinking narrows as it becomes proper, moral, appropriate. And all of its power is aimed at maintaining its position and proving that it is worthy of love and acceptance—or faking it.

In fact, the Butler has become so entrenched in its assumed identity that it becomes unwilling to relinquish control. So the Master needs to send in his Henchmen. They appear to the Butler as obstacles to its work: moods, such as anger or depression and feelings of futility; fears of inadequacy or of losing control; projections onto others, making them the source of its problems. The Butler now feels afraid all the time: afraid it will be found out, afraid it won't have enough, afraid it will be left alone. Soon the Butler may dream of being attacked or killed by unseen enemies.

Eventually, by facing the Henchmen and undergoing many experiences of great pain and struggle, the Butler is humbled and forced to surrender to the Master's greater power—that is, to the voice of the authentic Self. The false ego can no longer reign supreme in the household; the call of the Self must be heard. And the Shadow, via the Henchmen, provides the means by which the ego is humbled, seeing its own limitations and reluctantly bowing to the greater wisdom. Jung articulated this point when he said, "the experience of the Self is always a defeat for the ego."

Finally, we use the term "soul" to denote our immanent human value. Unlike Self, which denotes a connection to transcendent spirituality, soul implies relatedness, complexity, and vulnerability. Frequently, we are forced as children to abandon the tender, authentic needs of our souls. As James Hillman has pointed out, soul offers an approach to life as sacred, an orientation toward depth. It brings a quality of awareness that is reflective, imaginative, and downward, engaged with the dailiness of things.

Today, through the democratization of spiritual teachings, more and more people appear to be remembering the Self, the divine essence. We sense that a limited identity that used to be comfortable is no longer enough; we feel a dissonance between who we are and who we could become. We are beginning to hear the whispering voice of the Self.

This is the first clue that the journey of spiritual ascent has begun. However, there are few warning signs of the risks of a flight into spirituality. Like Icarus, many young seekers, flying unbound by attachment to this world, whether through meditation or psychedelics, have burned their wings and fallen to the valley below. And some holy men, who seemed immune to the frailties of the rest of us, have grown inflated by identification with the Self, losing contact with their own shadows and inflicting great pain on their loving but perhaps naive students.

Conversely, the descent to soul, untouched by the rarified air of the Self, holds different risks: Like Hades, lord of the underworld, we can remain bound in the darkness of depression or overly attached to the ephemeral things of this world, ruled by fears of abandonment or feelings of isolation.

Thus, when the Self, in its expansion to the heights, denies the needs of the soul, something essential is lost. And when the soul, in its extension to the depths, denies the needs of the Self, something essential is lost. This book attempts to build a bridge between the Self's upward longing and the soul's downward dive through shadow-work. *Romancing the Shadow* teaches you to honor the call of the Self, deepen and widen the range of awareness, and enjoy the moment-to-moment personal life of the soul.

The Promise of Our Book

By reading this book—a comprehensive look at the appearance of the shadow in all areas of life—you will discover that the consequences of romancing the shadow can be transformative:

- Individuals can find the sources of their deep-seated feelings of fraudulence or self-hate and come to know a deeper authenticity. You can uncover the roots of your own self-sabotage and begin to untangle the shadow's hidden purpose in seemingly destructive behaviors, thereby becoming more self-directed. You can storm the walls of denial and learn to see yourself and others with greater clarity and compassion. Eventually, you can turn self-hate into self-acceptance and shame into pride (see Chapter 1).

- Family members who seek deeper reconciliation and greater authenticity with parents, children, or siblings can reduce family persona by opening family secrets, exploring family sins, and learning to break this dark legacy to the next generation (Chapter 2).

- Next we examine four potential patterns of development that result from a parent's betrayal of a child's soul: father's son, father's daughter, mother's son, and mother's daughter. By becoming aware of these unconscious patterns and examining each parent's light side and dark side, you can reclaim masculine and feminine soul (Chapter 3).

- Single people who suffer with the shame of dating as a series of rejections and failures can find a way to use dating to gain self-knowledge, break old relationship habits, and move toward intimacy with a partner (Chapter 4).

- In this climate of epidemic divorce, couples can learn to defuse negative emotions and step off the roller-coaster ride of seemingly purposeless, painful, repetitive fights. You can break long-term patterns of pursuing and distancing, criticizing and punishing, and move toward conscious partnership. By understanding how your projections color your perceptions of others, you can resolve long-standing shadow issues around sex, power, and money and learn to know one another more deeply (Chapter 5).

- Committed couples can move from shadow-boxing to shadow-dancing, from illusion to authenticity in a committed relationship. You can learn to honor and care for the Third Body, the soul of the relationship, which in turn nurtures and sustains you. And you can create a shadow marriage, vowing to sustain and support each other's full range of potentialities (Chapter 6).

- Friends can deepen feelings of safety and intimacy with one another by learning how to use shadow-work to explore feelings of anger, envy, and competition, thereby healing your sense of isolation and finding places where you don't have to hide (Chapter 7).

- Anyone who works can reimagine the purpose and meaning of their work. With shadow-work, even tedious activities can become soulful, an opportunity to deepen self-awareness, which can lead to greater authenticity on the job, an entrepreneurial or creative venture, or a separation of employment from soulful work. In addition, the search for soul on the job can become a way to break old patterns and deepen self-knowledge (Chapter 8).
- People in midlife who awaken suddenly to the loss of their unlived lives can learn to break free of the constraints of their well-trodden paths, becoming reinspired to live the mystery more deeply. Midlife depression can become descent, and ascent brings the resurrection of lost gods (Chapter 9).

Most people, regardless of beliefs, can begin to make sense of their suffering by learning how to turn their most painful experiences into wisdom—by turning their baser elements into gold. By seeing the shadow's patterns and purpose at work in your relationships, you will uncover an order in apparent chaos, a deeper meaning that ties together individual, family, and cultural stories. In effect, you will make room for soul.

Although highly practical in its approach, *Romancing the Shadow* offers no easy answers. We believe that, in dealing with the unconscious, there are none. One simple experience of telling a patient what to do leads any therapist to discover unconscious resistances. So, instead, we pose questions of a certain kind, questions that lead the reader down into a contemplative state of mind, down toward soul. We use questions like meditation objects to uncover precious shadow material. We use questions like koans, to open the imagination to the mystery.

Turning the questions around, we discover that everything with substance casts a shadow. This book teaches you how to look at what is hidden, how to live with light side/dark side awareness, which means learning to live with ambiguity, paradox, and complexity. In fact, living with shadow awareness by definition precludes easy answers; it demands holding the tension of opposites, which Carl Jung viewed as a sign of developing consciousness.

Most psychologies and self-help programs, which seek to repair individuals from one dysfunction or another, hold an unspoken attitude toward the shadow. If they represent the ego's point of view, as the vast majority do, then they seek the ego's objectives: feeling in control, looking good, getting things done. Instead, this book makes an effort to represent the shadow's point of view, to uncover the gold in dark places. It does not offer a mechanical, five-step method for "owning" the shadow; it does not advocate shadow-work for the sake of ego needs.

Whereas the ego weaves together the world, the shadow unravels the world. Whereas the ego acts as a catalyst of creation in the world, the shadow acts as a catalyst of destruction. Whereas the ego supports the status quo, the shadow is an agent of transformation.

Although this book does not promise a quick fix, it does promise a slow turning, a renewed orientation toward life, toward the depths, toward a fuller sense of authenticity. *Romancing the Shadow* offers an approach to life, a way of being in the world, being with others, and being with oneself that acts like a long drink of hot coffee—it opens the eyes and makes the skin tingle. It breaks through the wall of fatigue. It puts us slightly on edge. It prepares us to meet the shadow around the next corner.

OUR
STORIES

CONNIE'S STORY:
A TALE OF SHADOW-WORK

L et me tell you a story from my own life, a particular rendering of a
universal pattern that demonstrates shadow-work and introduces
you to some of our book's main themes. Like the book, my tale weaves
together a tapestry of personal, cultural, and archetypal realms.

Like the Greek goddess Athena, I was born out of my father's
head, with little awareness that I had a mother at all. Like Athena, I
am a father's daughter, a woman who, at some stage, unconsciously
identifies more with her father and the masculine element within her
than with her mother and the feminine. Father's daughters tend to be
adept in society, competent, and confident—except, perhaps, about
their own femininity, which is not expressed in stereotypically attractive ways and so instead may be banished into shadow.

As the warrior goddess, Athena appears in myth carrying her
sword and shield, and she is a virgin—that is, a self-contained woman.
Known for platonic friendships with heroic men, such as Odysseus and
Perseus, she aids them rather than bonds with them. Until midlife, I,
too, felt no desire to bond permanently with a man, partially because,
to me, the traditional roles of women appeared to carry an unspoken
inequality, and I have greatly enjoyed my freedom and independence.

Yet I always had a close male friend, a soul friend, whose creative efforts I supported and whose love I cherished.

As a young girl, the first daughter of two, I was very close with my mother, who was lovingly devoted and attentive. In our house, we made a game of dividing the family into "teams," pairs of family members who shared similar tastes and appeared to be most alike. I was teamed with our mother, my sister with our father, because we physically resembled one another, respectively, and shared more interests: We liked to gossip about human nature, watch love stories, and shop for clothes. They liked sports, action adventure movies, and slapstick humor.

In the myth, Athena's mother, Metis, was devoured by Zeus. My mother, too, was swallowed by my father's Zeus-like power. She sacrificed her life as an artist to become a full-time wife and mother and slowly disappeared into depression, becoming in some way invisible to me. Although she remained a constant, loving presence, as her power diminished in my child's perspective, so did her visibility. As a result, the archetypal wife and mother were banished into my shadow. And, at some unknown crossroads, the force of my father's impressions on my plastic young soul seemed to take more deeply, so that I appeared to become a father's daughter.

I can recall feeling in early adolescence that being a girl seemed somehow irrelevant to my identity (a shocking idea in retrospect). My father would tell me that with my abilities I could do anything, implying anything a man could do. Throughout my childhood, in fascinating, wide-ranging, combative dinner-table conversations, he groomed my mind to be, like his, a ruthless sword, to discriminate fact from fiction and soft feelings from hard reality.

My mother's feeling world seemed increasingly remote, chaotic, and out of control. The desire of other girls to marry and have children seemed to me the death of possibilities; I remember intuitively understanding early on the use of the word "nuclear" to describe both the family and an unwinnable war. As I watched my girlfriends adorn themselves to be attractive to boys and to play increasingly sophisticated games of flirtation, I felt mystified. I wondered why they bothered. In this way, many feminine qualities were banished into my shadow.

Because our culture is structured around the masculine principle, many people find little value in conventional feminine qualities, which therefore carry cultural shadow. For many men, this means banishing into the unconscious those parts of themselves that are deemed feminine—nurturing, vulnerable, and caretaking qualities—and even overdeveloping those parts that are deemed masculine—aggressive, competitive, productive qualities. As a result, many men seek those buried shadow qualities outside of themselves, in women, while at the same time unconsciously devaluing them until, one day, they devalue their partners.

For women, this second-class status of the feminine makes it difficult to identify with our very natures. So, unknowingly, we adopt a certain set of characteristics to survive, which, like makeup, covers another set of qualities that may be less suited to survival. One lovely woman client told me that, in order to deflect the constant seductive pressures of men that began in her early teens, she intentionally neutered her appearance and learned to act gruff, like one of the guys. Her experience, mirrored in my own, eventually leads to an internal conflict between feeling powerful in the world and feeling attractive as a woman. Until recently, we faced a forced choice: either power or femininity goes into the shadow.

In retrospect I see my identification with the masculine and rejection of the feminine as a root of my one-sided development. Its costs were high: Because I valued men and the masculine over women and the feminine, I had few women friends, often patronizing them and considering their concerns trivial. This included my own sister, whose interests in fashion and style seemed superficial to me. Without a global sense of sisterhood, I could not share the social and political concerns of other women.

Instead, I retreated into a spiritual community based on a patriarchal, monastic model. For nearly a decade during my twenties, I practiced meditation intensively and taught it to hundreds of people, encouraging in them a transcendence of this world and of the body. Like Athena in her virginity, I cultivated self-containment by turning inward. But when the cycle was complete and I returned to my senses, moving back into my awakening body and burgeoning emotions, I faced a difficult transition.

Suffering for many years with a lack of intimacy, I was unable to be vulnerable with others or to find a community of like-minded souls.

Instead, I threw myself headlong into journalism with a dedication that previously had been reserved for my meditation practice. After moving into publishing, I could imagine myself striding brazenly through the world of commerce much like Athena with her sword and shield, symbols of a rigid, heroic boundary that protects the illusion of a separate self. In these ways, she served me as I served her for many years. And my tender feelings of vulnerability and dependency remained concealed in the shadow.

However, in my mid-thirties I began to long for a more nurturing, sensual, intimate life. I imagined living another kind of femininity, which did not require the sacrifice of my hard-won independence.

I got my first clue to healing the Athena pattern in a dream: *I found the bloody head of my father in the bathroom sink. I knew in the dream that my mother and I had done the murderous deed.* In working with this dream in Jungian analysis, I came to see that my alignment with my father—and through him with the male-dominant bias of society—had to be sacrificed. I needed to sever the connection with the logical masculine mind that had run my life like the captain of a tight ship. As I pushed my father from the pedestal until he fell far enough to crack, the young girl's eyes cleared, and I began to see his flaws: My hero suffered from a serious addiction and abused his power out of secret feelings of powerlessness. As his shadow side came home to me, turning the hero into an all-too-human Dad, his authentic gifts came to light as well: a brilliant, loyal, generous man with a hunger for knowledge, whose legacy to me is social conscience, a compassion for all humanity.

Recognizing these multiple realities in him permitted me to see them in myself, to have a more direct relation with my own darkness and my own light. Eventually, I could see how my childhood image of my father also had affected my choice of lovers, as well as my choice of a spiritual teacher. Before shadow-work, I had been, in both instances, trapped in a dynamic determined by unconscious intense feelings about my father, not by conscious adult choices.

I also needed to discover who lay sleeping in the shadow of Athena. For I, like many women who live out this pattern, had remained intoxicated with power and intellect, forgetting my more erotic, soulful connection to my body and to nature. The Greek story of Medusa begins when, as a beautiful woman, she is raped in Athena's temple. But Athena, instead of aligning with Medusa, had a knee-jerk identification with the male aggressor. She punished the victim by turning Medusa into a snake-headed Gorgon with a petrifying gaze. Whether this was an act of envy or revenge, the creation of the Gorgon concretized the image of the shadow through projection. Forever after, Medusa's gaze turned to stone anyone who fell prey to it.

I, too, have petrified people with my gaze, halting the natural and spontaneous flow of feeling between us. Cut off from my heart, I have played the role of the wrathful goddess, judging and condemning others to an inferior status. It pains me now to think of the suffering that I caused others with my Medusa looks.

Just as Athena turned Medusa into a Gorgon, she also played a role in her destruction. When Perseus, an arrogant young hero, vowed to behead Medusa, Athena offered help: She gave him a polished shield that served as a mirror, enabling him to kill the Gorgon without having to look at her directly and become petrified. In creating a reflection, the goddess's mirror shield enabled him to see the shadow—an image of that which is too terrible to see directly. In this way, Perseus was able to vanquish Medusa. From then on, Athena wore the snake-haired head on her chest, an outer emblem of her own wrathful, death-dealing energies for all to see.

I, too, did the difficult daily work to reclaim aspects of my shadow and my lost feminine heritage by seeking to understand my conscious identification with my father and the masculine principle. Then I turned to face my mother in an effort to make conscious those aspects of myself that I had absorbed unknowingly from her. Although I had come to believe that my identification with my mother had been broken early, it had only been buried.

One day I asked a friend, Jungian analyst Marion Woodman, what she thought about my wheat allergy, a mysterious problem with food that had appeared several years earlier. She replied, "Wheat is the food of the Great Mother, Demeter. When you have more fully differentiated from your own mother, you'll be able to eat wheat."

I was stunned. Differentiate from my mother? I was nothing like her! A classic Demeter woman, she had lived for her children, whereas I had lived an independent, professional life. But, in Marion's words, I heard the call of my own Self. At that moment, my shadow-work changed direction. I began to focus on the early fusion with my mother, which had been covered over by my more conscious father's daughter pattern.

My mother, like her mother before her, has a passion for bread. She craves dark bread full of raisins, light brown bread full of seeds, twisted toasted blond bread with warm butter. All my life I had witnessed her struggle with this craving and, eventually, her addiction became my allergy. My body, at the level of the immune system, had rejected Demeter and all that she implies. In an effort to differentiate from my mother's suffering and avoid her traps with food and marriage, I had become allergic to wheat *and* to relationships. I had been forced to find new forms of sustenance as an Athena woman, an independent warrior.

As I raised my mother from the curse of devaluation and did shadow-work to understand my unconscious rejection of the feminine, she began to take on grace and beauty before my eyes. My mother's gifts, which had remained hidden to me, seemed suddenly startling: An artist of extraordinary talent, she is a lover of beauty who is dedicated to her craft. And, as an inquiring fan of psychology, she is a student of human nature, whose lifelong journey to heal her own soul modeled shadow-work for me and bequeathed the greatest gift: the hunger for consciousness.

Today I can raise Athena's sword and shield when I need them for self-defense. But I can also lay them down when I need a more open, vulnerable stance and a connection to the deep feminine. In addition, I continue to honor Athena in other ways: As a psychotherapist, I use her mirror shield to provide a reflection for my clients. As a writer, I call on her as the goddess of weaving: She helps me to unravel the threads of the old life by breaking my identification with the masculine, by accepting my dark sister, Medusa, and by knitting together a larger story, which is the book you hold in your hands.

Several years ago, my mother began painting seriously again, creating huge colorful canvases that bring her viewers great joy. It had never occurred to me to hang a painting by my mother in my home. But, one day, while considering the gifts of shadow-work, I had the feeling that I wanted to live with one. I asked my mother how she felt about it—and she was thrilled. Today my living room wall is filled with her creative work, a symbol of the tie between us and of the separation, of the unity of mother and daughter and of the diversity of individual life. These are the promises of shadow-work.

STEVE'S STORY:
A TALE OF SHADOW-WORK

Sometime near midnight one evening during my eighteenth year, I was driving down a dark street in New York City when I caught sight of a man out of the corner of my left eye. I lost him for a moment, then I heard a *thunk* on the hood of the car and saw his body flying up into the air like a rag doll. My first thought: My insurance rates will go up. In that moment I was aware that I had no sadness or remorse for the man I had hit. I should have felt something, but I did not. My feelings were asleep. My vulnerability, fears, and empathy for others were hidden in the shadow. This troubling incident set me on my path: I knew I needed to awaken my ability to feel, so I enrolled in psychotherapy.

I had a special birth: The firstborn son to Holocaust survivors, I entered this world on a high holy day. Like a young prince, I was loved and cherished and had the doors of opportunity opened for me. But when I entered adolescence, I began to feel secretly unworthy of these privileges, physically unattractive, and inferior to others socially. Deeply alienated throughout my teenage years, I suffered a loneliness of the soul. I later came to see these feelings in part as a shadow inheritance of my parents' pain from the Holocaust, which I carried in me for many years as my own unacceptability.

In a famous twelfth-century myth, the legend of the Holy Grail, a young man is born whose name, Parsifal, means innocent fool. When Parsifal was ready to leave his mother's house, unknowingly to follow in the footsteps of his father and brothers who had died as knights in battle, his mother grieved. On his departure, she gave him three instructions: respect fair maidens, go to the Church for food, and don't ask questions.

I, too, set off on my journey from my parents' home with similar instructions. When I left for college, I understood that my task was to assimilate into society, to act like others act so that I would not stand

out: I was told to be polite to women, open the door for them, and protect them from danger. I was advised to stay within the Jewish tradition to gain my spiritual nourishment. And, my elders said, there was
no need to ask questions: Everything to be known was already known;
I needed merely to memorize it. For the first few years of college, I followed these instructions. I placed women on a pedestal, adoring them
but treating them with polite distance. I identified with my Jewish
roots and with my father's highest value of gaining financial security.
And, remaining an average student, I did not ask questions. My curiosity and aliveness were buried in the shadow, beyond my reach.

Beneath a mask of bravery and independence, I hid my feelings
and acted tough and invulnerable. With sarcasm and an acerbic
tongue, I kept people from getting too close to me. When one woman
said that she felt afraid of me, I secretly liked the feeling. I had
achieved my goal: to hide my vulnerability and fears of rejection. I also
got a glimpse into my shadow's hidden purpose: a desire for power.

One day, while traveling in Europe, I climbed an alpine peak that
overlooked a breathtaking vista. In that moment, I was overwhelmed:
The beauty of the natural world and the unity of all life filled me with
awe and bliss. Like Parsifal, who stumbles into the grail kingdom while
still young and naive, I had no way to integrate the experience and it
disappeared like a dream. When I failed to ask the key question that
would have opened a spiritual doorway—What is the meaning of this
experience?—the landscape of my life remained desolate. And my
spirit remained asleep, concealed in the shadow.

When I fell in love at age twenty-two, I innocently married as my
father had done: for life. Projecting my soul onto the goddess, I held
my wife aloft, adopting a role as her caretaking partner but unable to
give her intimacy or authenticity because I was cut off from my own
shadowy vulnerability.

Entering graduate school, I chose to study psychology essentially
to avoid participating in a war I did not support. At this conventional
school, behaviorism reigned: Carl Jung was viewed as a madman, and
psychology meant running rats in meaningless experiments. I put one
foot in front of the other, but my mind remained asleep. My inquisitive-
ness and ability to think for myself remained in the dark. Eventually, I
completed my course work—then dropped out before writing a disser-

tation. I came to realize that, in all of this schooling, I had never had an original thought or asked a meaningful question. Perhaps, like Parsifal, I was unknowingly fighting my father's battles.

In my twenties, I took a job as a clinical director in the New York City prisons and set up therapeutic community programs for the prisoners. Deep in the underworld belly of the prison, I felt afraid and disillusioned and faced a crisis of confidence: I did not know enough about myself to be able to heal others. Acknowledging that I moved through life in an unconscious, mechanical fashion, I reasoned that perhaps I was a good tadpole doctor—but I knew nothing of becoming a frog. Transformation eluded me.

At age twenty-five, I had my second dramatic wake-up call: My young wife had an affair. With this betrayal, my illusions shattered and my feelings came alive as my heart broke open, exploding in tears of grief and overwhelming rage. The world as I knew it dissolved around me. I had been thrown out of the grail castle and into the emotional streets. I had previously believed in my ability to read people, to see others as they were. But now, because I had remained unaware that my most intimate companion had been living a lie, I could no longer trust that my mind provided me with valid impressions. I was so confused that I had no idea what to believe; I admitted, silently, that I needed another way of knowing. And I realized that my grail was not to be found in a romantic projection.

I also recognized that, although my feelings had awakened through the breakup, I still lived in my head. As a result, my body was asleep. Slowly, I began to awaken to my senses through meditation and tai chi chuan and later introduced these practices into the New York City prison system.

Still overcome with the sorrow of losing my marriage and with it my identity as a man, I hungrily pursued my own healing in Jungian analysis. For the first time, I uncovered the layers of my own vulnerability, hurt, and anger in relation to my mother and other women. I faced my wounded masculine generativity as it related to self-acceptance, sexuality, and creativity. During this time I came to understand the suffering figure of the Fisher King, who appears in the grail myth as the king who presides over the grail but cannot be healed by it. For him, the healing miracle is just at hand but out of reach. An unhealing wound on his thigh leaves him cold and dry, so his kingdom, like my experience of life, lies arid. He is too ill to live but unable to die, which describes precisely how I felt upon the breakdown of my marriage.

In analysis, my curiosity was awakened. My values suspended, I began to explore humanistic and transpersonal psychologies, as well as Eastern philosophies. One day, I decided to take a psychedelic: Lying on the grass, the sun shining on my face and a quiet rain falling on my body as a spider walked across my chest, I experienced deep within my soul a unity with all of nature. I spoke aloud: The purpose of my life is to achieve this state of unity without drugs.

With this mystical experience I also found my relation to young Parsifal, whose ascent to spirit contrasts with the Fisher King's descent to soul. I began to recognize and embrace these two characters within my own soul. Parsifal is an image of the *puer eternus*, or eternal youth, who soars to the heights by cutting off memories of pain and limitation via meditation and altered states. In this way, he avoids his feelings of shame and his needs for intimacy and loses his masculine standpoint. The Fisher King is an image of the *senex*, or rigid old man, who falls into the depths, bearing the pain of loss, sorrow, inadequacy and personal limitation, but remains cut off from his own larger potential.

Like the Fisher King, who gained relief only by fishing in deep waters, I, too, was relieved only by reaching into the depths of the unconscious for meaning. In analysis, I came alive, as if waking up from a deep sleep. I discovered a personal relationship to the archetypes, mythology, and fairy tales. I began to write poetry and play with clay. My curiosity burst forth and I began to ask my own questions, eventually discovering my relation to a larger story. As I identified less with the conventions of the outer world, I set aside my parents' instructions and turned within for an inner source of guidance.

My new intense aliveness awakened a well-buried fear of life itself. I was afraid of the pain of remaining a tadpole, but even more scared of becoming a frog. I admitted that I needed a teacher, a guide for the journey of transformation that had begun. Like Parsifal, who meets a hermit who provides him with instructions for finding the grail castle, I met Oscar Ichazo, founder of a mystical school known as Arica, who offered similar instructions. Under his guidance, following a path clearly marked, I learned how to reexperience the ecstatic states that I had stumbled onto earlier. Asking the right question—Whom does the grail serve?—I entered the grail kingdom for the third time. And by acknowledging my own woundedness, I was prepared to receive the healing. I learned that the grail is as near as my own Self, whose voice can be heard at any time.

Continuing to awaken my body through Chinese martial arts, I grounded the meditation practices. My heart opened and I discovered love again, more prepared for the struggles on the path of conscious relationship. Then one day I was put to the test: While I was camping in the wilderness with my second wife and young son, a huge black bear appeared at our camp. Like Parsifal battling a pagan knight, I fended off the hungry animal to protect my family. But just as Parsifal discovered that the knight was his own dark brother, whom he then embraced, I discovered that the bear was alive in my own wild instincts, which I had reclaimed from the shadow.

With this initiation, I felt ready for the return. Armed with the maps of consciousness from the Arica training, I could see how spirituality completed Western psychology as a natural part of adult development. My quest to integrate Eastern philosophy and altered states of consciousness with Western models of psychological development had led me to a new land. I re-enrolled in a doctoral program in psychology and completed the degree that I had begun twenty years earlier. With the self-knowledge I had gained from a rich, adventure-filled life experience, I felt ready to participate in the larger society, develop my craft, and dedicate myself to serve humanity as a clinical psychologist who had personally experienced the benefits of both psychological analysis and spiritual practice.

As a provider for my wife and son, I underwent another initiation into masculinity: healing the *senex-puer* split at a deeper level. At the end of the grail myth, when Parsifal hears news of the Fisher King's death, he returns to the castle and is crowned king. He marries and reigns in peace for many years. The story teaches that rulership of the grail kingdom passes to the person who, after many trials, has gained both self-knowledge and compassion. Similarly, when a man has done shadow-work and the old king or father complex dies within him, he can become a conscious king, uniting the *puer* and *senex* energies on the inside.

As I left behind the world of my father and found my own way, doing spiritual work and repairing psychological wounds, I also left behind the *puer*'s flight and began to experience a kind of masculinity that is large enough to contain the wisdom of spirit, the depth of soul, an empathic relatedness to women, the worldly responsibilities of work, and the blessings and demands of fatherhood. As a husband and father, I continue to undergo daily challenges to my masculinity. In my gratitude, the land is bountiful again.

CHAPTER 1

ME AND MY SHADOW

One need not be a chamber to be haunted—
One need not be a house.
The brain has corridors—surpassing
material place.
Far safer, of a midnight meeting
external ghost,
than its interior confronting—
that cooler host.
Far safer, through an abbey gallop
the stones a'chase—
than unarmed, one's self encounter
in lonesome place.
Ourself behind ourself concealed—
should startle most.
Assassin hid in our apartment
be horror's least.
The body borrows a revolver—
he bolts the door
o'erlooking a superior spectre—
or more.

—EMILY DICKINSON

One hundred and fifty years before Carl Jung wrote about the shadow, Johann Wolfgang von Goethe wrote a vast work on

Faust and Mephistopheles, the story of one man meeting his devil, which has rung dark chords through the halls of Western civilization. Henrich Faust is a scholarly man who thirsts in the desert of an over-intellectualized life. Dissatisfied with the knowledge he has gained, he longs for meaning. Despondent in his isolation, he longs for an end to his feelings of estrangement and alienation. Disillusioned and alone, he yearns for faith in something greater than himself.

In a moment of desperation, Faust turns to magic to gain meaning and power. When the specter of a black poodle appears, he falls under its spell and makes a blood pact with the devil: He trades his soul for youth and pleasure, agreeing to become the devil's servant after death if Mephisto will be his servant during life. In this way, Faust becomes possessed by his shadow, surrendering his will in a quest for gratification.

As the story unfolds, Faust appears to have lost all sense of moral responsibility. But in his confusion he slowly begins to wrestle with the two aspects of his human nature: spirituality and sensuality, conscience and desire, ego and shadow. Following a series of trials and misdeeds, Mephisto's influence on Faust's inner life begins to wane, and a psychological awakening takes place within the protagonist as he faces the split between the divine and the diabolical in his own soul. As Jung puts it, "Faust is face to face with Mephistopheles and can no longer say, 'So that was the essence of the brute!' He must confess instead: 'That was my other side, my alter ego, my all too palpable shadow, which can no longer be denied.'"

Like his more contemporary brothers, Frankenstein, Mr. Hyde, Darth Vader, and the Terminator, Mephistopheles lures Faust with promises of power and conquest and the hope of usurping the dominion of god. He is the incarnation of Faust's desires for power, sex, and money; he offers the end of greed, envy, and jealousy with the glowing fantasy that Faust can have it all.

Like Faust, each of us longs for meaning and an experience that connects us to something larger than ourselves. Like him, each of us yearns for an end to loneliness. And like him, each of us has sold out to a devil, sacrificing our complexity and authenticity in an effort to feel safe, earn money, or win love.

Contemporary Faustian bargains take many forms: We trade off our tender feelings of intimacy for a marriage of convenience. We trade off a rich family life for success and influence in the marketplace. We trade off peace of mind for persona, building up a large debt to attain the symbols of external status. We trade off authentic relationships for hot anonymous sex, or we trade off sex for the appearance of purity. We trade off autonomy for financial dependency, remaining childlike under a family system or a welfare system. Or, we trade off the lifelong struggles of soul-searching for the temporary pleasures of an addiction.

Of course, we make these pacts unconsciously, without knowing the sacrifice involved: the loss of vulnerability, intimacy, authenticity, imagination, and soul. But, at some point, perhaps when detecting a lie we have told ourselves or facing a lost dream at midlife, we wake up to the cost of the bargain. Previously, we believed that by paying the devil its due we could avoid suffering; we would not have to acknowledge our own darkness. Then, like Faust, we realize that we have committed the ultimate betrayal: We have betrayed ourselves. At moments like these, when we meet our own inner Mephisto, the shadow seems large and overpowering. From the ego's point of view, it is life-threatening: When the shadow takes over, the ego is pushed into the backseat and a forbidden, even repulsive part of us moves forward and appears to take the steering wheel.

In these crucial moments, we see that forces much larger than ourselves shape the events of our lives. And that which was clear becomes ambiguous; that which was Other becomes our own. Jung wrote of this phenomenon in this way:

> The meeting with oneself is, at first, the meeting with one's own shadow. The shadow is a tight passage, a narrow door, whose painful constriction no one is spared who goes down to the deep well. But one must learn to know oneself in order to know who one is. For what comes after the door is, surprisingly enough, a boundless expanse full of unprecedented uncertainty, with apparently no inside and no outside, no above and no below, no here and no there, no mine and no thine, no good and no bad. It is the world of water . . . where I am indivisibly this *and* that; where I experience the other in myself and the other-than-myself experiences me.

This chapter introduces the internal figures of the shadow in each of us. In it we will examine how they develop naturally and inevitably within us and how they appear to sabotage us later in our lives. We will trace their roots in personal psychology and in culture, as we invite you to do when you engage in shadow-work.

For an extended discussion of how to do shadow-work, see "A Shadow-Work Handbook." It includes a centering practice that can help you to step back and regain your balance when you are confronted by a shadow character, several ways to identify the appearance of shadow characters, and a suggestion for how to realign with the voice of the Self, which permits the shadow character to recede from the seat of power. In the next chapter, we explore in greater detail the roots of shadow-making in the family. And in the following chapters we move from the inner world to the social world, emphasizing the appearance of shadow in relationships and the promises of romancing it.

Meeting the Shadow: Abusers, Abandoners, Addicts, Critics, Thieves

Typically, the meeting with the shadow occurs in small ways quite often, even several times a day. When we feel humiliated by an unacceptable aspect of ourselves—the addict, the critic, the thief, the miser—we meet an interior saboteur, a shadow quality. When we walk into a party and feel an immediate dislike of a stranger ("He's so stupid," "She's so fat," "He's so arrogant," "She's so seductive"), we meet a projected shadow quality. At these times we may feel as if our conscious intentions are crossed by unknown, unconscious opponents.

Because by definition the shadow is unconscious, we cannot gaze at it directly. Because it is hidden, we need to learn to seek it. And to do so, we need to know where to look:

• The shadow hides in our secret shames. To uncover the feeling of shame is to discover an arrow pointing straight toward shadow material, toward sexual taboos, bodily defects, emotional regrets—perhaps toward that which we would not dare to do but would secretly love to do. When shameful feelings are tucked away from those we love or even from ourselves, the shadow remains in the dark, out of sight of loving eyes and therefore unavailable for healing. What private thoughts or feelings most embarrass you? What trait do you wish to be rid of? In what ways do you feel unacceptable, dirty, or shamefully different?

• The shadow disguises itself in our projections, when we react intensely to a trait in others that we fail to see in ourselves. If we feel disgusted ("Gee, she turns my stomach!"), incredulous ("I can't believe he would actually do that!"), or embarrassed ("That makes me really uncomfortable") by another's trait or behavior, and our response is exaggerated, then we may be seeing an aspect of our own shadow indirectly, out there where it's safer to observe it. We project by attributing this quality to the other person in an unconscious effort to banish it from ourselves. Whom do you hate or judge the most? What group of people most repulses or terrifies you? What is it that you cannot *stand* in a friend or family member?

• The shadow lurks in our addictions. When we are in the grasp of compulsive behaviors, we aim, even unknowingly, to deaden shadowy feelings and to fill an invisible emptiness. Whether through alcohol, drugs, sex, work, or food, we disguise our deeper needs by creating the symptom of addiction and becoming deaf to the call of the Self. What do you crave most deeply? What desires do you attempt to control or limit when you succumb to the addiction?

• The shadow blurts out in slips of the tongue. When, like the archetypal Fool, we make embarrassing misstatements, the shadow slides past the gates of consciousness momentarily and reveals unintentional feelings or thoughts, such as sexual innuendo, sarcasm, or cruelty. Caught with our masks down, we smile in embarrassment. For instance, in describing a gift of cuff links from a father-in-law, which previously had belonged to the donor's own father, a client said, "I just can't believe he gave me those handcuffs." Unknowingly, the client revealed that he felt trapped too quickly in this man's line of descent and resented such a presumption of intimacy. What do you secretly wish you could say but believe that you cannot?

• The shadow erupts in humor, especially cruel jokes at another's expense and slapstick antics. We howl at off-color remarks and laugh at the clumsiness of others, then shake our heads in wonder at our own responses, as if taken over momentarily by a surprisingly cold or cruel

inner character. When have you been surprised or ashamed by your reaction to another's demise?

• The shadow wears the camouflage of physical symptoms. We
may lie, but the body does not. We may forget an abuse, but the body
does not. Like shock absorbers, our bodies absorb the wear and tear of
emotional experience. We may defend against it, but our bodies take
the heat. And slowly, over years, the patterns of stress and trauma accumulate. Inevitably, if we do not become conscious of the shadows
lodged in our muscles and cells, they begin to tell their tales. What is
your body trying to say? If your cells could speak, what secrets would
they reveal? What betrayals?

• The shadow rears its head at midlife. During that time, we do
not need to go in search of the shadow; it comes to find us. Whereas
the tasks of the first half of life typically involve creating stability in
love and work, the tasks of the second half involve creating consciousness of that which has been neglected and ignored. Thus a midlife crisis often feels like the notorious dark night of the soul. Frequently, the
result may mean instability in love and work, the feeling of running
out of gas, the urge to flee for the unlived life. We suggest that the first
half of life is for developing the shadow, while the second half is for romancing the shadow. What god or goddess is summoning you to a new
life? In what ways do you yearn for a change? Where is the Trickster
turning your established values and customary habits upside down?
When you are eighty years old, what will you regret having done or
not done?

• The shadow dances through our dreams. Perhaps the most elo-
quent voice of the unconscious, our dreams can reveal unknown feelings and unseen attitudes that cannot be discovered in any other way.
Thus, in a dream, a shadow character may enact forbidden wishes as a
sadistic figure or break strong taboos as a criminal, which the dreamer
could not uncover in conscious waking life. Who appears in your
dreams to contradict your waking self-image? What do these characters do and what do they need?

• The shadow reveals its gold in creative works, which build
bridges between the conscious and unconscious worlds. The arts have
the power to loosen the tight grasp of the conscious mind, permitting
unknown moods and images to arise. Writers and artists alike have

helped to lift the veil and allow others a glimpse of the infinite rich-
ness of the shadow realm.

The encounter with the shadow also may be dramatic, even life-
changing: A man, feeling out of control, hits a woman and faces his
raging killer instincts, meeting the archetypal tyrant or abuser. A
woman, feeling trapped and desperate, leaves her children for a more
unconstrained life, meeting the dark mother or abandoner. Each of
these moments is a shocking encounter with an internal stranger.
Each has roots in the individual psychological history of the person,
but each also has roots in the cultural context in which it occurs, as
well as in archetypal or mythic reality.

In a contemporary Faustian story, a woman client, who was driven
by a need to understand everything, had maintained an over-
controlled, highly intellectual lifestyle as a philosophy teacher. In this
way, she had successfully avoided the chaotic emotional world of her
mother. But, at midlife, an untamed, uncivilized, shadowy feeling began to pull at her. And a whispering voice could be heard, calling her
away from the predictable world of academia and toward an unknown,
uncertain life. We suggested that she do shadow-work by imagining
this feeling as a wild part of herself and writing in the third person
about allowing it to take possession of her life. This is her journal
entry:

> She became all that she was not. All she had worked to de-
> velop, strived to create, came undone. The threads of her life
> pulled. The story unraveled. And the one she had despised,
> the one she had disdained, the one she had burned at the
> stake of her fury was born. Born in her. Born of her. Torn from
> her. Like another life, a different life, yet her life, its mirror
> image, its twin.
>
> She walked away then. She packed very few things,
> turned her back abruptly, and walked away then, away from
> the words, away from the morning light, away from the lemon
> tree. She walked away from the smiles, away from the shoes,
> away from the hum of machines. She entered the wildness,
> where the words stayed in her throat, and the sky remained
> dark, and the faces were fierce. She entered the wildness,

where the feet were bare, and the sound was of owl and coyote
and bear.

In these moments, when we become strangers to ourselves, face-to-
face with an unknown, unsuspected Other, we turn and, in an instant,
glimpse our own blind spots. Immediately, our preprogrammed response is to turn the other way. We shift quickly into denial, hardly
noticing the white flash of humiliation, the red heat of rage, the cold
wave of grief. They pass fleetingly and go unacknowledged.

Like letters left unopened, their messages remain mute, their gifts
unreceived. Romancing the shadow means opening the letters and
hearing the messages from hidden parts of ourselves. Romancing the
shadow means listening to the voices that have been silenced and
honoring what they have to say. To learn to romance the shadow we
need, first of all, to be able to imagine the shadow characters hiding in
our own souls.

ROMANCING THE SHADOW: KING ARTHUR AND THE KNIGHTS OF THE ROUND TABLE

Many people awaken in adulthood to a growing desire for greater self-
awareness and authenticity and for a deeper intimacy with others,
both of which can be achieved with shadow-work. We suggest that
this awakening desire is part of a natural developmental process that
occurs in adults, which has been charted in the transpersonal and
spiritual literature. Unlike the transition from adolescence to adulthood, which occurs biologically and therefore automatically, the transition to greater consciousness must be chosen and then enacted
intentionally.

This change involves, first of all, a shift in focus from the exterior
world to the interior one. In young adults, this shift may occur as a result of difficult family problems or serious betrayal by a family member.
It may occur as a result of painful disillusionment with a romantic relationship, which brings emotional chaos and self-reflection in its wake.
Or it may occur as a result of an experience with altered states of consciousness, which bring a more internal orientation. For people in midlife, this developmental shift often takes place once again and signals a

descent to the underworld, the search for a fresh perspective and a renewal of meaning.

Also, this awakening desire may occur at any age with the beginning of psychotherapy. When people enter therapy, they turn within and begin a rite of passage that signifies a change in attitude, a willingness to accept greater responsibility for the consequences of their choices. Psychotherapy, like ritual, may represent a quest for the lost gods.

Typically, people come to therapy to tell a story from their lives, a narrative of certain events and their feelings about them. They describe a set of problems as they perceive them; they seek empathy, insight, or concrete advice. As psychotherapists, we, in turn, tell them the story of King Arthur and the Knights of the Round Table in the mythical kingdom of Camelot, which helps us to imagine together the shadow figures living within.

As the story goes, Arthur, a wise and worthy king, had a great table constructed so that all of his knights could have a place to discuss their individual perspectives on the kingdom. The king sat in the seat of power, which belongs to the ruler or, psychologically, the Self, because it alone holds the perspective of the entire kingdom, thereby protecting it and giving it direction and purpose. Each of the knights, in contrast, has particular interests to defend.

In our metaphor, the kingdom represents the psyche as a whole, including the individual's needs and the interlocking needs of others in his or her life. The knights, or characters at the inner table, represent the personal and archetypal patterns of functioning that influence our behaviors, shape our decisions, and color our feelings. At any moment, one of them may usurp the seat of power from the king, taking over the ruling authority during an inner coup—perhaps as a needy child seeking affection and security or as a harsh critic afraid of imperfection or as a compulsive overeater whose hunger cannot be satisfied. Then the inner kingdom falls into disharmony and suffering under the reign of a knight or shadow figure.

So, we do not see the psyche as a solid, unified front surrounded by a Teflon wall. Instead, it is a dynamic, fluid, multiply intelligent world populated by myriad characters that may quickly appear on center stage or retreat from moment to moment. During these shifts, the whole of us may seem to be possessed by a part, while the other parts remain backstage. While one part acts out, it may not feel like "me" at all.

Each of these parts or characters at the table has a personal history or creation myth. Also, like each god and goddess, each has a wound to bear and a gift to give. The more unconscious and less differentiated the characters, the more tightly they can hold on to the seat of power, possessing us like alien forces and stealing our free will. But as we begin to make them conscious and differentiate or personify them in our imaginations, the less tight their grasp becomes and the more our range of choice expands.

Archetypal psychologist James Hillman writes of the link between the characters, which he calls our pathologies, and our compulsions, which he calls Ananke, the goddess of necessity. When we feel as if we are claimed by a foreign power, held hostage by a character that causes us to act in irrational, unfamiliar ways, we are caught in the circle of Ananke. The less we can imagine the force that drives us, the more compulsive and unconscious our activity will be. But the more we can imagine it and relate to it, the less we will be possessed by it. Eventually, with ongoing shadow-work, we can offer it a place within the divine order, a sanctuary in Camelot, where its power can be honored and its voice can be heard. We begin shadow-work by tracing the roots of the characters in our personal history.

TRACING THE ROOTS OF THE SHADOW IN PERSONAL PSYCHOLOGY

Each shadow figure or character at the table has a story to tell with a similar plot line: At a young age, our full range of aliveness, feeling, and dependency was too much for our caretakers to bear. Unknowingly, they betrayed our young souls again and again, inflicting the wounds of neglect, intrusion, cruelty, and shame. To survive this wounding environment, as children we made a Faustian bargain, concealing the unacceptable parts of ourselves in the shadow and presenting only the acceptable parts (or ego) to the world. In an ongoing, subtle series of feedback loops with parents, teachers, clergy, and friends, we learned, over and over, how to present ourselves in an attempt to feel safe, accepted, and loved. In this way, ego and shadow are inevitably created in tandem within us all.

This universal creation of the shadow figures takes place via the following coping strategies or defense styles, which act archetypally like guardians at the gate of the soul. They help us to survive in untenable situations by protecting us from the anxieties of rejection and abandonment. But, paradoxically, just as we defend against shadowy feelings and behaviors, the shadow is formed. Just as we attempt to protect our vulnerable young souls, we lose contact with them.

The disavowal of our thoughts and feelings (denial) begins at an early age as we discover that our parents may withhold love if we cry or punish us if we are wrong. As wounded children themselves, our parents defend against the return of their own difficult, buried feelings when they are stimulated by a child's natural spontaneity, raw emotion, and eroticism. As their defenses flounder, the parents often protect themselves by unknowingly judging and condemning their young ones through shame and rejection.

If, as children, we internalize our parents' critical voices, shame and self-loathing get built into our self-concept. We learn to feel insufficient, fraudulent, unacceptable. The quality of our parents' feelings and values then shapes our later defense styles. We tell them "I am not like that" or "I didn't do it" in an effort to avoid judgment, blame, and punishment and to feel acceptable. In this way, so-called negative shadow content, which is deemed unlovable, is stuffed into the unconscious (repression), buried in the body (somaticization), or attributed to others (projection), while so-called positive traits, which are deemed acceptable, turn into our ego ideal (identification).

For example, when we bury uncomfortable feelings to avoid dealing with them (suppression or repression), we pay the price of our aliveness. Our client Carol came to therapy struggling with a midlife depression. As a young girl in the rural Midwest from a farming family of seven children, she learned to appear happy (character 1) and hide her feelings of sadness in an effort to protect her parents from feeling failure or helplessness. As a result she concluded, even unknowingly, that her feelings were not acceptable. She developed a persona with a narrow range of feeling and behavior that has caused her to appear superficial, like a Barbie doll. Internally, continuing to protect her parents, she feels overly responsible and acts moralistic (character 2), compelled by Ananke to obey the command of a punishing, wrathful god. As a woman, she has continued to live out the girl's persona, so that when she married she believed it was her job to be her husband's caretaker, to keep him happy by being a proper wife.

Later, in a natural developmental process, partially as a result of the safety of her marriage and as a result of entering midlife, her hidden feelings unexpectedly erupted. In this way, she uncovered Moody (character 3), the name she gave to the character at the table who contains her parents' message that sad feelings are not acceptable. Moody has usurped the seat of power and Carol, still unable to tolerate her feelings, has become seriously depressed.

We see moods as undifferentiated feelings; the mood of depression, embodied in the character Moody, contains the undifferentiated feelings of sadness, grief, loss, hopelessness, despair, and even rage, which became suppressed together. With shadow-work Carol began to recognize that her depression was not merely about dissatisfaction with her external life or a hormonal imbalance. It stemmed from her disconnection with the depths of an authentic soul life. When she began to attend to the difficult, banished feelings, she found the gift of a richer, more authentic emotional life.

When we unconsciously adopt the characteristics of a parent or other authority figure (identification) to reduce the pain of separation or loss, we also defend against our own separateness and vulnerability. When a child says proudly, "I'm smart just like Daddy," he drinks in the values of his father, defending against feeling stupid and small. When he grows to adulthood, Daddy's Boy may still operate within him and contain the roots of his father complex, the inner voice that tells him how to take a stand in the larger world, how to be powerful, visible, and productive. The shadow appears when his training to avoid feeling small and powerless leads him to self-sabotage as a compulsive workaholic, which requires that he sacrifice his marriage and his authenticity on the altar of productivity.

For instance, our client Anthony, now forty-two, had been terrorized by his father and brother as a young boy. Today, he cannot tolerate men who are weak and powerless, judging and criticizing them as victims. As an alternative, he developed an overly responsible character with a workaholic lifestyle and two professions so that he could feel strong and powerful. But when he reached forty, Anthony began to suffer from exhaustion and lethargy, and he grew depressed and hated himself for being weak. His protector had become his saboteur.

Eventually, he began to see that through identification with his father/aggressor he could feel strong; however, he had become a tyrant not only over others but over himself. Through projection, he could expel his weakness and disgust onto others, treating them the way he had been treated. Yet in doing so he had cast into shadow his own vulnerability, which returned to haunt him at midlife.

When these kinds of defenses break down and anxiety-provoking feelings begin to break through the surface, we feel flooded with fear. At those times, we may adopt the behavior of an earlier stage of life (regression) in an effort to ward off the anxiety. In regression, we time-travel into the past, longing to be adored or cared for by another, free of adult responsibility. On those occasions, we may give up the voice of our authority, become unable to act independently, yearn for a former lover, disappear into a depression or illness, or literally return to live at our parents' home.

Or at difficult times we may attempt to self-medicate (denial), anesthetizing ourselves through substance abuse and distracting ourselves through compulsive activities. Denial also acts as a platform for the creation of extremely autonomous characters in dissociative disorders, such as multiple personality disorder. This splitting off (dissociation) of a particular thought or feeling during a traumatic event, such as sexual abuse, results in creating one or more autonomous characters with lives of their own, which are unrelated to the authentic Self. In these myriad ways, the inner characters are born, living outside the boundaries of conscious awareness but secretly influencing our moods, responses, and life choices.

Defending Ourselves with Shields: Power, Sex, Money, Addiction

As we develop, our shadow characters pick up swords and shields—power, sex, money, addiction—to protect their identities, compensate for feelings of shame, and defend against further injury. First of all, the characters seek to compensate for their feelings of weakness, inferiority, incompetence, and powerlessness and for their fears of nonexistence. So they devise ways to gain invulnerability by using a power shield to banish these uncomfortable feelings. They may resort to violence, verbal abuse, emotional control, or withholding love and approval. But the result for them is the same: Those internal characters who carry the more vulnerable feelings move deeper into shadow and become more entrenched in the unconscious.

At the same time, the ego grows stronger and stronger. Like a reigning monarch, it builds empires via status, authority, or fame. And the shadow character, who appears to speak as a friend, actually inhibits the authentic voice of the Self and speaks as an enemy. Using power to serve the ego, the shadow character turns the archetype of power into a power complex, a demon hungering for satisfaction. Soon, we do not have power; it has us. (Because this is such a central theme, each of the following chapters has a section on the *power shadow*.)

We make a distinction between two kinds of power: *authentic power*, the ability or willingness to stand for the authentic voice of the Self, which also has been called empowerment; and *inauthentic power*, which stems from the ego and serves to reinforce a defense or coping strategy of the persona. At times, an individual's expression of authentic power may look like a power trip or an inability to adapt to an outer authority. But each of us must learn to make this distinction for ourselves, differentiating between an inner tyrant, ogre, or witch and the assertive voice of the Self. In other words, we need to learn to use the power to act without an act of power.

In myth, the god of power and war, Ares, is the lover of Aphrodite, the goddess of sexuality. Power and sex go hand in hand; they are a matched set. Within us, the characters at the table use sex, like power, as a shield to defend against feelings of isolation, impotency, or unattractiveness. Sexuality carries the life force from one human being to another. As creators of human life, we experience one of our most intimate connections to the creator, to the gods, in sex.

However, for millennia, the sexual archetype has been split: It is worshiped for its powers of creating life, and it is damned for its powers of connecting us to the shadowy realms of the body and instincts. Therefore, sexual shadows pervade our intimacies. Eros, the god of love, opens the floodgates of desire and shuts them just as rapidly. Or he directs them down back streets, through dark alleys, and across unknown byways. One vampy seductress character may act out sexu-ally to hide deep shame about her body; another Don Juan character may seduce a series of women to feel young and powerful and to hide his fears of intimacy and vulnerability. (Each of the following chapters has a section on the *sexual shadow*.)

In addition, the characters use money as a shield to bolster a weak self-image or to inflate low self-esteem. Like sex, money has archetypal origins, and it is reduced by becoming the ego's tool. Money carries soul, the projection of divine energies. We long for money as we long for love, even as we long for salvation. We sacrifice for money, our life blood in exchange for coins. We fight for money, even with those we cherish the most. We worship money like a false god.

The word "money" derives from the Roman goddess Moneta, whose temples were mints where the first money, as we know it, was made. Moneta was considered an aspect of Juno, the mother goddess of Rome, who also served as protectress of women, marriage, and child-birth. As a fertility goddess, Juno Moneta acted as the mother of money, from whom plenty issues forth.

Today, as the sole currency of exchange, money is a potent symbol of transformation, of the power to turn one thing into another, like the alchemist's quest in reverse: turning gold into matter—food, cloth-ing, shelter, pleasure, status, mobility.

But like other archetypes that carry soul, money also carries shadow, hidden meanings, forbidden feelings, unknown forces. In our public seminars on shadow-work, we have found that asking people to tell others how much money they have in the bank provoked more anxiety than the most intimate questions about sex. People who thought they had too much money felt intense guilt; those with too little felt intense shame. Either way, money acted like a dirty secret, containing feelings of "worth."

So, money is also a split archetype in the culture: It's the root of all evil; it's the grail we seek. In some ways, our relationship to money re-veals our relationship to our life purpose, even our fate. Depending on which myth we live by, we may spend all our lives ignoring it, or we may spend all our lives pursuing it. Either way, money has a tightfisted grip on us that needs to become conscious. For money lives in the shadows of our lives, in the secret greed of our own Midas-like selves, in the family battles that divide parent from child, in the wrenching divorces that separate lovers, in the lifelong friendships that turn dark after money changes hands. (Each of the following chapters has a section on the *money shadow*.)

Finally, the characters use addiction as a shield to numb the pain of a rejected character and to escape its dark feelings. Addictions act as camouflage, a way of hiding from and protecting against our real needs, which remain unconscious. But as psychological dependency becomes physiological habituation and then abuse, the user becomes filled with guilt and shame for the self-destructive behavior. So instead of escaping shadowy feelings, addicts find themselves face-to-face with them, believing themselves once more to be bad, unworthy, and unlovable. In this way an addiction creates more shadow content by failing to address the shadow directly, allowing it to erupt indirectly and therefore to remain unconscious.

Once the addiction is in full force, it becomes a glaring symptom, diverting attention from the dark and difficult feelings beneath the behavior. And the struggle with the demon gets all of the attention. The demon addiction is a shape-shifter, taking the form of white cocaine or Russian vodka or sexual obsession. In any case, the user's life becomes oriented around craving it, scoring it, using it, coming down, and starting all over again. The person is taken over, possessed by the demon, so that the rest of life pales, losing its color and significance.

Addiction camouflages a vast inner emptiness, a gaping hole at the center of the person. But cocaine covers it with a heady rush of power, an inflated sense of potency like a balloon filling with helium. Addiction may conceal a terror of intimacy, a fear of losing oneself in the unknown territory of another person or of being seen as a small, selfish individual who needs love. But sexual obsession wrenches the person's attention away from these shameful feelings and fixes it on the shining love object, the man or woman who holds the mana to heal the addict, to make her feel safe, to make him feel like a man.

Dionysian intoxication, which appears in most cultures, fills a natural human need. Wine-drinking can be a sacred act; chewing or smoking psychoactive plants can open a doorway to divine reality. But in the West, as the Christian church purged itself of "pagan" rites, becoming increasingly earnest and joyless, it turned the god of wine into the god of darkness, the devil. In so doing, it turned divine intoxication into evil addiction, a possession by the dark side of the neglected archetype. For instance, highly rational, controlling Apollonian women may use alcohol and become vulnerable to sexual shadow attacks by Aphrodite or rage attacks by Kali; highly logical, controlling men may use drugs and become susceptible to invasion by seductive Eros or martial Ares. In this way, some people may use substances to release repressed aspects of themselves, permitting them freedom of expression.

For us, addiction can be seen as a search for an experience of soul that is always sought but never maintained through drugs. For this reason, the user pursues it with ever-larger doses. And an opportunity for rebirth is stillborn. Instead, the addict confronts the inner demons, invoking the agony of Job as he cries out in despair against the divine for its indifference to his affliction.

Thus, as the gods speak to us through power, sex, and money, they also speak to us in our addictions. Or, more accurately, they speak through us. But we do not know how to listen or how to respond because we are caught in an unconscious complex, cut off from the divine archetype.

Besides their personal roots in individual and family psychodynamics, each of these defenses and their accompanying shields have deep cultural roots. Personal psychology is a necessary but insufficient explanation for shadow issues.

Tracing the Roots of the Shadow in Culture

The *cultural shadow* is the larger framework in which the personal shadow develops. It helps to determine on a large scale—via politics, economics, religion, education, the arts, and the media—what is permitted and what is taboo, thereby shaping individual and family personae. In our fast-changing contemporary culture, many images and ideas that could not be spoken about two decades ago have been publicly disclosed: childhood sexual abuse, wife battering, alcoholism, addiction to prescription drugs. In this cultural moment, the shadow is also breaking through in the violent lyrics of rockers and rappers, in a growing number of books on Satan and evil, and in cyberspace, where

Internet users take on shadow identities to experiment with their multiple selves.

Although the archetype of the shadow is universal, shadow content is always formed within a cultural context—that is, within the beliefs, values, language, and myths of a given group. Cultural differences in relation to competition and winning, for example, yield different shadow content: Dutch children, who need to be prepared to live in an egalitarian society, are taught that coming in first is not necessarily a virtue; they learn to keep low profiles, thereby banishing their ambition into the shadow. Children in Mediterranean countries, such as Greece and Italy, are taught to feel special and unique, even superior, thereby burying their more communitarian feelings. And British children are taught that it's acceptable to finish first—but only if they do not appear to work harder to achieve their goals.

Distinctions in moral behavior also reflect different cultural attitudes toward the shadow. In Catholic countries, the world of darkness is starkly set against the world of light, and moral behavior is prescribed according to the Seven Deadly Sins—anger, envy, pride, avarice, lust, gluttony, sloth. The roads to heaven and hell, then, are clearly paved. But in Hindu Bali, the world of darkness ritually interweaves with the world of light in shadow puppet plays from the Vedic scriptures. The distinctions between gods and devils may blur. And in Buddhist Tibet, the demons have no objective reality but are viewed as misunderstood energies within the human mind. And prescriptions of moral behavior are replaced by contemplative spiritual practices for transforming the five poisons: anger, pride, jealousy, ignorance, greed.

Given these vast differences on "the deadly sins," it's imperative to make our cultural frame more conscious and to point out that the view of the shadow in this book stems from an American or Western European, white, post-industrial social context and thus inevitably reflects this time and place. We assume, for instance, a respect for the individual rights of a child and the civil liberties of an adult rather than tribal or communal needs, which might be emphasized in a non-European culture. We assume a respect for social and economic equality among men and women rather than a model of dominance and submission, which might appear in a Middle Eastern society. We assume a respect for multicultural views and a tolerance for diversity rather than a monolithic view of religious or ethnic values, which might be advocated in a single-minded religious community. Our perspective on the shadow cannot escape our own cultural frame; our attitudes toward power, sex, money, and addiction, for example, are formed within this mind-set.

Furthermore, even our language reflects this problematic issue in the use of the words "shadow" and "dark side," which unfortunately have racial overtones and imply the superiority of whiteness. James Hillman has pointed out that, etymologically, *whiteness* is associated with heaven, purity, innocence, and lightening up, whereas *blackness* is associated with hell, pollution, evil, and drawing down. In psychological terms, white is consciousness, which is cast as positive; black is unconsciousness, which is cast as negative, dirty, perverse, forbidden. But this kind of splitting, or linguistic apartheid, does not reflect psychological reality, in which light side and dark side are intimately intermingled.

Our cultural shadow projection—we are light, they are dark—falls upon different groups at different historical moments. In the name of the one right way, whole populations cast their darkness onto others with holy zeal, reenacting the ancient tribal heritage of Isaac and Ishmael. During the Holocaust, the Nazis advocated the ethnic cleansing of those who did not belong to "the Aryan race." More recently in Bosnia-Herzegovina, more than a quarter of a million people died, caught in a web of ethnic hatred.

American soil also is poisoned—with the genocide of Native Americans, the slavery of African Americans, and the slaughter of the Salem witch-hunts. And today, gays and lesbians, especially those infected with the HIV virus, have been turned into the Other and forced to hide their sexual orientation or, instead, to flaunt it in an effort to end feelings of self-betrayal. In addition, we attempt to turn a blind eye to homeless people, who form a kind of untouchable caste that carries shadow projection. And illegal immigrants, who appear to threaten security by transgressing our borders and consuming our resources, have been officially deemed the new enemy.

Like our culture, our nature contributes to shadow formation. In myths and fairy tales throughout time, the human shadow has been imagined as a brutal Beast, an unruly savage whose tireless aggression and bottomless appetites stem from his animal origins. Animals themselves have been demonized to stand in for the Other: the predatory wolf, the restless jaguar, the crafty fox, the devouring hunter in search of its prey. The shadow, like the animal, cannot be controlled; it lives under a law of its own. As culture rejects biology and our animal nature is exiled for the aims of civilization, the *biological shadow* is formed: Our creatureliness is banished for higher purposes, and we are taught to identify with mind over body and to honor spirit over flesh.

All of these layers of shadow projection might be imagined as nested dolls: The personal shadow is nested within the family shadow, which is nested within the cultural shadow, which is nested within the global shadow. As a result of these interrelated forces, biological factors, and family dynamics, we make our individual version of the Faustian bargain, and the shadow robs the riches of the soul. We lose the range of our original energy or aliveness and the connection to our authenticity. But the lost riches return when the banished shadow character, like an outsider trying to make a place for itself in the kingdom, appears at the boundaries of awareness at the most unexpected moment. And, once again, we meet the dark side.

THE SHADOW AS REDEEMER: FINDING GOLD IN THE DARK SIDE

Toward the end of Goethe's tale, Faust owns all the land the eye can see except for one small parcel with a chapel, which is owned by an elderly couple, Baucis and Philemon. Swallowed up by his own greed, Faust orders Mephisto to take the land by force. Acting autonomously, Mephisto kills Philemon and Baucis and burns their land.

Jung studied Goethe's work intently and extended it into the psychology of the shadow after having a dream while reading Faust. According to some sources, Jung may have been Goethe's great-grandson, but, in any case, the psychologist continued the literary genius's tradition when he named his own inner guide Philemon, perhaps to repent for the sacrifice required by Faust's ego. As described in his autobiography *Memories, Dreams, Reflections,* Jung discovered the reality of the psyche through the wise figure of Philemon.

In Jung's story we can see that shadow-work may be a multigenerational process; certainly, it is a lifelong one, a metamorphic struggle that portends renewal in arid times. To Jung, Mephisto carries not only Faust's dark side but also the scholar's energy, vitality, and imagination. Without him, Faust is dry, wooden, lifeless. Yet by wrestling with him, Faust is resurrected. So, although Mephisto appears to be a Judas, in the end he is a savior.

Each of us wrestles with the dark giant in our own way. For some, doing shadow-work may mean sacrificing niceness for honesty; it clearly means sacrificing ego appearances for the authenticity of the Self. For others, it may mean sacrificing grandiosity for humility; it clearly means sacrificing naive innocence for the promise of mature wisdom.

As each layer of shadow is mined from the darkness, as each fear is faced and each projection reclaimed, the gold shines through. And we begin to realize that the task is ongoing: The mine has no bottom floor. Yet, somehow, in a compassionate embrace of the dark side of reality, we become, like Lucifer, bearers of the light. We open to the Other—the strange, the weak, the rejected, the unloved—and simply through including it, we transmute it. In so doing, we awaken to the larger life. We sense patterns within patterns. We begin to hear the call of the Self. We no longer simply believe in magic, we rely on it.

CHAPTER 2

THE FAMILY SHADOW: CRADLE OF THE BEST AND THE WORST

Sometimes a man stands up during supper
and walks outdoors, and keeps on walking,
because of a church that stands somewhere in the East.
And his children say blessings on him as if he were dead.
And another man, who remains inside his own house,
stays there, inside the dishes and in the glasses,
so that his children have to go far out into the world
toward that same church, which he forgot.
— RAINER MARIA RILKE

Shadow-making happens in families and makes us who we are. It leads to shadow-work, which makes us who we can become.

Families are our origin and, for many of us, our destination. We are born into families, contained in families, nourished by families, and cherished by families. At the same time, we are neglected by families, betrayed by families, and witness violence in families. In the end, we die among family.

The family holds mythic power—the source of all good, the defense against evil. It's exalted as a sacred ideal, which promises roots, blood relations, future generations. It ties each individual life to its fate, imprinting it genetically, biochemically, and psychologically with blessings and curses. To imagine life without family is to imagine life in free fall, without a container, without a ground on which to stand.

In the last thirty years, as a society, we have come to realize that our image of the family is just that, an image. But it's not *just* an image. It's a fantasy that drives us because the archetype of the family is at the center of this image. And it compels us to follow it, to bond, to love, to re-create ourselves, thereby forming family. So, we long for a vessel of blood relations; we yearn for a community of kin that understands us implicitly, that offers safety and acceptance. And, wherever we find family, we find home: More than a place, home is a dwelling for the soul.

Recently, as family secrets such as childhood abuse, wife battering, and epidemic addictions have emerged from the cultural shadow, our fantasies of the perfect family, à la Norman Rockwell paintings, have been shattered. In fact, many families appear to deliver us into the very kinds of suffering from which they promised to protect us. If we open our eyes and look closely, instead of averting our gaze, we will see that, everywhere, love and violence, promises and betrayals go hand in hand. Home is also a dwelling for the shadow.

In addition, many forms of family that have been tainted with darkness in earlier generations today have become the norm. Single-parent households, blended stepfamilies, multicultural relationships, and gay marriages have changed forever the face of the American family, exposing previous taboos to the light of day.

As a result, many people lament the breakdown of the traditional family structure and blame it for a larger cultural malaise that includes the rise of drug addiction, teen pregnancy and suicide, and gang violence. Grieving the loss of traditional values, some long for a return to the old image of a stable, patriarchal, nuclear family, reminding us of another time, another place. For them, this image is like a finger pointing upward toward the heavens, toward the promise of a better life.

But we do not believe that the dissolution of the family and the concomitant lack of moral order we see around us stem primarily from an absence of moral order imposed from the outside. Instead, we suggest that in many homes the *family soul* has been sacrificed to maintain the illusion of the *family persona*. As a result, the *family shadow* erupts, ripping apart the fabric of life for its members.

Like each individual, each family has a persona, a proper mask worn to gain acceptance in a unique subculture. Those families who have internalized a traditional Judeo-Christian image may wear the appearance of nice, honest, hard-working, churchgoing, charitable folks. Others, whose image is shaped more by an experience of the 1960s, may wear the clothing of free-spirited iconoclasts and reject the work ethic of the larger culture. Others, whose standard of behavior is shaped by a poor neighborhood in the inner city, may wear the mask of cool, indifferent underachievers who refuse to play society's unjust games. Still others, who hold an ideal image of a highly educated, highly cultured family, may wear the appearance of wealth and elitism, force-feeding their young ones academic skills or extracurricular classes regardless of their individual tastes or talents.

In each case, so-called negative behaviors and traits (rage, jealousy, adultery, greed, laziness, alcoholism) as well as devalued or latent talents (artistic, athletic, intellectual giftedness) lie concealed just beneath the surface, masked by the family's proper presentation and forming the family shadow. This family shadow develops naturally and inevitably as the group identifies with ideal characteristics, such as politeness or generosity, and buries those qualities that do not fit their family image, such as rudeness or self-centeredness. In this way, the family persona and the family shadow develop together, creating each other out of the members' life experiences.

Parents, children, teachers, clergy, and friends add to the mix, helping to determine what is allowed to be expressed and what is not. For some families, emotional vulnerability and crying are encouraged; for others, they are banished into shadow. For some families, anger and conflict are tolerated; for others, they are the worst taboo. For some families, nakedness and natural bodily processes are accepted; for others, they are banned. For some families, artistic talents are supported; for others, they are considered a waste of time. In this way, anything can become shadow content; it's not determined by the nature of the material but by how family members relate to it.

If a young child feels violent toward another child and is told "Get over it" or "Stop that," he will be forced to banish the difficult feelings into the shadow, along with the authentic part of himself that contains those feelings, as a natural defense against the pain of disapproval and abandonment by the adult. On the other hand, if an adult tries to understand and honor the child's feelings, teaching him to talk them out or redirect them toward a constructive outlet, such as physical activity, the feelings are less likely to be banished into darkness only to erupt later as violent rage, dark depression, or alcohol abuse.

Just as individuals remain unconscious of their personal shadow material, so family members remain unconscious of the family shadow, which contains buried secrets like a treasure chest stowed away in the attic. Like the personal shadow, the family shadow may appear unexpectedly, acted out in the breaking of family rules ("We don't use that kind of language here"), impulsive acts (a child is caught stealing), compulsive behaviors (a teen suffers from an eating disorder), or mood disorders (chronic depression and anxiety). It also can be projected, such as when one member angrily blames another for a trait he cannot accept in himself ("I can't stand when you cry like a baby and don't act like a man") or when one parent disowns a child's bothersome trait ("That comes from *your* side of the family").

Families expel or hide from the shadow in another inventive way: family triangles. Partners may avoid conflict or reduce anxiety by focusing on a third person and projecting the shadow *over there*. A husband may displace tyrannical anger at his wife by routinely punishing a child. A wife may bond too closely with a young son, turning him into her idealized spouse and leaving her adult spouse holding the shadow. A woman may get rid of her own nagging witchiness by attributing it to her partner's ex-wife, "that other woman." A family unknowingly may turn one child into a "bad seed," a scapegoat for the whole group, so that the others may carry on business as usual. As a result, the third person becomes the Other, the identified problem, keeping the temperature down between the partners and thereby maintaining the status quo, which camouflages deeper underlying patterns.

In these ways family persona and family shadow play against one another like Dr. Jekyll and Mr. Hyde, in an ancient antagonism that keeps family members concerned with the outer props of life—an appearance of decency, financial security, the children's education, caring for the next generation. But privately, deep in their souls, many feel as if they have missed the boat; they suffer with the suspicion that they have failed as partners and as parents. They surmise that there must be something more to family life than this facade.

THE MISSING INGREDIENT: FAMILY SOUL

We suggest that this missing element is family soul, a natural environment or psychic space that allows for the deepening and unfolding of family members' individual souls. When the family soul is present, the members feel contained; they carry an internal connection with one another, rather than an imposed or obligatory relationship. When the family soul is palpable, the members feel deeply at home, seen and accepted for who they are. When the family soul can be felt, its members do not have to hide.

When the family soul is present, the members feel genuinely loving toward one another and loved by one another. The Greeks had a term for this kind of family love: *storgé*. It refers to the naturally occurring devotion and affection that arise among family members, as distinct from *agapé*, spiritual love, or *eros*, erotic love.

A soul-centered family honors individual differences and may even welcome, rather than repress, conflict as grist for the mill. It encourages learning and exploration of new attitudes, feelings, and competencies, rather than imitations and conformity. It works together to meet challenges and plays together to share the joys of life. The family soul creates a safe psychic space in which to do shadow-work and recharge individual soul.

Family soul may be linked to the virgin goddess Hestia, who symbolizes the hearth containing the fires at the center of the household, the city, and the earth. There are no myths about Hestia; she merely stands firmly at the threshold of the home spreading calm, protection, and dignity. She turns the house into a home, a dwelling place where family members can feel that their own natures are accepted. When Hestia's fires go out, as they have in so many homes today, there is no place for family soul, no calm that radiates out from the center. Instead, order may be imposed from any direction, creating a facade of togetherness.

When this facade or family persona is strong, the space for soul shrinks. Members' capacity to be present with each other in an authentic, vulnerable way is limited. Instead, they begin to act habitually, even mechanically, with each other, losing honesty and vitality. A five-year-old boy begins to act "like a little man"; a woman barely out of school behaves like a dutiful wife. Unconsciously, they fear risking disclosure because their feelings will be seen as unacceptable to those whose acceptance they depend upon. They fear risking nonconformity because they will be shamed and punished. Eventually, they feel that they have to hide from the very people who could offer them healing acceptance.

Like precious heirlooms, the mother's family shadow and the father's family shadow become woven together, creating a tapestry of artificiality, disappointments, secrets, lies, and betrayals. If this is not recognized, it gets passed down to the next generation, bequeathing another legacy of pain. Without shadow-work, family members remain trapped in this web of parental complexes, homebound no matter how far away they travel.

But with shadow-work the unconscious wounds of the family can set us on the path toward consciousness. Instead of remaining profane wounds, instilling feelings of bitterness or thoughts of revenge, which restrict awareness from the ego's point of view, they can become sacred wounds from the soul's point of view, opening our awareness to a higher order. Instead of unconsciously learning to bury our wounds, we can consciously learn to carry them, identifying our projections and deepening our empathy for others and for ourselves. In this way, the betrayal and its wound become a vehicle for soul-making.

If one person in a family begins to make these wounds conscious ("Yes, I can see I failed you in that way"), then that individual can bring reconciliation to the group, creating the potential for a greater family awareness and for the emergence of family soul. Learning to use the experiential tools of shadow-work, he or she can fulfill the Jewish proverb: "A son wishes to remember what his father wishes to forget." For instance, when a man can feel the rage of his father well up in him in the presence of his young son, but instead of expressing it he can observe and contain it, he spares the next generation. When a woman whose mother remained disconnected from her own feminine beauty can discover the nature of that disconnection in herself, she can learn not to inhibit the feminine in her daughter.

✫ What lies in your family shadow? How is family soul sacrificed in your home?

Facing these intergenerational family shadows, we can begin to redeem the family soul. The first step is to identify the sins of our fathers and mothers.

Sins of Our Fathers and Mothers: Shame, Envy, Depression, Anxiety, Addiction, and Self-hate

Once upon a time, at the very beginnings of Western civilization, our most distant ancestors, the Titans, set a terrible precedent. Ouranos, god of the sky, and his wife, Gaia, goddess of the earth, bore six sons and six daughters. But the father hated his children and hid them in the dark hollows of the earth, where the light could not reach them. Infuriated, Gaia fashioned a great sickle, enlisted the help of her son Cronos, and plotted revenge. When Ouranos came at nightfall and lay across the earth with ardor, Cronos seized his father and used the mighty sickle to castrate him.

Cronos later married Rhea, who bore three daughters and three sons, the first generation of Olympian gods. Cronos, whose name means time, reigned over a Golden Age with the orderly passage of seasons and the cycles of birth, death, gestation, and rebirth. But Cronos struggled against the very cyclical laws that he inaugurated. Told that he was fated to be overthrown by a powerful son, he, too, got rid of his progeny, flinging Hades into the underworld and Poseidon into the sea. Rhea grieved terribly, so when their third son, Zeus, was born she hid him in a cave on Crete and instead offered Cronos a stone wrapped in swaddling clothes, which he swallowed instantly. Zeus grew up in secret and, with force and cunning, ultimately overthrew and castrated his father.

But this shadowy pattern did not end here: Zeus was trapped by the same fate. Taking many consorts and fathering many children, Zeus believed that the offspring of Metis would be wiser and stronger than he. So, to avoid being overthrown, he swallowed Metis during her pregnancy, and the armored warrior Athena sprang forth from her father's head.

These three generations of devouring fathers have characteristics whose dangerous qualities reappear today in ancestral sins such as sexual incest, emotional incest, and even the murder of children by their parents. Or we might imagine these mythological fathers' gruesome acts as stemming from envy of their children's growing potentials, which evokes a power shadow. The terrible result: the emerging willpower of the new generation is cut short.

This reenactment of family sins seems to be the shadow's cruel way of challenging us to learn the lessons that our ancestors failed to learn. If we, in turn, fail to change, we perpetuate the family curse, as illustrated by adults who were abused as children who then abuse their children, and so on through the generations. Either we do some form of psychological work, like shadow-work, or the issues continue to haunt us. As Jung wrote: "When an inner situation is not made conscious, it happens outside, as fate." It also appears in the lives of our children and in the lives of our children's children.

Certainly, intergenerational sins may be passed on in biochemical predisposition, such as in fetal alcohol syndrome, endogenous depression, or schizophrenia. But we are not using "sin" in that way. And we are not using it in the conventional way, as the breaking of religious or moral law. We refer here to sin as maintaining destructive unconscious patterns that keep us trapped in the family shadow. If individual development has meaning and purpose, as we suggest in this book, then the etymological root of "sin" applies: To sin is to be off the mark, that is, to inhibit development, contracting backward into regression rather than expanding forward into growth.

In the psychological transmission of sins, unconscious feelings and attitudes are passed on from grandparents to parents to children or from older siblings to younger ones. The elders' hidden conflicts, anxious worries, and buried wishes are absorbed by vulnerable young minds, leading to the same attitudes, gestures, and emotional states. Like little sponges, children pick up hatreds, depressions, fears, and addictions, even if they have never been mentioned aloud.

These sins are transmitted in a variety of ways. If a man continually makes belittling looks or degrading remarks about his wife's appearance, he shames her in front of the children. They, in turn, begin to devalue her, naturally identifying with the more powerful parent. At an unconscious level, the children absorb sexism, perpetuating a collective shadow; both boys and girls learn to devalue the role of wife and mother. But, at the same time, even though the shame is not directed toward them, because they love and identify with their mother they internalize her reaction. In this way, they themselves are shamed, and they learn shaming behavior.

Eventually, they may develop a shame complex, becoming sensitive to rejection, eager to accept blame, and hungry for acceptance and approval. At the level of soul they feel unworthy, debased, and unlovable, anxiously anticipating the next shaming moment. At the center of the complex sits an archetypal image: a worm, a termite, a dark spot or glob of black goop. As a result, a shame-based person longs to be invisible, to remain hidden like a sea anemone which, when touched, quickly closes up.

Shame, then, is a gatekeeper of family shadow. It props up the family facade and reinforces denial. It encourages projection and guards against any new knowledge that might puncture the family image. Shame divides us from ourselves and from those we love. It banishes the family soul. For all of these reasons, arenas of shame point toward healing; they carry the potential for the restoration of authentic feeling.

Who shamed you? Who is the character at the table who carries your family shame? Whom do you shame? What is the deeper need lying hidden in your shaming behavior?

Envy also transmits family sins. A man who strives to provide for his family may envy his nonworking wife's solitary time. On the other hand, a woman who sacrifices her career opportunities to be a stay-at-home mother may envy her husband's achievements. In addition, she may succumb to the danger of envying her children's opportunities as well. If she lives vicariously through her daughter with conscious pride, she also may suffer with unconscious resentment and express it with unconscious anger. If her own dreams and ambitions have gone unrecognized, if she regrets her unlived life and feels herself to be a failure, she may develop a vested interest in shaping her daughter's direction. Her daughter, in turn, may feel trapped by the mother's need to live through her. She may silently rage against the older woman, eventually sabotaging her own success with self-destructive acts, such as eating disorders. Or she may accommodate her mother's wishes, becoming an obedient daughter but sacrificing her own authenticity.

The shadowy feeling of envy, then, arises from the discontent and resentment aroused by obstructed desire. We feel that if we lack a coveted possession or a prized opportunity, we are less than the person who has it and less than who we can be. As a result, we kneel and bow before the object of desire, placing ourselves in an inferior position, creating the two poles of have and have-not. For some, to envy a person is to project a god, missing altogether their human foibles and limitations.

★ Whom do you envy? What is the deeper desire lying hidden in this feeling? Who envies you? How does it feel to be envied?

Anxiety also transmits family sins. If a parent did not feel safe as a child and became distrusting of others, fearful of simple behaviors such as flying or driving, or unable to relax or sleep properly, her child is probably susceptible to this same anxiety. One woman, a highly successful screenwriter from Chicago, had so internalized her anxious mother's fear of life that she thought constantly about the impending disasters that would arise from any decision she might make. She lacked any kind of spontaneity and felt dread about the smallest risks. She developed intricate perfectionistic behaviors for fending off the shadow. And her own self-worth remained inaccessible until she acknowledged her long-concealed rage at her mother's imperfections.

★ Who in your family carries the anxiety? What makes you nervous, anxious, afraid? How does an anxious shadow character sabotage your intentions? What do you need to feel safe?

Depression is also a carrier of family sin. A parent may look at a child without hope or touch a child without warmth. A mother may not get out of bed for days at a time; a father may withdraw into television night after night. Through repetitive behaviors that suggest feelings of emptiness, helplessness, or hopelessness, a parent unknowingly leaks depression into a child. In this way the pain of depression is perpetuated through the generations, much like a contagious disease.

Family therapist Terence Real has written eloquently of this transmission of family shadow from fathers to sons. He distinguishes between overt male depression, which has debilitating but highly visible effects, and covert male depression, which may be chronic but well hidden by denial in heroic behaviors and addictions. Real points out that an epidemic of male depression has remained undetected due to cultural shadow issues about gender: Women are raised to internalize pain and blame themselves for distress. Therefore, they typically suffer from overt depression, which can be viewed as internalized oppression or the experience of victimization. On the other hand, men are raised to externalize pain and blame others for their distress. Therefore, they typically suffer from covert depression, which can be viewed as internalized disconnection or the experience of victimization that is warded off through grandiosity and perhaps victimizing others.

The unconscious, unresolved suffering that stems from the depression of previous generations operates in families like an emotional debt, according to Real. "We either face it or we leverage our children with it."

Who in your family carries the depression? Who denies it? What is the depressed character at the table trying to tell you? What are its deeper intentions?

When anxiety or depression threaten to break through the threshold of conscious awareness, many people suffer addictions; they turn to alcohol and drug abuse, or compulsive sex and work to avoid their feelings. One woman reported that she felt so polluted by her alcoholic father's blood running in her veins that she feared she could not escape her family's fate. Both her older sister and twin brother succumbed to alcoholism, while she fought desperately to avoid the gravitational pull of her family shadow.

Who is the family addict? Who takes care of this person? Who denies the problem? What shadow issues are camouflaged by the addictive behavior?

Of course, some sins are brutally enacted within the walls of the family home. A child who witnesses a man battering his wife or a mother beating a child may not appear to be the victim per se; however, this child's soul is brutalized. She or he loses a sense of innocence and safety, as well as the freedom to feel fully and to express feelings, out of fear of becoming the target. Becoming passive and depressed or anxious and hyperalert, a witness to violence may unknowingly banish authenticity and aliveness into the shadow.

Other sins are not so cruel or concrete but may be passed on in a silent attitude or an invisible projection. A family with a lineage of strong women may imply to children that men are ineffectual, creating disrespect at a young age. A high-achieving family may teach that "we are what we accomplish," so the children do not learn to value feeling or interiority. Another may teach that those with less socioeconomic status are trash or that those with higher status are evil; or they may teach disrespect and disdain for their elders. In every case, the soul of the child is diminished as the child identifies with the parents' feelings of inferiority and superiority.

The inevitable result of the transmission of these sins is some form of self-hatred, which may be experienced as a tormenting inner critic, a disdain for the body, or a rejection of an essential part of our nature. Our client William, twenty, for instance, had absorbed his father's shadow projection of homophobia. A small, effeminate, artistically gifted man, William had not yet told his family that he was gay; he feared that his strict, religious father would disapprove and never speak to him again. As a teenager, he had begun to use alcohol and marijuana to hide from the lie and dull the pain of his inauthentic life. Then he turned to heroin, the ultimate escape.

In therapy, William slowly wrestled with his sexual orientation. He began to realize that he was not inherently flawed, disgusting, and perverted, but that a character within him constantly delivered that message from his father. He began to see and feel the beauty in his sweet, artistic nature; it was merely his internalized father's voice that told him that his temperament was better fit for a girl. But William's homophobic character, who drew strength from cultural and religious taboos, tormented him with self-destructive thoughts. And William succumbed to the undertow of heroin. Despite his hard-won awareness, he could not make the required sacrifice: He could not allow the homophobic character to die so that he could continue to learn to accept himself. Instead, he died of a drug overdose, a casualty of hand-to-hand combat with his shadow.

In addition, as carriers of the collective shadow projection of racism, many people of color will pass on some form of low self-esteem or self-hate to their children. Today, Caucasian children who live as minorities also suffer this kind of projection. As one client put it, "I feel like white bread in my neighborhood." Similarly, many Jewish survivors of the Holocaust internalized some form of anti-Semitism, which their children and grandchildren unconsciously pick up as self-loathing or unacceptability, despite mighty efforts to assimilate or achieve success.

Sometimes the sins of our fathers and mothers are shrouded in secrecy. Family secrets may remain hidden not only to outsiders but to family members as well. Indeed, through the powers of repression and denial, secrets may be hidden even from ourselves.

FAMILY SECRETS:
THE SACRIFICE OF AUTHENTICITY

Family secrets are the shadow's tools for keeping lies, addictions, and violence—the family's multigenerational sins—in the darkness. Typically, the secret comes about to protect a vulnerable part of a family's history ("We escaped the Holocaust" or "Our grandparents had African-American blood" or "My sister was schizophrenic" or "We were dirt poor") or a member's questionable behavior ("My mother was a pill addict" or "My uncle molested me" or "My brother committed suicide" or "My wife had an affair").

One Asian-American client revealed, in an offhanded remark, that when she was six months old her parents immigrated to the United States, but they could not support the whole family. So they kept her brother here but sent her back to Taiwan to be raised by an aunt for one year. And the experience was never spoken of again. She repressed the feelings, minimized this experience, and does not see its link to her terrible fear of abandonment today. A beautiful young black woman tells her therapist that her mother denies their African-American heritage, living in disguise as an Indian woman in a sari. The client, who lives with a white man, admits that she has no black friends. Finally, a woman who attends an expensive private college tells her therapist that her younger sister is anorexic, though no one else in the family has noticed. With the perpetuation of these family secrets, authenticity between family members becomes increasingly difficult, and family soul is diminished.

However, to tell a family secret is no simple task; its repercussions may be earth-shattering. For some, the family container cannot hold, and it breaks apart. For others, the powers of denial stand like a fortress around the family secret, and the secret teller cannot be heard. Like Cassandra, the prophetess who was cursed to be disbelieved in the Greek tragedy *Oresteia*, the secret tellers are not given credibility and may even be banished from the fold.

These days, as the public corridors ring with family secrets of abuse, it's commonplace to assume that all secrets should be told as loudly and as quickly as possible. But the hero on an archetypal journey often cannot speak of what he has seen until his task has been completed. So the urge to keep the secret may at times be as strong as the urge to tell.

In other cases, telling the family secret is required to lift the family curse, even though the consequences for the secret teller are high. Miranda, admonished by her parents never to speak the family secret aloud, kept silent for forty years. Like an obedient child, she lived life with her mouth shut, certain that if she told the truth her parents would abandon her, disinherit her, or perhaps even die. Then Miranda was diagnosed with breast cancer, and her brush with death acted like a wake-up call. She felt compelled to live with greater authenticity. She decided to speak the truth and risk losing her parents in an effort to take back her own life.

Her mother, at twenty-one pregnant and unmarried with two children, had given her up for adoption. A wealthy couple from the Upper East Side of Manhattan adopted her at birth. She remembers clearly being told at six years old that she was adopted—and that she was never to discuss the matter with anyone, or she would be sorry. Miranda acted the part of the perfect daughter and kept the secret. But by the time she was a teenager, she hated herself. Although she was a star in school, she took drugs after class, which was the beginning of her double life.

When she married in New York City at age thirty, she also began an affair in Los Angeles. So in her thirties she was bigamous and bicoastal. And she had two sets of parents as well.

On the outside, Miranda wore the trappings of success: She drove a BMW, owned a house in a wealthy neighborhood, and climbed to the top rungs of her career ladder. But, on the inside, she rejected herself the way her mother had rejected her; unconsciously, she had buried her self-worth in the shadow. She also hated and resented her adoptive parents, because they would not allow her to speak of the secret and be herself. She resented her husband for the same reason; she felt controlled, self-conscious, and inauthentic around him. So her authenticity and personal power remained hidden in the shadow.

When Miranda finally decided to look for her biological mother, she found her in a small town near the city where she was raised. After a long internal struggle, she told her adoptive parents about the meeting with her mother—and they were furious, threatening to disown her if she ever discussed it again.

As Miranda continued to do shadow-work, she came to understand that although she was forty years old, she projected her power onto her parents and husband as a child would. Naturally, she resented and belittled them, feeling no choice but to hide herself and continue to depend on them emotionally and financially. In order to discover her own authenticity, Miranda needed to connect with her own rage and power and to stop projecting them outward. That is, in order to become an adult with a positive sense of herself, Miranda needed to accept her own origins—by betraying her adoptive parents and telling the family secret.

Miranda identified the shadow character that had taken over her life as "the rejected one." She imagined her as a small, waiflike girl who was filled with shame. Archetypally, Miranda saw herself as an orphan, an exiled, hopeless child who would never find her way home.

As she connected more deeply to her own authentic Self, she had the internal experience that the character of the rejected one was not *her*, but merely a part of her, a shadow character which had taken control. Miranda herself was not an outsider, a powerless victim; however, her early life experiences shaped a part of her to identify with feeling that way. By making a more conscious relationship with the character and acknowledging her feelings without identifying with them, Miranda was able to slowly uncover some sense of pride and entitlement. Eventually, she began to develop her own creative voice by writing poetry.

Miranda disclosed to her husband that she had been living a lie and wanted a divorce. In grieving the loss of her marriage, she began to tell her story to friends as well. Two years later, she met Gary, an engineer, and the powerful combination of shadow-work and their honest relationship enabled her to accept the limits of her relationship with her adoptive parents. The growing love between Miranda and Gary also enabled her to consider motherhood, which had always been cast in shadow due to her painful birth circumstances. In fact, Miranda could consider giving birth to a baby because she had given birth to herself. By facing the family secret, she had lifted the family curse.

What are your family secrets? Who keeps them from whom? How does this reduce authenticity among family members and decrease family soul?

Now that we have explored how family sins are transmitted from parents to children and how they may remain concealed in family secrets, we turn to siblings and their unique shadow issues.

Shadow Sisters/Shadow Brothers

We have been using King Arthur and the Knights of the Round Table as an image of the internal world of shadow characters that can take over the seat of power. Externalizing the metaphor, we might view the family as the kingdom and the characters as the siblings around the dining room table, each vying for love, attention, and resources. When the kingdom is in balance, the goddess Themis abides: She regulates the proper order in human relations, establishes boundaries, and prevents the shadow from intruding.

In this atmosphere, each individual feels his or her needs honored. Therefore, there is less need for siblings to act out. However, with an absent or alcoholic king or a tyrannical or depressed queen, the kingdom is thrown into chaos. As a result, the sibs enact the shadow with each other in an unconscious effort to reestablish harmony.

Felice, a landscape architect, had a dream about this image: *I dreamed of getting up from my seat at the family table. When I returned, my seat was missing. I went down into the basement.*

Felice grew up with six sisters, each struggling for a fair share. She felt that she disappeared in the crowd. In fact, one of her sisters literally disappeared—she died of anorexia. Felice's survival strategy was more subtle: emotional suicide. Having been beaten by an older sister and undefended by her parents, Felice surrendered: Out of fear of attack, she did not speak up or disclose her feelings. As a result, she felt unseen and misunderstood. When she was ten, her father returned from a trip with key chains for the girls. Felice offered her older sister the choice between them. After choosing one, the sister changed her mind and wanted Felice's chain. Felice felt defeated again and unworthy of keeping her gift. Her own sense of entitlement was banished into the shadow.

Years later, as an adult, Felice repeated this pattern: When their mother died and the family inheritance was doled out, Felice could not bear to open her safety-deposit box. It took a full year before she could look inside.

Slowly, with shadow-work, Felice came to realize that she deserved to have needs and desires of her own and that she deserved to have them met. In addition, she could not continue to feel responsible for her sister's jealousy. She had to take her own seat at the family table. And in this way she found the gold in her dark side—her sense of self-esteem and capacity for assertiveness.

Some sibling pairs develop by pushing against each other in opposite directions until they seem, as adults, to carry the projection of the Other for one another. Like the mythological sisters Eve and Lilith, or Psyche and Orual, each holds the mirror reflection for the other: one is artistic, the other athletic; one is smart, the other beautiful; one is accommodating and well behaved, the other rebels and acts out. This kind of splitting can trigger terrible envy between sibs, causing one to reject the other or to idealize the other and reject herself. Brothers, too, may appear to be opposite, yet they are complementarily linked at a deeper level: Like Jesus and Judas, Abel and Cain, Osiris and Set, one creates, the other destroys; one becomes godlike, the other devilish.

We suggest that this strange but significant phenomenon—the one who is most like us is also the most different—stems from a key family dynamic: the division of the pie of family shadow. During the birth and early years of each sibling, differing pressures on parents may lead to distinct shadow content. As each sib absorbs a parent's shadow in a unique way, they unconsciously split the pie: each sib cuts off parts of him or herself, such as aggression, sadness, or ambition, in an effort to preserve the family persona and to belong. Then the indigestible parts are played out among them, as they fight with each other in the pain of self-denial, suffering from cutting off their budding potentials in order to keep the family together.

For instance, the birth and development of a gifted "golden child" in the family may mean that others feel they cannot compete. So they hide their own talents or give up the fight altogether, ashamed of their lack in the sibling's reflection. On the other hand, the gifted child may suppress her own self-expression out of the discomfort of being envied, or she may shine as the family star.

The story of Gloria and Toni, two sisters now in their forties, illustrates this splitting of family pie. Gloria and Toni have not been close in their adult years. Although their mother says they were inseparable as children, Gloria primarily recalls their differences, their otherness. "She's such a stranger to me—stranger and kin," she says.

A perpetual reader, Gloria takes great joy in thinking about ideas; her sister did not finish college. Whereas Gloria is awkward in her body and disinterested in physical activity, Toni is a star athlete in whatever sport she tries—baseball, tennis, golf. And whereas Gloria, as a child of the 1960s, rejects all concerns about image, her sister dresses to the hilt, as if fashion designers put together her wardrobe. A student of yoga, Gloria looks for natural highs and spiritual solutions; Toni believes that life is so full of suffering that depression is the only authentic response.

Gloria wonders aloud how two children of the same gender, raised by the same parents only two years apart, could develop such distinct abilities and follow such divergent paths. She remembers that their father, the authoritarian head of this Latino clan, used to talk about La Familia as if it were one monolithic structure, as if it were a sacred name that, when invoked, could keep out enemy intruders. He saw the family as one single entity, no individuals, only the sacred group, the tribe, the clan. The boundary around the family was secure, but the boundaries within the family were lost. And the opportunity for family soul was limited.

Perhaps, Gloria says thoughtfully, she and her sister developed such contrary qualities in a desperate effort to differentiate from their enmeshed family. With so little space for individual soul, they used each other to push against, to find a separate name, to carve out a separate purpose or fate. It's almost as if they developed the two opposing sides of one psyche, like ego and shadow. Although their differences appear to be irreconcilable, at a deeper level they may demonstrate an alliance of opposites which, like yin and yang, together make a whole.

For example, Gloria disclosed that ever since she was a young girl she often felt envied by other girls and later by women. "They envied my independence, or my family's closeness, or my career success, or my intelligence. But it always made me a little uncomfortable, as if they wanted something from me, as if they felt inferior to me somehow." And in that moment, Gloria stopped and, taking in a breath, looked at her therapist and said, "Oh, I guess I secretly felt superior to them, too. All the way back to my sister, I unconsciously held the superior position—maybe that's why people felt inferior and envied me all this time."

To break this lifelong pattern and open up the possibility of more equality in her relationships, Gloria does not need to give up her self-esteem; however, she may discover that her feelings of superiority mask their opposite: feelings of inferiority, which have been carried by her sister. Similarly, her defenses against her own depression have permitted her to live a life with less suffering; her sister, though, may know a depth of feeling she can only imagine. By uncovering her own feelings of inferiority and depression, Gloria can discover her separate self beyond the split attributes with her sister. In this way, she will be more free to explore into her sister's territory, thereby ending their lifelong turf war.

By acknowledging in herself those qualities that she disowned and projected onto the Other, by doing shadow-work with the internal image of her sister as a character at the table, she can enrich her own self-image, as well as feel more compassion for her actual sister, perhaps one day cultivating a more authentic relationship with her. Gloria's ticket to individuation can be found in her lost, rejected traits. Her shadow sister, then, may be her redeemer.

How is the pie of family shadow split among your siblings? Does a sibling carry a quality that might enrich your own treasury?

In the end, siblings are part of our fates; we are part of theirs. Some of us spend all our lives standing in each other's shadows; others discover there a beloved friend.

SEXUAL SHADOWS: INCEST AND INITIATION

Family members carry divine or archetypal energies for one another. The child is always the Divine Child; the mother, the Great Mother or Queen; the father, the Great Father or King. For this reason, parent-child incest is more than a personal betrayal; for the child, it's an encounter with the dark side of a god. Thus an abusive mother as goddess of creation becomes goddess of destruction, dancing like Kali on the corpses of the dead. Or she transforms into Medusa, whose stare petrifies her child into stony silence. In the same way, the father as lord of the house becomes Lord of Darkness, taking on the face of Hades, who steals the young Persephone away from her mother and penetrates her in the obscurity of the underworld.

With incest, a timeless taboo that lives in the collective body of humanity is broken. With incest, a household is cursed with a psychic affliction. With incest, a child's natural erotic warmth and authentic openness turn cold and hidden as shame, like the original fig leaf, covers over a naked vulnerability.

Although the act is sexual, some of its consequences are deeply spiritual. When a parent sexually violates the trust of a child, the young one's spiritual wholeness is violated. Betrayed, robbed of innocence by those who should be the protectors of her innocence, the child responds unexpectedly: with self-blame. Because a child is dependent on the adult for its very life, the shadow makes a U-turn, transforming the offending adult into a good parent and the victim into a bad child. In psychology, this internal act has come to be known as identification with the aggressor. The child's soul is so vulnerable that it must protect the parent as the wrongdoer, thereby taking on the blame. To her, she is not simply engaging in bad behavior, she *is* badness itself. This is the root of the intense feelings of shame and contamination that are epidemic among survivors of abuse, ingrained at the level of identity. And this is the root of their ongoing mistrust of others and their lack of faith in life itself. Finally, in this internalized parent, the family pattern is carried on.

If the family's religious orientation reinforces the offending parent's rule as divine law, then the child's obedience is sanctioned by higher powers. If the parent denies the behavioral reality, then the child is confronted with an untenable situation, a Faustian bargain: to deny his or her own bodily experience. At the soul level, this calls for the survivor's sacrificial death: the surrender of identity, the loss of will, the end of reality testing.

Tragically, experts estimate that today a shockingly high percentage of girls and boys are molested. As more and more adults have recalled episodes of childhood abuse in therapy, the validity of their memories has been called into question and dubbed "the false memory syndrome." For us, the actual reality of these incidents is less significant than the reality of the psyche: If a boy was not sexually molested but has a felt sense of intrusion, he may have been emotionally molested. Either way, his soul was violated and cries out for healing. If he does not receive it, he may identify with being a victim and, in turn, become a victimizer of the next generation, spreading the wound like a virus. In this way, the shadow of the victim/perpetrator returns to the scene of the crime, re-creating the past in the innocent young ones.

As the cycle of abuse recurs again and again, the child tells herself: "This is really happening," creating a character at the table. Another part of her responds, "It can't be happening," creating another character. Eventually, her memory gives up, banishing the event and its attendant feelings into the shadow. It cannot retain the truth and allow her to survive. The defenses of repression, dissociation, and denial are at work.

We suggest that these same defense mechanisms that arise in the survivor are at work in the perpetrator and may be reinforced by alcohol. With these reinforcements, the perpetrator can banish the event into the shadow, perhaps becoming rigid and moralistic to defend against it, and thus creating a rigid family persona. If the perpetrator recalls the event, he may feel mortified, frightened of his sexuality, and suffer from compulsive urges to act out. His guilt and regret become self-hatred, perhaps turning into depression or cruelty to himself or others.

Without minimizing the crippling effects of this trauma, we would like to suggest that incest, as the most heinous violation, can also be an initiation into shadow. For many survivors today, its discovery is the first step in the long journey toward redemption. It evokes the poignant question: How can one best live, like the Fisher King in the grail myth, with an open, unhealing wound?

This has been the journey for our clients Trudy and Sheila—to establish an honest, living relationship with their molestation and to understand what it requires of them. Trudy, a highly competent executive secretary with an infectious laugh, told her story. Her father died when she was nine. She remembers longing for him, like a prince who would return to rescue her. But the next year, her mother married Joe, a physician, so the young girl turned to him as her new father with hope and trust. But Trudy's trust was betrayed when, two years later, Joe began to enter her room late at night and molest her. She began to dread going to sleep; she would hear the squeak of the door and jump in alarm. During the day, she would suffer panic attacks; at night, she would suffer nightmares.

Trudy recalls being terrified of saying no to Joe. She was afraid that he would leave her two younger sisters, her mother, and herself, as her dad had done. So, in her version of the Faustian bargain, she became their protector, a child-wife who pleased him to make him stay.

Trudy's stepfather swore her to secrecy with a threat of violence. And she held the secret for five years. But with puberty an additional conflict arose within her: Trudy began to be flooded with feelings of arousal against her will. She fantasized about Joe and, at the same time, felt disgusted with herself. When she started to enjoy the sex, she also started to feel a secret competition with her mother for Joe's affections. At the same time, she felt tormented with terrible guilt because she began to believe that it was her fault that Joe turned to her rather than to her mother. She began to feel that if he were not aroused, he might go away. If she did not wear attractive clothes, he might lose interest. Like Persephone, Trudy had been pulled down into Hades, her innocence lost, her childhood never to return. And her rage, which would be directed against men, banished into shadow.

When Trudy turned fifteen, she began to stay away from home for longer and longer periods, discovering a budding identity outside of her family. She became infatuated with a girl her own age who returned her feelings and respected her sexual limits, so that she could give and receive affection without concomitant feelings of hatred. Soon, she told her stepfather that she would call the police if he ever entered her room at night again. The molestation stopped—and so did Trudy's interest in men. She turned to women for a safer experience of sexuality, especially gentle women with whom she could be the aggressor and act out the powerful role.

At thirty, Trudy met Malcolm, a younger and rather innocent man who had not yet established a career. When he wished to begin dating her, she felt frightened and uncertain. Respecting her limits, Malcolm proposed a friendship instead. After spending time together for about a year, slowly and tentatively, they fell in love and eventually married.

During this time, with the support of her husband and therapist, Trudy allowed herself to feel her buried rage at her stepfather, Joe, and to confront him with her memories. He admitted the full truth, disclosing that Trudy's mother had withheld sex from him all those years. Trudy had to face yet another harsh reality: her mother's collusion.

Doing the difficult steps of shadow-work, Trudy separated out the characters at the table: "the whore" (character 1) was the adolescent girl who felt aroused by her stepfather's touch, becoming a seductress and enjoying her power over the older man. When "the whore" took over, Trudy felt dirty and ashamed (character 2), but this character seemed safer than feeling vulnerable and receptive. So she became more tough and bossy (character 3), using her power shield to protect her wounded soul, which then became a pattern in her marriage as well. As she made these distinctions and learned to witness the characters, she slowly began to feel less defended and more vulnerable with Malcolm.

As the emotional intimacy of their marriage deepened, however, Malcolm felt threatened. He began to make excuses about avoiding intimacy and rejecting Trudy's sexual advances. A few months later, he began to sense memories of his own molestation by his father. He was not certain if these memories were real or imagined. But he realized that he was becoming controlled and rigid around sexuality when Trudy initiated it, and he did not know why.

When Malcolm confessed his memories to Trudy, she was stunned. But this was not the final blow. Three months after Malcolm's discovery, his father was caught molesting a young niece. With the help of her therapist, Trudy reported the incidences to the Department of Social Services and, in shock and retribution for telling the family secret, the family began to shun her. No one wanted to believe this horrific tale. DSS sent a Catholic caseworker to interview Malcolm's dad, a practicing Catholic. The caseworker believed that he had repented—and DSS dropped the case, leaving the young niece in harm's way.

In facing her feelings of rage and helplessness, Trudy told her therapist, "It feels like a never-ending story. The theme of abuse haunts me wherever I go." But it did not end there. Malcolm got a job assignment in Trudy's hometown. Moving back, they brought her secret home with them. "It's as if my presence is a constant reminder of the abuse to everyone," she said with finality.

Trudy continues to feel pain and sadness about what happened to her, but she no longer suffers from denial or shame. She carries her wound openly, honoring herself and her healing process. She tells her own truth in her adult relationships with her stepfather and her husband, and she has keen antennae for those who have lost their authenticity and live in denial. She continues to reclaim her rage from the shadow and, with it, she has uncovered her capacity to be vulnerable.

Another client's story portrays the long-term effects of trauma and their relation to shadow-work. Sheila, twenty-five, who works at a local bookstore, sits in an oversized T-shirt and sweatpants in the therapy session sobbing, holding her head in her hands, her long blond hair falling over her face. "Last night I felt so crazy, I couldn't sleep. I felt small and dirty, so I stayed up cleaning the house, just scrubbing walls and floors and sinks. It's filthy, I couldn't get it clean. I thought I was losing my mind."

Sheila had been looking at childhood photos of her brother, her sister, and herself when she recalled, for the thousandth time, a painful act of betrayal that changed her life when she was eight years old: Her father, as usual, was away on a drinking binge. Her mother was preoccupied in the other room. A male neighbor, age eighteen or twenty years, stood in the bedroom with his pants down, forcing Sheila's ten-year-old brother to perform sexual acts. Then the neighbor picked up Sheila and placed her on the big bed. The neighbor told her brother to get on top of her or he would tell everyone what they had done a moment before. She felt small and helpless, petrified with fear, pinned down under her brother's body. Then she felt a terrible piercing pain, and she cried softly to herself.

Sheila told her therapist that the images would not stop coming. They filled her mind so that she couldn't think about anything else. "I just feel wrong," she said. "I feel dirty, ugly, and polluted. I can never get rid of it." Like the scarlet letter "A" for adultery, Sheila wears her identity as a victim of childhood sexual abuse. She feels ugly, although she's quite attractive. She feels false, a phony, although she comes across as natural and sincere. She feels distrusting of others, although she trusted the therapist quickly. And she deeply distrusts herself, remaining frightened of her own impulses and desires.

Sheila continued her story. Later that night she lay in bed with her live-in boyfriend, Teddy. When he began to kiss her, she felt swept away, flooded by archetypal content. "I left my body. Some part of me didn't want to be there, didn't want to be touched or feel turned on. I mean, if I had stayed present I would have felt outraged at him. And it's not his fault."

Blessed by Mnemosyne, goddess of memory, Sheila first remembered her molestation in a dream when she was sixteen. At that time she asked her mother and sister about the event, triggering memories in her sister and corroboration from her mom. Sheila felt that she had uncovered a dirty secret that had been buried under her other issues, much like the fairy-tale pea under the princess's mattresses: her dislike of her own body, her discomfort with sex, her tendency to space out and lose track of time, and her fear of her brother, now an active alcoholic like their father.

When Sheila's therapist took a summer vacation break, the young woman felt abandoned and alone. She was caring for her young nephew when her mind filled with intrusive thoughts: She imagined herself molesting the innocent young boy. "Dark shadows crossed my mind, taking me over until I lost myself and imagined doing bad things to him. My mind got worked up, with the gears spinning but not engaged. My heart was pounding. I kept wishing these thoughts would go away, but they wouldn't. I was horrified, completely ashamed of myself."

Sheila called this part of herself "the dark side." The therapist asked her to identify the sensations she feels in her body when the "dark side" appears. Then she can become aware of it, slow down, and do her breathing exercise so that it doesn't overtake her. Then Sheila began to hold a dialogue with that part of herself that might hurt a child, robbing him of his innocence. It told her in a cold, uncaring voice: "I want to do to him what was done to me." Sheila's brother had overpowered her, leaving her feeling like a helpless victim. Now, some part of her wanted to identify with the aggressor and take the power back by becoming an aggressor against her nephew, attempting to vanquish the victim.

Then another character at the table spoke up, her "protector."

"This part protects me from the dark side, but it goes too far—it doesn't let me trust myself about anything at all." Again, Sheila identified the sensations and thoughts associated with this character.

When these two characters show up and Sheila unknowingly identifies with them, her adult ego gets paralyzed. "I get lost because I think *they* are me. They just take over, and I don't know how I think or feel. So I feel crazy."

Sheila came to understand that her fundamental unconscious feeling about herself—she is bad—was influencing her to commit an act that would prove her right, that would justify her sense of badness. The shadow may lead us to act in a way that evokes a particular character to help us get in touch with deeper feelings about ourselves. When we identify with the character, we lose control and unconsciously make choices that may be destructive. But when we uncover this feeling consciously, we may be able to avoid having to act it out unconsciously. And by centering on the breath and reconnecting with the authentic Self, we can disconnect from the complex, become more aware of repressed shadow influences, and discover our freedom of choice again.

Doing ongoing shadow-work, Sheila struggled for several years with her self-hatred, her feelings of contamination, and her efforts toward spiritual perfectionism. But as she witnessed the dark side character and experienced that it was not her, she slowly gained a deeper self-acceptance and self-trust.

If you believe that you were molested, how does the victim or bad child character at the table influence your adult life? Who does it blame and who does it protect? What does it need for healing at the level of soul?

Like sexuality, family money may also carry the projection of family soul and become tainted with shadow.

MONEY SHADOWS:
INHERITANCE, SELF-WORTH, AND GREEDINESS

Family money holds such numinous archetypal power that some members may become obsessed with it, experiencing a loss or gain of money as a loss or gain of soul. Money is linked with the life force; it circulates like blood in the family system. When there is a lack of money, family members feel deprived and suffer with shame. When a young child wants to participate in family money matters, offering to lend Dad his allowance or to earn small change with his chores, he seeks participation in the exchange of family energies. When an older child leaves home for college and refuses family money, she seeks separation and differentiation. Rejecting family money may mean rejecting participation as a child in the family system—that is, taking a step toward adulthood.

Because much wealth is inherited, most self-worth is inherited as well, like a family sin. For many, to have financial worth is to have self-worth, regardless of the source of the money. Ruth, thirty, discovered this link between financial and emotional inheritance when her grandmother left her a large sum of cash. When she told her therapist that she felt terrified of accepting the gift, she began to untangle the threads of family shadow. Her wealthy family had offered her every opportunity as a child: classes in art and ballet, designer clothing, and private schools. Propping up the family persona, Ruth had developed into a nice girl with nice parents in a nice house. But they had not offered her an opportunity to be authentic, to discover her own likes and dislikes, to express her own feelings and opinions. Instead, they told her constantly that she was a lucky child; she had so much that she had no right to complain.

The burden of her parents' expectation grew heavy. When Ruth behaved like a nice girl, she felt trapped. When she expressed herself even a little, she disappointed her parents and felt terribly guilty and responsible for their feelings. Then she felt regret for causing their suffering.

In her twenties, Ruth left home and did not look back. She became an extremely independent young woman, who fended for herself and needed no one, a condition sometimes known as counter-dependency. If her wall of autonomy were punctured even for a moment, she felt humiliated and smothered. Ruth came to believe unconsciously that if she accepted anything from her family, she would lose her own boundaries and her newfound identity, becoming once again a child without a voice, a subservient, well-behaved daughter.

But when she turned thirty, Ruth became depressed. Her tender feelings of vulnerability, her natural need to love and rely on others, surfaced with a vengeance. And as these shadowy feelings sought the light of consciousness, she began to miss her family members. Slowly, Ruth came to understand the deeper symbolism of the gift: If she avoided receiving the gift, she could remain alone and avoid having to risk an authentic relationship with her family. But if she could accept the gift and allow herself to maintain some boundaries, she might have an opportunity to develop a more authentic family intimacy.

Family money may be shrouded in secrecy, carrying potent shadows of greed, envy, shame, and low self-worth. One therapist friend, who works with cancer patients, told us that the discussion of money seems to be more stressful for his clients than the discussion of preparing for death from cancer.

Paulette, thirty-two, who worked long hours as a waitress, hid her financial situation like a dark secret. Her parents lived on a fixed income and could not offer her support. She earned barely enough money to pay her bills each month and felt as if she lived "one step from the streets." But when she socialized with friends, she acted as if she had plenty of discretionary income.

When Paulette began to sabotage her work by arriving late and performing poorly, she grew anxious about her welfare and dreamed one night about becoming a "bag lady." With shadow-work, she came to see that a rebellious inner character, who resented her family poverty and felt entitled to more money, undermined her efforts. If she allowed this character to take over, she might lose her job and end up in desperate straits. Paulette needed to befriend this saboteur and find its appropriate place at the table, so that it might lead her in a new direction while she maintained her daily responsibilities.

Roger, forty-five, a social worker who had been in therapy for two years, arrived one day to say that his father had offered to give him $8,000 toward the purchase of a new car. Initially, he told us, he felt this to be a generous offer. But Roger had been working with his shadow issues and, when he listened more intently, he reported that he heard another voice within saying, "See if you can get some more" (character 1). Instantly, on saying this, he identified it as a greedy character at the table and felt ashamed at his own greed (character 2). He looked down at his shoes, unable to look his therapist in the eye.

Roger noted that this greedy voice sounded familiar; it had instructed him in the past to take more from his father. In fact, this inner character felt entitled to more. The therapist asked when he had felt this entitlement earlier in life. And Roger then confided that as a boy he used to steal money from his father.

As a result of discoveries in therapy, Roger realized that he took money from his dad because it was that which he believed his father loved the most. And as a child he had wanted more of his father, feeling angry and neglected most of the time. As a compensation, he unconsciously wanted to take something of value from his father for himself.

Roger became aware of this pattern when he explored the mythological figure of Hermes, a trickster god who acts as a guide between the worlds but is also a liar and a thief. He identified Hermes in himself with a quality of desire that rises up in his chest. He experiences it as a craving, a compulsive urge to have something even if it does not belong to him.

As a boy, Roger had equated that which he could steal with receiving love. So he felt fulfilled through the act of stealing, an admittedly twisted way of getting his needs met. Although his ego felt gratified that it could take what it needed, his soul went into hiding. At a deeper level, Roger felt ashamed of wanting money; he was ashamed of having any needs at all. And stealing only temporarily made him feel better. Eventually, he felt more unworthy than before.

Over time, Roger came to see that the internal costs of stealing were high: anxiety, guilt, and the feelings of being dirty and unworthy. As he grew more aware of these negative consequences, he became more capable of negotiating with Hermes when he appeared. When an opportunity to take something or to avoid paying for something arose, Hermes would jump at the chance to get away with it. Roger struggled with his new awareness, using the creative arts to listen to Hermes without surrendering control to him and thereby avoiding the internal consequences. When he succeeded, he returned the greedy Hermes to his proper place at the table and uncovered the gold in this shadow character: an ability to raise his fees to earn what he was worth and to spend money on himself without feeling undeserving.

In childhood, Hermes had been his protector; he had given Roger a way to calm himself and maintain his feelings of being loved by actively taking the love he craved. Later, that same friend became an enemy. As an adult, it was no longer acceptable for him to compensate for his lack of self-worth by attempting to accumulate more money in a dishonest, secretive way.

We stayed with the issue for several weeks and discovered in it an element of intergenerational family shadow. Roger's father had called on Hermes as a Polish immigrant escaping to Switzerland after his army was defeated in World War II. He set up a smuggling ring to steal gold from the Nazis, using the gold to transport his family out of Europe and into the United States. So, in his aspect of thief, Hermes had saved Roger's father and family; in his aspect of guide between the worlds, Hermes had brought them to a new life. Working together, we came to realize that today Roger could call on Hermes as a guide to the inner world of his underprivileged clients.

✦ Does your family money carry more shadow or more soul? What is the nature of your emotional inheritance? Do you have family secrets about money?

LEAVING THE FAMILY HOME: CULTIVATING INDIVIDUAL AND FAMILY SOUL

Some people live their entire lives within a ten-mile radius of their family homes. Internally, too, they remain in position in the family constellation, forever the provider, the dutiful child, the critical outsider, or the family scapegoat. Unable or unwilling to examine family sins, these people pass them on with the family jewels.

Others leave home at an early age. Called away by romantic or spiritual longings, they heed the voice of the Self, as described by Rilke in the opening poem. However, although they physically move far away, without shadow-work these people remain caught in the clutches of family shadow or family secrets.

For those who leave and do shadow-work, another opportunity arises: to return home with the gift of consciousness and offer it to the family in a spirit of reconciliation. The result may be a more authentic intimacy and a deepening of family soul. This intergenerational development is expressed in this aphorism by President John Adams: "I was a warrior, so my son could be a farmer, so his son could be a poet."

How can you maintain your individual identity yet remain deeply connected to family members? Do you need to leave home in a more complete way? Or is this the time for you to return and cultivate family soul?

In the next chapter, we look more deeply at a particular family sin: the parent's betrayal of the child's soul.

CHAPTER 3

A PARENT'S BETRAYAL
AS INITIATION INTO
SHADOW

I am not a mechanism, an assembly of various sections.
And it is not because the mechanism is working wrongly
that I am ill.
I am ill because of wounds to the soul,
to the deep emotional self
and the wounds to the soul take a long, long time,
only time can help and patience,
and a certain difficult repentance
long difficult repentance, realization of life's mistake,
and the freeing oneself
from the endless repetition of the mistake
which mankind at large has chosen to sanctify.
—D. H. LAWRENCE

Well-known science-fiction writer Ursula Le Guin wrote a short story that centers around a stunning image of the scapegoat, a tortured soul who is exchanged for the happiness of an entire community. In her tale, the residents of the seaside city of Omelas appear to be unusually cheerful. They are not naive, like children, or bland, as if drugged. They are simply and genuinely joyous. They do not use swords or keep slaves, she says, as if to tell the reader that these people have no shadows.

However, in the basement of a public building a young child sits in

88

a locked dark room. Abandoned and undernourished, it grows thin and feeble-minded. Having screamed for help to no avail, it only whines occasionally now. This wretched one remains in the dark until a resident of Omelas arrives to bring cornmeal and water.

The people of Omelas know that the child is there. They know that it *has* to be there. The people's happiness, the beauty of their city, the tenderness of their friendships, the health of their children, and the abundance of their harvest depend on this child's misery. It is the existence of this child and their knowledge of it that makes possible the nobility of their architecture, the poignancy of their music, the profundity of their science. If the child were to be brought up into the light, cleaned, fed, and comforted, the prosperity of Omelas would disappear. And so, day after day, they exchange the blessings of their lives for the suffering of this one small soul.

Viewed in light of the parent-child relationship, the abandonment, betrayal, and sacrifice of the child has deep mythic roots. Etymologically, to betray means to serve up, perhaps to serve up to the gods, as in a sacrifice. To sacrifice, in turn, means to make sacred. Mythic fathers throughout time betray and sacrifice their children. In the New Testament, God sacrifices his only son, Jesus, on the cross. In the Old Testament, Abraham agrees to sacrifice his son, Isaac, in an effort to follow God's commandment. In Greek history, the king of Troy abandons his infant son, Paris, to die of exposure, but the prince returns to lead the Trojan War. During this same war, King Agamemnon, leader of the Greek forces, sacrifices his daughter, Iphigenia, to gain fair winds for his fleet.

Mythic mothers, too, betray their children for questionable causes: Princess Medea, deserted by her lover Jason, who gathered the golden fleece, slays their sons to take her revenge. And Agave, mother of Pentheus, king of Thebes, slaughters and dismembers her son in a Dionysian revelry.

In a parallel way, contemporary fathers, unconsciously perpetuating family sins, may judge and condemn their young sons as rivals to be pushed aside, as obstacles to their freedom from responsibility, or as weaklings to be turned into men by any means necessary. Like the gods banishing Hephaestus for a defective foot, these fathers may express their hostility through verbal abuse, corporal punishment, competitive aggression, or neglect and abandonment. Or they may idealize their young daughters as trophies for their own sense of pride or devalue them as objects for their own selfish pleasures. For some, the betrayal is malicious and intentional, simultaneously a betrayal of the natural order of parent-child love. But for most, the betrayal is covert and unintentional, a breech of trust, a failure to mirror, a transmission of his own shadow.

And mothers, too, betray their young ones in a variety of ways today: Medusa-like mothers stare down their daughters with a cold, perfectionistic glare. Or they trespass on a young boy's body with hands that seek to fill their own emptiness. Some mothers rage like the three Furies, who punish sinners of all kinds. Others devour their children, holding them hostage physically or emotionally, until they have no will of their own. And many play the shameless virgin mother, a saint whose children have to carry her invisible shadow.

Looked at on the inner plane, Le Guin's abandoned child is our very soul, whose tender feelings and vulnerable needs are sacrificed by parents in just the way that their parents sacrificed theirs. Banished from the inner kingdom, these feelings become shadow characters, who, like Paris of Troy, later fight for a place at the table. Marion Woodman points out that the soul child, radiant with light, often appears in dreams to be abandoned among bulrushes, in a tree, or in some other forgotten place. One of our clients dreamed that her soul crouched in a dark dungeon that shone with one beam of light.

The parent's ego, then, uses the repression of the child's soul to maintain the position of power in the family and to prop up the image of family persona. In a strange twist, the child unknowingly identifies with the powerful parent, whether it is the same-sex or opposite-sex parent. As a result, the child develops an ideal image of this parent, a fantasy of father or mother that is compelling because the archetype of Father or Mother lies at the center of this image. And in this way the child unconsciously models him or herself after this parent, resulting in the formation of particular ego patterns, such as father's daughter or mother's son. At the same time, the child unknowingly rejects the less powerful parent, burying his or her qualities in the shadow, resulting in the formation of particular shadow patterns.

Unconsciously, our parents want to create us in their own image. And we, as children, want this identification process to work. However, a parent's response to a child rarely lives up to the ideal image;

even with the best of intentions, even with the highest moral effort to nurture, support, and mirror the child's authentic nature, the parent fails. An inevitable betrayal occurs, and the child's ideal is shattered, initiating him or her into a parent's shadow. As the child meets the parent's shadow and continues to try to become acceptable by repressing unacceptable feelings or behaviors, she rejects authentic aspects of herself, repeating the betrayal internally and forming her own ego and shadow. And, in this way, another human child develops psychologically into an adult.

This fall from innocence, however, is not a simple, obvious, or avoidable evil. We do not refer here to the insensitive act of a cruel parent in physical or sexual abuse but to the subtle, inevitable moment in the life of a child or, more accurately, a series of moments, in which a parent turns away, attends to other pressing needs, or conveys an unintended, unconscious message. It is impossible to maintain a child's innocence according to a standard of perfect parenting—that is, the parent cannot meet the child's longing for love, desire for safety, and needs for mirroring at every given moment. The parent, whose soul has been wounded, is bound to fail. From the point of view of the child's soul, the betrayal is inevitable, and the parents are the instrument of that betrayal.

Archetypal psychologist James Hillman points out that betrayal can be seen as a necessary turning point that permits an individual to move out of a childlike state of naive trust and innocence into an awareness of the complexity of every human being, including the dark side. When a father betrays a son, for instance, by divorcing his mother, gambling away the family funds, or disappearing into depression, the boy faces not a godlike, idealized image of the older man, but a naked, limited human being who in some inevitable way cannot be trusted.

If, as adults, we continue to long for relationships that are free of disappointment, Hillman says, we may never grow up but remain in the position of the innocent child. This position, which he calls primal trust, carries the seeds of betrayal. Just as faith carries doubt within its nature, or a taboo carries the possibility of transgression, so primal trust activates its opposite—betrayal. In those moments, we reexperience the fall from grace; we move from fusion to separation, from innocence to knowledge.

Our parents as our betrayers, then, also act as agents of consciousness. We do not say this to excuse the tyranny of abuse or minimize the pain of injury but to deepen our notions of the parent-child relationship. Despite our assumptions that betrayal is evil, despite our deepest wish to live life without being wounded, betrayal has the hidden potential to open us to something larger. Thus it involves more than personal psychology: It's a gateway to an archetypal, perhaps fateful reality. In our betrayers we recognize our own capacity to betray. In this way, betrayer and betrayed are tied together in an alliance of opposites. The Other who carries the shadow then becomes a vehicle of the gods, requiring from us a richer ambivalence, a capacity to love and hate.

In this chapter, we will explore four of the many possible patterns of development that can occur as a result of shadow-making in families: father's son, father's daughter, mother's son, mother's daughter. Our portraits may appear to be oversimplified, but in life each has many versions, such as an Artemis- or Athena-style father's daughter, or a Hephaestus- or Hermes-style mother's son. These stories, based on our clients' lives, serve to illustrate how identification and repression work together to shape ego and shadow, respectively. As a result of this developmental process, the rejected qualities reappear as characters at the table with their respective shields. Each pattern is an attempt to meet the challenges of personal development in a given family. Each has its gifts and its limits. And each has a destiny that unfolds later in life as an individual's patterns of ego, shadow, and soul emerge in romance, friendship, and work.

The title of the Ursula Le Guin story mentioned at this chapter's opening, "The Ones Who Walk Away from Omelas," reveals her conclusion: From time to time, when a young adult visits the abandoned child and witnesses its plight, that individual may not go home again. He or she may walk away from Omelas and just keep on walking, perhaps to find another home, one that has not sacrificed a child to maintain its happiness. This individual can no longer consciously live with the betrayal. It is often the very wound to the soul itself that becomes the catalyst for the developmental leap away from the family and toward a more authentic individual life.

What aspect of your soul has been sacrificed? As a parent, how have you sacrificed your child's soul?

The Father's Son:
Reclaiming Feminine Shadow

In a story from the oral tradition surrounding the Old Testament, Abraham's father sold ceramic religious idols to support his family. One day the father asked his son to tend the shop for him. Abraham obeyed, but while he surveyed the idols before him, he became angry at his father's hypocrisy for taking money for the false gods. In his rage he smashed them all, except one. His father returned and, outraged, demanded to know what his son had done. Abraham lied: He said the one remaining idol had smashed all of the others. But his father replied, it has no power; it's only a statue. So Abraham told his father the truth. And in that moment of smashing his father's idols and revealing the hypocrisy, he sacrificed his childhood obedience and his unconscious bonds to his father complex, becoming an individual perhaps for the first time.

In Western post-industrial society, the pattern of the father's son stems from the boy's unconscious ego identification with his father and the masculine world over his identification with his mother and the feminine. Supported by the heroic ideal of a patriarchal culture in his same-sex identification, he becomes a boyish boy, primarily interested in trucks, sports, and competition. If his childhood is traditional, it is in many ways like a hazing for manhood. If he observes physical abuse of his mother by his father, he is more likely later to abuse his wife than a son of nonviolent parents. If he himself is physically abused, he may perpetuate the pattern with his children. If he enters the armed forces, he is encouraged to learn how to kill or be killed. Even if he is not abused or drafted into the military, a father's son may absorb patriarchal attitudes toward women and other men from the hypermasculinized men around him.

Like his dad, he banishes the more sensitive, nurturing, vulnerable qualities into the shadow. In this way, his persona may become rigid, angry, dogmatic, and resentful in an unconscious effort to appear strong, independent, and heroic. The father, whose soul was sacrificed to his father/god, requires the same sacrifice of his son, and an innocent child loses his capacity to be gentle or dependent. We do not wish to imply here that a father's son cannot be kind, generous, or supportive. Rather, we wish to emphasize that his greatest fear is weakness and dependency.

Our client Wayne, thirty-six, told his individual version of this universal story. As European immigrants, his traditional parents had an arranged marriage when his father was thirty-two, his mother eighteen. His strict, authoritarian father worked hard to support the family and took charge of the money and of the emotional atmosphere in the home: He permitted no sign of weakness in his son, disdaining incompetence and shaming uncertainty. He permitted no talking at the dinner table so that he could watch the evening news. He permitted no display of emotion among family members, except for his own Poseidon-like explosions of rage, which created trembling aftershocks in other family members. And he disliked music, so it was forbidden. Whenever Wayne asked for an explanation, his father slammed his fist on the table and replied, "Because I say so."

Wayne's father was highly influenced by the archetype of the *senex*, who in its positive aspect represents the wise old man and moral sage, but in its negative aspect represents the old, rigid, castrating king, a conservative, cynical figure who is cut off from youthful idealism. One archetypal image of the *senex* is Cronos, or Father Time, and, synchronistically, Wayne's father worked as a watchmaker. He also ran every aspect of his life on clock time, tyrannizing his wife if dinner was not served at six o'clock and punishing Wayne if his chores were not complete on schedule. The father's relationship to time was transmitted to his son, who came to feel that he could never be productive enough because there was never enough time. Unlike Demeter-style time, whose seasonal, organic cycles have a natural rhythm and serve as our ally, Cronos-style time is mechanical and contrived; it creates a life of busyness and devours its subjects, so that it comes to feel like an enemy, even like the Grim Reaper himself.

Wayne remembers that, as a young boy, his job was to go to school and perform well to make his parents proud. He played sports, although he was not particularly coordinated and felt no passion about the games. He pushed his body through the motions of football, treating it like an object that needed to learn to obey his mind. By the time he was twelve, he had broken both arms and legs.

Wayne's father unknowingly betrayed his young son in several ways: He was emotionally abusive, shaming the boy's vulnerability and neglecting his authentic feelings; he was intrusive, controlling Wayne's bodily rhythms and cutting him off from his own instincts. In effect, Wayne was emotionally neglected; his father was present but deprived him of deep contact and of a rounded image of the father. Like Abraham, another image of the *senex* archetype, the father sacrificed the son, whose tender, vulnerable soul had gone into hiding.

Wayne's mother did not object to her husband's dominant style; she presented a calming, understanding presence in their traditional home. Whereas the father was the provider of security and order, she was the provider of family feeling.

Unknowingly, Wayne identified with his father's position of power in the home and created the persona of a responsible, superior man (character 1). He remained in graduate school to become a professional until he turned twenty-five, dominated his women companions, asserted his opinions with a forceful logic, and acted as if he were invulnerable like his hero, James Bond. But internally he felt powerless, inadequate, and unworthy of his own standpoint.

Wayne lived in a black and white universe in which his father's critical *senex* voice (character 2) told him that any feeling of uncertainty made him look inferior and any trace of vulnerability made him look feminine, which formed another shadow character (character 3). Like Hamlet, the voice of his father's ghost haunted him for many years. Wayne remembers the few times that he felt deeply, all instances when he saw his mother cry.

In addition, Wayne struggled with secret sexual compulsions (character 4). Like the child in the basement demanding to be fed, he fantasized constantly about anonymous sex with women. But he felt too unattractive to approach them. Wayne met Roberta in grad school and became sexually involved without much emotional contact. But after six months he believed that he had real feelings for her and proposed marriage because he thought it was the right thing to do.

He became, like his father, a responsible, goal-directed provider who from time to time felt overwhelmed by what he believed to be feelings of love. But he gave his young wife no intimacy; he had no sense of how to reach her when she became moody and cried. Cut off from his natural bodily eros, their sexuality remained mechanical and without feeling. Their conversations remained dry and aloof, so he withdrew further into his own mind.

When Roberta asked for a divorce, his world shattered. He trusted her and never questioned her commitment; he had never really thought to question her about anything at all. Suddenly and with great intensity, Wayne felt overcome with grief. He sobbed uncontrollably and could not get out of bed to go to work. Like his father, Wayne was struck by Poseidon, god of earthquakes and the ocean depths. His persona as a father's son was reduced to rubble; his towering facade could no longer hide his secret wishes. His forbidden feeling came flooding in with the force of a tidal wave.

His psyche flipped to the other side of the archetype—the *puer*. He quit his job, left his hometown, and joined a spiritual community for the next fifteen years, which closed the door on responsibility but opened the realm of possibility. He experimented with psychedelics, explored intimacy with women, and learned to speak his mind with lovers and friends. Finally, he broke the stranglehold of Cronos when, through resting when he felt tired and practicing yoga to enliven his body, he discovered his own natural timing and began to live by his own rhythms. Having lived out his father's pattern without fulfillment, he then lived out his father's unlived life.

Without knowing it, Wayne was doing shadow-work by exploring those qualities that he had banished as a father's son. It would, however, be several years before he understood that flipping to the other side of the archetype—from *senex* to *puer*—is not the answer; rather, he would need to become the father of a young daughter to uncover his own way of holding the opposites, of being a stable provider and an emotionally available husband and dad.

THE MOTHER'S SON (THE PUER): RECLAIMING MASCULINE SHADOW

Other men, who do not identify with an overly masculine father, may begin their lives as a *puer*, or soft male. In his first therapy session, Charles, twenty-eight, disclosed that he felt as if he came from another planet or at least as if he were born into the wrong family. He had suffered all his life from feelings of isolation and alienation; he often had dreams of flying high above the earth, free and unattached, soaring away from the limits and responsibilities of daily life.

Mythologically, the one who flies high over the world is the *puer* (or, in a woman, *puella*) *aeternus*, the eternal youth who will not or cannot grow up. Under the controlling influence of the dark side of this archetypal pattern, a man may suffer tremendously from an inability to mature in socially conventional ways, such as an inability to commit to work or relationship. He may remain innocent and childish, caught in fantasies of spiritual perfection and unable to accept the limits of mortal human life. Or he may be seduced by drugs and alcohol into living on a constant high. On the light side, this divine figure, when in its proper place at the table, can keep an individual connected to ideals and lead him to a genuine spirituality.

Charles was raised by a depressed, emotionally intrusive mother who turned him into her confidant and caretaker. His childhood purpose became to cure his mother's wounds. When she felt upset, he would make her tea; when she felt lonely, he would listen to her speak, sometimes for hours. Charles learned, even as a boy, that if he had separate outside interests or became willful, his mother would belittle him and tell him that she felt depressed. In effect, Charles was a victim of emotional incest.

Charles's father, a welder, seemed to be a quiet, introverted, ineffectual man who drank vodka at night and disappeared into his room. He also remained close to his own mother, which created conflict with his wife, Charles's mother.

Charles expressed disappointment that his father did not teach him sports, so he did not feel a sense of belonging with other boys at school. He tried to compete academically but received only mediocre grades. With some of the more traditional masculine traits buried in his shadow, he developed other gifts, such as artistic interests. But, sadly, they were devalued by both his parents and teachers, who betrayed his creative spirit. Socially, Charles felt awkward and shy. He was too ashamed to bring friends home because he did not know when his father would be drunk. And he was too frightened to approach girls because unconsciously he felt that his mother would feel abandoned. In this way, she betrayed his independence.

After high school, his parents encouraged him to become a welder, following his father's footsteps and taking over the family business. An obedient son, he heeded their request. But after five years, he felt dry and depressed. He suffered from sexual impotence and had suicidal thoughts and feelings of emptiness.

Unlike Wayne, whose adaptation as a father's son fit his more remote, analytical nature, Charles, as an emotionally sensitive, artistic mother's son, could not adapt to the overlay of the traditional male role without great suffering. His sense of inferiority stemmed from this lack of fit between the family and cultural expectations of him—"buck up and act like a man"—and his own gentle nature. His critical inner voice, a shadow figure absorbed from these sources, told him that he was not masculine enough, assertive enough, or potent enough to be a real man. Tragically, having identified with the parental voice, he learned to devalue himself as he had been devalued by his parents.

Doing the slow, daily tasks of shadow-work, Charles uncovered his devouring mother complex and his consequent terror of women's power. Eventually, he learned to separate out her voice from his own and her needs from his, thereby finding the gold in his dark side: his own unique style of independence and masculinity. Working with his flying dreams, he found within himself a deep spiritual longing, which led him to a meditation teacher, a substitute father for the one he never had. In time, Charles returned to his passion for the arts, studying design and becoming reinspired with life. He found work as a graphic designer and later became head of the art department for a major fashion company.

In addition, Charles joined a men's group and found the support and reinforcement for his particular style of masculinity that he never felt at home. In these untraditional ways, over a period of several years, Charles uncovered his authentic nature as a sensitive artist. Gradually, his self-respect began to return as he reclaimed his rejected vulnerable soul.

There is debate in the Jungian community about how to interpret the appearance of the *puer* archetype. Analyst Marie-Louise von Franz focuses on the dark side and characterizes *puers* harshly as immature, ungrounded men who are unable to make commitments. She believes that they have excessive spirituality and a head-in-the-clouds attitude, which can blind them to shadow issues. This problem, she says, stems (for men) from an excessive attachment to the personal mother and a failure to separate from her, which leads to an inability to make other attachments. Von Franz points out that the *puer* receives from his mother a feeling of being special, which in turn evokes an inferiority complex because he can never live up to her expectations. For those in the grasp of this character, she prescribes shadow-work to avoid hubris and to help face the disappointment of lost ideals.

James Hillman, on the other hand, focuses on the light side and assesses the *puer* positively, claiming that it represents "the spirit of youth and the youth of spirit. . . . It is the call of a thing to perfection; it is the call of a person to the Self." Therefore, he says, the *puer* is not meant to walk but to fly.

It's only from the point of view of the ego that the *puer* is a problem, Hillman says. The ego wants it to adapt, succeed, be powerful and heroic. For this reason, all the influences of socialization collude to clip its wings. Therefore, Hillman continues, the *puer* should not be seen solely as a pathology with its basis in the mother complex. His solution: The *puer* needs to pair up not with the mother but with the father in an imaginal relationship. He does not mean here the personal father, but the *senex* or wise old man.

Poet Robert Bly has also explored a version of this pattern, which he calls the "naive male" and identifies by several traits: The man assumes that others are sincere and fair, without seeing their shadows. With this kind of blindness, he has special, prized relationships only with certain people. In addition, he may be passive in relationships, not aggressive. Typically, he responds to the troubles of others in a nurturing way rather than by saying what he wants, which may cause trouble. Finally, he may lose that which is precious to him, "giving away his gold" because of a lack of boundaries.

The archetypal story of the *puer* appears in the Greek myth of Icarus. Daedelus, father of Icarus, was jealous of one of his helpers and killed him. Forced to flee from Athens to Crete, Daedelus then offended the king while in exile and was imprisoned with Icarus. In his solitude Daedelus designed two pairs of wings to enable them to escape across the waters that surrounded the prison tower. He cautioned his son not to fly too close to the sun because the wax that held the wings together would melt. But once in flight, the boy disobeyed his father and arrogantly soared off to the heights. As the father watched in horror, Icarus's wings melted and he plunged into the sea.

Today, we see an epidemic of *puers* among people living on the margins of mainstream culture, especially in more growth-oriented or spiritually based subcultures. From the point of view of the larger *senex*-oriented culture, the *puer* appears naive and childlike, too internally oriented, and dangerously disinterested in the work ethic. In addition, he or she seems to carry fantasies of specialness or grandiosity.

In their dreams, *puers* fly over the sea without constraints. This flight represents their rejection of human limitation, their love of spirit, high ideals, and open-ended possibilities. Like Icarus, they may have been divinized by a mother or father and given wings to soar above others. They, too, may have lost their connections to the body and the earth.

If they become involved at a young age with a spiritual teacher or religious community, they may become insulated from the difficulties of the larger world, avoiding its limits and even professing that it is illusory. They may enjoy the safety of a like-minded group that serves as a surrogate family. And they may feel special, even chosen, as their parents had implied. Finally, they may find a target for the projection of the Self, becoming part of a divine twinship with an "enlightened" teacher that confers special status.

Despite the dangers of the *puer's* flight from reality, from the point of view of the cultural shadow the *puer* stands for youth and openness, as against age and rigidity; spirituality, as against materialism; creative possibilities, as against mere production; and imagination and talent, as against conventionality and uniformity.

For the man who is strongly influenced by this pattern, shadow-work does not mean merely getting tough or getting serious; it does not mean simply making a shift to its opposite, the traditional form of masculinity or *senex*. Instead, it involves finding an appropriate place at the table for the *puer* character, who can dream of future creative possibilities while the man, who works to become more deeply connected to his masculine body and soul, also builds a grounded life in the world. This developmental task can be achieved through the rigors of psychological work, intimate relationship, and creativity, each of which can give voice to the banished characters and connect the conscious mind to the unconscious depths.

THE MOTHER'S DAUGHTER: RECLAIMING MASCULINE SHADOW

Whereas the man who identifies with his same-sex parent carries traditional feminine qualities in his shadow, the woman who identifies with her mother may carry certain masculine traits in her shadow.

Vanessa was born to an unmarried woman in her forties who worked as a librarian. Her mother's mother also raised her daughter alone. In both households, the message was conveyed that men cannot be trusted. In this way, Vanessa's natural attraction to men and the masculine was hindered, even betrayed.

Throughout her childhood and teen years, Vanessa and her mom were inseparable. They studied together, shopped together, and went to the theater together. They both enjoyed doing pottery and, in these ways, Vanessa's mother transmitted the creative spirit to her daughter. However, like Charles, Vanessa came to feel responsible for her mother's happiness, learning to be a generous and polite caretaker. But, on the inside, both women suffered from low self-worth, fear of poverty, and loneliness.

When Vanessa turned sixteen and wanted to learn how to drive, her mother refused, saying that it would not be necessary because she would always be there to drive her daughter. Reluctantly, Vanessa obeyed, extending the natural period of her dependency and denying her yearning for independence.

Vanessa remained an innocent maiden or *kore*, in her mother's home as her mother's best friend, until she was twenty-two. Like Laura, the daughter of Amanda in Tennessee Williams's play *The Glass Menagerie*, who remains trapped in her mother's fragile glass images, Vanessa at times felt like a hostage. But perhaps because she knew so little of the world, much of the time she felt complacent in her self-enclosure, contained in her mother's warmth and affections.

And then, one day, she encountered Bret, a high-strung young man whose black-leather, motorcycle-riding charisma captured her attention. Like Hades, who abducted Persephone in the Eleusinian mysteries, he arose from the underworld to seize her youth and wrench her away from a sheltered, mother-centered life. Initiated into the wildness of new sexuality and the adventures of an independent life, Vanessa stayed away from home for longer and longer periods. Her mother entered a period of Demeter mourning, feeling as if she would rather die than face the loss of her daughter.

Like this mother's daughter, many children today are caught in a web of enmeshed family patterns. Invaded by incestuous fathers or controlled by intrusive mothers, they are forced to become alternate spouses, feeding love to monstrous, all-consuming parents. In some cases, only the sudden, threatening appearance of a Hades-like under-world figure can tear them away. Hades may wear the face of a drug dealer who seduces a young teen into another kind of dependency. Or he may use the sounds of heavy metal music or the lure of dangerous sex to break the hold of a tyrannical parent. Hades also speaks through the violent images of film and television, which offer a vicarious, sym-bolic journey through death and rebirth. For some, Hades is a violent rapist who steals our innocence at great cost, resulting in trauma and even suicide. For others, he is a depressive mood that pulls us down from the light world of ego into the dark world of shadow.

For the fortunate few who have an underworld guide and the tools of shadow-work, Hades can be the initiator of independence, an agent of self-discovery. Fortunately for Vanessa, she found her way to therapy and began to do shadow-work on her relationship with her mother, sorting out light side from dark side. As she uncovered the shadow qualities that she had absorbed unknowingly from her mom, she could hear the negative voice of her mother complex as a character at the ta-ble: She should not trust men; in effect, she should not trust anyone but her mother. The original betrayal had served as the catalyst for her development; it brought her into therapy and forced her to face her desire for and fear of a relationship with a man, which became the fo-cus of her shadow-work.

Slowly and cautiously, at age twenty-three, Vanessa began dating. She did not wish to replicate her family pattern of a life without men. And, like Persephone, who returns to her mother in spring and to her underworld husband in winter, eventually Vanessa learned to hold the opposites of light and dark, no longer a *puella* girl but a queen in her own realm.

THE FATHER'S DAUGHTER: RECLAIMING FEMININE SHADOW

Whereas the mother's daughter identifies with her same-sex parent, the father's daughter identifies with her opposite-sex parent and thereby banishes certain traditional feminine qualities into her shadow. Deborah, forty-six, began shadow-work when a relationship with a younger man ended after two years and she admitted to herself, perhaps for the first time, that she would never have children. Depressed and suffering from insomnia, she drank three cups of coffee to awaken each morning and smoked marijuana or drank wine to relax at night. As she sat in a large, overstuffed chair and sobbed uncontrollably during the first therapy session, surprised and embarrassed at her outburst in front of a stranger, she looked a bit like a lost child, except for the cigarette burning in her right hand. Although she was an accomplished actress and a politically active feminist, Deborah felt anxious, alone, and, above all, disoriented by her recent self-reflection.

She had never before told her life story, and it flowed from her like a river that had been dammed up for years. "We lived on a large ranch outside of Denver and, as a young girl, I was left alone a lot with the animals. Always in blue jeans and dirty shirts, I helped to plant and harvest the garden and loved to watch the horses and cows give birth. As I got older, I began to ride the horses and liked nothing better than to ride all day. I felt most alive outdoors and, long after dark, my mother would have to convince me to go inside for dinner.

"My dad worked as a doctor in town and stayed away a lot to go to the theater at night. When he did come home, we took long hikes and talked about the theater, which led me to dream about becoming an actress. I adored him and thought of him as the perfect gentleman. He dressed in expensive clothes and frequented the best restaurants. A pillar of the community, he sat on the board of the local charity and just looked like the ideal father. He pretty much left my mother, whose family had owned the ranch for three generations, with a couple of staffers to run the ranch. But when he returned, the mood in the house changed. We would all have to sit down to dinner together at seven o'clock and try to be a family.

"My parents seemed more unhappy when they were together than when they were apart. They weren't alcoholic or abusive or anything like that. But my dad would make subtle, cutting remarks about my mother's appearance or about the dinner, and she would become sad. I remember one incident in particular when I was about seven years old. He instructed my mother to set the table differently and, hanging her head, she obeyed. I think this moment left an indelible mark on me: I told myself that I did not want to be anything like my mother. I couldn't *stand* her subservience. And if that's what women do to be married, I would rather remain single."

With that remark, Deborah took a deep breath and looked up. "Well, I guess I got what I wished for." Then she continued, "But I really don't understand how it happened, how I never married or had a child. I mean, my family was not all that bad, compared to most. How could I be such a failure at relationships?"

Without knowing it, Deborah had identified deeply with her powerful father and the masculine world over her mother and the feminine. She had become a father's daughter, a girl whose idealized relationship with her father results in an unconscious alignment with him, causing her to reject and devalue her mother and her own feminine qualities, which are exiled into the shadow. Deborah's father, whose upright persona and superior ways won her heart, had overshadowed her mother in their home. As a result, many of her mother's hidden abilities remained lost to Deborah.

Deborah lived out one image of this archetypal pattern of the virgin, the Artemis-style father's daughter. Unlike Athena, who is also a father's daughter of Zeus, Artemis does not develop her mind in her self-containment; she develops a connection to nature, a sense of sisterhood with other women, and a brotherly affection for men, beginning with her twin, Apollo.

The Greek goddess Artemis was born on an isolated, uncultivated island to her mother, Leto, a nature deity who was impregnated and abandoned by Zeus. Artemis had little nurturing or supervision by either parent and, like Deborah, raised herself in the outdoors. When Artemis met her father at age three, Zeus granted her wishes for a bow and arrows, a pack of hunting hounds, mountains and wilderness as her special places, and eternal chastity.

Like Artemis, Deborah's experience of mothering was primarily archetypal. She ran wild with the horses and cattle and rested in the arms of Mother Nature. And, like the goddess's father, her glamorous, all-powerful father remained remote and belittled women. Finally, like Artemis, Deborah unconsciously wished for a solitary life: As a witness to her mother's humiliation, her ability to identify with traditional femininity was betrayed. She rejected outright the stereotyped roles of women, saying, "I'm unwilling to live through a man or in service to a man." Vowing not to be vulnerable or dependent, she instead lived out her mother's unlived life, becoming a vocal feminist who stands for what she called the authentic female voice.

Today, at midlife, Deborah faces the high price of her inviolability: Her nurturing, vulnerable feelings and her capacity for a healthy dependency have remained in the shadow for so long that she is terrified of releasing them. Even today, she cannot imagine a relationship with a man that does not require her to give up her identity as an independent woman. As a result, she will remain childless.

Slowly, with shadow-work, Deborah discovered that her contempt for traditional femininity had contaminated her feelings about her own feminine self. She uncovered her mother's unspoken rage in her own collective projections at men. In her grief about her unborn children, buried beneath her independent persona, she uncovered her own Demeter mourning and thereby came to value her Demeter-style mother, who had been banished long ago by the father's daughter. Using imaginal writing to explore her grief, she tells of the link between her father's daughter pattern and her childlessness:

> As I write this piece, I am in midlife, sitting by the warm fireplace in my beachfront home. I let the music go still. I add a log to the fire and step back into the soundless container, pen in hand, facing the empty page, feelings of grief and loss welling up into squiggly lines meant to transmit this moment of my very private life to another, an unknown other, perhaps a woman like myself who also has no demands of feeding schedules or dirty diapers, no breasts that fill at the cry of a small one, no baby-sitters to find or preschool to choose. Another perhaps who is grateful for the absence of these messy interruptions but who wonders, too, in her quiet moments, about small smiles missed, small hands and feet unseen, silky skin untouched, and the first step not taken.
>
> Does she feel as I do that childlessness is a separate state of consciousness from having children, as distinct as waking is from sleeping? Does she feel as I do that she has taken from her father his most precious dream?
>
> To my father, childlessness is a stain on my womanhood, a blemish on my worth, a failure of maturity. Adulthood for a woman means in some profound way to birth and care for young ones, helpless and dependent ones, so that to remain childless means to remain a child. To remain childless means

to avoid fulfilling a female mandate, to betray a biological gift. I refer here to an inner wound, as if we were meant to grow two arms but grow only one—an amputation to our potential as women.

The feminist in me rages at this feeling—I was not born to breed. I am enough as I am. I can live independently—without a child—and I shall. But as a single woman coming to terms with not having a child, now incapable of having a child, I carry a secret terror of meeting new men, assuming they all seek to impregnate the one they love; they all seek to re-create themselves; they all dream the dream of family life.

And I carry a secret shame that no matter what I could produce or create that would make my father proud, I have utterly failed him because he has no young ones playing at his feet as he grows old. This is my fate, and so it is his.

I ask myself in this moment, How do I stop seeing the world through the eyes of a daughter without becoming a mother? How do I become a woman who did not give birth to children—but did give birth to herself?

Finally, Deborah returned to the ranch to visit her mother after a decade away. Frail and facing death, her mother admitted for the first time the pain of her own sacrifices, rather than pointing out her daughter's failures to form a family. And together the two women mourned the end of their family line and jointly planned how to sell the family property.

To sum up, these four archetypal patterns of ego development and shadow formation emerge inevitably as we are shaped by family and cultural influences. They are a few of the many stories we may tell with our lives, or we are the vehicles through which they express themselves.

Which parent is your model of ego identification? Who is your shadow parent? Do you fall into one of these four patterns? If so, which archetypal version of the pattern do you live most fully? After you contemplate these questions, you may have a sense of how to reclaim lost aspects of your own soul.

Reclaiming Masculine and Feminine Soul

To reclaim authentic masculine and feminine soul, we have several tasks ahead of us: We need to begin to make conscious the hidden dynamics of identification and repression that formed our egos and shadows, respectively. For a father's son and a father's daughter, this work involves, first of all, clarifying our more conscious relationships with him and with the masculine principle. We need to look closely at how we have become like our fathers and disowned our father's qualities, how we have idealized him and rejected him. We need to become aware of how we listen to the inner voice of our fathers as a shadow character who lays down the law like a wrathful god, so that we relive that relationship day after day as his child, his victim, or his rebel. In the end, we must be consciously willing to carry our fathers within us as they once carried us in their arms.

For example, a child may have adopted some of his traits or tried unsuccessfully to fulfill a career wish that belonged to him. Another may have veered off in the opposite direction to thwart a father's will. In the one case, the child tries to live the father's unlived life; in the other, the child tries to escape his influence. Either way, the child is trapped in a dynamic that is determined by unconscious intense feelings about the father, not by conscious adult choices.

Second, shadow-work for people who are living out these father-dominant patterns involves uncovering the influence of the rejected parent, the mother and the feminine. We can begin by trying to make conscious those aspects of ourselves that we unknowingly absorbed from our mothers, such as an artistic sense or a love of business, wilderness, or children. And we need to examine our mother's shadow qualities, which we may carry as excess baggage, such as dependency, substance addiction, or deeply buried resentment and rage. We need to become aware of those disliked and rejected qualities in her that we have struggled to disown, because they probably continue to influence us below the boundaries of awareness as shadow characters. And they hold a key to unlocking the depths of soul.

Our sorrow for the lost mother and our lamentation for the lost feminine goddess have a cultural component as well: Although the personal mother may be present to raise a child, her role may be devalued and her soul diminished in the family, making her psychically absent to a father's son or a father's daughter. Or she may have entered the world of work herself and struggled to return to the home with her feminine soul.

For a mother's son and a mother's daughter, shadow-work involves clarifying our relationships with her and with the feminine principle, including those qualities we have idealized as well as those we have devalued. We must be consciously willing to carry our mothers within us as they once carried us in their bodies. Then, we need to explore the more covert influence of our fathers, their blessings and their curses, which we hear in our minds like the whispers of a stern ghost.

Our sorrow for the lost father and our lamentation for the lost masculine god have a cultural component, too: Many fathers have been called away from their families by the Sirens of sex, work, alcohol, or drugs. Caught in a compulsion, they run toward it and away from their young ones, who suffer their absence and the loss of masculine soul.

In Edgar Allan Poe's story "The Tell-Tale Heart," a man feels haunted by the look in an older man's eyes. Each time he feels seen, his blood runs cold and he wants to be rid of the eye. We can imagine that he feels looked at too directly when he wishes to remain hidden, that he feels humiliated in his nakedness. So he begins to plot revenge. Slowly, he becomes obsessed with how to kill the old man. One night he peers into the old man's room and hears his heartbeat, a low, dull thud, which sounds like a watch in cotton. As the beat grows louder, the man grows furious until he pulls down the bed and crushes the old man to death. Then, slowly and methodically, he cuts his body into small parts and buries them beneath the floor.

When the police arrive to investigate the death, the man shows them to the murder site, assuming that the evidence is well hidden. But he begins to hear the low, dull thud of the old man's heart. It grows louder and louder until, crying out in anguish and fury, the man admits his crime.

Poe does not make clear in his story the nature of the relationship between the older and younger men. Perhaps the victim is a grandfather or father whose hypervigilant stare gives the younger man no peace. In his rage, the son or grandson dismembers his victim, but like Osiris, he rises again in the sound of the beating heart. In an analogous way, we identify with one parent and bury the remains of the rejected one under the bed—that is, under the layers of conscious awareness. But one day, the rejected parent, like the banished soul child, returns in the sound of our own heartbeat, announcing that it's time for shadow-work.

These are the first steps in re-mothering and re-fathering ourselves, separating out our identities from those of our parents, from our inner parents' voices, and from the larger cultural and archetypal influences. Only then can we provide ourselves as adults with those essential qualities and authentic feelings that we may have missed as children and that will nourish our souls.

Later in life, as we are attracted to lovers and mates, our fathers and mothers (now internalized as characters within us) continue to vote on our choices. Some women seek their fathers in other men, forever searching for the one that got away. Others seek their fathers' opposites, their shadow qualities, because they are determined, even unknowingly, not to re-create the original father-daughter relationship. Similarly, some men seek their mothers in other women, forever searching for the unconditional love and adoration they missed as children. Others seek their shadow mothers, longing for a different quality of feminine love. This is where we turn our attention in the next chapter.

CHAPTER 4

LOOKING FOR THE BELOVED: DATING AS SHADOW-WORK

The minute I heard my first love story
I started looking for you, not knowing
how blind that was.
Lovers don't finally meet somewhere.
They're in each other all along.

—JELALUDDIN RUMI

When Cupid struck Apollo with a golden arrow through the heart, he fell hopelessly in love with a nymph named Daphne. But to Apollo's chagrin, Cupid had struck Daphne with a leaden arrow, causing her to abhor the thought of love and despise marriage as a crime. So Apollo pursued her, inflamed by the chase and pleading his intentions. And Daphne fled, her hair streaming behind her and feeling no wish to be caught, even by the god of song and healing.

As Apollo gained upon her and her strength began to fail, Daphne called on her father, the river god, for aid. Instantly, her limbs grew stiff, her body became enclosed in bark, her hair turned to leaves, her arms to branches, and her face to a treetop. Apollo embraced the nymph, now a laurel tree, and proclaimed that he would wear her for a crown.

This story of Apollo's first love and its pursuit motif contain some of the themes and images of many people's early dating experiences: They act as if they are under a spell. One person, longing for love, chases the Other. He or she, longing for separateness, runs away. There's very little authentic contact between them. If they meet to spend time together, the first typically pursues intimacy while the Other keeps a distance. In generations past, this dynamic typically occurred along gender lines, with the male pursuing and the woman holding the boundary. But today that distinction has broken down. Some women are in Apollo's position, aggressively pursuing a man, while some men play Daphne's role, running away from getting involved.

In this chapter and the next two we will explore these ideas in the context of shadow and soul. First, we will consider dating and some of the painful shadow issues that single people face today: the feeling of being unacceptable, the terror of being hurt and rejected, and the fear of commitment. Dating, as the timeless search for a romantic partner, may be led by the persona in its quest for the image of the perfect Beloved in human form. In its search for image, the persona also seeks companionship, pleasure, and sexuality from dating partners. As in Apollo's case, the pursuit may end in failure. When the god of rationality is overcome by intense, primitive sexual attractions, he, too, struggles to make a meaningful connection.

But, with a deeper understanding, dating can become an ideal forum in which to explore unknown aspects of ourselves by doing shadow-work. Whether as one who is not yet married but remains hopeful, or as one who is divorced or widowed and suffers with feelings of grief, we can view being single as an opportunity to cultivate self-knowledge. Rather than avoid the cycle of living as a single person by frantically looking for someone—anyone—to date, we can use these periods to find our own internal sources of stimulation, build sustaining friendships with both women and men, and draw upon our creative inspirations, all of which may get eclipsed with the demands of a full-time relationship.

In Chapter 5 we will examine romance, the divine madness of finding an erotic partner, which may be choreographed by the personal shadow in its quest to re-create the familiar feelings embedded in the way we were raised as children. For this reason, in adulthood, people abused as children often find abusive partners; children of alcoholics often are attracted to drinkers; children who suffered parental neglect may find themselves with neglectful lovers. When the shadow arranges a marriage, it puts us face-to-face with our unresolved childhood issues.

We consider dating, then, typically to have less depth and entail less commitment than romance, which emerges when a mutual attraction is acknowledged and a shadow projection finds its target. In dating, we long for an end to loneliness, a companion in joy and sorrow. But the shadow also contains those missing parts of our authentic nature that were rejected in childhood. So, beyond the persona connection, in romance we long to complete ourselves in the Beloved. And the shadow leads us to retrieve those rejected parts, which seek acceptance so that we can feel whole again.

In Chapter 6 we will look at marriage, the gifts and struggles of living authentically in a long-term relationship with the soul of the Beloved. We will reimagine committed relationship and suggest that, with shadow-work, it can become something larger than the sum of its parts—a transpersonal field in which love and consciousness grow. At that time, the object of the quest changes: from the beauty of image and the ideal Beloved to the beauty of depth and the real Beloved.

In these ways the search for an authentic relationship mirrors the search for the authentic Self, as told in the Sufi tale in our introduction. During dating the Master leaves the Butler in charge of the house—that is, the Self goes dormant and the ego takes over. But as the romantic relationship deepens and becomes increasingly conscious, the Self returns and demands more recognition and authenticity. If the ego resists relinquishing control and continues to dominate the dating process, we seek again and again an ideal image of the Beloved that reinforces its fantasy expectations. As a result, the relationship ends, and we search for yet another partner.

However, through the pain and frustration of failed attempts at bonding, the Master's henchman, the shadow, eventually may force the ego to see its limitations and to relinquish control. With shadow-work, we then hear the call of the Self, the Master. And, as a result, a conscious relationship really can begin.

Whom do you desire and pursue? What authentic shadow need threatens your developing relationship?

Shame and the Single Person

Some people, of course, enjoy the light side of dating; these people view the single life as an opportunity to experiment socially and sexually, to feel the freedom of their own rhythms and to maintain their own privacy. They may wish for a committed relationship in the future but recognize wisely that they are not ready for it. Or they may dread commitment, imagining it as a jail sentence.

For others, the dark side of dating is oppressive; these people suffer with feelings of isolation, alienation, and sexual frustration. For them, to be single in a culture of couples is to be a carrier of shadow projections, to feel the pain of being seen as strange, a loser, an outsider. It is to feel the banishment of the one who is not chosen. It is to feel perpetually awkward, caught in a sustained adolescence, not yet belonging among the grown-ups who have mated and formed families. To be a young single is to be seen as inexperienced, naive, one who has not yet begun to live. To be an older single, especially if he or she has never married, is to be seen as eccentric, tainted, one who has failed the test of maturity. In a culture that defines people in relation to others even on simple institutional forms—single, married, divorced, widowed—the life of the single person is filled with daily reminders of being tainted with shadow.

Even though they may enjoy several intimate, ongoing friendships, some single people suffer terribly because they feel the stigma of being alone. When they feel lonely, they may devalue their deepest friendships rather than cherish them, as if these heartfelt connections cease to exist and the only valid relationship were a sexual, monogamous one—a couple.

Some observers of single people eating alone in restaurants or sitting alone in movies may feel uncomfortable as well, projecting their own fears of solitude or abandonment. The singles may, in turn, sense this attitude from others as discomfort, disdain, or even pity. On the other hand, married observers may feel the mournful discontent of envy around singles, imagining the joys of free time, free choice, and self-reliance. One woman, unmarried into her fifties, noted that her close married friends frequently imagine that she has a busy, fascinating social life that is off limits to them. She chuckles as she recounts this and then, turning serious a moment later, tells us that she is so ashamed to be home on Saturday nights that she never answers the phone.

Of course, the single person at twenty-five, whose college friends have coupled and cocooned, has a different perspective from the single person at forty-five, whose friends have married, perhaps divorced and remarried, and given birth to children by then. But in both cases, the single person may feel the same pain, raging against others ("All of the good men are taken") or against social institutions ("The women's movement has made women hard and angry"). For them, potential partners never match the internal romantic images. Each one fails to meet their standards of beauty, intelligence, success, or sensitivity, as they project their own inferiority onto others. If a relationship forms and they continue to judge and blame the other person for being inadequate, they risk becoming critical, nagging mates.

Instead of blaming others, some single people may blame themselves for their fate, feeling inadequate, unlovable, even hopeless. In this case, they themselves are not enough—thin enough, successful enough, smart enough, sexy enough. For some, this shame leads to endless routines of diets, workouts, therapy, singles events, and self-help books. All of this compulsive activity may cover up a deeper self-loathing and a desire to fix some secret flaw, which feels as if it's been there forever. This feeling—it's been this way forever—signals the legacy of a family shadow, a self-hatred that is absorbed from one or both parents, whether spoken or unspoken, and passed down from generation to generation.

Some singles reason that they have been cursed by an incident, such as molestation or abandonment, that bars them from trusting anyone. Or they have been branded with a bodily trait that makes them feel unattractive, thus undermining their confidence and capacity to make contact with potential partners. Bonnie, an Artemis-style father's daughter and art director in her mid-forties, disclosed that she had never felt comfortable in her own body. After years of feeling ashamed for her failure to mate, she noticed that her mind would move around her physical form at times, becoming obsessed with various bodily traits. In her twenties, she felt intensely embarrassed about her large breasts and was convinced they kept men away. Later, her legs became the problem: They were too short, too muscular, too pale to be seen as attractive. Finally, at midlife, as small lines appeared around her mouth and her cheeks began to sag, the voice of her inner critic concluded that the aging in her face held the key to her isolation and loneliness.

Bonnie's mother had told herself the same critical messages about her own body. She felt chronically overweight, stodgy, unfeminine, and very different from the cultural standard of beauty. Although her mom had never spoken critical words to her daughter concerning her appearance, Bonnie unknowingly had absorbed this aspect of her mother's shadow as her own critical voice.

When she became aware of this pattern and began to witness it, learning to root her identity in her Self, she could laugh at the noise of her own mind, which told her that the "moving fatal flaw" had ruined her life. Gradually, she separated from this character and grew more accepting of her body image, felt more attractive, and as a result became more attractive to men.

Then, to her surprise, Bonnie found herself rejecting those men who desired her. As her critic turned the negative, inner-directed messages outward toward her pursuers, she became judgmental: He's not smart enough; he's not rich enough; he's not psychologically developed enough, the critic told her. With the advent of real opportunities for a relationship, Bonnie uncovered a previously hidden shadow figure, the assassin, who unknowingly protected her Artemis nature. With even more judgmentalism and perfectionism than the critic, this character would maintain her independence at any cost by killing off those who wished to share her life.

In order to pursue her dream of a committed relationship, Bonnie needed to find a place at the table for the assassin, the protector of her vulnerability and independence. She needed a way of relating to this character so that it would not push away the very men she might truly desire. Eventually, she found the gold in her dark side when she realized that the perfectionistic assassin could be useful at work, where she critiqued the fine detail of award-winning television ads. But in her love life it sabotaged her deepest longings, eliminating potential romantic partners.

What is it about you that you fear will be rejected? What do you fear that others will find out about and consider unacceptable? And what do you suspect in them that will force you to become rejecting?

Single Women and the Shadow

All too often, people who blame themselves for an absence of intimacy suffer with an intense longing for love and the fantasy that, if only they could become better, love would appear. They live in hope—hope that if their flaw can be fixed, the right person will appear just around the corner. Hillary, who came to therapy in order to understand how she sabotaged intimacy, spoke in a rapid, breathless tone of that part of her which continues to hope:

"I can see my thirtieth birthday coming round the bend. It looks like a big red No U-turn sign. I'm terrified—thirty, not married, and no prospects. Thirty and living alone.

"But I know he's coming. I can feel it now. The perfect guy is going to show up soon, and I've got to be ready. I've got to look great so he'll notice me. Not too much makeup so that my skin looks natural. But enough makeup to cover these lines around my eyes. And the right outfit—one that shows my small waistline but doesn't accentuate my large breasts.

"And I want my mood to be just right. I mean interested but cool, open but not too available. I'll show him I'm glad to meet him, make contact for a moment or two, then rush off, in demand somewhere else. When he takes my number, I won't ask for his. I'll let him make all the moves, at least for a few weeks. I'll do whatever he wants to do—restaurants, movies, dancing. But sex—I won't have sex for the first month. It always ruins everything. I make a vow in this moment—please, God, help me—not to have sex. To make him wait. Feel his desire. If I want a relationship, slower is better. I've got to get to know him first. See if I really want him.

"But I get so afraid—afraid he'll stop calling if I don't have sex. Afraid he'll disappear if he doesn't get what he wants. And what if the right guy, my ideal mate, shows up and I won't sleep with him, and he gives up? I mean, he just disappears like all the others?

"But the truth is, I sleep with them and they disappear anyway. Men are such a mystery to me. They say they don't want a relationship, but a month later they're shacked up with some blond. I wonder sometimes, after fifteen years of dating, how I go on, how I keep hoping. But I know it will happen. Maybe tonight, if I just look right and don't act too pushy or too smart or too eager—maybe tonight he'll take me in his arms and I'll be home."

Hillary's romantic dreamer character kept hope alive, but she used it as a shield to defend against intractable feelings of grief and inadequacy. As she fantasized about cutting and trimming her own traits to fit a man's inner pictures of beauty and availability, she enacted the Greek myth of the innkeeper Procrustes, who tied his victims to an iron bed and stretched their bodies or amputated their limbs to make them fit its given size. In trying to fit herself into an imagined mold designed by others, Hillary moved farther away from her authentic Self and from an authentic human encounter.

While she gave lip service to the adage that "slower is better," she did not understand that it is more than a tactic or ploy to reel in a man. Many relationships burn out quickly with too much sex, too many demands, or too much neediness too soon. To go slowly is to allow for time itself to influence the process: time to relax together, time to see the Other and be seen, time to get past initial projections and gain a sense of each other's authentic identities.

Suzanne, a father's daughter and journalist for a local newspaper, suffered great pain at midlife after a series of abusive relationships. She felt extremely depressed, even futile about creating the kind of partnership she dreamed about. In expressing the lack of positive models for intimacy in her own life, she said: "I look to my left and I see a married couple fighting constantly. I look to my right and I see a man abusing his girlfriend. I look behind me and I see my parents, who divorced when I was three. And I look before me, into the future, and I have no image of a creative, fulfilling relationship."

In therapy one day, Suzanne reported overhearing her mother say on the telephone: "Oh, Suzanne never married." She stopped cold at the simplicity and finality of her mother's statement. She felt as if, by not coupling, she had become a Crone twenty years too soon. The therapist asked her to examine her feelings by writing the story of a visit with the character of the hopeless single woman within her, the one who never married. Her story follows:

She doesn't go out much anymore. She doesn't answer the phone. The machine is unplugged. To speak to her, you have to drive up the mountain, wind around the curves, and climb to her front door, past the wild jasmine and the broken stairway. There's no bell, no way to get her attention. You just call out her name—she's always there. And slowly, if she feels like it, she finds her way downstairs, opens the door a crack, and lets her eyes and eyebrows ask what you want. When you say you want to speak with her, she doesn't say much. "Not much to tell these days."

The signs of another, busier life still lie around the house. A computer and its printer, hardly used. A fax machine, unplugged from its source of life. She's not dressed, of course. She wears a sheer flowing gown, purely for comfort. She sits without speaking, waiting without eagerness, without curiosity even. She sits, a vacant kind of look on her face, no rush to get on to something else, no question to fill the empty silence.

She lifts her hands and refolds them in her lap. "I never married," she says quietly, to no one in particular. "It's because I never married."

I get up to leave. She sits while I let myself out, knowing somehow that I had received the answer to my question.

By expressing her hopelessness and helplessness through creative writing, Suzanne slowly uncovered the rage that was buried deep within her. She was enraged at her father for rejecting her feminine beauty at a young age, turning her into a tomboy. And she was enraged at her male lovers, who also overlooked her particular kind of beauty in their search for a more stereotypically feminine woman.

After writing this piece, Suzanne had a clearer image of this hopeless part of herself, differentiating it as a character at the table. She began to realize that the hopeless single woman was not her entire identity, but only one character of many. She discovered that her underlying rage—her fear of destroying her father or of being destroyed—was the key shadow issue. As she learned to witness and center herself while she explored her rage and her deep desire for intimacy, her depression lifted. And the one who never married gave up the seat of power and began to take more of a backseat. As she began to deal with her rage, tentative feelings of hope returned and, with them, she began to recover her passion for life.

Both of these female figures—the ever-hopeful one and the hopeless one—are shadow characters in the single woman's inner world. Each one keeps the dream alive somewhere in the chambers of the heart; each one lets the dream die from time to time, while the woman turns her focus elsewhere, such as to work or friends. Each one pretends to be an authentic voice. But, in fact, both use shields to defend against the appearance of the authentic Self, which lies hidden beneath the shadow.

If you are single and ever hopeful, what loss do you defend against? What do you need to grieve? If you are single and hopeless, which character blocks your larger passion for life?

SINGLE MEN AND THE SHADOW

Many single men also suffer with similar feelings of isolation and futility. Noel, thirty, a youthful, athletic-looking mother's son who worked as a metal sculptor, came to therapy with the following story. One evening in New York, when rain was pouring outdoors, he felt restless and decided to go out despite the weather. He walked to the elevator, descended, walked outside, and then changed his mind, abruptly returning to the apartment. But he could not sit still with his feelings indoors, so he put on his jacket once more, returned to the elevator, and walked outdoors. Then, again, he returned to his apartment—startled at his own behavior.

He spoke slowly, shaking his head, "When I realized what I was doing, going back and forth like that, I started to feel nuts. I just wanted contact, I told myself. But in reality I was trying to avoid my feelings of panic. I was unable to be alone in my apartment, alone with my feelings, my unceasing desire for sex and my terror of failing at sex. I wanted women so much, but I hated them for having so much power over me." Noel had discovered within his feelings of panic an obsessive character that, in the past, had protected him from experiencing just those anxious feelings.

Like many heterosexual young men, Noel had spent years in emotional turmoil obsessing about women and acting out sexually. He had fantasies of having anonymous sex with women on the street, wondering if they were attractive enough for him, then wondering if they would desire him in return. His pain was so great that he had decided to put his life on hold because he did not feel loved for who he was. He had even made a decision to postpone a career until he found a woman to love him as is, "without the props of material success," as he put it.

Noel explained that historically woman had liked him for his intelligence; many wanted to be his friend, but not his lover. And this pattern of physical rejection had caused him great pain, reinforcing his lifelong feelings of homeliness and insecurity. At some point he decided that he would not befriend a woman unless she agreed to have sex. He no longer wanted to feel liked but not desired.

Like the craftsman god Hephaestus, who was thrown out of Olympus for a physical deformity and betrayed by his wife, Aphrodite, Noel felt banished from the heavens of erotic love and was rejected as a lover. He had tried to escape into his labor of love, sculpture, which sustained him for a while. But before long Noel could not tolerate feeling isolated from women, so unconsciously he tried to deal with his fear and rage by proving himself sexually with more than a hundred partners rather than by learning how to be intimate. Like Hephaestus, who shaped Pandora from the materials of his burning forge, Noel longed to shape the woman of his dreams and bring her to life.

Eventually, he became so anxious and confused that he stopped dating and started therapy. During the first year of shadow-work, he began to unravel the complexities of his mixed feelings toward women and toward himself. Using the breathing practice to witness his thoughts and feelings, he began to see his fear of sex and his problem with premature ejaculation as symptoms of his fear of intimacy. He discovered that his passivity camouflaged buried aggression, which was unacceptable and so stuffed into the shadow.

Slowly, with time, Noel learned to listen for his own needs and to honor them. His addictive sexuality decreased, and his erotic desire became more internalized and more related. As a result, in order to become aroused, he needed to feel connection and intimacy with a desirous, receptive woman. He was no longer aroused simply by the appearance of a woman's body part. In effect, he had integrated his sexuality in a deeper way, becoming a more sensitive lover. Then he was ready to resume the search for a partner.

Single homosexual men also feel the loneliness and hopelessness of a single life. But these issues are often compounded by shame, ambivalence, and confusion about their sexual orientation. Jungian analyst John Beebe describes the quintessential feeling of being gay: a strong sense of destiny to place one's life in the hands of a person of one's own sex, as well as the uncertainty of how to find that person.

Many of the Greek gods are attracted to same-sex lovers, although none is exclusively homosexual. And in most cases, the immortal is drawn to a beautiful mortal man, who is assigned the receptive role. For example, Zeus seduces the innocent Ganymede, becoming an emblematic older man–younger boy pair. Eventually, Ganymede is taken to Olympus and made immortal, becoming a cup-bearer to the gods and remaining eternally young.

The life of Apollo is also filled with stories of homosexual passion. When he pursues the handsome youth Hyacinthus, son of the Spartan king, his eros is returned. The two hunt and play together until, one day, in competition Apollo throws a discus, which hits the younger man full in the face, killing him. Apollo's medicinal art fails, and Hyacinthus dies in his arms. From his blood Apollo causes a purple flower to grow, which bears the name of his lover even today.

If you have felt isolated and unattractive seemingly forever, what family sin do you carry into dating? If you are sexually obsessed, what deeper feelings lie hidden in the compulsion?

AN ARCHETYPAL PERSPECTIVE ON DATING

As these case histories illustrate, people's shadow issues become the catalysts for their development, bringing them into therapy and deepening their self-awareness. For people like Hillary, Suzanne, and Noel, who are not single by choice but seek a loving partnership, we prescribe a little shadow-work. They might explore which myth they are living out as a single person. They might ask themselves which gods are alive in that myth and which are banished into shadow.

To put it psychologically, they need to befriend those parts of themselves or characters at the table that they have rejected and repressed into shadow. And they need to acknowledge and contain those persona parts that they have unconsciously chosen to play out, those characters that have usurped the throne, which keep them from attaining their desire. At different stages of life, one archetypal pattern may be in the seat of power and determine our intentions and behavior during dating, whereas at another stage a different god or goddess will influence a choice of partner.

For instance, some women believe consciously that they want marriage or children, yet remain caught in the pattern of a virgin goddess who thrives on independence and invulnerability. Like Artemis, a woman may flourish in the great outdoors, unbound by the tasks of home and family or the ardor of a lover, but bound intimately to her own brothers. In her twenties and thirties, she may resent her suitors and keep them at a distance or choose only those who would never qualify as lifelong partners. For her, dating partners may be temporary liaisons to share an adventure, men who need a lot of distance, or female lovers.

Then, in her forties, she may be shocked to find herself feeling lonely and depressed as Artemis recedes from center stage. Her developmental needs may suddenly contradict the ruling archetype, requiring the emergence of a new pattern, such as Demeter, the goddess of motherhood. If her ego remains identified with the old pattern, this transition can be confusing and painful.

One woman, whose erotic beauty had seduced many men into short-term encounters with Aphrodite, suddenly found herself trying to get pregnant in her late forties with a totally inappropriate partner. This impulse swept her away like a strong wind. She reported: "My god, I can't believe I did that!" She had not recognized the swift emergence of Demeter, whom she had scorned all her life. Rather than reduce her desire simply to biology and hormones, she came to understand that these urgent unconscious needs to feather a nest, which could have ended in disaster, reflected a changing of the gods in her psychology. And she began to hear the authentic voice that required her attention.

Other women desperately want to bond with a man but remain single into their forties or fifties for other reasons. These women may have rejected Hera, the archetypal wife whose primary relationship is to her husband. With the advent of the women's movement, Hera was banished to the cultural shadow, disparaged as dependent and self-sacrificing. So for a woman to allow herself to experience this pattern, she must go against the cultural grain of feminism, feeling her options too constrained, or fearing her loss of identity by aligning with a man. For some women, the long-term rejection of Hera brings depression, emptiness, and a feeling of incompleteness if it is a self-betrayal, a rejection of the voice of the authentic Self. For others, Hera does not need to be lived out and alternate sources of satisfaction suffice, such as single motherhood, friendships, and creative work.

But, at the same time, many women were raised by Hera mothers who gave up education or career to marry, so a rejection of her involves personal shadow issues as well as cultural ones. Women who tell themselves emphatically that they do not want to be anything like their mothers, that her choices and her suffering are reprehensible, may have unknowingly exiled Hera from their lives, and, perhaps, alienated an aspect of their own souls.

Similarly, women who want urgently to have a child but have failed to create the circumstances to support this wish may have an injured relationship to Demeter, the archetypal mother whose primary bond is with her child. Demeter, or motherhood, may be sacrificed if Hera, or being a wife, is too threatening because she reminds us too much of the mother who has been banished into shadow. In recent years, some women have chosen single motherhood and in that way allowed Demeter to emerge without Hera's binding relationship to a man. Or they may uncover an Athena-, Aphrodite-, or Artemis-style of mothering, which is more suitable to their independent natures.

Some men who seek a loving relationship but fear the commitments and responsibilities that accompany it unconsciously may be living the *puer* pattern: They are drawn to the freedom of creative possibilities but are frightened by the limits of long-term relatedness. These men feel that they are being suffocated by commitments and can only imagine what will be sacrificed if they commit to one love for a while. They cannot conceive of what will be gained.

Like the woman who unconsciously rejects Hera, the *puer* man who is unwilling or unable to become a husband or father may outwardly express a desire for a long-term relationship. But when a potential partner appears or the time for commitment to a relationship approaches, the *puer* character steals the seat of power. Then the man

feels ambivalent and confused, rejecting that part of himself which desires a committed relationship.

Some men also deny their own desires to become fathers, perhaps
fearing or resenting the provider role and cherishing freedom over
responsibility. Certainly, there are few mythological or cultural models
for fulfilling fatherhood. When Paul's lover became pregnant unexpectedly, he uncovered a deep desire for a child that he did not know
lived within him. "I didn't want to become a dad. In fact, it involves
everything I don't like about becoming a more mature man—the financial limits and responsibilities, the sexual monogamy, the settling
down in one place. But with the pregnancy, I melted. I discovered that
I was ready." Paul chose to give up his independent, jet-setting lifestyle
in order to create a family and welcome his child, thereby uncovering
gold in his dark side.

★   What gods or goddesses live in your shadow? How do they sabotage your efforts at authenticity and bonding? How can you encourage
their expression or begin to meet their deeper needs?

DATING: THE SHADOW'S SEARCH FOR SHELTER

On the outside, dating may look like a pursuit in which, traditionally,
the woman runs away just fast enough to get caught. The man pursues
her image of beauty, while she chooses him for his power, money, and
resources. Each seeks sexual attraction, compatibility, and security on
a conscious level. But beneath the boundaries of awareness, another
process of dating is taking place.

We define this inner process of dating as the shadow's search for
shelter in a projection that fits early childhood patterns. By re-creating
the past, the shadow tries to help us to feel safe, cared for, and loved. It
attempts to achieve these ends by re-creating with a lover the primor-
dial unity we felt in early life with a parent. Then we unconsciously
transfer responsibility for our survival from our parents to our partners.
And we imagine that our partners will love us the way our parents
never did, nurturing our deepest needs and fulfilling our deepest
desires.

At the same time that the shadow is pulling us into the past, re-creating imaginary early bonds that we had with our parents, the force of the authentic Self is pushing us toward development, toward more consciousness and freedom. We propose that, with shadow-work, dating can become a conscious, meaningful process, rather than an unconscious, seemingly meaningless series of failures. Dating as shadow-work requires a willingness to look within and identify early childhood patterns and characters at the table, those sources of family shadow that influence our attractions and responses to potential partners. In addition, it requires a willingness to identify the wounds of previous relationships so that we don't unconsciously repeat the same patterns, becoming wounded again and again in the same ways.

Instead of blaming others for not making the grade ("There are no men who know how to be intimate"), or blaming ourselves for a fatal flaw ("I was molested by my mother so I can't trust women"), we can learn to identify when a particular character takes over and re-creates the same old patterns of pain. We can stay tied to the breath, learn to honor the needs of the shadow without surrendering to them, and follow the call of the Self by risking greater authenticity. With this practice, we can become more authentic in our encounters, seeking real contact with the other person in a mutual exploration rather than showing a false front to achieve a preconceived outcome. As we become less defended and more vulnerable, we can learn at the same time to honor our own limits and protect our own boundaries. Finally, if we can trust the magic of the process, rather than strive with ego to make it happen in a particular way, it may rise to another octave— romance. And we may find a relationship that nurtures soul.

When our client Patricia, thirty-five, learned about dating as shadow-work, she reported that she had met a man who seemed kind and compatible; in fact, she thought about him every day. Yet she never called him. Instead, she continued to casually date another man who verbally belittled her. In response, she put her leg on his lap and seduced him. But after having sex with this man, she felt ashamed and regretful.

With shadow-work, Patricia came to realize that her old patterns did not allow her to choose men with whom she could bond. Instead, a shadow character, who had learned to protect her from intimacy, now sabotaged her efforts. And another character, which secretly felt inferior, used sex as an aphrodisiac to equalize the power. The result: Without being put down, Patricia does not feel seductive or become aroused.

After these discoveries, Patricia did the difficult work of learning to witness the voice of the character that compels her to approach men who are using a power shield. When she disobeyed it, the character receded from the seat of power, and she could begin to hear the whispering voice of the Self, which guides her in a more appropriate direction. Perhaps eventually she will meet a man with whom she can feel safe and vulnerable.

For us, success at the dating stage is not primarily about whether a particular relationship will work out; if "work out" means marriage, it probably won't. Rather, it's about learning how to experience vulnerability and intimacy with another human being—and to gain the awareness that comes with it. In our view, a relationship at an early stage is a process, not a product; it's a verb, not a noun. In these days of serial monogamy, the faces of the people involved may change, but the process goes on.

If one does not understand shadow-work and the notion of process, serial monogamy can seem meaningless and feel futile. But with the understanding that each of these seemingly unrelated relationships is part of an ongoing developmental process, providing grist for the mill in the next relationship, one can gain real meaning and value, as well as have more fun. The price of admission is emotional vulnerability; the payoff is the wisdom that comes with it. In this way, even a short relationship can enrich your life, in spite of not fulfilling your romantic dreams. And each experience can better prepare you for the next romance with the shadow.

A STORY OF DATING AS SHADOW-WORK

The story of our client Brad, forty-five, an extremely good-looking, charismatic corporate executive, illustrates this inner process of dating as shadow-work over several years. Brad had been leading a Don Juan life when he came to therapy, dating and seducing a series of women he called "upgrades," one beauty after another who served to elevate his own sense of self-worth. But eventually Brad began to imagine something more; he began to long for deeper, more meaningful contact with a woman. And then his search after an eternal feminine ideal began to feel like a meaningless series of defeats. At that time he began to suffer bouts of anxiety from an unknown source and to feel emotionally bankrupt.

Upon beginning shadow-work, Brad was dating Alice, a real estate broker. Although she was extremely attractive and treated him well, Brad knew somehow that she was not intelligent enough for him and was not the partner he sought. Nonetheless, he called her daily, "just to check in," and took her out on fashionable dates. From her side, Alice experienced Brad as distant and condescending, in spite of his perfect manners and attentive phone calls.

When the therapist asked why he called Alice so regularly if he did not have strong feelings for her, Brad responded that he felt obligated to call out of a sense of guilt. He felt guilty because he wanted sex without intimacy, which caused him to feel out of integrity with himself. This behavior, in turn, caused him to feel anxious and ashamed, so he checked up on her to appear like a gentleman, thereby attempting to avoid his own discomfort.

Brad brought in the following dream: *My mother is flirting with a younger man, but she won't introduce him to me.* Historically, Brad's mother had suffered from severe depression when he was a boy and confided to him some of her deepest problems, including her secret desire for divorce. He had felt overwhelmed by her neediness and afraid that she would leave him, abandoned and alone. So, he had felt responsible for her happiness and for keeping their family together, which created the shadow character of a desperate, insecure, obligated child. At the same time, he felt repulsed by her efforts at intimacy.

As an adult, Brad, the gentleman, experienced a sense of duty to women when, unconsciously, he projected his mother onto them. This mother complex, in turn, triggered a deep fear of emotional involvement because it aroused frightening feelings of dependency and resentment in him. So Brad resented Alice because of his imagined obligations, yet at the same time felt terrified that he would fail her and be abandoned. These fears undermined his ability to risk entering into an authentic relationship: intimacy equals obligation, dependency, and the terror of abandonment.

In therapy, Brad expressed pent-up anger at his mother for seducing him into being her confidant and caretaker and for violating his emotional boundaries. He had a right to be angry—it's not a child's job to advise a parent about divorce or to keep her from depression. The dream had forced him to acknowledge that his mother was far from perfect; the trapdoor to his mother complex had opened and with it the access to his forbidden feeling world, which was populated by these shadow characters.

Brad's persona, the character with an uncaring, freewheeling spirit without needs of his own, defended him against his devouring mother and his terror of losing himself with other women. Through shadow-work, he began to recognize his behavior and attitudes as characters at the table. He imagined his mother as a thirsty vampire, who sucked life from him as she lived vicariously through him. As a child he had felt helplessly swallowed by this devouring aspect of her, and this is what he had feared in women ever since.

Brad had moved thousands of miles from home to get away from his depressed, critical mother. But unknowingly he took her along— she had become his internal critic. It was she in his own mind who told him that no woman was intelligent enough. It was she who told him to call every night and act like a gentleman so that women's feelings would not be hurt. This two-dimensional critical voice now came alive as a three-dimensional creature with its own vested interests. The life of the critical vampire was dependent upon his failures with other women. If Brad were to succeed in forming a satisfying relationship, the critic would no longer have a lifeline.

Although maintaining his obligations helped him to avoid the difficult feelings of guilt and resentment, they cut off access to his positive feelings as well, prohibiting him from knowing whether he felt authentically interested in someone. If Brad could give up these obligatory relationships and risk being alone, he might rediscover his tender, soulful, but well-hidden feelings. This key task provided another dimension to his dating experience.

To break the obligatory pattern, Brad needed to recognize the gentleman character as a saboteur of authenticity. The therapist encouraged Brad to call Alice only when he really wanted contact. The following evening, on a prearranged date with her, Brad became angry because, although he had tried for an hour to bring her to orgasm during lovemaking, he "failed." In his anger, he went into the bathroom, full of resentment, and looked in the mirror—only to discover that his obligatory relationship went beyond phone calls and extended to love-making. He felt guilty if he did not satisfy her and angry at her when he was unsuccessful. He also identified the obligatory character within him and realized that this drama took place within his own mind, and that it may have had nothing to do with her expectations of him. At that point, he knew that he was angry at himself, not at her, and he ended the relationship that evening.

Several months later, Brad fell in love at first sight with "a god-dess," Joanne; he became captured by her image. He cracked up on the rocks, losing his sense of himself and performing again as the perfect gentleman because he felt insecure and deep within believed himself unworthy of her love. Brad felt worshipful around her and quite awk-ward, like a toad who needed to be awakened by her kiss. His anxiety returned, and he lost sleep worrying about whether she would care about him.

But this time Brad was more prepared to deal with his patterns and witness his emotions. He began to spend time alone writing in a jour-nal about his experiences with women. With Joanne as his internal muse, he explored his feelings of vulnerability and powerlessness, his dislike of obligation, and his fears of isolation and commitment. Brad suffered deep discomfort and bouts of painful depression. But through this process he came into a deeper relationship with his own authentic feelings and uncovered a dormant aspect of himself, some gold in the shadow—his creative, poetic side. In this way, his infatuation with the outer muse began to lessen.

Soon he was ready to risk giving up a fantasy relationship with a goddess for an authentic relationship with a real woman. Sacrificing his defensive role as a suave gentleman, he asked Joanne directly about her intentions toward him. She responded that she was busy and would call him, but she never did. As painful as it was to be rejected, Brad had an epiphany: He saw himself through the eyes of Alice, his former girlfriend. He realized that he was being treated by Joanne the way that he had treated Alice—with avoidance and disdain.

His illusions shattered: The goddess was flawed, distant, and un-caring. In addition, he now saw that she drank so heavily that she was probably an alcoholic, which he had not allowed himself to acknowledge previously. In seeing her limitations, he uncovered his own projections and became prepared to meet her and be met as two mortal human beings. But she had disappeared.

However, Brad had been empowered and, by risking his feelings, he was now behaving with a higher degree of authenticity in the dating process. He began to recover his self-respect and feelings of equality with women. In addition, he had discovered a law of relationship—we must be willing to risk a relationship as it is in order to allow it to become something else.

Most recently, Brad began dating Diana, a high school teacher. Despite a strong attraction, he could feel the love without falling into it; he could hear the music and stay centered on his breath. In other words, he had established a sense of identity beyond the feeling of fusion. Brad's centeredness and expanded range of feeling were new to him, but he did not assume that he knew what the feelings meant. Despite his strong emotions, he did not project into the future because he understood that he and Diana did not yet know each other deeply. He felt apprehensive about not being in control as a gentleman, but he also felt excited about the possibility of a deeper intimacy. Brad was finally capable of vulnerability and of beginning to explore the realm of conscious relationships.

Continuing to write in his journal, Brad looked through the rearview mirror to gain self-knowledge from exploring the pattern in his dating relationships: He identified the obligatory behavior of the gentleman character in which he lost an authentic connection to his own Self. He identified the character of the critic and the projection of shadow in which he saw the lack in others, his unconscious attempt to remain superior in order to protect himself from intimacy. He identified the projection of soul onto his goddess lover, which uncovered his inferior shadow character. And he discovered his mother's shadow hidden in the recesses of his own mind, like a Sphinx guarding the entranceway to his vulnerable, soulful feelings.

To an observer Brad may have appeared as a contemporary Don Juan womanizer. However, on the inside, he was undergoing a continuous process to which he became deeply committed with a high degree of integrity. As a result, he learned to turn his experience into wisdom, becoming more and more conscious of his own unconscious dynamics so that he could move toward a more authentic, soulful partnership. Finally, in building a relationship to his inner critic, he solved the riddle of the Sphinx.

SEX, MONEY, AND POWER SHADOWS

In many relationships, money, sex, and power shadows get woven together in a web of unconscious patterns. In dating, for example, they may work together to disguise the deeper shadow issue of dependency. Some people use sex or money to gain power in a relationship, so that they can feel safe enough to get their needs met without feeling vulnerable. To be vulnerable is to risk falling into dependency, attachment, and fear of abandonment. They may engage in emotionally detached sex to avoid intimacy yet maintain a connection. Or they may use money as a cover-up for feelings of low self-worth, maintaining a safe, superficial persona and reinforcing a desired image.

However, despite our shields, after we begin to receive love, acceptance, and sex from another person, the fear of dependency begins to emerge. We may fear being overpowered ("I'm powerless if I'm dependent because you have what I need more than anything. It's worth even more than taking care of my own authentic needs." These are the roots of codependency). Or we may fear being abandoned ("If I'm dependent on you and you leave me, I'll be devastated and alone again").

Clearly, this intense fear of feeling our dependency needs stems from early childhood experiences, but it also has a cultural root. Our collective worship of independence or heroic autonomy puts dependency in the cultural shadow, tainting it with fear and shame. Therefore, some people develop counterdependency, a terror of intimacy with the appearance of autonomy; whereas others develop codependency, a terror of autonomy with the appearance of intimacy. In the first, the possibility of authentic relationship is sacrificed for the needs of the individual; in the second, the individual's authentic needs are sacrificed for the relationship. In both instances, authentic, valid dependency needs lie in the shadow. Perhaps one of the aims of the dating process is to explore the potential for healthy interdependency with the other person.

Sexual Shadows:
Erotic Intoxication and Risky Behavior

Sexual shadows abound during dating and the early stages of romance. For some, a terror of sex renders physical intimacy impossible; for others, a terror of intimacy leads to compulsive sex. Epidemic numbers of people suffer from low sexual desire, having banished Aphrodite or Dionysus into shadow; many others suffer endless craving, like our client Noel. While many women worry about an inability to have an orgasm, many men worry about self-control and premature ejaculation. And members of both sexes keep sexual secrets: One client told her therapist that she dated a man for four years before he disclosed that he was bisexual and having unprotected sex with men during the time he slept with her. It took her years to recover from the betrayal.

When Tom, a software salesman, met Dory at a party, he felt immediately intrigued: She radiated self-confidence and sensuality. He told himself that she seemed refreshingly different from the more insecure women of his past, refreshingly free. Later that night, Tom dreamed of making love to Dory with a sexual charge that overtook him. A few days later, they spent a splendid evening in her candlelit living room dancing and necking until midnight; then they went upstairs, following Eros into the bedroom.

Tom and Dory fell headlong into the most intense sexual relationship of their lives. Dory, who had been sexually abused, needed heavy stimulation, thus evoking a sexual aggression that had been buried in Tom. Once given permission to express his sexuality so freely, he became obsessed with her, fantasizing about their sex games day and night. He was under her spell.

After several months, however, Tom had a rude awakening: He and Dory had nothing much to say to each other. And she frequently responded insensitively to his needs. In the end, he realized that he had mistaken sexual intoxication for a relationship; he had confused the release of his passion with love. With disappointment, he told Dory that he wished to stop seeing her. And, with the understanding that he could resume dating as shadow-work, he took up the challenge to discover his erotic nature in a less compulsive way in the next relationship.

In another story of sexual shadow, Joyce, the youngest of six children, was taught to be nice and not to make waves. Her mother told her that if she would just keep quiet and willingly lose at tennis most men would like her. The underlying message: You are your persona.

Joyce came to therapy as a thirty-year-old journalist who had married her first lover seven years earlier. Like many young people who marry as virgins in their twenties, she had done what was expected of her as a young Catholic woman and become a wife. But at that time Joyce had no will of her own, no real sense of herself or of the contribution she might make. And although her husband was kind, they shared little passion or deep connection with each other. Joyce said she felt like a robot, "not living life, just sucking air."

Nonetheless, within the security and safety of her marriage, Joyce naturally matured and developed her own opinions and explored her own needs, like a caterpillar in a cocoon. As she became more aware of her own authentic needs, she gradually became dissatisfied with the superficiality of her relationship. During the final year of the marriage she asked her husband to join her in therapy, but he declined. Eventually, the container of the relationship felt too small for her—she needed to fly. So, with sorrow, she ended the marriage. When she came to therapy, she had dated only one man briefly since her divorce and felt that her sexual passion had been suppressed for years. Although she felt unseen and untouched, she desperately wanted to play, to make up for lost time.

Joyce began to shop in high-style boutiques and to adorn herself to attract wealthy men. She reported that she chose them like "ornaments" and just wanted to be seen on their arms. In fact, she was trading sex for attention. She felt used and disrespected most of the time and would come into therapy feeling angry and hurt because of how they had treated her. In fact, she expected men to respect her when she did not respect herself.

After a few months, Joyce pronounced that she dreaded the hour. It felt like the confession of her youth. She had thought of lying but, in the end, told her therapist the following story. That week, on a second date with a man, she had had sex without a condom. She had thought about her therapist during sex, fearing that he would be disappointed and she would feel guilty. She felt angry about the danger of AIDS and its constraints, she reported; she consciously chose to ignore it. She didn't want to deal with reality, she said. She just wanted to have fun for a change. Besides, she said, she didn't like condoms—although it turned out that she had never tried them.

The therapist asked her which character at the table rebelled against authority. She called it Risky, the one who rebels impulsively against her strict Catholic upbringing and her mother's insistence that she remain invisible. Because Joyce was told repeatedly that she was a boring, unexciting child, Risky gets her into trouble so that she can have another identity. But her unthinking rebellion is as dangerous as her unthinking conformity; either way, her authentic Self is not in charge.

When asked how she would deal with condoms on the next date, Joyce decided that she would share her internal experience, telling him that she felt disturbed by her own carelessness. However, if he refused to use a condom, she feared that she would have sex anyway, out of her fear of abandonment.

For Joyce, this process of self-discovery turned what appeared to be a series of random events into self-knowledge. Despite its dangers, her sexual acting out served to raise her awareness about who she is and what she needs. By learning to witness her impulsivity as a character and using the breathing technique to stay connected to herself, she began to make different choices. She realized that when she unconsciously allowed Risky to lead, rebelling against others' guidelines, she was dismissing her own values. In addition, she felt bad about herself, going out of authenticity and regretting it later. In particular, she began to recognize that she grows attached to men after sexual intimacy, yet she does not choose men who would honor her vulnerability. So she ends up feeling rejected and hurt, as she did with her mother. And she blames them and then blames herself.

To break the pattern, Joyce began to date without having sex, experimenting with becoming more outspoken and opinionated. She felt positive about being more prudent with her sexuality, despite her rebellious attitude toward her early religious training. In fact, she dated Raymond for two months before getting intimate, holding out for trust and friendship before sexuality. When the time came to become intimate, she discussed using condoms with Ray ahead of time. Today, they enjoy a conscious, committed relationship.

Who lives in your sexual shadow? How does this character use sex to defend against intimacy or to resolve other family shadow issues?

MONEY SHADOWS:
SUCCESS OBJECTS AND SUCCESSFUL FATHERS

Sara had not yet awakened to an inner life and remained unaware of the princess who sat in the seat of power at her inner table. An attractive young law student, she was highly concerned with her clothing and her car. She scouted bars at night in search of her "success object," a man whose high-style image would match her own. Her first requirement of him: a six-figure salary.

Sara met Will at a gala party one night and told her therapist that their chemistry was electric. After two months of ecstatic sex, she agreed to marry him. "He meets all my criteria," she said. "He earns a lot of money, and I love the way he treats me like a princess."

But during the few months before the wedding, Sara began to feel worried and anxious. Will did not speak to her much and, on occasion, treated her so insensitively that it felt like cruelty. He seemed preoccupied and did not participate in planning the wedding. When Will dismissed her concerns about music for the celebration, she suddenly realized that he reminded her of her father, also a wealthy but insensitive man who frequently patronized her. In that moment, Sara knew that she would have to betray her own sense of dignity and self-respect to marry him. She suggested they try joint counseling, but he refused. With heartbreak and remorse, Sara canceled the wedding and returned her engagement ring to Will. Facing the death of her dreams, she entered therapy to try to understand why she had chosen to marry a man who treated her in these ways.

Several weeks later Will called and told Sara that their separation was extremely painful for him. He wanted to work on the relationship and invited her to enter therapy with him. Having risked the fantasy of marriage, she had gained her own self-respect and allowed the relationship to become something better. For Sara, this self-affirming act helped to equalize the power in their relationship and permitted it to truly begin.

Our client Barbara, thirty-three, also discovered that her

unconscious relationship to money shaped her attractions to romantic partners. A flourishing motion picture producer in Hollywood, Barbara always wondered why she was drawn to less successful men, including those who earned a lot less money than she did. In an effort to uncover a secret hidden in her family shadow, the therapist asked her to describe her dad.

Barbara's father had been a successful executive in the movie industry, a dominant presence at work and at home. He had reigned in the living room as he had reigned in the boardroom, lecturing rather than conversing, expounding on every topic with the black and white morality of a priest. Barbara loved her dad, but she observed the destructive consequences of his communication style, his lack of relatedness, and his alcoholism on the family.

In addition, her father controlled the family through money. He showered them with gifts to win their love, unable to be vulnerable or tender with them. Unknowingly, Barbara had come to believe that money had given him his power, turning him into a tyrant. So from the time that she began to date, she felt attracted to men who were more sensitive and artistic, better listeners, and certainly less ambitious. In effect, she was drawn to her father's shadow. Yet this pattern kept her in a reactive mode, open to only a narrow range of partners.

Curiously, whenever she ended up in a relationship with a man who was strikingly unlike her father, some part of her always felt disappointed. On the other hand, whenever she dated a powerful man with money who wanted to spend it on her, she fell into her father complex, feeling controlled and inferior. She could not allow herself to be treated well without feeling that there were strings attached.

In therapy, Barbara did the slow, steady work of sorting through her father complex: She recognized how much she was like him and how much she disowned him. Eventually, she discovered that she could respect some of his traits without becoming him. And she could be attracted to some of his traits in a man without feeling trapped by him. Through ongoing shadow-work, Barbara continues to date a wide range of men and to explore her own feelings about money and intimacy.

How do you or did you use money as a shield during dating? How do your family shadow issues around money affect your choice of partners?

POWER SHADOWS: VICTIMS AND VICTIMIZERS

Our cultural worship of the powerful, invulnerable hero persona has resulted in a collective tendency to bury vulnerability and victimization in the shadow. Struggling to maintain an image of perfection and triumph, we have tended to blame the victims, whether they are poor welfare mothers, battered wives, or drug addicts. Our policies have suggested that if the disenfranchised strive harder, they, too, can achieve success or accommodate their abusers. If they do not succeed, they have brought on their own fate.

Several decades ago, the women's movement challenged our collective tendency to ignore the more complex truths of victimization, which was followed by challenges from advocates for people of color, gays and lesbians, and children. And, slowly, another response to abuse and exploitation has emerged, which points to cultural blind spots and rationalizations. But today some social commentators suggest that we have swung to the other extreme, becoming a culture of victims. In this paradigm, individuals who form a victim persona are seen as childish, manipulative, and unwilling to take personal responsibility. Within this cultural split, neither the hero nor the victim can confront the reality of the power shadow and its insidious effects.

At an individual level, the consequences of this split for finding a romantic partner can be devastating. Patterns of power may be laid down as early as a first date. Typically, the hero-identified person abuses power, while the victim-identified person relinquishes it. But these two sides of the power complex also exist within each person as an interior power struggle between two characters—the overpowering tyrant or victimizer and the powerless victim.

Justine, thirty-five, an executive buyer for a fashion retail chain, had given up meeting men in conventional ways, such as at parties, because she often felt shy in groups of people. Instead, she decided to place a personal ad in the local paper. When George called, he sounded interesting and asked to meet her at a bookstore near his home, some thirty miles from Justine's neighborhood. In response, Justine suggested a site closer to her home, but George was adamant about his choice. Immediately, Justine felt uncomfortable. Their first joint decision became a power struggle.

The daughter of a tyrannical and abusive father, Justine had learned at a young age to accommodate men in an effort to feel safe. So, while dating, she tended to surrender her own preferences and give up power. But Justine had been doing shadow-work, so she identified this victim character and, in this case, could listen to a different voice. She chose not to meet with him after all.

Three days later, George called back and agreed to go to her meeting place. Reluctantly, Justine joined him for coffee and they spent a few hours in casual conversation. A few days later, George called and told her that he had won two free airline tickets to Hawaii, inviting her to join him. Justine hesitated, but she was tempted. She was bored at the time, eager for an adventure. She asked to go out with him again before she decided. During their date, George disclosed to Justine that he was involved in a lot of lawsuits. Instinctively, she found him a little dangerous; however, she found him exciting as well, so she overrode her fears and agreed to travel with him.

That night Justine dreamed: *she was flirting with a black-haired man who seemed imposing and intense.* In the dream she felt that he was enclosing her, "like the kind of man who could kill you, but won't." She felt attracted to his strength and power but, at the same time, she was afraid of the danger.

On their next date, Justine found out more about George's lawsuits: He earned his living in petty litigation. She felt disgusted and afraid and canceled the trip. George was furious and applied intimidation tactics: He told her that he would sue her for $400, the price of the plane fare, because her name was on the ticket. A lawyer advised her not to be concerned, and, after a few more harassing calls, George disappeared.

In her encounters with George, Justine had tried not to give up her power, as she had done in the past. However, a deeper pattern of victimization remained: Out of her own feelings of inadequacy, she had responded to a man who had shown a slight interest in her, ignoring her own ambivalent feelings toward him and banishing her instincts. After this troubling experience Justine recognized that she could be seduced by danger, so she needs at least three dates with a man before she can trust her own evaluation of him. In this way, she honed her instinct and faculties of discrimination while she learned to protect herself from her tendency to give up power and make snap decisions.

Whereas most conventional power struggles are about ego, others that may resemble them are, in fact, quite different.

INTRODUCING CRISES OF COMMITMENT

As two people begin to date regularly and spend more time together, growing closer and relaxing into intimacy, their defenses relax as well, and they start treating one another more like family. With a growing feeling of safety and familiarity, they live less in persona and more in authentic feelings. Eventually, they make decisions about how much time to spend together, when to begin sexual intimacy, meet each other's friends and family, become monogamous, become engaged or live together, get married, and, perhaps, have children. These decisions appear as crises because one partner may present the other partner with an ultimatum. However, we view them not as conventional commitments to an external form but as a series of natural internal conflicts that arise between the call of the Self for greater safety in intimacy and the ego's fears of dissolution or abandonment.

Although this direction toward deeper commitment is not universal, it is what many people seek. We believe that it stems from an authentic need of the Self to feel seen by and secure with a loved one by creating a mutual bond of trust. At some point, one of the partners feels an internal pressure for more safety, recognition, and commitment, which needs to be addressed. We call it a "crisis" because if this inner voice is not heeded and shared with the other person or defused internally, the pressure builds, creating internal consequences, such as depression or resentment. We tend to tolerate these negative feelings for as long as we can, suffering them to avoid the risk of expressing them. But at a certain point we cannot stand it any longer; we must risk losing the relationship as it is in order to allow it to evolve into something new.

If the crisis of commitment is honored, then the relationship can jump to a new level of intimacy. If it's not honored, the partner expressing an authentic need at least has honored himself or herself, regardless of the outcome. And that act is empowering and self-affirming, preparing that person for the next step.

Crises of commitment appear around a range of issues, each requiring a responsibility to the Self: honesty about our experience, sexual limits, and desires; commitment to monogamy; the need for separation; the readiness for engagement, marriage, or pregnancy. In honoring a call of the Self, the relationship moves forward, and another crisis of commitment inevitably follows. Or the relationship ends.

For example, if a woman goes out on several dates with a man and feels subtly emotionally abused, she may face a crisis of commitment: a conflict between her need to speak up and describe her experience and her fear of losing him and feeling alone again. If she does not heed the call, she may begin to feel like a victim, become depressed, and resent his behavior. If, like Sara, she heeds the call and risks giving up the relationship, the power shifts—and it will become something else. It needs to produce more mutual respect and equality or, in all probability, it will end.

In another circumstance, if a man has dated a woman for ten months and feels ambivalent about her request for a commitment to a monogamous relationship, they face a crisis. A client described this dilemma: "I do care about her, but there are so many difficulties. I don't feel in love with her. I'm only twenty-six years old and I am not ready to commit to the future from my heart. And she's always late, which drives me crazy. I can't stand waiting around for anyone. Yet there's this sweetness between us. And we share a passion for the arts." The therapist helped this man to explore his ambivalent feelings for this woman. In the end, he decided that it was not his fear of intimacy that blocked the commitment; he did not wish to commit to this particular woman.

Another man, thirty-eight, had been through a crisis of commitment concerning monogamy in a long-term relationship three times before. He decided, at that point, that this problem involved a lack in him, not in his partner, which caused him to avoid commitment. By doing shadow-work to take responsibility for himself and clarify some of his negative projections, this man moved toward commitment with his partner. His pattern, which was to stay in ambivalent relationships and blame his partners for not meeting his expectations, was shattered with this decision. And the vector of his destiny moved forward.

Thus the key to working through a crisis of commitment is to acknowledge the authentic demands of the Self to keep the relationship process alive and evolving to another stage. It does not imply commitment to the current form of the relationship; at its highest level, it implies commitment to the internal process of development.

CRISIS OF COMMITMENT: WHEN TO HAVE SEX

With the cultural shift from sexual freedom to sexual caution, which stems primarily from the AIDS epidemic, many singles today take more time to get to know one another before becoming sexual. But besides the danger of sexually transmitted diseases, there are internal reasons to consider before becoming sexually intimate with someone. Bruce and Sally had been dating for a month, talking intensively and discovering shared passions, as well as necking lovingly for long hours. When Bruce suggested that he was ready to make love, Sally realized that she was not. She felt unsafe for a number of reasons: Bruce still spoke daily with his ex-wife and maintained strong feelings for her. He spoke adamantly about not wanting to make a premature commitment to monogamy, not wanting to feel tied down after a twenty-year marriage.

Sally, on the other hand, had been single for a long time and longed for a strong bond with a man in which she could feel loved and safe. They began to wonder whether, despite their affections, they had met at the wrong time.

In staying with her feelings of vulnerability, Sally waited and watched to see how Bruce responded. Fortunately, he did not pressure her or threaten to end the relationship. But he did mention that he felt unaccepted in some deep way and probably would until they could have sex. Sally felt his pain and agreed that evening to begin an intimate relationship soon.

In therapy, Sally wondered whether she was overriding her own tender feelings in order to please him. Her Zeus-style father had overpowered her, as well as her mother's, feelings routinely. Perhaps the character within her that had learned this habit from him was now in full gear. In this case, she would have sex for the wrong reasons and would suffer the regret of feeling inauthentic and out of alignment, betraying her own soul. She wondered whether she was complying with a man's desire, feeling her own soulful desire, or really becoming ready.

Sally needed to look at her relationship to sex in the present moment and explore whether she could be vulnerable without promises or whether a shadow character was making a Faustian bargain. The therapist asked her whether she would make love if she knew now that the relationship would not last. Sally applied what we refer to as the Principle of No Regret: She imagined herself one to three years into the future, looking back at this moment in time and asking herself whether she regretted her choice. This practice, which can help us to live life with the least amount of regret, can also help us to gain an authentic perspective on a range of decisions.

Eventually, Sally realized that she deeply enjoyed feeling courted by this man and that something would be lost when this stage of dating ended. She would lose the archetypal power of the virgin goddess when she had sex with him. She feared becoming a routine lover, a withholding wife, or a disappointed, rejected woman. Thus she uncovered deep mythic roots to her concerns about making love. This was not a simple problem, such as a fear of rejection alone. She would be changing status in the eyes of this man, from Virgin to Aphrodite, and she did not want this moment to be undervalued.

Nor did she want to undervalue her authentic need for security. She wished to honor her anxiety without bulldozing her way through it; she wished to hear the voice of the character that needed to be heard. Her therapist asked her how she could have sex with Bruce and also honor the sacred aspect of the voice of hesitation.

For Sally, raised to be an independent thinker and a career woman, this desire for security and the dependency needs that go with it live in her shadow—that is, they feel unacceptable to her. She did not know how to feel these needs without feeling ashamed. After identifying these underlying issues and listening to the voices of the characters at the table, she expressed them to Bruce and felt seen, heard, and understood by him. She then felt her authentic desire to make love with him without regret.

In this chapter, we have tried to reimagine dating as a journey toward self-knowledge through shadow-work. For many people who long for a Beloved and suffer the loneliness and shame of being single, or the feeling of failure that may result from the dating process, we offer our compassion. And we suggest that doing shadow-work on personal issues, family issues, and archetypal motifs may ease your suffering and offer signposts along the way, guiding you toward your destination.

In the story of Apollo's pursuit of Daphne, she calls on her father to rescue her. By turning her into a tree, he pulls her back into an earlier state of nature, insulating her from adult intimacy with men, rather than forward into culture, which is represented by the god Apollo. In many romantic liaisons, the opposite-sex parent has a powerful pull on our attractions and on our underlying patterns of intimacy. We will explore this idea in Chapter 5.

CHAPTER 5

SHADOW-BOXING: WRESTLING WITH ROMANTIC PARTNERS

How do I love thee? Let me count the ways.
I love thee to the depth and breadth and height
My soul can reach, when feeling out of sight
For the ends of Being and ideal Grace.
I love thee to the level of every day's
Most quiet need, by sun and candle-light.
I love thee freely, as men strive for right;
I love thee purely, as they turn from praise.
I love thee with the passion put to use
In my old griefs, and with my childhood's faith.
I love thee with a love I seemed to lose
With my lost saints. I love thee with the breath,
Smiles, tears, of all my life! and, if God choose,
I shall but love thee better after death.

—ELIZABETH BARRETT BROWNING

In a famous Greek myth of romance, Eros insists that Psyche make love to him in the dark. Like Eros, many of us want to remain hidden when our passions loosen the reins of the ego's control. We long to know the Other, but not to be known. We ask probing questions, but reply with half answers. In a myriad of ways, we run from being seen and avoid becoming vulnerable, disguised in tight personas and baggy clothes, hiding in sordid addictions and clandestine habits.

And yet, right alongside the urgent longing to know the Other and the refusal to be known is the converse longing: the urgency to be known and the refusal to see. Like Psyche, we open our arms to love, but we may not open our eyes. We consent to temporary blindness, giving our sweet love to unknown others, people who are not what they seem, people who become strangers with the light of dawn. Like Psyche, we follow the lead of Eros, god of love—and when we light a candle in the dark, we are shocked at his Otherness.

For this reason the divinity of desire has been called Eros the bitter-sweet. With the sweetness of love, the bitterness of shadow is evoked. And our desire, which seems to be such an intimate friend, comes to appear as a hostile enemy that brings longing, envy, and even hate in tow.

We long for wholeness, a greater unity that stems from meeting the Beloved, our other half. Eros, our archetypal longing, causes us to reach for that which is missing; our desire is organized around this radiant absence. And we yearn to melt into the Beloved, to find there the missing piece, and to lose ourselves in a paradise of everlasting love. Jung expressed this universal quest of the human soul in this way: "The soul cannot exist without its other side, which is always found in a 'You.' Wholeness is a combination of I and You, and these show themselves to be parts of a transcendent unity whose nature can only be grasped symbolically."

Yet as the god spreads its wings of desire, it blinds us to the reality of what is there. In this chapter we move from the tentative exploration that defines dating to the spell cast by romantic love and the infamous blindness that results. We will learn, through the stories of many couples, how romance leads us through dark alleys to the meeting with the Other, the stranger who appears in our most intimate moments to sabotage our feelings of familiarity, safety, and love. And we will show how shadow-work can transform the painful consequences of romantic blindness, so that eyes blinded by persona can see ever more deeply into soul. By reexamining relationships from romance to marriage in the context of the shadow's hidden needs, eventually we can move from shadow-boxing with the Other to shadow-dancing with the Beloved. We can pierce the veil of illusory projection and see our partner with clear perception. Then we will discover that the Beloved is both the solution and the problem;

the Beloved is the answer and the question to be asked again and again.

Who do we spend our entire life loving?

Meeting the Other:
Projections Hit Their Targets

When two people meet and feel a deep connection, their hearts open like flowers. So do their imaginations. Five-year-old Ned, a blond-haired blue-eyed cutey, played in the park with his parents when a young girl, about his age, approached. She said, "You look just like John Smith in the *Pocahontas* movie." Ned grinned and his little chest filled with air. He announced to his parents that he had a new girlfriend.

Projection begins at a young age. We view it as a natural, unavoidable process, not a pathological problem to be rid of or a symptom to be cured. Through projection, the unconscious mind expels both positive and negative traits, attributing them to other people, whereby they can become conscious. Because by definition the unconscious is hidden, like the dark side of the moon, we need to discover indirect ways to catch glimpses of it. And projection is a primary way of doing so.

Rob, an architect in his forties who has been married to his second wife for ten years, recalled how he met his first in an instantaneous romantic projection. "I walked into a college dorm and saw this blond-haired girl sitting on the couch. She was swinging her legs, wearing bobby sox and loafers, to the music of Simon and Garfunkel. I walked up and told her that we would be married one day. She told me I was nuts. But two years later, we were husband and wife." Five years later, they were divorced.

Carrie described a first date with Vince, who appeared on a motorcycle in black leather boots and jacket. She stood on the balcony above and said to herself, "My Romeo has arrived."

Projection is like shooting an invisible arrow. Each of us carries a kind of archer's quiver strapped on our backs. Every so often an arrow shoots out unpredictably, and we say something nasty or we fall in love. When we turn around to find out where the arrow came from, the quiver moves out of sight.

If the receiver has a soft spot to receive the projection, it sticks. For instance, if we project our anger onto a dissatisfied mate or our seductive charms onto a good-looking stranger, then we hit the target and the projection holds. From then on the sender and receiver are linked in a mysterious alliance, which could feel like erotic passion, intense disgust, or unbearable envy.

Julia, twenty-nine, a slight, wiry woman who works as a pastry chef, reported breathlessly that she had found the man of her dreams two weeks before. She knew nothing about him, but because of the look in his eyes and the sound of his voice she was certain that they would be married by the end of the year. The therapist asked her to write a short piece about her internal experience of the moment of their encounter:

> Her eyes seek the Fit, the match between her world and his. The parallel lines, the flush corners, the edges that rub up against each other. She feels for the Fit, the mesh, the weave that joins her with him.
>
> She saw him in a moment across the empty, white-walled room. She saw him with her whole body. It cried out with the Fit. It moved her toward him relentlessly on a one-way vector; no return. He sat still, waiting. Her body sat nearby and began to pulse. The air between them felt thick, resonant, palpable. The Fit was screaming from her cells.
>
> She looked into his eyes and said slowly, "I've been waiting for you for so long." He nodded and said slowly, "I know." The Fit smiled in her cells. Nothing had prepared her for this moment. She was perfectly prepared.

We might wonder why the sender shoots these arrows into others. Poet Robert Bly uses the following metaphor: When we were very young, we had a 360-degree personality, which radiated energy from all directions. But the adults around us could not tolerate this much exuberance. So, in their own discomfort, they unintentionally but inevitably betrayed us by shaming and humiliating us for certain feelings, such as vulnerability, or behaviors, such as competition, which we then learned to hide. Our teachers may have scolded us for other behaviors, such as daydreaming, or our priests may have imposed terrible guilt for our sexual feelings. These denied, disowned parts of our souls—anger or depression, jealousy or resentment, intellectuality or sensuality, athletic or artistic ability—get exiled into the dark. As a result, the full circle of energy that was our birthright is sliced away piece by piece, leaving only a thin, proper facade to greet the world.

When we begin dating, as a natural part of development the shadow goes in search of its lost traits in others in an effort to recover the full range of our personality—the gold in the dark side. Like *Star Trek's* Dr. McCoy (aka Bones), who does a high-tech DNA check on his patients within minutes of their first contact, the shadow scans for a love fit, looking for the "one." When we find romance and fall in love, our unconscious fantasy image of the Other often is a composite of familiar parental qualities, which we inherited through identification, and our own neglected traits, which we banished into shadow through repression. When we feel a harmonic match with another person, a seemingly magical feeling of familiarity or resonance—the Fit—a part of us begins to believe that our soul's dream of acceptance and belonging can be fulfilled.

Without our knowing it, the shadow is at work attempting to recreate early childhood relationship patterns with a secret mission—to heal old wounds and feel loved. We view this inevitable childhood projection as the first stage of romance, a kind of fusion that may feel like living inside of an eggshell, an enclosed form in which the couple feels nurtured and self-contained. Like two chicks in the shell, they feed one another on love, which speeds the growth and development of both. Other friendships may fall away as the partners imagine meeting all of each other's needs and fulfilling all of each other's desires.

Then, one day, inevitably, the shell cracks—and the relationship breaks down. The old rules, often unspoken, which previously provided security ("You are all that I need" or "I pay for everything, so we have sex when I want it" or "You carry the feelings for both of us") no longer hold, and the partners face a crisis of commitment. Once the shell has been cracked, it cannot be put back together again. The partners may try, but they have entered a new stage of relationship: They are now too well developed to remain fused. For those who do not know that this is a natural developmental crisis, the relationship will end, and the partners inevitably attempt to re-create the eggshell with the next person. But for those who can negotiate the new rules, which allow for greater individuality and authenticity, the partners can go play in the chicken yard—a larger psychic space with more room for individuality and clear boundaries—and yet remain a couple. Then the relationship can begin again.

What traits does your lover carry for you that creates the unconscious attraction between you? What do you give to him or her that might be returned to your own treasury? How would that influence the way you live your life?

COMPENSATING THE OTHER:
TWO PARTS MAKE A WHOLE

At the same time that we send projections, we also carry them for others. Some people tend to draw certain kinds of projections toward them. The receivers' shadows also try to heal old wounds through being seen deeply, feeling adored or respected. But those who receive the arrows of projection pay as steep a price as those who send them—being seen via projection is not being seen authentically. For example, women who carry Aphrodite energy speak about the pain of feeling objectified as an image of beauty and of being envied by other women; at the level of soul they often feel unseen and misunderstood. And men who are chosen for their Adonis sex appeal or their wealth and power also may question whether they are viewed as objects or seen in their authenticity.

The shadow's aim of completion via the new partner explains why opposites attract—optimists and pessimists, pursuers and distancers, extroverts and introverts, artists and scientists, pragmatists and spiritual seekers together make one whole. Consequently, through an unspoken division of labor, many couples operate like one person, trading strengths and weaknesses with the Other throughout a period of compensation.

Then they may discover, at some point down the road, that just those traits in the partner that seemed the most attractive—part of the shadow's solution—become the least attractive—part of the problem.

"He's so strong and commanding" becomes "He's such a power freak." Or "She's so sensitive and nurturing" becomes "She's so overly emotional and dependent." Of course, because we have rejected these qualities in ourselves, at some deep level we are repelled by them in the other person.

Without shadow-work, shadow-boxing is inevitable: As the partners reject their disowned qualities in the Other, they get drawn into painful, repetitive fights, inevitably ending up hurt and angry and perhaps separating from each other. In defending against the pain, we also defend against the love. But with shadow-work, a partner may rediscover his or her own rejected traits in the projections and learn to romance them. In this way, the sources of conflict can be viewed as sources of opportunity; the relationship becomes a means to find gold in the dark side both in ourselves and in our partners. As a result, our partner, who felt like an enemy, becomes an ally to our soul. And the relationship deepens.

But other problems may arise as well. When one partner begins to retake possession of lost parts of him or herself, the Other no longer needs to compensate for a lack and therefore no longer serves as the source of the partner's sense of wholeness. Ted, who was attracted to Carol's outdoor Artemis qualities, her love of nature and animals, is now a competent camper himself and no longer depends on her to blaze the trails outdoors. If their relationship were based, even to some degree, on her competence and his incompetence, chaos could result. The two would need to discover deeper sources of connection.

Shirley believed, since she was a young child, that she was unintelligent and uncreative, so she used a sexual shield to feel and appear attractive and to compensate for her feelings of inferiority. She habitually became romantically involved with highly creative but unavailable men, seeking that which she yearned for outside of herself. As she gradually discovered her own creative voice, her unconscious attraction to creative, unavailable partners faded. Eventually, she used her seductive powers less and her authentic feelings more to establish contact with men.

Joel, a forty-six-year-old screenwriter, was divorced by his homemaker wife after a twelve-year marriage. Accustomed to intimacy and a supportive woman, he felt surprised at the strength of his attraction to Ellen, a stockbroker, who clearly thrived in her autonomy. During their first six months of dating, they enacted the Daphne and Apollo myth: He pulled her in, while she pushed him away.

As they became more romantically involved with each other, they entered the eggshell stage: Joel did not wish to face his separateness and independence and tried to feel safe through fusion with Ellen. In response, she created a power shield and clung to her separateness for safety, judging his dependency needs and her own as unacceptable. Whereas he feared abandonment most of all, she feared being overwhelmed by his neediness.

Their patterns quickly became problematic: Joel felt that he could never get enough love from Ellen, as if he stood at the watering hole but was not allowed to drink. Ellen, self-contained like an Athena-style woman, felt smothered, unable to breathe her own air. When her emotional claustrophobia reached a peak, a destructive part of her picked up a metaphorical sword and lashed out at Joel with cruel words, cutting their intimacy in an effort to restore her sense of safety. Each time this pattern recurred, they faced a crisis of commitment.

Slowly, with the help of their therapist, the partners discovered which characters were at work: the fuser and the distancer. They found that this pair of opposites had been split between them, each side carried by the Other and shadow-boxing with one another. So, their shadow-work involved making them conscious of their disowned traits. As Joel slowly learned to find an authentic sense of security within himself, he began to uncover a shadow character that held his need for separateness and a healthy distance. He no longer panicked when he felt alone, fearing that he might disappear; he even gradually grew to enjoy solitude. Eventually, he could tell Ellen that he loved and honored her independence, even though it felt shadowy to him. As a result, she could feel more deeply accepted for who she was, not simply for his fantasy projection of her.

As Ellen slowly allowed herself to feel loved, she began to feel more emotionally dependent on Joel, even to need him, uncovering a shadow character that held her own need for intimacy. She was deeply afraid of these vulnerable feelings, which she had repressed for a long time. And sometimes, when Joel pulled away, she felt humiliated by her own feelings of dependency. But the authentic nature of their growing love allowed her to build trust in herself, in Joel, and in the relationship itself. Eventually she learned to witness her automatic tendency to brandish the sword and power shield. At times she would backslide and separate from Joel in an abrupt way, hurting him deeply. Then, together they would remind each other that Athena, not Ellen, had taken control and issued a call, and they would seek to hear her deeper need.

With ongoing shadow-work, they continued to bring more of themselves into conscious awareness and thus into their relationship, exposing denied aspects of their personalities and opening up new avenues of intimacy. Eventually, the two discovered together that Ellen's fear of fusion is just the other side of Joel's fear of abandonment.

✱   Where does the shadow sabotage your intimacy? When does your fear of fusion cause you to appear distant and aloof? When does your fear of abandonment cause you to surrender your authentic voice and your independence in an effort to feel safe?

These disowned compensatory traits, when projected onto a partner, can become threatening because they stir up taboo shadow feelings. For example, initially a man may be drawn to a woman's open sexuality, then find her behavior inappropriate as his wife. This pattern may stem from the archetypal split known as the Madonna/Whore syndrome, in which a woman may carry either the elevated projection of mother—purity, kindness, and compliance—or the devalued projection of mistress—sensuality, instinct, and bodily hungers. During dating, a man may be attracted to the "whore" quality of a sensual woman, but he would never take this character home to his family. And he may feel that the mother of his children must be "pure," like his own mother. With this split the man may find himself lamenting the loss of his sexual desire and unconsciously rendering himself incapable of maintaining a satisfying sexual relationship because to have sex with mother is taboo. Thus his underlying negative attitudes toward sex and intimacy may have been buried together in the shadow during dating and only become evident during later stages of romance or marriage.

This pattern has deep cultural roots in religious teachings, as well as individual roots in a man's psychology. If a man with a puritanical character at the table has cast his own bodily eros into the shadow to live a "pure" life, banishing the wildness of Dionysus and labeling others as hedonists, then he cannot tolerate these energies in his partner. As a result, he may turn her into a mother figure, a sexless caretaker who is supposed to love him unconditionally and display no shadow of her own. In some cultures, where this pattern is seen as the norm, men may turn to a mistress to fulfill their more sexual Dionysian needs. Or a woman initially may be attracted to a man who appears to be upbeat, optimistic, even ecstatic. As our client Lorraine put it, "When I met Josh, he had a radiant sparkle and boundless energy. He just seemed to live life so fully and was not brought down by petty problems."

But after a few months Lorraine wanted more vulnerability from Josh and could no longer tolerate his high energy and seemingly automatic positive attitude. In fact, she came to believe that he habitually denied his more difficult feelings and defended against them with learned optimism. As they spent more time together, she noticed that he drank several cups of coffee in the morning and again in the afternoon. When she suggested that he was addicted to caffeine, he denied it and agreed to cut down his coffee intake to prove her wrong. But as his energy level dropped, he grew weary and moody and had to admit that she was correct. Lorraine, in turn, needed to support the less energetic, more moody Josh if she wanted more emotional authenticity.

In these cases, a partner may begin to discourage a troublesome quality or shadow character in the Other: He may shame her sexual desires; she may criticize his lack of emotional range. In response, the receiver of the projection may begin to feel judged and diminished in just the way that he or she did by a parent, which caused the wound in the first place. In this way, the shadow achieved its goal—to re-create the past.

Compensation is only the most obvious solution to the shadow's dilemma. Many couples have more complicated unconscious dynamics than a simple balancing act of disowned traits. In what psychologists call projective identification, one partner unconsciously identifies with the other person's rejected part, or shadow character, and acts it out. For instance, if a husband has cast his rage into the shadow and never shows angry feelings, the wife may grow angrier and angrier, unconsciously carrying them for the pair. Just as family members split the pie of shadow material among them, the couple splits it between them. As a result, one appears highly emotional, the other highly rational, such as a feeling-oriented mother's daughter paired with a thinking-oriented father's son or, alternatively, a sensitive, intuitive mother's son bonded with an intellectual, independent father's daughter. Other combinations: one partner appears upbeat, the other depressed; one appears neat, the other messy; one appears to need intimacy, the other to need distance. One may even become an alcoholic, the other a tee-totaler. In this way, a process that is actually internal to both people is externalized, becoming an interpersonal conflict and creating the Other, the worthy opponent, the shadow-boxing partner.

Consequently, the sender is protected from seeing those traits in himself and can instead criticize and try to change them in his mate. The receiver, who carries the dirty laundry that doesn't fit with the sender's persona, then becomes "the problem," the person who needs to be fixed. From the ego's point of view, the lover may seem strangely unfitting—too unhappy, too messy, too loud, too shy, too indulgent, too prudish. But from the shadow's point of view, the lover may seem strangely familiar, like a parent or even like the flip side of oneself.

If the shadow did its work of finding an appropriate fit with a part-ner, the relationship re-creates early patterns—and thereby provides an opportunity for consciousness. Thus we suggest that the early stages of romance are determined primarily by the shadow's needs; they form the bases for the initial attraction and for the development of later, more conscious stages of relationship, which occur in real time with a Beloved, rather than as a repetition of the past with a projected Other.

☆ Who lives in your lover's shadow? A slut, an artist, a helpless child, a violent tyrant, a reclusive monk, a free spirit? How do you re-late to these characters in him or her? How do you subtly discourage their expression in your partner when they do not fit your image of him or her?

Partners as Parents: The Psychology of Love

Randy, thirty-two, a tall, lanky, boyish-looking property manager, had a troubling childhood. His mother was addicted to painkillers and often drifted off into a world of her own, betraying him through ne-glect and abandonment. When his mother was awake, she became ex-tremely critical and accusatory, blaming him for a dirty house or an unprepared meal. At times, the verbal abuse would escalate until Randy felt overwhelmed and cried, covering his ears and begging her to stop. He did not know which of her extreme behaviors was worse: her withdrawal and neglect or her raging accusations.

Either way, he experienced his mother as crazy and out of control. So he learned to survive as a teen by using his mother's shield and retreating into drugs and later by retreating into books. In these ways he avoided feeling vulnerable to her rage and responsible for her unhappiness. In fact, he avoided feeling anything at all by anesthetizing his soul.

By the time he left home, Randy had identified with his academic father and developed an intellectual shield, which caused him to be hyperalert and self-protective. He learned that by relying on this character, he could think things through analytically and avoid the swirling tides of sadness, anger, and guilt. He could remain alert and above water; he could find neat answers to messy problems, thereby banishing his mother's chaotic emotional world into shadow.

In his thirties, Randy discovered in himself a deep spiritual longing and a hunger for an orderly, meaningful universe. As he explored various methods of positive thinking and Eastern philosophy, he found corroboration for his disdain of emotional life. And slowly he began to feel safe with his newfound answers, continuing to fortify his intellectual defense against feelings of sadness, guilt, shame, and isolation with an intricate spiritual philosophy.

Living out the character of a charismatic *puer*, Randy acted like a magnet for young, attractive, spiritually oriented women. He had lived with six lovers before coming to therapy and reporting that each was not spiritually committed enough for him; each was too distancing or too emotionally volatile. As he told the stories of these relationships, a pattern emerged.

The lovers initially felt a deep spiritual union and moved in together within a few months. Randy was finely attuned to any lack of harmony between them, such as a difference of opinion. In those moments, a shadow character emerged: He panicked with a sense of abandonment if his partner separated or asserted herself even a little. An independent move, such as making a social plan without consulting him, which felt to her like a one on the psychic Richter scale, felt to him like a nine—and threatened seismic catastrophe. Randy's shadow character could not tolerate a feeling of separateness; he needed his lover to be present to him at all times and felt extremely anxious if she turned to her own reality.

Although he thought of himself as a calm, sensitive, emotionally available man, Randy panicked if his partner became what he called overly emotional. He would feel irritable, angry, or depressed. Because he was unconsciously avoiding his own feelings out of fear of falling into chaos, he could not tolerate disturbing feelings in his partner. At those times, he would begin to analyze her problems in an attempt to fix her and re-create the harmony he so desperately needed. He projected his mother's loss of control onto his partner, and his desire to fix her covered up his inability to deal with his own internal chaos, which threatened to emerge when he felt emotionally overwhelmed.

Randy currently lives with Betsy, twenty-nine, a petite blond songwriter who was abandoned by her father at a young age and raised by a dominant, intrusive mother. To assert herself with her own mother, Betsy unconsciously felt that she would have risked abandonment. So, instead, she developed a quiet but resentful, rebellious shadow character. With Randy, she re-created this pattern: Unable to express her need for quiet in the mornings, she felt that he would abandon her if she asserted herself. But, as a result, her resentment built up a head of steam until she told the therapist how she felt.

Randy gets up early in the morning to go to work. He tries to tiptoe around quietly, but Betsy awakens and experiences his sounds as an intrusion. As she describes the situation, "When he enters the bedroom and I'm asleep, he's being incredibly insensitive, selfish, and invasive." Thus she projects aspects of her own shadow, inherited from her mother, onto Randy.

Caught in the clutches of her mother complex, Betsy freezes: She has no idea how to communicate her needs to Randy in a constructive way, so she sees a choice between two extremes, each reflected in a shadow character: to sacrifice her need to sleep, becoming tired, resentful, and withdrawn; or to become combative, making demands and risking his rejection.

Betsy replicated her relationship with her mother: If she asserts herself, she believes Randy will abandon her. In therapy, she learned to describe her dilemma in the context of each character at the table: the frightened little girl who fears abandonment, the overly independent woman who cannot express her vulnerability, and the mature woman who has valid needs of her own. As she separated out these characters, she was able to witness each one in her relationship with Randy.

Of course, Randy also replicated his relationship with his mother. When Betsy becomes emotionally reactive due to the buildup of her own unexpressed feelings, he panics; he experiences her as judgmental and is terrified that she will lose control. In his panic, he unknowingly distances from his own feelings and retreats to his intellectual shield by analyzing her, projecting onto her the source of their problems. But even when he's accurate in his description, she feels attacked, "as if he's shoving himself down my throat." So she rejects him, defending herself against the attack. And their joint objectives—to communicate in an effort to feel safe and loved—are lost.

The couple's parental complexes are shadow-boxing with each other, feeding off one another's fears and anxieties in an endless downward spiral until they can put on the brakes only by taking responsibility for their own feelings, romancing their projections, and moving out of the past into present time. Ideally, Betsy needs to identify the cues that indicate that she is caught in a complex: She feels shut down and deadened; she becomes humorless, unable to laugh and play. Then she can learn to say, "I feel invaded and it angers me. But I don't say it out of fear that you will judge and reject me." Ideally, Randy also needs to identify the cues that indicate that he is caught: He feels irritable and anxious and becomes critical. Then he can learn to say, "I feel cut off and attacked by you." In return, Betsy might tell him, "I feel overwhelmed with responsibility when you feel cut off. I'm not your mom and I can't take care of all of your needs. I have needs of my own." As Randy begins to witness his feelings of disconnection, he can become more able to respect Betsy's boundaries. As she begins to witness her silent victim character and separate out from it, she will feel better about herself and less resentful of him; she may one day feel safer to move toward greater intimacy.

Other people who have a pattern of creating long-distance relationships or longing for unattainable lovers, such as married women or men, also may be turning their partners into their parents. Peter, a high-tech entrepreneur, believes that he remembers feeling unwanted even in his mother's womb. He has faint memories of reaching out to her and feeling rebuffed both in utero and as an infant.

When he came to therapy, he claimed to be in love with a French-woman whom he met while visiting Paris. His long-distance yearning for her aroused deep passion in him. He believed that she was his ideal woman—except that she wasn't there. When he uncovered the connection with his yearning for his mother's attention, he was more able to end the fantasy relationship and prepare to meet a woman who would be more available to him.

Childhood sexual abuse also imprints our parental projections onto lovers. Camille, an African-American college student who was molested by her father for nearly ten years, explains that she feels safe only in romantic triangles. "I tend to be attracted to men who are already in relationships, because they want me but not too much. They're not too needy, so there's no real risk involved. And I can feel the excitement of competition, jealousy, and fear that I felt with my parents at a young age. I just have no interest in monogamy, no vision of being intimate with one other person for a long time."

Most intimate relationships have some version of this story: one partner (or both) turns the other into a parental figure. In the grips of a complex, he or she feels hurt and angry, then numb and deadened. As a result, a mechanical, repetitive process gets played out in which each lover believes that the problem lies in the other person, blaming the Other's moods or behaviors endlessly. Therefore, the solution to the problem lies in that person's waking up and changing. We call this negative downward spiral the roller-coaster ride because the lovers get on at the same place, seem to spin out of control, but end up getting off at the same place—and nothing has really changed. They had a wild ride, which always ends in aggression or withdrawal, another form of aggression.

When faced with a repeating roller-coaster ride, the sweet, simple words that used to heal wounds now feel thorny. They begin to further irritate the wound until one or both partners feels deeply hurt, disappointed, and betrayed. Eventually, the partner feels like an enemy, and both feel hopeless and defeated. This feeling of hopelessness ("He will never love me in the way that I need"; "She will never change"; "This will never work out") may at times seem endless. And without fresh awareness, suffering may increase until one partner ends the relationship. Even if the two find their way to forgiveness, in time the cycle repeats itself.

The roller-coaster ride can, however, become a vehicle for shadow-work: The projections can reveal an aspect of a woman's internal shadow in the partner's actions, such as her punishing, controlling side. Or a man may see his own darkness on the partner's face—that is, his unconscious, angry, critical nature, which lies hidden behind his passive retreat. To romance the shadow we need to recognize our projection; admit that it exists within us; and identify and communicate our feelings in the moment, thereby relating to a real-time person, not to a ghost of the past. When each partner sees the other accept full responsibility, the blame game can recede. Then, both can relax and Eros returns.

In this way, as a result of the healing power of love and the gift of shadow-work, the couple becomes a vehicle for developing awareness in the partners. As we begin to feel more safe and secure within ourselves and with a partner, the soul is nourished and the relationship transforms: a new kind of trust and internal strength appears. As a result, each individual develops, and the eggshell cracks, allowing for more individuality, risk taking, and vulnerability. Therefore, the partners can achieve a deeper integration of opposites, a capacity to accept and even value both darkness and light within ourselves and our partners.

PARTNERS AS GODS: THE ARCHETYPES OF LOVE

Besides the two sources of the projected image of Other that we have discussed—our disowned parts and parental traits—there is a collective, archetypal aspect to the image as well, as described by Robert Bly. When a vulnerable baby boy first feels disappointment with Mother as she fails to respond adequately with love or nourishment, he may rage with a tantrum, imagining that his all-too-human mom, who represents for him the all-powerful source of life, turns into a death-dealing archetype such as Kali, the wrathful Hindu goddess of birth, death, and transformation. If the projection sticks, throughout the man's life his mother and lovers may at times wear the face of the devouring, critical, demanding goddess. In order to survive, he may put on the face of a kind, submissive caretaker in an effort to avoid her threatening rage.

Later, when the man falls in love, this projection gets handed over like a family legacy to his female partner, who unknowingly dons the mask of Kali. Therefore, in her marriage, a woman actually may feel herself become more pushy, greedy, or hostile than she ever was before. At the same time, the man may grow kinder, which enrages his wife still more. As she carries all of the Kali energy for both of them, he grows calmer—and tells her that she needs therapy.

The same process takes place for women: At an early age a girl may begin unconsciously to pick up various images of masculinity and project a bossy tyrant onto her all-too-human father, eventually seeing in him the face of a killer warrior or a dark, domineering god. When as an adult she commits to a partner, he unknowingly takes over the projection from her father, becoming more controlling, rigid, and kinglike in his decrees. She, in turn, survives by submission, unable to hold her own tyrant character within.

Unlike the personal shadow, which can be understood as stemming solely from our parents, these archetypal images are more complex and ineffable, stemming from a confluence of factors: The feminine pattern, as embodied by our personal mother, contains images of women from childhood fairy tales, religious stories, films, television, advertising, and other cultural sources. The masculine pattern, as embodied by our personal father, contains images of men from the same sources.

In addition, each archetype is represented by a dyadic image with two sides—light and dark—like Christ and Satan or the merciful and wrathful aspects of Yahweh, the Persian Ahura Mazda and Ahriman, and the Egyptian Osiris and Seth. The female godhead also has two sides: The Hindu Durga, omnipotent mother who combats demons and blazes with the splendor of a thousand suns, is the flip side of Kali, the black goddess who wears a necklace of skulls and wields weapons in her many hands. The Egyptian Bast, goddess of joy, is the sister of Sekhmet, goddess of divine retribution, who has a lion's head and a woman's body. And in the Judeo-Christian tradition, Eve, the second wife of Adam, only came to power because the first, disobedient wife, Lilith, refused to lie beneath him and so was cast out into the realm of wild dogs and screeching owls.

In a discussion of male psychology, Jungian writer Robert A. Johnson has pointed out that it's a difficult but necessary task for a man to differentiate the various aspects of the feminine projection: mother, mother archetype, mother complex, goddess, wife, romantic ideal, sister, daughter, and friend. If a projection contaminates a relationship inappropriately, such as a mother complex or goddess projection onto a wife, it can wreak emotional havoc.

We would suggest that a woman, too, can strive to differentiate the various aspects of the masculine projection: father, father archetype, father complex, god, husband, romantic ideal, brother, and friend. Our client Marsha had been sexually abused as a child and later raped as an adolescent, so her sexual passion had gone into hiding. But so had her intense anger at men. Today, at age thirty-four, she finds herself extremely enraged at her fiancé, Guy, when he tries to touch her, even for simple affection. If she succumbs to his advances in an effort to please him, she wells up with anger, which overtakes her, and she ends up feeling like a helpless victim, reenacting her abuse.

Guy, in turn, reports, "She stares at me with a coldness that I can't describe, like she's hating me. I don't understand what I've done to deserve that. And I'm starved for sex. We have no erotic life at all."

Marsha is not simply angry at Guy for something he has said or done; she is caught in a negative archetypal projection, enraged at all men and especially at male sexual desire. In those fits of rage, she is overtaken by Lilith, who traditionally was seen as a dangerous she-demon, seductive witch, and child-killer. For women today who have been victimized and rendered passive and obedient, there is gold lying hidden in this shadow character: She can represent a woman's capacity to say no, her desire for equality and independence, and her natural, wild instincts, which may return with healing.

In a similar way, the positive archetypal projection both blesses and curses us: Through its deep resonance in our souls, it carries us past the persona and puts us in contact with the Beloved's spiritual essence, pulling us toward a deeper love. At the same time, it blinds us to the dark side of the individual, who, as a result, carries the light projection, setting us up for a fall when the projection shatters. During his thirties, Ron, a Jewish attorney from New York, fell in love six times in one year with thin, blond, youthful, athletic women. He would see one of his goddesses and instantly his heart would go out to her. "She has my heart. I want her," he would say to himself with a sigh, as if he actually gave away that part of himself to another human being. Pretty soon, there was a long lineage of Ron's goddesses living in downtown New York City.

Ron kept following this image of womanhood until one day he saw her, a stranger, on the street and, in one moment, he understood the meaning of projection. He realized that his intense feeling had nothing to do with her. He did not know who she was or what she valued. Instead, the attraction was all in his mind. He was falling in love again and again with an invisible aspect of himself, his soul, which like a prince could feel complete only by bonding with a princess. Although he still admired these goddesses, the spell was broken: Ron was free to explore a more authentic connection with a different kind of woman.

In therapy Ron found several keys in the darkness of the shadow. He confessed that all his life he felt ugly and unlovable. In seeking the goddess, he was attempting to make peace with this wound. At the ego level, he sought to be with an attractive woman so that he could be perceived as attractive. But at a deeper level, he was in search of his own acceptability, which would heal his soul.

His healing came when he fell in love with a goddess one last time and, looking into her eyes, saw her soul. In a moment of grace, the woman told him that she, too, saw his beauty. He believed her, and in receiving that reflection from her, like the Beast receiving Beauty's love, he broke his identification with being unacceptable and connected with his own soul. Soon after, he met a dark-haired Jewish woman who has been his partner for three years.

In a similar way, Mindy, thirty-three, a lovely San Francisco artist who lives in a loft, kept falling in love with the same kind of man—a dashing, charismatic, highly intelligent, highly self-involved entrepreneur. In a strange twist of fate, all three of Mindy's men were named David. She reports that she would meet him and feel dizzy, as if her feet were lifting off the ground. But when she would go out with him, she would feel frightened and her body would grow tight as she relinquished the kingdom to another character, who is self-conscious and rigid. Then she would lose her sense of humor and gracious personality. Mindy would feel abandoned if the man needed to attend to other people, even on phone calls. She felt as if she were always waiting, "waiting to see if they liked me so I would know who I am." Like

Sleeping Beauty in her glass coffin, she waited to be awakened by her prince.

Both Ron and Mindy projected their souls onto other people, investing their lovers with the archetypal powers of gods and goddesses. For Ron, the thin blond woman became a carrier of meaning and validation, a guide to another world. He followed her as Dante followed Beatrice, as the poet follows his muse. But he never knew her—he was blind to her individuality, deaf to her needs. He was caught in his own idealized projection, living a mythic reality, not a personal one.

Mindy, too, attributed magical powers to the men in her life. Like King David, they were charismatic, noble creatures who offered her an identity simultaneous with their acceptance of her femininity. Like a puppet on a string, a character would come alive with a nod of their heads.

Heterosexuals don't have a monopoly on projection. It's a universal human process that inevitably appears in gay relationships as well. Lee came to therapy for grief counseling several months after his mate, Manuel, died of AIDS. He spoke emotionally of their meeting twenty years earlier, each man recognizing a deep and soulful connection with the other. Moving in together soon after this encounter, Lee reported that the patterns of their relationship dynamic set in quickly. Manuel, more extroverted and competent in the outside world, became head of the household; Lee, more introverted and artistic, became more subordinate.

Today, having nursed his lover through the long, terrible illness, Lee recognizes that a certain kind of projection underpinned their behavioral roles. "I saw Manuel as my lord, a saint, really. In private, I wanted only to serve him. Raised as a Catholic, I didn't seek to be God but to serve God. And Manuel stood for Christ for me. I felt special by humbling myself as his servant, especially near the end of his life when my sole purpose was to care for him."

These archetypal projections may initially pull us into the arena of relationship; however, they eventually evoke the shadow. Like the many priests who have been caught recently in clandestine sexual escapades, those who carry the idealized projection suffer under its weight. When Ron married one of his ideal women, she felt idolized, not loved; held at a distance, not held closely. Eventually, she had an affair with a friend, and this betrayal opened his eyes. He told his therapist, "I was married to Lil for three years, but I couldn't tell you how she felt about things or what she thought. I could only tell you what she looked like. When I realized this, I knew that I needed help."

Conversely, the one who projects the ideal suffers diminishment and loss, identifying with the inferior, unworthy position. Lee, for example, came to realize that he "gave away his saint" in a projection onto Manuel out of fear of owning his unique kind of greatness. After Manuel's death, Lee did the slow, difficult work of taking back elements of his projection by wearing his lover's clothes, assimilating some of his traits, and eventually learning to face the world as a more independent, competent man.

★ Which gods and goddesses lie sleeping in your partner? Do you wish to wake them up?

THE BREAKDOWN OF PROJECTIONS: MEETING THE WITCH AND THE TYRANT

These two kinds of romantic projections—partners as parents, partners as gods—inevitably rattle and break down, often causing a crisis of commitment. At that crucial moment in every relationship, the most familiar person becomes a stranger. Then one or both partners proclaim, "This is not what I expected." "This is not the person I married." "I thought I knew you so well, but I was wrong."

The partners may suffer shock and disbelief. Then the feeling of betrayal sets in. We suggest that there are three reasons for this series of events: First, the romantic partner *is* not who we thought she or he was. Yet if the shadow did its work, our partner is exactly the right one—and exactly the wrong one. As one couple put it: "She has everything I need—and everything I hate." "Yes," said the Other in response. "He has everything I need—and everything I hate."

In short, the ideal projection of parent or god rattles—and another face appears suddenly on the loved one. As one woman said, "He's like a stranger with secret desires that are not like him. But it *is* him." The quiet, nonthreatening woman turns into a jealous, demanding, nagging complainer—her partner's worst nightmare. The strong, efficient man turns into a needy, dependent control freak—his partner's bad dream. When these shadow characters emerge, shattering the illusions of romance, they reveal such unknown, unexpected aspects of personality that the observer may feel, all at once, that trust between them is broken. The partners face a crisis of commitment.

Second, the romantic process is not what we thought it was. We are no longer at home in old, comfortable patterns that feel familiar. Instead, we are face-to-face with the Other, the stranger, the unpredictable one who lives inside the Beloved. And the process, which had been moving toward greater and greater safety in intimacy, seems to be halted.

Finally, *we* are not who we thought we were. The humbling revelation of our own shadow sides can be as abrupt and disconcerting as the discovery of our partner's. One woman told her therapist that she habitually used sarcasm as a shield, out of her fear of having her feelings rejected. But when her partner reported that her sarcastic tone hurt him deeply, she felt great sadness and remorse. In discovering these aspects of our own shadows, we feel humiliated in our own nakedness and rush to hide, thereby creating obstacles to intimacy and another crisis of commitment. Or we may feel overwhelming guilt and responsibility for the disillusionment and suffering of our loved ones.

The shattering of these illusions may happen gradually, like peeling off the layers of an eggshell, so that bit by bit, even over many years, we come to have a clearer perception of our partners and ourselves. For instance, a man may keep an alcohol dependency hidden from his wife or a woman may use tranquilizers or antidepressants secretly to control her moods. When the mate finds clues to these behaviors after years of secrecy, he or she may be outraged and betrayed, feeling as if life had been shared with a stranger.

Or the shattering may happen suddenly, like the eggshell cracking open, so that in one moment we feel we know one another, and in the next we are living with a foreign intruder. A friend told the story of walking into her kitchen where her new husband stood in his bathrobe with his back to her. She looked down and saw his "bony knees" sticking out from under the robe—and in that moment her perception of him shifted from a refined, elegant musician to a vulnerable, limited man.

Just that part of us which may project perfection onto our partners may, in turn, become critical of all that is not perfect about them. That's why the goddess can shift so quickly into the witch, or the king can pick up the whip of the tyrant, or the hero in an instant can seem ordinary, fading into insubstantiality like a dream figure. Like Randy, a mother's son who projects spiritual purity onto Betsy but uncovers in her a volatile, distant mother; and Betsy, a father's daughter who projects a spiritual hero onto Randy but unearths in him a controlling, invasive father, each of us seeks the light and unwittingly finds the darkness.

As projections break down and we meet our partners' shadow characters, as well as our own, the tasks of relationship become more complex: to romance the dark side and to hold on to the soul connection, the archetypal unity that joins us together; to see through the illusion of Beauty to the Beast and to see beyond that to the authentic beauty that lies at the heart of our loved ones. To be able to contain both the light side and the dark is a great developmental step—and a promise of romancing the shadow.

Our objective, then, is not to live without projection; that is an impossible task. We will naturally and automatically turn our partners into our parents as the shadow tries to make us feel safe and loved. To uncover the gold in this personal projection, we need to continually see through it while mining it for insight, and at the same time stay related to the other person as a real human being.

We also will naturally and automatically turn our partners into gods as the powerful archetypes sweep us off our feet. To uncover the gold in this archetypal projection, we need to continually see through it while staying related to the other person as a mortal human being—*and* honor our deeper vision, which can see god in the Beloved, a transpersonal reality and an ongoing source of aliveness and inspiration.

Power Shadows: Shaming, Deprivation, and Entitlement

The power shadow has many faces. It may appear, for example, in a disparaging look or fleeting remark that sends a loved one into shame. Jackie, an actress and father's daughter, and Grant, an attorney and mother's son, had been dating for nearly a year when he asked her to spend more time with him. When she asked how frequently he wanted to get together, he said five nights a week. Jackie felt so desired that she beamed with delight, but deep inside she panicked. She was terrified of Grant's neediness—or was it his great capacity for intimacy? She felt loved and wanted—but what about time for her creative projects?

In the next few days, Grant cleared his schedule of clients and children to make more room for intimate time with Jackie. She, however, had other things on her mind. She felt a production deadline hanging over her head like a guillotine. In the past, she rehearsed for long hours into the night. Now, that option was gone. In addition, she felt annoyed and irritated about several recent events, but she had put on a shield, suppressed her feelings, and chosen not to discuss them with Grant. In doing so, she identified with a compliant, unassertive character that had been modeled by her mother.

One weekend they attended a formal event together. Grant mentioned that he wanted to wear a new tuxedo; Jackie felt uncomfortable but did not say anything. After they arrived, a friend mentioned that Grant looked attractive in his new tux. Jackie added, "Just don't mistake him for the waiter and order herb tea."

Grant's body froze. Jackie felt him pull away from her, as if he were shriveling up. When they sat down together, he didn't take her hand; he looked straight ahead. And for the rest of the evening he acted aloof and cold. Driving home in the car, Jackie asked him what was troubling him. "I'm furious. You shamed me in public," he said. "Once you do that, you can't take it back."

Jackie was stunned. A passing joke had caused her lover to feel disgraced and humiliated. She quickly understood his experience and apologized, but the damage had been done. Grant felt betrayed; the shaming incident triggered earlier feelings of belittlement and abandonment, and he withdrew from Jackie. She told him that she would try to understand why her shadow had emerged.

In therapy, Jackie reported that recently she had been feeling trapped and smothered by Grant's relationship style. She resented sacrificing time from her acting and her friends. Sometimes she would agree to see him when she was preoccupied with other affairs out of fear of disappointing him or being abandoned by him. In effect, she was doing what her mother had done: giving up her voice in the relationship and projecting the power of decision-making onto him, and then resenting him for it. Her shadowy issues of dependency and abandonment lurked below the surface of consciousness, beneath her persona of independence. And her rage seethed below the compliance.

Gradually Jackie realized that, underneath the struggle with priorities, she was beginning to feel very attached to and vulnerable with Grant, which made her feel frightened and small. "I think I understand now why I shamed him. I was feeling small and seeing him as big. When I made the joke, I felt big again, just for a moment, by making him small." But the trouble with shaming is that it actually achieves the opposite of the desired result: When Jackie became conscious of what she had done, she felt very small again, embarrassed and ashamed.

To review this variation on the theme of power shadow: Jackie withheld communication and acted compliant out of fear of rocking the boat. She did not want to jeopardize the security she had begun to feel, thereby diminishing her own sense of power in the relationship and resenting him for it. In effect, she no longer felt entitled to a voice that honored her own authentic needs. In addition, she projected power onto Grant, making the problem his fault and causing her unknowingly to want to reduce him. Her power shadow emerged unconsciously as a shaming character to equalize the power. But, instead, it created pain and distance. Fortunately, Jackie and Grant wrestled with this shadow issue until they felt safe with each other again. And having addressed their hidden shadow needs, Eros returned.

SEXUAL SHADOWS:
DEMANDING AND WITHHOLDING INTIMACY

Strange as it sounds, sexuality can be an arena in which we turn our partners into our parents. We may carry on family sins unknowingly by perpetuating a parent's repressed feeling or behavior ("My mother never enjoyed sex; she saw it as her duty"; "Oral sex is unnatural") or by enacting family taboos such as incest ("My father did it to me and I ended up okay") or affairs ("My father was unfaithful and my mother survived"). We may arduously long for partners who are in other committed relationships, becoming the child who longs for the opposite-sex parent and plays out the Oedipal drama in romantic triangles for years.

Or we may enjoy sexuality without intimacy until we begin to become emotionally involved. Then a mother or father complex erupts, turning the partner into a parent and evoking the sexual taboo so that the fire of desire is suddenly snuffed out. One man in this predicament could express his sexuality until he began to feel emotionally attached. Then he could not stand to be touched on the genitals, which felt too intimate and threatening to him. Another lived for five years with a woman whom he loved deeply but for whom he felt no sexual desire. He did, however, have intricate masturbatory fantasies about anonymous women in the street.

In our sexual intimacies we may discover Aidos, goddess of modesty, self-respect, and shame. Traveling with Aphrodite, goddess of love and desire, Aidos enfolds her dark wings around lovers and their sexual secrets, protecting their *authentic shame*, their instinctive need for privacy and boundaries. In this way, Aidos serves soul. But she can be co-opted by the ego or by a shadow character, who criticizes, disparages, or humiliates our desires, resulting in self-deprecating, *inauthentic shame*.

To do sexual shadow-work is to open Pandora's box, to release sexual afflictions, erotic mischief, and endless craving. Some will find there a terror of being devoured or eaten alive by the lover's insatiable appetite. Others will find a habitual, mechanical response that disguises bodily numbness and covers over the deadening of natural erotic feeling. Still others may discover a will to power, a need to dominate and control a loved one in order to feel safe enough to become aroused.

But like Pandora's box, which contained sorrows and plagues, the sexual shadow at bottom also contains hope: to shed light on our sexual revulsions, inhibitions, and shames is to shed light on the full range of our erotic potential as well. People who can open the lid may begin to reclaim a sexual identity that offers more pleasure and more freedom from a parent's constraints.

From the day he was born, Rory's mother had been charmed by her darling son. Whatever he asked of her, she would surrender if he would only ask long enough and lovingly enough. So, naturally, when he fell in love with Margaret, he continued this strategy even unknowingly, believing somehow that it would continue to fulfill his needs.

But when Margaret did not wish to have sex, a problem arose. Rory would persist, asking as long and as lovingly as he could. But if Margaret held her ground and continued to say no, he became angry and his critical character emerged and called her names. He expected to get the answer he wanted if he asked in just the right way. And when Margaret did not adore him as his mother had, he felt totally abandoned and interpreted her response as proof that she did not love him or value the relationship. He believed this issue was her problem—she was cold and unloving. But she also carried his cold, unloving shadow, which erupted when he felt rebuffed.

Margaret, however, had a secret chemical dependency, which was even a secret from herself. Using three cups of coffee to wake up in the morning, two glasses of wine with dinner, and sleeping pills to rest at night, she had numbed herself to her own feelings. As a result, when Rory approached her for intimacy, she could not feel vulnerable; he felt forced to demand the sexual intimacy to which he was entitled.

Also, Margaret had been verbally abused by her mother. So when she heard Rory's accusations, she withdrew even more, launching a roller-coaster ride in which each could see the Other's shadow: He sees his self-centered, insensitive, ungiving side in her, and she sees her judgmental, critical, attacking side in him. Both partners despise these qualities in the Other and, until they did shadow-work, both remained unaware of them in themselves. Eventually, Margaret discovered that her inability to share intimacy called forth the very emotional abuse that she wished to escape.

Larry withheld sexual intimacy for other reasons. A gifted artist who earns his living in the advertising industry, Larry had had hundreds of sexual escapades before he met his current partner. But no one had touched his heart deeply, opening him to the tender feelings of love. Instead, he had created a gruff and aloof persona as a tough guy who used women sexually but suffered secretly from a lack of intimacy in his life.

When Larry met Claire, he wanted to protect and care for her. But he did not desire her sexually. When he begins to have sexual feelings or fantasies, he's not drawn to make love to Claire but to masturbate to pornographic pictures. This fantasy activity, however, typically leaves him feeling ashamed, guilty, and empty, as if he has a secret life full of lies. Larry finds actual sexual contact with Claire too messy for his liking, but he feels saddened that Claire receives so little contact from him.

In an early betrayal, Larry was abandoned by his mother as an infant when she left him twice with his grandparents. When she retrieved him later, in his teenage years, she would drape her legs around him, making him feel aroused and disgusted. But he would not ask her to stop because he feared hurting her and being abandoned again. She also exposed herself by wearing very little clothing around the house and often told him to rub her naked back, exposing her breasts inadvertently to his curious young eyes. These early experiences created the roots of Larry's split between sexuality and intimacy. His sexuality became a "bad" character at the table; he could only enjoy sex furtively. But in doing so he felt terrible shame, as if he himself were bad.

In this context, Larry's shadowy fantasy life served him well. He permitted his "bad" sexual character expression through flirting, peeping, and pornography, while maintaining a "good" or pure character with Claire by avoiding sexual intimacy for five years. Unconsciously, he knew that if he became sexual he would have to deal with his guilt and rage. And if he became vulnerable, he believed unconsciously that he would become dependent, smothered, and eventually abandoned. So, to be safe, he maintained the split.

Larry disclosed that at times he felt impulses to move toward Claire, but he would get busy or distracted. Then he would feel a wrenching guilt for failing to meet his obligation to her; he would be caught in his mother complex. The therapist explained that there are two kinds of guilt: *inauthentic guilt*, which arises from the ego as a historical complex; and *authentic guilt*, which arises from the Self in the present time as a valuable signal from the unconscious. When Larry gets busy in an unconscious effort to distract himself from sexual feelings and to avoid following his impulses toward intimacy, his guilt is a cue that he is failing himself, not her. Understanding this distinction, he can now use the guilt as a reminder to acknowledge his sexual feelings in the moment or witness his resistance to them. Uncovering these memories of early erotic stimulation and opening the traps of his parental complexes helped Larry to understand his behavior and to begin to heal the split between sex and intimacy.

✶   What shadow character in you demands intimacy and what are its deeper needs? What character withholds and why?

An Archetypal Perspective on Romance

Within our fantasies of romance there are timeless mythological images of sacred union. Aside from the personal aspects of our parents and our own missing parts, these archetypal forces shape our partnerships. They can reveal the nature of the Other as well the kinds of qualities that the Other may being forth in us. And they offer a glimpse into the nature of the relationship itself, the particular quality of the bond that may emerge as a result of the story that underlies it.

So, for people seeking a deeper look into their romantic relationships, we suggest exploring the myth at its core: You may be living an erotic bond like Psyche and Eros, which begins in blindness with a stranger and leads to an awareness of the divine. You may imagine living a complete spiritual union like Shiva and Shakti, whose ecstatic merger is all-consuming and overcomes their individuality. You may be struggling with a rivalrous battle for power like Zeus and Hera, whose marriage seems to feed on ongoing conflict, which permits them to remain together but feel separate. You may have forged a brother-sister marriage like Isis and Osiris, in which you feel that you belong together for the purpose of mutual reliance without dominance and with or without sexuality. You may have found an older man–younger woman alliance like Merlin and Vivianne in King Arthur's Court, who mentor and caretake one another, respectively, awakening each other's dormant gifts. Or you may have created an older woman–younger man alliance like Inanna, a mother-goddess, who initiates Dumuzi, her son-lover, revitalizing them both with life. Or you may have discovered an older man–younger man bond like Zeus, whose passion stirs the handsome mortal Ganymede to respond and, as a result of their love, he becomes a god. You may have found yourself, like Ariadne, abandoned by a hero-lover, dejected and alone, and later partnered with the god of ecstasy, Dionysus, who ironically becomes a faithful husband. You may be a single mother like Demeter, whose primary role is to care for children with an absent father. Or you may find yourself facing the death of your loved one, like Orpheus grieving inconsolably the loss of Eurydice.

Each of these stories, and many more, tell of a way to love and be loved. Each opens onto a vast expanse of possibilities, and each has its shadow side, its dangers and limitations.

In your myth, which gods are being honored? Which are being sacrificed? Do the gods or goddesses that are being expressed match the myth you desire to live?

When Relationships End: The Shadow's Moving Target

As the divorce rate so glaringly shows, at times the centripetal force of love and the magnet of mutual attraction are not sufficient to hold two people together during a crisis of commitment. When the love bond snaps, one partner or both may end the relationship abruptly. Then the shadow begins the search once again for the perfect fit.

During the dating stage, for instance, an individual may know instinctively that a given person is not a potential long-term partner. In that case, an internal crisis may precipitate an end to dating, such as when Brad, who remained in obligatory relationships due to his fear of being alone, his need for sex, and his desire to be seen with beautiful women, ultimately felt that he was losing his own integrity and self-respect by continuing this pattern. A few weeks or months later, the search would begin anew.

At other times, a shadow character may step in to end a relationship by acting out a betrayal, thereby making the person seem unacceptable. One man told his therapist that he could not stop screaming abusively at his partner, then felt humiliated by his own outburst. But he was not surprised when she packed up and left. In retrospect, he realized that unconsciously he had wanted it to end. A woman client confessed to a sexual liaison with her ex-husband, never consciously suspecting that her current partner would find out. But when he did, she made no apologies. She felt as if her actions had been choreographed by some unknown, alien part of herself. In addition, under the influence of a new drug, such as a diet pill, sleeping pill, or antidepressant, another character may emerge, leaving a partner to feel as if he or she is living with a stranger. In these ways, we may cheat, lie, become abusive or depressed in such a way that our partner has a rude awakening: a positive projection shatters and the connection breaks.

Alternatively, a relationship may end for developmental reasons—that is, one partner leaves the eggshell, while the other is not ready. Doris, who was raised by a strict single mother of six children, ended a difficult marriage after thirteen years. The following year she began to date a man and found herself falling into the victim pattern that she had learned from her mother and perpetuated in her own marriage, thereby betraying herself again. Some part of her wanted to crawl back into the eggshell, to let this man take charge of her life and make decisions for her. But Doris saw the cues: She began to feel small, as if she were disappearing. And she began to feel irritable and angry. After dating him for ten weeks, she told him that she wanted more from the relationship. She needed him to acknowledge her feelings and to listen to her more considerately. This man could not honor her request, so she ended the relationship. Although externally the relationship failed, internally it succeeded. Whereas it took Doris thirteen years to emerge as an adult in her marriage, it took her only ten weeks to recognize what she needed and ask for it in her next relationship.

Because of the cultural bias toward maintaining marriage and honoring commitment and the ego's bias toward permanence, this ending typically feels like another failed effort, rejection, or abandonment. A partner may be deeply disappointed in himself or in the Other, feeling betrayed and abandoned. New salt adds to the sting of old wounds, and the promise of love goes unfulfilled.

If the shadow's objectives, which were instrumental in generating the attraction, remain unconscious, then the patterns will probably repeat themselves in the next relationship, again re-creating old wounds without awareness. If the relationship has served an individual by bringing the shadow's motivations into consciousness, then the relationship can be considered at least partially successful. Eventually, if we do not deny the loss but allow ourselves to grieve it deeply, we may one day feel gratitude for the awareness gained at the cost of great emotional pain over losing a relationship.

From the soul's point of view, any relationship that generates feelings of being seen and loved can be considered a success, even if it lasts only a few weeks. For we believe that love heals. And human beings evolve through sharing love and expanding awareness together. When the soul is nurtured in a conscious, caring way, we are more willing to risk showing those more shameful, vulnerable aspects of ourselves to a partner and thereby discover a deeper sense of our own authenticity.

For longer-term relationships, commitment may become the crisis issue. After a year or so, a woman may be headed for marriage and children, while a man may still feel unprepared for monogamy or family. If he says he's not ready, and she says she needs to take this step for her own integrity, they have a serious crisis of commitment: The authentic needs of one conflict with the authentic needs of the other.

If he values the relationship over his own needs and agrees to her request but is not internally ready, he betrays himself and resents her for feeling manipulated into giving up his power. Perhaps they can find interim agreements, such as six months of monogamy as an experiment. If that's not enough for her internally but she agrees to it anyway, she steps out of authenticity with herself and ends up resentful of him for giving up her self-respect, which causes her either to withdraw or attack him. Their differences in timing and the way they handle these differences could signal the end of the relationship.

For couples who do shadow-work to reduce conflict and deepen their relationships, we hold a particular attitude about ending relationships: Stay as long as possible, attempting to bring shadow issues into awareness. In the end, if the relationship terminates, you will know that you gave it your best effort. And you will feel that you honored your highest intentions, as well as romancing a bit more of your shadow.

REDEFINING SUCCESSFUL RELATIONSHIP: FROM SHADOW-BOXING TO SHADOW-DANCING

A conscious relationship does not breed complacency; it does not offer the security of a warm blanket. Instead, a relationship is a cauldron in which to cook the soul. Its aim is heat, not warmth; movement, not rest. The goal of a relationship, then, is not to make order or to sit back and relax in an idyllic paradise. Rather, it aims to share the mystery of evolution—and evoke evolution through confrontations with the shadow.

In this context, we would call any relationship successful that brings forth love, healing, and awareness, even if it ends after a few dates. If one partner identifies a new character and awakens to shadow awareness, he or she may not repeat an old pattern in the next round. And that new quality of consciousness may help to create a much more satisfying intimacy the next time. If one partner feels a deeper sense of authenticity, recovering buried parts or unrealized gifts, then healing has taken place. If one partner learns to see through a particular projection and view the Other with greater clarity, then both have a better chance of knowing what they want in the next relationship.

As two partners make the transition from noncommittal, experimental dating to the safe enclosure of the eggshell, the projection takes hold. They make agreements and maintain relationship rules that permit them to feel more safety and intimacy. But eventually the shadow erupts and they face a crisis of commitment. Romancing the shadow, they may move into the chicken yard, experiencing more intimacy and independence. Continuing to do shadow-work at times of conflict, eventually they may move from shadow-boxing to shadow-dancing, the topic of the next chapter. To make this transition, each partner will want to remember the needs of the soul, which offers depth and a connection to the sacred dimension. If we can learn to differentiate between the needs of ego, shadow, and soul, we will have a key to a deeply rewarding life of intimate partnership.

In the opening myth, Psyche vowed to Eros to make love with him in the dark. But her curiosity took hold of her and she lit a candle in their bedchamber, illuminating the god in all his splendor. Betrayed, Eros fled, the love bond fractured.

On one level, Psyche did not have the faith to keep her agreement to remain in the dark. When she broke it, the relationship ended. But on another level, Psyche, whose name means soul, refused to remain in the garden of the unconscious. Like Eve, she chose knowledge and sacrificed the innocence of the original relationship, enabling it to become something more. This act set Psyche on her own path of consciousness; she underwent difficult trials, including a journey to the underworld, until she was reunited with her Beloved once more in a deeper bond, which is the topic of the next chapter.

SHADOW-DANCING
TILL DEATH DO US PART

A man and a woman sit near each other,
and they do not long
at the moment to be older, or younger,
nor born in any other nation, or time, or place.
They are content to be where they are,
talking or not talking.
Their breaths together feed someone whom
we do not know.
The man sees the way his fingers move;
he sees her hands close around a book she hands to him.
They obey a third body that they share in common.
They have made a promise to love that body.
Age may come, parting may come,
death will come.
A man and a woman sit near each other;
as they breathe they feed someone we do not know,
someone we know of, whom we have never seen.

—ROBERT BLY

Relationship is a myth for our times. The quest for the ideal relationship has taken on legendary proportions, like the quest for the Holy Grail. We pay homage to relationship as our ancestors paid homage to the gods. Its story line grips us with hope and devastation in ubiquitous newspaper headlines, romantic novels, and movie plots. We long to fathom the ineffable mystery of relationship, to understand what makes it work, and to avoid what makes it fail.

If we don't have a primary relationship, we live haunted with self-doubt, questioning whether we are capable of intimacy and commitment, even questioning the value of life without it. We yearn for the sacred marriage, the union of souls that will endure the passage of time. We long for a partner who offers a shady oasis in a hot, dry world; a mate who provides a refuge of acceptance and understanding. We dream about the sweetness of love and speak constantly to friends about the urgency of the quest: how to find a relationship, how to change ourselves in order to attract the right person, how to keep that person interested in us, how to make it last for the long term.

Certainly, the isolation and fragmentation of social life in the Western world spur this search. Our general estrangement from others forces us to seek one with whom we can find intimate companionship. But beneath these untenable social conditions and the widespread fantasy of partnership as solution lies something more: an unconscious image that drives us because the archetype of marriage lies at the center of the image. And it compels us to follow it; it compels us to desire it.

If we have a relationship, we may be fortunate enough to feel moments of fulfillment in deep resonance with another human soul. But we also may long for more intimacy, more depth; conversely, we may long for more separateness, more time alone. For to be in a committed relationship is to hold the tension of opposites: the secret yearning for engulfment, the secret dread of entrapment; the fantasy of being rescued, the ongoing debt to the rescuer; the aliveness of creative partnership, the deadness of meaningless routine. And, of course, a marriage as a psychological relationship includes the sacred union of masculine and feminine in each of us.

Jungian analyst Murray Stein has suggested that by joining opposites, a relationship points toward the spiritual possibility of wholeness. According to Jung, the Self is the inner principle of direction and orientation toward meaning, which is awakened through holding opposites. So, Stein reasons, relationship today has taken on mythic proportions because it promises wholeness and symbolizes the Self.

Paradoxically, although relationship is our myth, we have no myth of relationship. That is, the old myths of romantic partnership reflect archaic patterns of human consciousness that do not match our current political, psychological, and spiritual development. Instead of helping us to form more conscious alliances with shared opportunity and shared responsibility, today's archetypal images can become shadow characters that sabotage our more innovative efforts to bond.

For example, if we turn to the Greeks, we find no stories of two partners who mutually contribute to the welfare and creativity of a family and who have the skills to resolve conflict and deepen their intimacy. Instead, we see marriage evolving out of the early goddess cultures into the patriarchal pattern of Zeus and Hera. Today, some contemporary women who choose the traditional role of full-time wife, like Hera, project the fulfillment of their desires onto their heroic husbands. If they stifle their own self-expression, they may grow resentful, depressed, or ill. Only a few women, such as those in traditional religious subcultures, find the narrow path of fulfillment in living out the Hera pattern today. Rejected by feminists who belittle her dependency and idealized by fundamentalists who overvalue her traditional ways, the character of Hera has difficulty finding an appropriate place at the table today. Yet she still reigns in the shadow of many women and may appear abruptly as a wild jealousy or keen possessiveness.

Like Zeus, some traditional men today, such as the Christian group the Promise Keepers, continue to fantasize a kinglike ruling power in the household, making decrees rather than joint decisions with their partners. Terrified of the epidemic breakdown of the nuclear family, they long for the old image of patriarchal stability, so they unknowingly pay homage to the archetypal king, husband, and father and thereby vanquish their own vulnerability into shadow. However, reports from men in power seem to indicate that, despite appearances, they often feel powerless internally. Although a Zeus persona sits on the throne of power, the soul of a man who is highly influenced by him may feel alone, isolated, and bereft.

Alternatively, a matriarchal family pattern centers around the maternal instinct for family and children. In millions of single-parent families today, in which the mother is both provider and caretaker, the children may have little contact with their own fathers. We can detect this pattern in the myth of Demeter, whose life revolves around her daughter Persephone, who has little exposure to men until she is abducted by Hades.

In addition, the early legends of the heroes no longer serve us in these postpatriarchal times, when male hegemony has given way to diversity. In these countless tales, a young male full of bravado makes a perilous journey, which typically includes a descent to darkness, and slays a terrible shadow-monster, winning a damsel as his prize. Interpreted psychologically, the hero slays the monster-Other within; the ego vanquishes the shadow but does not stop to recognize it as a dark brother, so the deeper initiation does not take place.

The shadow side of the hero's journey is now coming into awareness: Many men suffer with the emotional and financial burdens of heroic expectations. In attempting to heal, they are exploring new forms of masculinity that are both strong and nurturing, independent and emotionally related to women, productive and connected to soul. Many women have pointed out the violence and power-shadow that are inherent in this heroic vision, which have been enacted via domination over women and the environment. A heroine's journey would not simply replace the protagonist with a woman but might tell a different story altogether.

This chapter calls into question these archaic images of male-female relationship that go unnoticed but unconsciously rule over us like powerful gods. With the death of these myths comes the death of romance—and the birth of conscious relationship or shadow-dancing, the central theme of this chapter. We hope to renew the purpose of committed love by setting it in the developmental context of shadow-work.

The shadow challenges our longing for simple answers. Therefore, in this chapter, we do not present a simple how-to formula for happy marriages or a therapist's simple diagnosis of unhappy ones. As Albert Einstein reportedly said, "Everything should be as simple as it can be, but not simpler." So we explore the innate human wish for lasting love—and its seeming impossibility, often due to the emergence of painfully difficult shadow feelings and behaviors and our inability to form conscious relationships with them as characters at the table.

Thus far, Chapter 1 addressed issues of the personal shadow and authenticity—that is, taking responsibility for the Self by doing internal work. Chapter 2 examined the formation of shadow in family patterns and explored how to create more authenticity among family members. Chapter 3 looked at the effects of betrayal by parents, resulting in four parent-child shadow patterns. Chapter 4 looked at the influence of parent-child patterns during dating, when the shadow turns our partners into parents or ideal images of gods. Chapter 5 examined more closely the process of projection during romance, whereby shadow and soul are attributed to the other person and suggested how to take responsibility for these projections in order to separate Self from Other.

Chapter 6 raises the octave of responsibility to another level: We suggest that, as Robert Bly describes in his poem, a Third Body emerges in a conscious intimate relationship that becomes the container in which love grows. We call this the soul of the relationship. It is this larger force that we can choose to honor and cherish in the best of times and the worst of times.

THE THIRD BODY:
THE SOUL OF THE RELATIONSHIP

During dating and romance, two individuals meet and a chemical reaction occurs in which their missing parts overlap and their internal characters begin to shadow-box with each other. Fairly quickly, the *persona of the couple* develops. Jungian analyst Murray Stein calls this the uniform of adulthood. The partners may present themselves to others as two independent, unconventional individuals with separate interests and groups of friends, or as a united front with a traditional lifestyle and shared values. They may appear to be distant from one another or constantly clinging; they may seem relaxed and open or extremely private and exclusive.

Whatever the persona, the *shadow of the couple* remains hidden: their apparent compatibility may disguise conflicting values or even domestic violence. Their bon vivant lifestyle may camouflage near-bankruptcy. Their puritanical religious doctrines may belie split-off shadows that act out in sexual affairs or perversions. At a more subtle level, they may agree, perhaps implicitly, that they cannot be vulnerable, angry, or depressed with one another, thereby sacrificing authenticity for the status quo. For most people, this is the foreground or personal field in which relationships take place.

But at a background level, we propose that there is a transpersonal field that contributes to bringing two people together, thereby shaping their fate. From this perspective, the relationship is larger than they are, transcending their individual egos and shadows, perhaps acting like an invisible glue that holds them together. We call this the *soul of the relationship* or the Third Body.

As shadow-boxing with the Other gradually turns into shadow-dancing with the Beloved, authenticity between the partners deepens and they feel a palpable sense of safety and comfort. Some people might imagine this felt sense as a big, fluffy cushion on which to relax or a pliable container in which the relationship can grow. We have found that at this stage many couples become conscious of the presence of a Third Body—a new entity that is greater than the two separate individuals. With its emergence, the partners feel yet greater trust and can risk yet more vulnerability and authenticity, for they are bound together as if in a joint soul.

People have an intuitive sense of the Third Body and its containing function in their lives together. For each couple, it has a unique texture and flavor. It may feel sweet, soothing, warm, and loosely knit. Or it may feel cool and shady, like a protective covering. Couples know when the Third Body is nurtured because it feels like a positive vibration or loving air between them that hums quietly. And they know when it is wounded because it feels like a wrenching tear in the fabric of their love.

This field that is the Third Body knits together the various dimensions of our lives; it holds our egos, shadows, souls, and the larger world together in a common story. It contains the personal, interpersonal, and archetypal realms.

The care and feeding of the Third Body is an ongoing part of maintaining a conscious relationship. Like a plant, it is alive and responds to the correct amount of water, air, and light. If we take it for granted or attend to it only when a problem arises, it may become dehydrated and wither. In its weakened state, it cannot tolerate more stress. But if we nurture it and maintain its delicate equilibrium, it grows strong and supports the life of the relationship.

We suggest that, when the shadow erupts and we feel betrayed, instead of stepping onto the roller coaster of blame or caretaking each other like parents and children, we now have another option: to honor and nurture this larger field that is the relationship. In this way, as Robert Bly puts it in his poem, we make a promise to love that body, to feed someone whose presence we feel but cannot see.

For Stewart and Susan, the care and feeding of the Third Body became a key to deepening their sense of safety and intimacy. Stewart's father had avoided intimacy in his marriage by engaging in a series of affairs. Stewart also feared losing his identity in his relationship with Susan, so he carried on the family sin by frequently flirting and acting seductive with other women. During the stages of dating and romance with Susan, he made excuses for his behavior. But after their marriage, it wounded her deeply.

One evening, at a summer party, an attractive woman approached Stewart and asked him to dance. Having done shadow-work, Stewart became aware of a shadowy rebellious character that often feels an impulse to do something forbidden. This character in turn triggers another that feels guilty for abandoning Susan and resentful for feeling controlled. Stewart reported that his guilt arose simultaneously with his attraction to dancing with the stranger.

Stewart's actions with other women are shaped in part by the degree to which he values or devalues his own commitment to the Third Body. When he flirts with strangers, he is not attending to his relationship with Susan in the here and now; he's time traveling, reliving his parental complex by repeating his father's pattern and acting out his dependency and anger with his mother. Then he feels terribly guilty, which he believes stems from upsetting Susan but is in fact his passive-aggressive way of attacking her. So he ends up feeling like a bad person and resents her for "making him" feel that way. This feeling is a signal that he's turning his partner into a parent.

On the other hand, he says, if he rejects the other woman's offer, he will feel weak, as if he needs his mother's permission to dance. With this deepening awareness, Stewart is making conscious those parental complexes that shape his behavior. And he is beginning to romance the shadow projections that emerge from them, which opens the door to healing family sins.

In addition, he frequently projects the responsibility for the bond onto his partner. If he dances with the other woman as a rebellious act, this character creates his own guilt. If he refuses to dance out of self-sacrifice for Susan, this character will be caught in a parental complex.

But if instead he chooses not to dance out of his own free will in order to honor the relationship with Susan, he will be making a long-term investment in their joint account.

Armed with this new understanding, Stewart returned to therapy the following week and said, "I want to give *my* relationship a shot. I'm choosing to honor it now." In this way, he gave up the forced choice: be a good boy and take care of your mother, living with resentment; or be a rebel and disobey your mother, living with guilt. The choice to honor the Third Body can free us of deep-seated traps of obligation, caretaking, and control by enabling us to shift out of our personal psychology and attend to the larger relationship. As the soul of the couple is nurtured in this way, it gains strength and substance.

The mythic figure Queen Penelope of Ithaca, wife of the wandering hero Odysseus, embodies this loyalty and commitment to the Third Body. Portrayed as the Queen of Wands in the Tarot deck, the auburn-haired queen in a saffron robe and golden crown sits on a throne with a sleeping lioness at her feet and a flaming wand in her hand. While her husband, Odysseus, sails off to the Trojan War, she holds down the kingdom with faith that he will return alive. During the waiting period, many suitors assume her husband's death and seek her hand. She agrees to choose one only after completing the weaving of a shroud. But as she weaves the fabric by day, she unravels it by night. And, in the end, she welcomes Odysseus home. Penelope, an image of the loyalty of the heart, is more than a faithful wife or self-sacrificing victim; she rules her own world with inner strength and inspiration. And she has faith that her husband will return not out of enforced morality but from an inner conviction that the Third Body will endure.

How do you sense the Third Body? How do you nurture it? How do you betray it?

MEETING THE BELOVED:
TAKING PROJECTIONS HOME

These developmental stages of relationship—from the persona connection in dating through the romantic projection to the authentic soul encounter and the emergence of the Third Body—go unrecognized by most of us. Therefore, we may make an external commitment to marry in the first two stages before we have uncovered our own shadows, accepted our partner's shadow characters, or become aware that the process of relationship inevitably includes crises of commitments. However, without shadow awareness, we cannot make an internal commitment; we can only hold a persona wedding. Unknowingly, we vow to hold up each other's masks and to stand in place. When the roller-coaster rides lead us to great suffering, we feel helpless and disillusioned. We discover that we have no return ticket. Ultimately, divorce may seem the only way out.

The persona marriage typically results in a split projection, in which one partner carries the opposite qualities of the Other. Then one, the screw-up, is perceived as the problem: He or she is too emotional, too distant, too dependent, too independent. And the saint, who can do no wrong, offers sympathetic solutions from aloft.

If we marry in the grip of an intense romantic projection, the shadow may act out at any time in distancing behavior, unexpected moodiness, cruel words, physical violence, clandestine affairs, or a serious illness, causing us to feel as if we are falling from grace. Our innocence waning, we may wish for magical powers to ward off evil. We may rail bitterly against broken promises made in the original persona contract. We may suffer sleepless nights, bouts of anxiety or depression, addictions to food or drugs, headaches or other signs of psychosomatic tension.

But our fate has turned: When the persona and shadow processes meet, like two parallel lines that suddenly converge, we can throw up our hands and walk out the door, or we can stop and hear the call of the Third Body for shadow-work. Then we can discover that an inevitable developmental process is taking place, and that it is in our power to take the first step in shadow-dancing: romancing projections.

First, we will need to stop blaming the Other and examine how we contribute to the painful pattern. For example, Boyd, a house contractor, fell in love with a writer, Louise, except that he could not stand her so-called weight problem. With a haughty impatience, he disclosed, "She's at least twenty pounds overweight. I mean, why doesn't she just get it under control? I control my weight well enough. What's wrong with her, anyway?"

Despite this difficult issue, Boyd felt that he loved Louise and wished to marry her. He came to recognize that his judgmentalness was shaming and abusive to her and that he would need to accept her as she is or choose to leave her, because devaluing her was unacceptable to both of them. So, to do shadow-work, he turned within to examine his own judgments about her lack of control concerning weight. Boyd uncovered a saintly, superior shadow character that judged Louise as inadequate by projecting his own inferiority.

Next, he traced the roots of this critical character and realized that he was afraid of his mother's response to Louise; she would not be good enough for him. When Boyd separated out his mother's perfectionistic voice as a character at the table from his own tender feelings of love, he could move past the crisis of commitment and eventually accept Louise with her own struggles and limitations.

This kind of difficult self-examination must take place when we are alone in the dark. It feels as if we are taking a long journey through a tunnel in a mountainside with a parallel tunnel on the other side of the wall. Each partner can only hope that the Other is out there digging, too. But, at times, each loses the connection to the loved one and feels alone in the darkness. They only hope that, if both do the work and dig through the mountain, they meet again on the other side and rekindle their love.

As a result of this internal shadow-work, we see how we create the very problems that we perceive as caused by the Other. When we pull back our projections, the saint discovers his own screw-up, and the screw-up discovers her own integrity. The victim awakens to his own tyrant; the tyrant uncovers her own fear of being helpless and out of control. The fuser discovers her own separateness; the abandoner finds his own need for intimacy.

In this way, we romance our shadow projections and eventually recognize the Beloved in the Other, his or her authentic nature without our coloration. And we take home that which belongs in our own treasury, discovering the Other in ourselves, where it was all along. Gradually, in honoring the bond that is both within us and between us—the Third Body—we find soul in our complexes. That is why we say: Shadow-work is soul work.

✳   Who is the Other in you? Who is the Beloved in your partner? With these discoveries, it's time to talk Turkish.

French and Turkish:
The Art of Conscious Communication

Recently, a married couple came to therapy feeling confused and bewildered by each other. Abe said to Stephanie: "Yesterday I was so angry that I was purposefully trying to insult you. I was fed up. And I was really getting nasty. And you did something that you haven't done in years: You sat on my lap and hugged me." The man sat and stared at her in shock and confusion. "How could you do this? I just don't understand."

Stephanie replied, "You were telling me your truth, something you really felt in that moment. So I just loved you. I came over to you because I just loved you for that honesty, even though you were angry."

She was not listening to the content of her husband's words or to how they affected her mind—the French. She was feeling the unacknowledged emotional backdrop of the language, the authenticity of the words and how they affected her heart and her body—the Turkish.

Most roller-coaster rides are launched when two partners try to talk French and don't realize that they are actually talking Turkish. The body speaks Turkish with subtle gestures, such as a turned-up mouth or a shrugged shoulder, eye movements, such as a wink, and symptoms such as headaches. The voice expresses Turkish with its rising and falling tonal qualities, which communicate sarcasm, condescension, or disbelief. Even our moods convey Turkish; depression may send a message of anger, so that the receiver feels as if her life spirit is being smothered.

In fact, Turkish is the medium of the shadow; it carries hidden meanings and their bodily impact. Sweet words can be felt in Turkish to be patronizing; polite words can convey judgment; intelligent words can transmit dissatisfaction. On the other hand, a bodily gesture can convey reassurance in Turkish; a silence can feel like a warm invitation. Honesty, however difficult to hear, can be received as a message of love. The Turkish is not *what* is said but *how* it is said.

So, this second language of communication is filled with subtle nuances. When faced with the ongoing pain of an unresolved issue, a partner may willingly enter the mountain tunnel to do inner work. But if, for a moment, she turns toward her partner with blame or puts the slightest pressure on him to respond or behave in a certain way, the communication is delivered like a hard ball from pitcher to catcher. On impact, the catcher has a visceral response—slapped in the face, punched in the stomach, stabbed in the heart, caught in a net. There is a moment of painful vulnerability, which may go unnoticed. Then, in retaliation, he returns the pitch—name-calling, patronizing, withdrawing, being late. And the negative cycle begins anew.

When the return pitch perpetuates the pattern, increasing alienation and carrying the couple into the arena of shadow-boxing, it's not important to figure out who started it. In our view, fifty-fifty does not make a successful relationship. For success, each person needs to accept 100 percent responsibility for creating and perpetuating these negative spirals. A man may make a belittling remark in the early morning because he still carries feelings in his body from an irritating event with his wife the day before or even from a disturbing argument the week before. The Third Body takes the painful punches, and both partners feel the strain when the relationship is threatened. In other words, the Turkish lives in the field, where the unresolved issues lie dormant like kindling that is ready to be ignited by the most innocent comment.

When the soul of the relationship is strong, the partners feel free to express themselves and to be playful and spontaneous. When the Third Body is firmly established, one partner can be withdrawn, critical, or sarcastic and the other person will not feel betrayed or threatened, even if she feels hurt. She will know that together they can work out the issues, even though they may feel great pain.

But when the soul of the relationship is fragile, the partners feel tentative, cautious, and unsafe. Then, the Turkish becomes loud and intimidating. And shadow-boxing goes round after round, leaving nothing but pain in its wake.

In many couples, the partner who is the screw-up feels the impact of the Turkish more clearly than the other. He or she needs to voice the shadow issues in order to feel authentic. She frequently may feel hurt, criticized, shamed, or wounded by her partner. Her sensitivity is the trip wire that activates the pattern.

The saint, in turn, displays compassionate understanding for the partner's suffering. But he may blame her for being overly sensitive and deny any responsibility for contributing to her pain. Or he may blame himself, apologizing over and over again, asking for her forgiveness.

We suggest the following guidelines (outlined further in "Shadow-Work Handbook" to transform shadow-boxing into shadow-dancing:

- Remind yourself that no one is right and no one is wrong. Both of you have your own experience and point of view and are entitled to be heard and understood.
- When you sense that conflict may erupt, sit down and begin with the breathing exercise (see page 309). As you center yourself, you can begin to hear the voice of the Self, which expresses your authentic feelings, needs, and values. In realigning with this voice, the shadow character recedes and you become more self-directed and able to communicate without blame.
- Identify the early warnings signals that a conflict is about to begin: the physical sensations and emotional cues that accompany the shadow character, which activate your own participation in shadow-boxing. Get an image of this character. Listen for the repetitive words and phrases that belong to this character.
- If the conflict heats up and you hear the bell signaling the next round, ask for time out. Remember that nothing positive happens during the conflict; it always ends in a hurtful attack or withdrawal. So, you may simply take a moment to close your eyes and breathe deeply. Or you may tell your partner that the conflict is escalating too quickly and you need time to calm down and would like to continue the conversation at another time and place. Be sure to tell your partner that you are not abandoning him or her. Rather, you wish to avoid mutually created pain. You intend to center yourself, gather your thoughts, examine your own shadow issues, and return fully present to the challenge. Hopefully, your partner will do the same.
- When you are alone, do your own shadow-work by taking 100 percent responsibility for your participation in the pattern—even if at first you cannot imagine how you helped to create it. Stay with the difficult feelings until you uncover your own wound, which was triggered by the Other's behavior. Remember that what you experience in the Other is a reflection of your own deep woundedness.
- Ask yourself how your Turkish may have contributed to the

conflict and whether you carry any emotional residue from earlier roller-coaster rides, such as ongoing resentment, anger, disappointment, or shame that may be influencing this experience. You might explore it creatively, through writing or the arts, and in this way uncover a secret, sabotaging character.

- Identify what you cannot tolerate about your partner's behavior, recognizing that this is the shadow character that has shown up. Recall an earlier time when you were accused of this behavior or experienced this character in yourself. In other words, romance the projections. (Clearly, we do not include physical abuse as a projection here.)
- Identify the historical patterns or family sins that led to the creation of this character or style of defending or attacking. Ask yourself who in your family of origin acted in this way.
- Return to your partner at the appointed time. Create a collaborative atmosphere in an effort to understand the Other's experience by listening to him or her without defending yourself or blaming the Other. Try to avoid interpreting your partner's behavior or describing how he or she contributes to the conflict. And try to avoid attempting to come to a conclusion (in French) at this time. Instead, focus on yourself. Tell your partner how you contributed to it and how your unacknowledged feelings came through in Turkish. Finally, explore how you might respond differently the next time.
- Finally, honor the Third Body, the soul of the relationship, which transcends your personal shadow issues.

Your partner is your best mirror. As you communicate your own experience clearly and without blame, such as by using the first person in your speech, you can get a reflection of how your shadow operates. When your partner says he feels attacked, you have a choice: You can believe he's wrong or lying and defensively reject the feedback. You can blame yourself for being hurtful and insensitive. Or, with humility, you can seek to recognize how your shadow contributes to the conflict and attempt to become responsible for breaking the pattern in this relationship and for the next generation. As one man said to his lover, "My pattern of feeling attacked didn't start here. But it can end here."

With patience and a partner who shares the responsibility for shadow-work, you may discover the gold in the hidden message of the shadow character: a greater capacity to accomplish directly what the shadow tries to accomplish indirectly.

Eventually, shadow-dancing may lead to soul talk. The partners are no longer on guard for projections and blame, anticipating criticism or judgment. Instead, their words soothe and heal each other. They go right in, touching the soul of the Beloved, so that the partners feel known and heard.

Who is the saint? Who is the screw-up? What signals in Turkish warn you of impending conflict? How do you sabotage the shift from shadow-boxing to shadow-dancing?

CRISIS OF COMMITMENT: MOVING IN, BECOMING ENGAGED

With marriage, the archetypes shift in unpredictable ways as each partner changes patterns, from single to spouse. If children are involved, one partner also shifts from a childless adult to a parent or an instant stepparent. As one man put it: "Marriage scares the hell out of me. When I married the first time, the moment the ring went on my finger I felt old tapes switch on that I didn't even know were there. I could just feel myself becoming my father. And my wife, who was such an independent woman, somehow expected that of me. She changed overnight, becoming needy and depressed."

We take spiritual vows and enter into another realm, relaxing into familiarity and a deeper level of safety, shedding persona and further disclosing suppressed aspects of ourselves. As one client said of his new wife, who disclosed her sexual abuse after the marriage ceremony, "We had a great sex life for six months. Then she disappeared." So, from the point of view of shadow and soul, slower is better; we suggest moving toward marriage with caution and shadow awareness.

There is an interim period that is often overlooked today which can ease the transition from being single to being married—being engaged. Engagement, as an opportunity to prepare for conscious marriage, offers another chance to see a partner and to be seen, to discover the Beloved and to disclose the soul. It's a time to explore a deeper authenticity, especially by exploring sensitive differences in power, religious beliefs, sexual habits, financial attitudes, parenting ideals, and lifestyle preferences. In particular, it's a time to experiment with French and Turkish for the bouts of shadow-boxing that inevitably will occur. A successful engagement will act like a pressure cooker, either strengthening the relationship as it moves toward commitment or uncovering irreconcilable differences before the partners exchange vows, thereby helping them to avoid greater pain in the future.

For example, when Dick, twenty-eight, a high-strung accountant, met Madeline, a widow at twenty-seven, he was immediately attracted to her. He had a list of relationship criteria in mind, but the list no longer seemed important. He wanted to become involved, even though she had three children and a low-paying job. He was caught by the projection and the sweetness of their sexual connection.

A year later, engaged to be married the following spring, Dick changed the location of his work in order to move with Madeline and the children into a house he bought "for us, not me." A sequence of events then unfolded in rapid succession that quickly became devastating for both.

First, one night Madeline told Dick that she wanted to cuddle without having sex. He responded coldly that she should sleep in the other room. Several days later, he informed her that on his recent trip to another town he had applied for another job. And finally, a week later, arriving home drunk, Dick turned toward Madeline with an eerie look on his face and, in an instant, violently pushed her against the wall, pinning down her shoulders and slapping her repeatedly in the face. Madeline was too stunned to respond, even to call out. She stood helplessly against the wall in shock until her four-year-old daughter walked into the room and called out "Mommy." On hearing the innocent voice, Dick swerved around, dropped his grasp, and ran out of the room in a panic. Madeline slid down the wall into a heap on the floor and sobbed.

To Madeline, the physical abuse felt like a shocking betrayal. Within two days, she had packed her family's belongings, left the house, and refused to speak with Dick. For her, the relationship was over; forgiveness was not an option. Having been sexually abused as a child, Madeline would not tolerate domestic violence.

Dick had no insight into what caused him to act in this way. He was a mystery to himself. "This isn't the real me," he kept saying again and again. But this *was* the real work of his shadow. Let's retrace the events from the perspective of Dick's internal experience.

Proceeding with marriage plans, they had met with a lawyer and struggled over a prenuptial agreement. The signing of the agreement was a particularly difficult event for Dick. Giving up his own voice, he had agreed to conditions that did not adequately represent his interests because he was afraid to tell Madeline what he really thought, fearing that she would leave him if he did.

As a child, Dick had been severely beaten by his mother, so he felt safe only alone in his room, withdrawn from the family. As a result, he developed a protector character that could not speak up for him or express his vulnerability. In a similar way, he had withdrawn from Madeline to protect himself from her abandonment. When she refused to have sex with him, he felt neglected and betrayed, experiencing this rebuff as another rejection and pushing her away. In addition, he became increasingly sensitive to how little time she made available to him, compared with the time she had for her children and friends. The green-eyed monster of jealousy had taken hold of him, but his vulnerable feelings remained out of reach in the shadow.

Dick's trip out of town was part of his escape plan. When he lied to Madeline about his travel intentions, she took it as another blow. In fact, after she heard about his desire to find a job elsewhere, she slapped him in the face in a moment of anger. He held her off and remained calm on the exterior, his persona intact. But on the interior Dick felt attacked as he had been by his mother. And for a brief, almost forgotten moment, a raging character appeared and fantasized tearing Madeline to pieces. But Dick's angry character was unacceptable to him, so it was quickly repressed in the shadow. Consciously, he had vowed never to treat anyone the way he had been treated.

Approaching the afternoon when he had too much to drink, Dick had been harboring internal resentment for months about having to hide his feelings. He had been living with fear of abandonment and feeling the need to protect himself. He also had been living with the rage of having been assaulted, as he had been as a child. And he had been living with a bitter jealousy of Madeline's young children. None of these feelings was acceptable to him, so they were carried out of reach of awareness by shadow characters. Under the influence of alcohol, which loosened his ego's control, these volatile feelings burst forth, resulting in his slapping her and speaking abusively.

Dick's shadow had, in fact, accomplished its unconscious purpose—to push her away. He had done the same with many women during the past decade. But with Madeline, his heart had been touched, so he felt crushed and devastated. His intense grief and feelings of self-hate led him to shadow-work.

During the next two years, Dick learned to identify his authentic need to be heard. Because it had not been honored as a child, he did not know how to honor it as an adult. Tracing his personal history, he recognized his shadow as a powerful ally that came to his rescue when he felt unsafe. The shadow had protected him for years against his mother and other women, helping him to hide when he felt overpowered. But the ally had become an enemy that sabotaged intimacy and stood in his way of creating a meaningful, vulnerable relationship. Dick entered a program for perpetrators of domestic violence and worked for many years to identify the triggers of his rage.

Engagement also contains an archetypal dilemma: the choice between loyalty to our mother/father or loyalty to our forthcoming wife/husband. This motif appears in fairy tales in which either a parent or a partner must die symbolically for the other to live. Michael Meade explores this theme in "The Lizard in the Fire." In the story, a man tells his son that if he sleeps with a maiden, he will die. When he does so, the youth does appear to die. His parents do nothing but weep, but the maiden finds a hunter who lights a fire and places a lizard upon it. Then he tells the people that the boy will remain dead if the lizard dies, but he will return to life if someone pulls the lizard from the fire.

When the father tries, he fails, driven back by the flames; when the mother tries, she fails, driven back by the flames. But the maiden jumps right into the fire, pulls out the lizard, and brings it back alive. The youth, too, springs back to life. Then he faces a dilemma: According to the hunter, if the young man kills the lizard, his mother will die. If he does not kill the lizard, the maiden will die. He must choose.

As Meade points out, the youth faces a ritual moment: He moves between mother and maiden. If he sacrifices the maiden and maintains his relationship to his mother, he continues to live as his mother's son; even if he weds, he refuses the call of manhood. In that case, he cannot see the authentic maiden but will unconsciously project his mother-complex demands and disappointments on her. On the other hand, if he sacrifices the mother and begins a relationship with the maiden, the spell of childhood will be broken. And he may be welcomed into the community as a man.

These tales of initiation always require sacrifice: When the boy and the maiden disobey the father, the older man's authority gets sacrificed. When the father and mother cannot save their son from the fires of life, their parental power gets sacrificed. When the maiden leaps into the fire, her helplessness burns away. If the youth kills the lizard, he sacrifices his attachment to his mother; if he does not, he sacrifices his independence. This is a more mythological restatement of our law of relationship: We must be willing to let go of it as it is in order to allow it to become something more.

Graham, forty, a real estate investor, faced this archetypal dilemma when he considered becoming engaged to a woman for the first time. When he had begun therapy two years earlier, Graham saw himself as an attractive, Porsche-driving, womanizing man who simply had not yet found the right woman to appreciate him. But he suffered secretly with the lack of intimacy that resulted from his insensitivity. With shadow-work, he began to recover some of his more vulnerable, tender feelings and to relate more authentically to women. When he met Molly, he felt prepared for a more conscious relationship.

One day, a woman who had been Graham's lover a year earlier called to reconnect with him. Graham, however, did not tell her that he was in a committed relationship and felt ashamed of the omission. In addition, he admitted that he felt guilty and angry at himself for not telling his closest buddy that Molly was more than just another woman, that he was feeling deeply involved with her. Finally, with his head down, he confessed that he had not yet told his mother about the importance of this relationship. "It would upset her that I made a decision without her input. She would be hurt because it would mean that she's not the most important woman in my life. And I feel so responsible for how she feels. On the other hand, I let down Molly for not speaking about my feelings for her. I let them both down."

When asked what keeps him from telling his mother about Molly, Graham explained that he was embarrassed to reveal his new persona, to expose himself as a caring, loving man. "I'm stepping out of character and revealing myself as more vulnerable. So far, only Molly knows me in this way."

For Graham to give up his identity as his mother's son and caretaker and become Molly's partner, he will need to face the required sacrifice: to break his identification with the character of the protective son and his obligatory behavior toward his mother. He will need to feel the fear of abandoning her and accept the guilt about her emotional response, trusting that he will not become overwhelmed as he did as a child. Finally, he will need to honor the relationship with Molly by disclosing his love and their decision to marry to his loved ones.

Women who are father's daughters face the converse dilemma: to shift allegiance from a father to a husband. One woman, whose father told her that men will try to use her and dominate her life, believed in some secret part of herself that she would die if she married, just as the fairy tale said. So, for many years, she dated men who were not potential partners, permitting herself to feel free. But when, in her late thirties, she felt her own desire to become engaged to a man she loved deeply, she finally faced her father's message. In Turkish, he had told his daughter that no one would love her as he did. Eventually, she realized that this father complex had to be sacrificed for her to become a partner in an authentic marriage. In effect, she had to risk the fear of dying, trusting that she would in fact survive.

✦   What shadow character sabotages your intentions to commit more deeply? What old loyalties need to be questioned for the new alliance to be formed?

The Ex-Spouse Complex

Just as our formative relationships with parents shape our choice of partners and our style of shadow-boxing, so do our long-term intimate adult relationships. In fact, we suggest that a first marriage may create deep loyalties and unconscious patterns that influence subsequent relationships because of what we call an ex-spouse complex. For example, Brent, a pediatrician who is currently married to Ginger, still pays one-third of his salary in alimony to his ex-wife, Joy, and still speaks with her every day. Allegedly, the conversations center around their four children and joint custody issues. However, Joy was Brent's first love. They shared their first sexual experiences, and they remained married for fifteen years.

Like Brent's mother, Joy was a full-time wife whose attentive and nurturing qualities made Brent feel right at home. And, like his mother, when Joy became depressed, a blaming and belittling character attacked Brent. Again like his mother, she unconsciously believed that if she kept him in his place, always doubting himself just a little, he would not become vain and leave her for another woman.

Although legally divorced for two years, Brent and Joy are not emotionally divorced. Like a pair of tuning forks, they react to each other's mood changes, even though they may not see each other for several weeks. And they continue to feel sentimental toward one another, expressing regret about losing their dream of lifelong marriage and breaking their mutual promises of fidelity.

Brent tells the therapist: "Joy is still there for me. She would give me anything I want. When I left, I was feeling so claustrophobic. But now I'm not sure that divorce was the right decision. With Ginger, it's totally different. She's so independent that now I have to take care of myself. And I often feel lonely and neglected."

Brent and Joy remained in the eggshell for the duration of their marriage. When he moved on developmentally, needing to cultivate his own independence, he did not have the tools to do so within the marriage, so the conventional form of their relationship broke down. Then he found Ginger, who forces him out of his mother complex and into a more autonomous life. But the familiarity of Joy's caretaking still haunts him and, at times, he blames his new wife for not being more like his first wife. Unable to face his own wounds, he activates another round of shadow-boxing.

Brent struggles to maintain a higher order relationship in the chicken yard, to be responsible for satisfying more of his own needs and for romancing his projections. With further shadow-work, he began to feel more rooted in himself and could risk further emotional and psychic separation from Joy, thereby allowing the Third Body to form with Ginger. Until then, Ginger felt at times as if she were "the other woman," standing outside of the Third Body of the previous marriage.

Brent's move into the chicken yard is not simply about shifting loyalties or choosing another mate; he is learning to welcome the pain that he avoided in his earlier marriage, in which his partner became a parent. Slowly, he is learning to recognize when he is falling into an old groove—that is, when the historical patterns with Joy are influencing his current relationship with Ginger, such as when he anticipates caretaking from his new wife, which is not forthcoming.

Similarly, if one partner marries an addict in a first relationship, he may adapt to the excitement of feeling out of control. But if he chooses a sober partner the next time, he may miss the drama of addiction. When he is not needed as a caretaker, he may wonder how to relate intimately to his mate. If a woman chooses a tough male partner without much sensitivity to her feelings in a first marriage, and then a *puer* in her second, she may enjoy the enriched communication with a more sensitive partner but miss the polarity of masculine/feminine energies. She may find, to her chagrin, that she cannot access her own femininity in the new relationship.

Shadow-work, then, includes sorting through the layers of past relationships, like a geologist differentiating layers of sedimentation in rock. Each layer tells a different story, but together they shape the ground on which we stand.

Crisis of Commitment: The Shadow Marriage

Most people recognize three kinds of marriage: the legal marriage, which describes the partners' standing under the law; the social marriage, which describes their partnership in the context of family and community; and the nuptials, which describes their spiritual intent. But we propose a fourth: the shadow marriage, in which the partners vow to accept and honor the full entourage of the Beloved's shadow characters. And, with this internal commitment, they acknowledge that they are engaged in uncovering their own shadows and taking responsibility for their own projections, judgments, and fears.

For some couples, this inner marriage may be enacted in ritual or ceremony with family and friends. For example, one client struggled with her husband's authoritarian, commanding side. She often felt, when confronted with this character, that she had to either react and rebel or to accommodate and disappear. Slowly, she began to empathize with this shadow figure, which she called the patriarch, and to uncover his deeper needs to be heard and to feel in control. Her husband, on the other hand, often experienced her as intrusive and unwilling to honor his boundaries.

In a small ceremony with her partner, this woman said: "I see the patriarch, I accept him, and I vow to empathize with his deeper needs. At the same time, I vow to try to take responsibility for my projections and reactions to your shadow character." And the man said to her: "I see the intruder, I accept her, and I vow to empathize with her deeper needs. At the same time, I vow to try to take responsibility for my projections and reactions to your shadow character."

Another woman, Kate, reported that her husband has a character that she calls the single guy. After ten years of marriage, from time to time he impulsively takes off for a few hours without letting her know his whereabouts. It's as if his family disappears, and he becomes single and thirty again.

Her husband, Billy, agreed: "I especially feel like the single guy in my men's group or at a poker game. I get to live an independent life for just a moment—in the context of being a couple."

Early in their marriage Kate felt rejected and abandoned by this behavior. She could not tolerate her own feelings of separation and judged Billy as incapable of behaving like a committed husband. Today, though, she acknowledges that he needs these times of separateness for his own soul and that she needs to be responsible for her reactions to them, without imposing her feelings on him. She reports that the idea of an actual separation from him is more difficult than facing his shadow parts, so she romances this character. "Welcoming all of him is more important than maintaining my idea of a marriage. So I look at the single guy as my teacher rather than as someone to battle."

When Billy's shadow character can be embraced in this way by Kate and given a place at the table, he will not have to hide out of fear of her reaction or slip into taking care of her hurt feelings. In other words, he will not fall into his mother complex by trying to please her or rebel against her. In this way, the shadow wedding frees the partners from serving as parents: A man can be freed of his mother complex because he can risk authenticity and feel known and accepted, rather than feeling trapped into hiding and behaving in a particular way to feel loved. A woman can be freed of her father complex because she can feel deeply known and accepted at the level of soul, rather than trapped into hiding and behaving in a particular way to feel loved.

With the shadow marriage, a partner no longer has to serve as a god: The longing for the romantic ideal, for the perfect image of the Other, which cannot be fulfilled by a mortal human being, becomes the longing for the Beloved who, like a mandala, carries both darkness and light. Then the marriage of the Beloveds can take place, evoking that aspect of the partners that transcends ego and shadow—the soul wedding.

Of course, even the most conscious commitment cannot save us from shadow suffering. At some point, difficult issues around commitment, autonomy, power, sex, and money will erupt. And then we will be grateful for the tools of shadow-work.

★ Who do you see in your partner's shadow? What is required of you to accept this character and empathize with its deeper needs?

POWER SHADOWS: ANGER AND DEPRESSION, WITHHOLDING AND WITCHINESS

Power struggles often erupt in the arena of home decor. But, psychologically, they are more complicated than they appear to be. Although Gordon, fifty-nine, worked as a designer, Kathy, fifty-five, his wife of twenty-two years, designed their home. She kept tightfisted control over the choice and placement of furniture and art. The long-term consequences of this division of labor were disastrous for Gordon, who kept tight-lipped control over his feelings. Having nowhere to hang his own paintings, he stopped creating them. Eventually, he began to suffer from depression, his self-expression blocked.

Kathy, controlled and abused as a child by her widowed mother, who suffered from depression, had developed an uncompromising, perfectionistic character who took the seat of power at her table in order to compensate for her feelings of low self-worth. Like this character, her home had to look just right, or she felt unworthy of being Gordon's wife. If the environment seems under control, she can defend against her chaotic feelings and instead complain about Gordon.

Kathy has no emotional rheostat, only an on-off switch: She is either happy and in control or depressed, out of control, and terrified.

Gordon responds to feeling controlled by becoming depressed. In Turkish, he punishes Kathy with his dark moods, getting even through a passive-aggressive character. Because his authentic rage is in the shadow and he remains unwilling to express it, he blames her for controlling him, while he holds himself as an emotional hostage by giving up his own voice. Gordon also has no emotional rheostat: He cannot discriminate between constructive assertiveness and destructive rage, so both get banished together. Depression is the result of his silenced voice, and the aliveness of their relationship is sacrificed.

Through the process of projective identification, Kathy expels her unwanted depression into Gordon, who unconsciously manifests it for her. He acts out in depression those feelings that she cannot face in herself. As a result, she cannot *stand* them in him. In fact, she is repulsed by his depressed moods and feels guilty for not being more empathetic. Her self-esteem plummets, and her worst fear comes true: She feels as if she is living with her depressed mother.

Conversely, Kathy manifests Gordon's disowned anger and his unexpressed power struggle. He hates himself for compromising around their home decor and refusing to take a stand concerning his paintings. He feels ashamed for failing to act like a man with his wife.

With the help of the therapist, Gordon finally spoke about his frustration to Kathy. In response, she suggested that he paint a green and yellow canvas of a certain size for a specific wall. He balked at her imposed limitations, his creativity stifled, his anger rising.

The therapist then suggested that Gordon take possession of one wall in the house to display his own work. When Kathy, sensing the importance of the issue, agreed to the plan, he began to paint hungrily again. Not surprisingly, his mood brightened, his self-expression increased, and the feelings between him and his wife warmed as well. When Gordon again felt resistance to painting at a later time, he could not blame Kathy for his inability to create. He had to face his own internal resistances, which initiated shadow-work on his power and rage.

As a result of this process, Kathy also began to look within, facing her lifelong denial of depression. At first, fearful of being overwhelmed, she could permit herself to feel only the slightest disappointments. Gradually, she could explore the meaning of her mother's depression and its impact on her own life, as well as her role in colluding with her husband's depression.

Jon and Jeannette also get caught in power struggles. Married for ten years, they live in a large home with their six-year-old son and enjoy an intimate family life with fairly open communication. Still, from time to time, they spiral out of control—and it's always for the same reasons.

Driving together recently on the freeway, Jon drove way over the speed limit, and Jeannette asked him to slow down. Lights and sirens followed. As a policeman asked Jon to sign a speeding ticket, Jeannette declared, "I told you so. If you'd just listen to me, you wouldn't have to waste that money on a ticket."

Jon clamped up in a silent rage. Certainly, on one level, his wife was right. But Jon heard more than Jeannette's words; he heard her hidden meaning in Turkish telling him that he was wrong, inadequate, inferior. He heard her saying that he can't do anything right. And this unspoken message was only the most recent in a long series of many such messages. He blew a fuse, telling the policeman: "I'd take a traffic ticket from you any time before signing up for her lecture series." The cop looked at him with a compassionate, sheepish smile and walked away.

Then Jon, a father's son who cannot easily express his feelings, withdrew into a dark, silent, punishing mood. When they arrived home, he felt withdrawn and unable to communicate. In fact, Jon closed down emotionally for several days. Initially, he liked the feeling of withholding affection from his wife; he had a powerful sense of being in control that way. Within his own cocoon, he also felt safe, immune to her reproach. This allowed him some temporary relief.

Jeannette was confused by the intensity of her husband's reaction to her. Whereas for her the communication was "just sharing feelings," a simple statement in French, for him it rang loudly in Turkish as criticism and attack by an outright witch. She felt that his response required her to stuff her feelings away. She wondered how the relationship could work if she could never express disapproval or disagreement because of his hypersensitivity and his short fuse. She told the therapist, "He seems so unwilling to hear me or to change his behavior that, no matter what I say, he will feel mistreated."

Jon's withholding behavior was not simply ego resistance. It served to protect his soul when he felt vulnerable to his wife's "witchiness." We all reach a point at which we are no longer able to stay open in the face of strong emotions. We shut down and disappear in those moments, whether into alcohol, depression, or a six-hundred-page book, delivering a return blow with the withdrawal itself.

With her therapist's help, Jeannette saw her part in the conflict and apologized for the eruption of the witch character. She gently held her husband in bed at night, even though he did not respond. She just held him and waited. Jon, in turn, still felt it unsafe to love again and needed to wait, allowing himself to open to her at his own pace. The healing process seemed out of his control. He sensed his ego saying, "No. I won't give her that. She's got to suffer a while longer for what she did." But with the passage of time and his positive intent, he was able to override his ego, allowing his heart and his arms to open again. In this way, they broke the pattern and strengthened the soul of the relationship.

Jeannette learned to express her feelings more directly ("I feel unsafe when you drive so fast; I don't like it"). She also began to recognize the impersonal or archetypal aspect of her rage at men, which stems from generations of women's oppression. She saw how this resentment gets aimed at Jon, which activates the roller-coaster ride. She felt embarrassed and humbled by this realization and began to befriend this attacking shadow character, which they called the witch. As a result, Jon found Jeannette to be more empathetic and became emotionally available to her again. At last, like a phoenix rising from the ashes, their love returned and the Third Body hummed again.

Who carries the anger? Who carries the depression? How does the witch emerge to wound the Third Body?

⋆

SEXUAL SHADOWS:
COMPULSIONS, AFFAIRS, AND DEMON LOVERS

Compulsive sexual habits—pornography, phone sex, or electronic liaisons—act like real extramarital affairs in a key way: They camouflage shadow issues in the primary relationship. Like Hermes, who chases nymph after nymph, Donald, thirty-five, remained with a woman until he felt her becoming dependent on him. Then he quickly found a new lover, told the first about her, and, eventually, left for the new relationship. In this way he could avoid their so-called dependency on him and feel like a stud, which is the nickname that he gave to his seductive shadow character.

But when he met Michelle, he felt deeply touched. After a few months she asked him for a commitment to monogamy and, to his own surprise, he agreed. They moved in together but, within six months, Donald had two sexual interludes. When Michelle discovered them, she felt outraged and kicked him out of the house. In turn, he promised to keep his agreement and returned home.

During the next month, Donald became involved in phone sex as a fantasy outlet. Michelle felt betrayed and, inflamed with jealousy, forbade it. Again, they faced a crisis of commitment around sexual fidelity, and Donald reluctantly agreed to her demands.

A few months later, he began masturbating to pornography, finding another innovative way to wander from the relationship. Again, Michelle became upset and forbade the activity. Don's sexual attraction for Michelle dwindled at this point. He found that if the stud could secretly watch pornographic movies and thereby assert his independence from her, he could become aroused and have sex with her without feeling a threat to his own identity. But when he obeyed her and put on a "good boy" character by cutting down his other outlets, his sexual desire for Michelle decreased. Furthermore, when Don felt that his particular form of voyeuristic eroticism was unacceptable to his lover and he was judged by her as "a degenerate creep," he felt unacceptable to himself. Then a passive-aggressive character emerged: He grew less willing to be aroused with Michelle because their eroticism, combined with emotional intimacy, forced him to face his own self-hatred. So he shut down and retreated into the safety of the stud with anonymous sex in the form of X-rated films, perpetuating his distancing and self-loathing.

Michelle did not judge Don as a "degenerate creep." Like Hera, the archetypal wife, she felt extremely jealous of Don's other objects of desire. In the past, when men had told her that they desired her alone, she had felt wanted. Now, she felt hurt and undesirable, a replication of her early family experience. When she faced her fear of being undesirable in order to sexually approach Don, she anticipated rejection. In effect, Michelle's constant expectation of rejection caused her to give up trying to meet her sexual needs with Don.

Eventually, Donald uncovered a monstrous mother complex within the history of his relationships and his compulsive sexual acting out. He needs to feel connected to Michelle in order to feel alive, as if she serves as an electrical ground wire. Without this connection to a woman, he feels lost and anxious. But then he resents that he needs her because his vulnerability and dependency needs are so shadowy to him.

If he has no psychological affair, via phone sex or pornography, he fears that he will lose himself and feel overwhelmed by her. In reality, it was he who was the dependent partner, and it was his fear of dependency that caused him to reject previous lovers. The stud was a shield, a cover-up for the horror of his own neediness and, ultimately, the terror of nonexistence.

Before living with Michelle, Donald enjoyed taking hikes and going to the theater, but he had given up those activities after they moved in together. Caught in his mother complex, he could not act on his own behalf, which increased his fear of losing his identity with her. As a result, his soul was being nourished only by the relationship, increasing his sense of dependency. The struggle over sex served as a camouflage for his lack of connection to his own creative life. He relied on her and rebelled against it instead of connecting to his own soul. When he began to explore his independence via creativity, his anxiety about dependency decreased and he could risk a bit more vulnerability with Michelle.

Eventually, Don recognized that, whether Michelle judged him or not, he was a dutiful mother's son, judging and condemning himself and thereby carrying on his family sins. As a result, he allowed his unconscious need to suppress his shame and dependency to destroy their intimate life. When he turned to his own soul to find his creative wellspring again, he struggled with his own resistances to tending to his own needs. But he also began to find a natural boundary for himself, and his fear of dissolution in the relationship lessened. A year later, he no longer needed to use affairs or compulsive sexual activities to escape his fears of intimacy. He had found the gold in the dark side.

The sexual shadow also appears in the form of a fantasized or actual affair, which is like a direct blow delivered in Turkish. It can trigger a crisis of commitment for either partner. Affairs reflect an imbalance in the primary relationship and can be used to compensate for a missing element: freedom, passion, spirituality, creative inspiration, masculine or feminine energies. Thus a god—Eros, Aphrodite, Dionysus, Artemis—who has been sacrificed in the marriage reappears in the affair, bringing feelings of expansion and delight.

Affairs are not a world apart from primary relationships but an intimate part of them. When a coupled partner has an affair with another coupled partner, there are four people involved, not two. And each remains aware of the invisible spouse who, like a ghost, haunts the lovers' interludes. In many cases, the lover and the invisible spouse carry shadow projections—"the other woman"—perpetuating negative fantasies of one another.

Recognizing that affairs serve a function in primary relationships in these ways, we typically encourage partners to end affairs, at least temporarily, in order to address the issues of their committed relationships. An affair in general, and sex in particular, can obscure the primary relationship's deeper problems, acting as camouflage by becoming the apparent problem so that the underlying root issues go unnoticed. Like an addiction that appears to be the problem while camouflaging the shadow's deeper needs, an affair may divert the attention from the less-visible developmental crisis in the relationship.

From our point of view, an affair should not be called a relationship if a person leaves the shadow behind in the mate, splitting the projection so that the mate carries only darkness and the new lover carries only light. The new encounter, in this case, is a bit like traveling in a hot-air balloon, while the ballast is left back at home in the primary relationship.

Elaine, a nurse, discovered this principle when she met a man through work during a dry spell in her marriage. Soon after she arrived for therapy, she began sobbing deeply about her inner turmoil. Slowly, the story emerged. She had lived with Stan for seven years in a comfortable kind of homeostasis, drifting toward a numbing indifference. To some extent Elaine was satisfied with their arrangement. Like Stan, her father had been distant and unavailable, so as a child she became used to yearning for intimacy, though not really expecting it. Unknowingly, Elaine had turned her partner into a parent, so that she lived in familiar territory, even though as an adult she felt a gnawing lack of fulfillment.

In addition, Elaine had grown up on a large family farm and was highly influenced in early life by the virgin goddess Artemis. When she married Stan, she unknowingly made a Faustian bargain, exchanging her independent spirit for a traditional married persona. Together, they appeared to others to carry an ideal couple persona: They looked attractive and amiable.

But when Dave, a medical supplies salesman, showed up at the office for the first time, Elaine felt as if she were awakening from a deep sleep. Her body tingled; she began to feel self-conscious about how she looked; she laughed more readily and looked forward to seeing him again. The attraction was so strong that Elaine got frightened and suggested to Dave that they speak only via e-mail. She hoped that such limited contact would keep her from violating her marriage vows.

A month later Elaine succumbed to Dave's invitation to go out for lunch. They discovered that they held deep religious and social values in common and shared their life dreams with one another. Elaine felt a spiritual bond that she had not felt before with a man. But she made it clear to Dave that she would not be sexually intimate with him. So, although she felt a kind of emotional and spiritual disloyalty, she could convince herself that, by avoiding sex, she was not having an affair; she was not an unfaithful wife.

In fact, that part of her which remained in the eggshell with Stan felt a terrible guilt about betraying him even in her fantasies; she felt worthy of contempt and punishment. So she worked harder to please him for a while, condemned to the prison of dutiful wifehood and trying to learn to live with her feelings of entrapment. But that part of her which was beginning to step into the chicken yard felt attractive, excited, and free for the first time in seven years.

As Elaine began to compare the two men in her own imagination, she grew increasingly depressed and hopeless about her options. In therapy, we named the split that was taking place in her projections between the spiritual man and the mundane man, between freedom and responsibility. Elaine was leaving her shadow projections—an absence of passion, authenticity, and honesty—behind with her husband, Stan, while she soared in the spirit with Dave.

This marital crisis was part of a natural developmental process. Elaine and Stan's marriage had been successful because they entered it at a young age to meet their dependency needs with each other and, after seven years, those needs had been met. At that point, Elaine was ready for more, which triggered the crisis of commitment. When she met Dave, she met her next challenge: the call to shadow-work with Stan. So, even though the tactics of Elaine's shadow seem self-defeating, its drives are essential.

Elaine also came to see that, while the mechanism of splitting the projection between the two men relieved the pressure from her marriage, lowering her pain and disappointment with Stan, it also maintained her image of him as a distant, punishing father who, she assumed, would reject her authentic feelings. By decreasing the pain in her marriage via the spiritual affair, she could continue life with Stan but without spirit.

Using an analogy from science, the therapist explained to her that this is not how breakthroughs happen. In physical systems, internal pressure must rise to a specific threshold for the system to change form. For instance, it takes one calorie of heat to raise the temperature of one gram of water one degree Centigrade. It takes 540 calories of heat to transform one gram of water at 99 degrees into one gram of steam at 100 degrees. In other words, a qualitative shift from one state to another, known as a phase transition, requires a buildup of heat or pressure.

Relationships shift in a similar way. If Elaine allows the pressure to leak slowly from her marriage container, the situation could continue for a long time. But if she remains with Stan inside the container and allows the pressure to build, some kind of breakdown may occur—which may lead to a breakthrough that she cannot predict.

In addition, this crisis of commitment proved to be a developmental step for Elaine, because previously the spirit had been exiled outside of her awareness. But since meeting Dave, she became conscious of it as a dynamic factor within her. Archetypally, Elaine discovered that her Artemis nature felt trapped in the early marriage and acted out its independence unconsciously. When she began to attend to the authentic needs of this character, such as spending time alone in the garden, she began to heal the split in the marriage archetype.

Elaine decided that she would remain in her marriage, hoping that, with the addition of conscious intention, the increasing pain and pressure would motivate her out of inertia. While talking with her husband, she found that she hesitated to move toward intimacy with him because of the fear that he would not desire her. If he did, she also feared that she would not be able to risk real physical, emotional, and spiritual intimacy with him after seven years of blocking it.

After another secret date with Dave, Elaine confessed that she felt like a "bad girl." This character fantasized about sex outside of her marriage and the freedom to be unattached. She then became increasingly aware of how much she permitted the "good girl" character to rule the kingdom at home with Stan, and she became the subdued, organized, self-controlled wife she believed he needed. Now this character felt suffocated and began to resent the constraints of her Faustian bargain with Stan, which sacrificed soul for comfort.

When the therapist asked Elaine about other situations in which she felt "good" or "bad," she disclosed that as a young girl she had felt unworthy and inferior because of her family secrets: debilitating poverty and her mother's alcoholism. Suddenly, as she spoke, she looked up and claimed that she had always tried to be a "good girl" at home but secretly felt "bad" because of her shame. In her early relationships with men, she would replicate this partner-as-parent dynamic and, at some point, her "bad girl" would come alive. Certain that her real feelings would be unacceptable to her boyfriends, she hid them and created the "bad girl" by acting out and feeling guilty, just as she had done with her husband.

Elaine saw the pattern. In that moment, she chose not to act out the affair with Dave but, instead, to recognize the "bad girl's" erotic desire for an Other as a signal to pay attention to the crisis in her marriage. Her inner work involved risking her authentic self-expression so that her marriage could move out of the cocoon stage, in which her partner served as a parent, and into an adult, real-time relationship. To achieve this, she had to speak with Stan about her secret erotic desires in an attempt to bring the "bad girl" into their marriage. When the therapist suggested that there might be a "bad boy" lurking in Stan as well, and that she might seduce him into coming out to play, she seemed shocked. She feared his rejection, but she feared repeating the pattern of looking outside of the marriage even more.

Many impulses toward an affair reveal the split archetype within marriage: bonded and free, attached and unattached. Each pole contains an authentic desire of the soul that may be carried by a shadow character: the one who seeks commitment and partnership and the one who seeks freedom and independence. To learn to use a temptation to have an affair as a wake-up call to heal the split archetype, we need to find an appropriate place at the table for each character. In this way, we can honor seemingly opposing needs of the soul and attend to the Third Body of the marriage.

An Artemis-style affair like Elaine's may have different traits and motivations than an Aphrodite- or Athena-style affair. For men, a Zeus-style affair would differ from a Dionysian tryst or a Hermes rendezvous. By uncovering who is motivating an affair and what this character is telling us, we may learn to meet its deeper needs, preferably without unconsciously destroying an ongoing relationship. Or we can choose more consciously to end a relationship without the pain of betrayal.

Who in you needs to feel more bonded? Who needs to feel more free? How can you meet the authentic desires of these characters?

Money Shadows: From Dating to Commitment

The story of one couple illustrates the development of money issues as a reflection of the development of a relationship. When Bob, thirty-six, and Hailey, thirty-three, began dating, he was earning a steady income as an accountant and she was between jobs. But they agreed that they would split the cost of dates fifty-fifty by taking turns on alternate evenings so that Bob did not feel taken for granted. In his previous two marriages, money had created emotional difficulties. After about a month of sharing costs he told Hailey, "I'm so glad that money isn't going to be an issue in our relationship."

As they became more romantically involved, each felt a spirit of generosity as the money flowed between them easily like the love. Hailey reported that she felt she was being vigilant about paying her way, especially when they traveled together. When she obtained a lucrative salary a few months later, she began to fantasize about buying Bob special gifts or treating him to a trip to the Bahamas.

Then their romantic projections began to rattle. Each partner felt little disappointments, then deeper wounds. One evening Bob turned the conversation to money. "You're not paying your fair share," he claimed. "I have the records from my credit cards. I'm paying about two-thirds of our costs and you're paying one-third. Those are the facts. Before you had the job, I didn't mind. But now we need to adjust our agreement."

Hailey felt shocked. She felt wrongly accused. But she had only her feelings to account for the money because she paid for expenses with cash. "I don't agree with you," she said. "But what would you like to do?"

Bob suggested that they split each bill fifty-fifty in the moment, rather than alternate evenings, "so that she could see how much meals and entertainment actually cost." Hailey could not believe his statement; she felt patronized for the first time. An independent career woman, she knew well the cost of a comfortable lifestyle. But she did not yet feel safe enough to express the shadowy feelings, so she swallowed her resentment and agreed to the new arrangement.

A few days later, Bob turned the conversation to sex. "Our giving and receiving in sex is not equal," he said in a forceful tone. "I'm making love to you every time."

Once again, Hailey went into shock and disbelief. But this time her response was more authentic. "I can't believe you feel this way," she professed. "It's just incredible to me. I give you massages and sexual pleasuring much more often than you give them to me."

Bob's accountant character suddenly had appeared in two new arenas, tallying up credits and debits in money and sex. Hailey felt hurt, insulted, and resentful, as she had in childhood as a frequently criticized father's daughter. With her natural spontaneity stolen, she realized that, like a bean counter, he was monitoring her every move. "The innocence is gone now that we're keeping track," she told the therapist.

At a deeper level, Bob and Hailey played out their shadow issues disguised as money issues. She felt frightened that she could not be enough for this man: nurturing enough, sexual enough, conscious enough. Because her father had measured her against an impossibly high standard, she always came up short. So, with her father's critical voice internalized, when Bob claimed that she was not giving him enough, she blamed herself.

He suffered the converse: As a mother's son, he felt unwanted by his mother. So he, too, struggled with the feeling of betrayal when he could not get enough. And he blamed Hailey for withholding that which he felt entitled to receive from her in order to feel loved.

Eventually, as Bob and Hailey moved toward marriage, they tried to create a relationship to money that reflected a conscious commitment to one another. For some partners, this would involve joining their financial lives together as the rest of their lives become united. But for others, like Bob and Hailey, money might require another creative solution. After opening a joint checking account, Bob found that he could not tolerate Hailey's negligence about balancing the books. Their attitudes toward money and their styles of banking simply did not mesh.

Eventually they decided that, for them, the best arrangement involved keeping their money separate. As a result, he no longer blamed her for her style of accounting because it no longer affected him. In turn, she no longer felt controlled or blamed for her more relaxed spending habits. And in general this solution eliminated a category of conflict attributable to clear differences in their respective relationships to money, which could have become a constant irritant.

CRISIS OF COMMITMENT: HAVING A CHILD

Cindy, thirty-eight, and Mitchell, forty-one, had career-oriented lives, freed of the burdens of commitment to spouses and children. Both had traveled internationally and held high-paying jobs when they met. Both also had developed elaborate defenses against feeling vulnerable in intimate relationships. They also shared a historical wound that led to these romantic patterns: Mitch had been abandoned by his mother at birth and raised by an adoptive family. Cindy had been shipped off to boarding schools and spent little time with her family of origin. Each suffered from feeling unwanted.

When Mitch met Cindy, the walls of Jericho came tumbling down. "There was something about her, a kind of gentleness, that just made me want to protect her and care for her. I had never felt that way before." The two became inseparable for eight months—and then Cindy discovered that she was pregnant.

Because of her personal history of early abandonment and adult independence, and because their relationship was so new, Cindy felt frightened. She asked for his reassurance, which was not forthcoming. So she told him, "If you don't want this baby as much as or more than I do, I'll get an abortion."

Mitch felt punched in the stomach. In Turkish, he heard her say that if he does not obey her wishes, she will take everything away from him. So he reassured her. But at the same time, he built up feelings of resentment, which began to leak out in sarcastic quips. With his sarcasm, Cindy felt slapped in the face. In Turkish, she sensed his distance and withdrew, telling the therapist, "If I don't push him to the brink of disaster, I won't get the reassurance I need. But then he resents me for pushing him."

Cindy believed that Mitch did not really want the baby but only claimed to want it for her. She felt terribly anxious about taking this step and, disowning her feelings, expressed them as concern for him and his anxiety. Mitch, in turn, felt snared like an animal in a pen. He did not want to risk losing the relationship with Cindy, yet he felt hemmed in and totally unprepared for fatherhood.

As they began to sort out the French and Turkish, Mitch could catch his sarcasm before it started a roller-coaster ride. And Cindy learned to identify her own anxiety and stop projecting it onto him. They both realized that their internal reactions to each other's defensiveness can be interpreted as a signal from the Third Body of the other's discomfort, which when unrecognized activates the roller coaster. Slowly, the partners learned to feel their own authentic desires, as distinct from their obligatory responses. And, as a result, Mitch realized that he would feel terrible loss and regret if they had an abortion. He discovered a deep desire to have a child that he did not previously know he had.

Cindy knew her bottom line: "I don't want to bring a child into this world unless it is totally wanted." Mitch knew exactly what she meant.

So a discussion about having a baby progressed to a request for a soul commitment. When Mitch told the therapist that he did not know how to be a conscious parent, the therapist pointed out that he already was doing it: questioning his motives, exploring his ego's needs, romancing his projections, and remembering his shadow wounds. The conscious relationship, then, can lead to the birth of the conscious family or family soul. With this commitment, the parents as partners begin to learn yet another step in shadow-dancing: parenting a child's shadow.

Relationship as a Vehicle for Soul Work

In this chapter, we have reimagined the range of possibilities for a conscious partnership. We have proposed that by doing shadow-work with a partner to romance your projections, you can uncover your family sins and, in this way, gain a deeper self-knowledge, as well as uncover your partner's family sins and, in this way, help to heal one another. The result: The Other becomes the Beloved, the cherished soul with whom you share your life.

By attending to the art of communication, you can learn to reduce the blows in Turkish that leave you feeling wounded and scared of one another. And by using engagement as a time in which to explore your differences and shift the loyalties of your soul, you can move toward the shadow marriage, vowing to care for one another's deepest needs.

Finally, by honoring the Third Body, you can nurture the soul of the relationship, which in turn nurtures you. Like the mythic Queen Penelope, you can trust that your love will endure.

These skills can also be applied to friendship, which is the topic of the next chapter.

CHAPTER 7

Shadows Among Friends: Envy, Anger, and Betrayal

I am as a spirit who has dwelt
Within his heart of hearts, and I have felt
His feelings, and have thought his thoughts, and known
The inmost converse of his soul, the tone
Unheard but in the silence of his blood,
When all the pulses in their multitude
Image the trembling calm of summer seas.
I have unlocked the golden melodies
of his deep soul, as with a master key,
and loosened them and bathed myself therein—
Even as an eagle in a thunder-mist
Clothing his wings with lightning.
—Percy Bysshe Shelley

The shadow lurks like an incredible hulk behind our dearest friends. At one moment, we may feel as if we have found an eternal ally, one who will go the distance at our side. We imagine that we are no longer alone but accompanied by a like-minded twin. We understand him or her without effort; we feel understood in return. We can speak to our friend as if we are speaking to ourselves.

Then, in a moment of shock and disbelief, we feel betrayed: We turn our heads and see, instead of a trusty comrade, a gossip or, worse, a liar, who tells our secrets to an unknown other; a seductive vamp, who allures a romantic partner; a cheater, who gets away with something illicit or illegal; a racist, whose bigoted, parochial attitudes disgust us. In effect, we see, instead of a friend, an enemy, and we fall from grace, our innocence spoiled, our love rent. The warm openness of friendship turns cold and contracts, leaving only feelings of disappointment, anger, resentment, even betrayal. We step onto a rollercoaster ride, making critical, hurtful comments, not knowing whether we will still have a friend at the end of the line.

At those times we may come to see that our fantasy image of friend, like the image of family or the image of the Beloved romantic partner, compels us to long for the ideal friend, the archetypal friend. We imagine an end to loneliness, a communion of souls, a joint destiny. We recall archaic rituals of blood pacts in which each person wounds him or herself, bleeds into a cup of liquid, and consumes the other's drink. Sacredly bound to our friend, the betrayal becomes even more potent: The betrayer carries the blood of the betrayed.

This archetypal image of the loyal friend carries multiple meanings of soul and shadow. Eros, god of relatedness, dwells here. He pulls us together, arousing empathy, admiration, even adoration; at times, he adds sexual desire to the mix. The fear of sexualized Eros among friends hinders intimacy between heterosexual men; they bear the collective wound of homophobia in their individual friendships. Heterosexual women typically have more permission to exchange physical and emotional tenderness, kissing one another and crying together; however, they, too, may suffer the sexual shadow in their affections for each other.

Typically, then, unlike a romantic partner, a friend is not a sexual partner, although the bond may arouse fearful erotic feelings. Unlike a parent, a friend is not a caretaker, although the bond may arouse uncomfortable feelings of mothering, dependency, and abandonment. Unlike a sibling, a friend is not typically rivalrous, although the bond may arouse shadowy feelings of competition, envy, and jealousy.

Instead, a friend offers us a place to feel special; a friend permits our *authentic specialness* to be seen. For many people, to feel special is forbidden because it leads to arrogance or hubris, the sin of pride. To feel special is dangerous because it means to stand out, to be separate from others, to be the object of envy or hatred. But it is only when our specialness is tied to ego that it looks like hubris or self-centeredness to

216

others or feels uncomfortable to ourselves; it is *inauthentic specialness*. On the other hand, our unique specialness at the level of soul is honored by a friend, who can see infinity in our particularity.

We attempt in this chapter to reimagine friendship and to revalue the specialness of the soul friend. We explore friendship based on affinity and friendship based on otherness. And we suggest that every friendship, at some point, offers an opportunity for shadow-work, an opportunity for widening the range of our own self-acceptance and deepening the quality of our own capacity for forgiveness.

The Loss of the Loyal Friend

For the Greeks, friendship, or *philia*, meant love of soul. For Plato, friendship as a form of Eros encompassed our longing for perfection. For Aristotle, an individual's capacity for friendship was a measure of the quality of soul. If you did not love yourself, you could not love a friend. If you did not treasure your own gifts and meet the obligations of having them, you could not treasure the gifts of a friend.

The ideal of male friendship is embodied in the Greek mythical twins Castor and Pollux, known as the Dioscuri. Their mother, Leda, had two sets of boy-girl twins: Castor and his sister had a mortal father; whereas Pollux and his sister had an immortal one, Zeus. The two boys became inseparable, sharing adventures and challenges, such as the quest for the golden fleece. But on one journey, Castor was stabbed and killed, and Pollux became inconsolable. He prayed to Zeus to permit him to die as well, so that he would not be separated from Castor and forced to return to Olympus alone. In compassion, Zeus allowed Pollux to share his immortality with Castor, causing them to spend half their days in Hades and half on Olympus. When that solution became unbearable, Zeus made them both immortal, and today they appear to us in the heavens as the constellation Gemini.

The twins reveal several aspects of male friendship: They are alike, brotherly, yet they are opposite, mortal and immortal, earthy and spiritual. They are action-oriented, yet they can be supportive and loyal. When one gets wounded, the relationship feels as if it fluctuates between heaven and hell. For some, it may not survive. But with grace it can become immortalized, a soul friendship.

217

If one brother is viewed as an inner figure within the other, he may stand for either the mortal shadow or the immortal Self. In this way, the bond can come to signify more than our need for mirroring; it promises to fulfill our deepest longing to be united with something larger than the individual ego by providing an experience of completion.

For most people, friendship implies loyalty, an allegiance to the bond that transcends circumstance, even life-threatening circumstance. We would like to believe, even unconsciously, that a true friend, like an alter ego, would take on our suffering, perhaps even sacrificing his or her life for ours. This timeless promise is illustrated in a tale of the Trojan War in which Patroclus, beloved friend of the Greek hero Achilles, dons the latter's armor to fight in his stead. When Patroclus is killed, Achilles is so grief-stricken that he slays his friend's murderer, even knowing that the act foretells his own death. The two men's bones are later placed in the same golden jar.

 Where do you witness this kind of loyalty? What engenders it between people? What is being sacrificed between two close friends? What is obligated? What are the limits of your giving?

Perhaps this loyalty appears today, from time to time, among young children who remain trusting and innocent. One seven-year-old boy who recently fell from a tree onto his head, which resulted in a concussion, told his father that he was glad that he took the fall, rather than his best friend. "I couldn't stand to see Carl in that kind of pain," he commented.

Today, only a few people experience the kind of friendship in which they offer to stand in for another's fate or to speak from their specialness. Instead, for many of us the word "friend" has degenerated to mean buddy, acquaintance, companion, neighbor, diminishing our fantasies about this potential bond. And, as a result, the deep reciprocity of soul friendship has been lost for us.

In fact, in interviews, author Lillian Rubin asked people to identify their best friend in an effort to discover whether their designations were reciprocal. To her surprise, she found that 84 of the 132 respondents did not mention the person who originally submitted their name. For all of these people, the feeling of friendship was not mutual. And only 18 out of the 132 people placed that mutual friend at the top of their list.

This shocking finding is reflected in many of our clients' stories. Frequently, one friend wants more from the relationship than the other—more time, more talk, more depth. The fuser, who seeks more intimacy, may feel deprived and disappointed when the other does not respond in kind; the distancer, who seeks more spaciousness, may feel intruded upon, even devoured by the love-hungry friend.

In long-term friendships, these boundaries may fluctuate with changing circumstances, such as a pregnancy in one woman. Then parental complexes can take over and result in shadow-boxing. For example, Lori and Frances had been close since elementary school, sharing the intimate details of their daily lives into their college years. Now in their thirties, their lives diverging, Lori still expects consistency in their intimacy but feels that Frances has pulled away, moving into her own world, which does not include her friend. For Lori, the Third Body of the friendship is wearing thin.

"We say we're best friends, but it's just a manner of speaking. I have to take all of the initiative; there's no reciprocity. When I sent her a birthday gift, I got no response. When I took my school exams, I got no phone call. Sure, we have a long past to draw upon. But you can use history for only so long. It's just a crutch if there's nothing happening in present time."

Recently, Frances had a baby and called Lori after a month had gone by, angrily asking her friend, "Why haven't you come to see the baby? It's been nearly five weeks."

Lori responded curtly, "Why did I have to find out about your baby from your secretary?"

Apparently, both women felt hurt and neglected, but neither risked the authenticity to say so. Their more proper personas sat in the seats of power. Unconsciously, Lori believed that if she spoke up and expressed unpleasant feelings, such as anger, the relationship would end. She had been taught as a child to be upbeat and sensitive to the needs of others, attuning to their souls, rather than nurturing her own. Unfortunately, she still obeyed this parental voice.

Of course, Lori secretly wished to speak with her friend about her feelings, but feared that Frances would respond with coldness and indifference. "I know that character in her. Her mother had the same cutting tone: end of conversation. And she hated it when her mother did that to her. Now she does it to me." When her friend slipped into the trap of this shadow character, Lori felt devalued, resentful, and angry.

She faced a crisis of commitment: Perhaps, she thought, it was time to let the friendship go. "We could save the friendship if I can really speak without editing. But the violence in her tone frightens me. It reminds me of my rageaholic father and causes me to clam up in silence. Then I feel no hope for our relationship."

A week later, with the help of her therapist, Lori told Frances about her bitter disappointment and her irritable feelings, deciding to risk the friendship as it is to see whether it could become something else. At the same time, she told her friend how much she cared for her. Frances was shocked; she had no idea how disturbed Lori had become. When she responded with loving concern, Lori felt as if a huge barbell had been lifted off her back. "Then I could feel the friendship underneath all of those feelings again, and it felt strong and cozy, as if I were coming home."

There are many cultural reasons for the loss of consistent, stable friendships, the scarcity of the cherished friend, and the lack of reciprocity between people. With the breakdown of the extended family and the disappearance of community, people have become more mobile, moving to urban centers, where they may meet many new people in a year, and allowing their bonds with older friends to weaken. Their work-centered lifestyles also demand the time that was previously available for leisure, which is required to cultivate and maintain friendships.

In addition, we tend to devalue people who are not romantic partners as "just friends," as if they are less important than our mates, as if only romance brings rich reward. When Alex divorced at fifty and lost his father soon after, he felt empty, alone, and a failure at relationship. When the therapist asked him about male friends, he began to tell stories about several men he had known since the 1960s, when they were political radicals together. When he reconnected with one man in a distant city, the friend flew into town for Alex's father's funeral, surprising him with a depth of concern. Speaking openly of these friends, Alex began to feel less isolated, more capable of friendship, and more accepting of himself.

Also, our worship of individual autonomy and shaming of dependency needs makes it difficult to admit our deep affections for others or to display our reliance upon them. Men, especially, tend to fear intimacy with one another; they are taught to deny their vulnerability, and they are often refused closeness by their fathers. As a result, they typically find it difficult to lean upon other men or to ask for help. Many rely solely on their wives or lovers for intimacy, which puts a tremendous burden on their romantic relationships.

Finally, deep-seated sexism makes it difficult for men and women to be friends. And institutionalized racism makes it difficult for people of diverse ethnic groups to be friends. Yet, for these very reasons, it's imperative to form these bonds and explore these collective shadow issues; friendship can be a potent antidote to enemy-making.

Despite these epidemic difficulties, many people fight depersonalization to maintain rich personal lives. They sustain long-distance relationships by phone or electronic mail. They form men's or women's groups and shadow-work groups to cultivate a sense of community. And they honor their bonds with weekly meals, monthly rituals, shared child-rearing, joint creative or political projects, and a desire to do shadow-work to nurture the relationships through difficult times.

Soul Friends/Shadow Friends

Members of other cultures hold rituals to honor the special bond of friendship. In India, each boy is married twice: once at puberty to a friend in a lifelong commitment and again at age sixteen to a wife, also in a lifelong bond. These rites offer the boy a sense of security in relatedness throughout a lifetime. In Germany, too, a friendship ceremony calls for the two people, each holding a glass of wine or beer, to become physically close by entwining arms, then to drink up after making a promise of eternal brotherhood.

This kind of friendship is not a *persona friendship*, which may arise from shared circumstances, such as those enjoyed by working colleagues, members of sports teams, or parents of school-age children. Typically, it does not arise from shared aims, such as those pursued by club members with common interest or members of a spiritual community seeking higher consciousness, who may share the transpersonal bond of spirit rather than the more personal bond of soul. In a persona friendship, we may be attracted to the other person's shields—money, sex, or power—and attempt to win them over for our own benefit, to use them for our own ends. We may get stuck in roles, in which one is the enabler for the other's addiction, or one holds a superior position while the other feels shame and envy, or the two may simply enjoy an activity together, such as shopping or basketball, without much intimate exchange. Finally, in a persona friendship the two tend to express sentimentality, a substitute, readily digestible form of the deeper, darker emotions.

Instead, in a *soul friendship*, we honor and recognize each other's essential nature. Our roles are more fluid; our respect is mutual; our deeply felt bond does not rely on *doing* as much as *being*. Soul friendship requires a loyalty to more than the passing feelings or opinions of the cherished one, a fidelity to more than temporary goals or appearances. It demands authenticity, or loyalty to soul. In effect, it demands that we honor the Third Body of the friendship. In return, it offers a place where we don't have to hide.

In addition, soul friendship will have different meanings in different contexts. For young girls who meet in adolescence and suffer a crush on one another, entering the eggshell phase, becoming inseparable, and remaining loyal friends through college, marriage, and child-rearing, a soul friendship survives the passage of time. It endures despite changing circumstances and developmental differences. It may lose its intensity, go latent even for years, or remain the one stable relationship in a lifetime, outlasting even marriage. For the women involved, each has a witness to her life story. If they are lucky, each has a refuge, a place where she belongs.

For these lifelong friendships, the memory of a shared history is key. Mnemosyne, goddess of memory, supports the bond by permitting the friends to connect through the past when the present-time tie wears thin. As mother of the Muses, Mnemosyne loves musing, narrative, rhyme, and myth, as well as the images that hold narrative together. When friends reminisce, they are less interested in facts and actual events than in symbolic memory, the recollection of intensely felt moments that are endowed with depth. Friendship, like psychotherapy, makes room for this subjective quality of memory.

Some friends who meet later in life feel as if they recognize one another at a deep, unspoken level; their affinity transcends their personal histories. So they do not need to look backward and recount the past. They simply step into the present moment together as if their bond is timeless, as if a Third Body existed before their meeting and glues together their fates.

Those who are attracted through affinity, or like meeting like, feel a sense of resonance with the other person, as if he or she is a twin. Like the Greek twins Castor and Pollux, in some African tribes twins are the ideal of best friends. Children born on the same day are considered twins who were somehow separated before birth but who share a lifetime bond. Friends, therefore, share their journeys before life and will do so after life; their destinies are intermingled. They embody the mystery of the two-in-one.

Others may not experience their affinity as primary. Instead, they may experience the friend's Otherness as the compelling quality, entering a differentiation phase in which they push against the friend to maintain their own separateness and uncover their own uniqueness. This is friendship as a *via negativa*, in which the friend is us, yet is not us. The friend is the loyal opponent, the Other who sets our limits and challenges our abilities. In the *shadow friend*, we meet the Other to find ourselves.

When Eve, a San Francisco artist and *puella* free spirit, met Myra, a Chinese-American law student, worlds collided: The combination of their personal and cultural differences was explosive. In reaction to a highly controlling mother, Eve lived a highly unstructured life, free of personal obligations, committed relationships, or work demands. Myra, on the other hand, believed in duty to family, friends, and work; she wished to serve others, to structure her time, and to maintain privacy and simplicity. Both women were drawn to the friendship; each felt mystified by the Other, compelled to explore their differences. Yet, having banished into shadow many of the Other's qualities, each felt quickly put off, irritable, then angry when hearing the other's needs in Turkish. As Eve put it, "It's painful to be at war with my very nature in my friend."

For their friendship to survive, Eve and Myra had to practice shadow-dancing; they needed to learn patience with one another and tolerance for their differences. They needed to observe their own shadow projections to see how they contributed to the repetitive cycle of mutual suffering, tie themselves to the breath, and romance those projections. If one had tried to convert the other to her ways, the friendship would have failed. So they slowly and gently explored each other's preferences in style, temperament, timing, and purpose. In this way, each discovered her own uniqueness, and each discovered the gifts of her shadow sister. Finally, each woman could begin to extend the range of her own repertoire.

For some pairs, the Otherness is too shadowy, too off-putting, and too uncomfortable. As a result, a friendship cannot even begin. When Brian, thirty-five, met Sam, twenty-eight, in a men's group and the latter reached out to be friendly, Brian was repelled. He did not know why the other's man's approach and the sound of his voice elicited such a strong negative response.

Brian said, "When Sam speaks, he's always gentle and soft, as if he doesn't want to offend anyone. And he talks nonstop about his new-age religion. He believes that if everyone meditated in just the way he does, there would be an end to violence and a new millennium. I can't *stand* his blissy attitude, his spiritual denial of the suffering of life. He's so self-righteous, as if he has all the answers anyone needs—it drives me crazy."

Brian, too, had been involved in a meditation community in his twenties and had become deeply disillusioned with its precepts and practices. Since then, he had married, had a child, and taken on the responsibilities of a working father. When Brian met Sam he also met a past part of himself, a *puer* character who now appeared to him to be naive and inauthentic. In Turkish, he heard his own past self-righteousness in the voice of the other man. So he summarily dismissed him.

But if, instead of shaming these feelings in himself, Brian had worked through them more deeply, he may have felt compassion for Sam, whether he chose to befriend him or not. By not doing so, he got caught in a shadow projection and was blinded to any value in the younger man's point of view. And he could not choose whether to be acquainted with him more deeply or not.

James Hillman has pointed out that the Other, who can become a friend or enemy, often seems to be given, rather than chosen. In this way the Other is an instrument of fate. This relationship between shadow friends requires the acknowledgment of deep ties and the fulfillment of mutual obligations. A failure to do so by one member can result in feelings of bitter disappointment.

Who is your soul friend? Who is your shadow friend? Who have you sacrificed as a result of a shadow projection?

MEETING THE OTHER:
FRIENDS AS PARENTS, FRIENDS AS GODS

In some friendships, family projections may play a key role; the shadow may scan for a fit to re-create childhood patterns and heal old wounds. A college woman, for example, may idolize her more mature room-mate of the same age, becoming dependent on her and gaining a model of femininity that was absent in her home. A man whose early life was shaped by a competitive brother who is close in age may feel rivalry and even antagonism with other men. Or an adolescent may form a bond because a quality that is rejected by her family is accepted by a friend. When she discovers that she can act out this repressed feeling or explore this forbidden behavior, and the friend can tolerate the intolerable trait, she forms a fast friendship.

When a mother or father complex is central to a friendship, and parent-child issues of dependency, control, or intrusiveness contami-nate the bond, shadow-boxing is inevitable. Jane and Laurel, now in their thirties, met in college and became best friends who spoke every day for ten years. Jane, an introverted woman who tends to become depressed and isolated, came from a family that was not generous with love or gifts. When she met Laurel, she was charmed by her extro-verted, nurturing, generous nature. When they began fighting and growing distant from one another, they decided to seek therapy to pre-serve their friendship, which was precious to both of them.

Jane disclosed that a recurring pattern or roller-coaster ride had interfered with her warm feelings toward her friend. She had begun to resent Laurel's constant questions about her emotional state, her wor-rying about the depression. Jane felt that her friend was intruding into her private world without permission, so she responded abruptly with a defensive, protective character.

Laurel responded, "I just wanted to help."

But, in Turkish, Jane heard Laurel as if she were saying: "I'm better than you. You have a problem and I can help you fix it. So I'm entitled to know your thoughts and feelings." As a result, Jane felt patronized and inferior and became angry. This character responded by asking her friend for a more distant, superficial kind of friendship. In addition, she told Laurel that their conversations were not reciprocal and asked her friend to disclose more of her own vulnerability.

Laurel, in turn, felt judged and unappreciated. She felt attacked for not exposing herself more in the relationship and unseen for her efforts to comfort and assist her friend.

As the two women sorted out their issues, Jane came to see that in some ways Laurel had become the mother she never had. In college, they had become fused, enclosed in an eggshell relationship. As long as Laurel carried the mother projection, acting in a Demeter orientation toward her friend, and Jane remained in a dependent character, the relationship worked. But the love generated in their bond had begun to heal Jane; she felt more self-worth and became more self-sufficient, eventually launching a career, finding a long-term relationship with a man, and no longer wishing to remain in a lesser role. When she broke her identification with the dependent character at the table, she grew restless, even claustrophobic in the old form of friendship with Laurel and wanted to break out of the eggshell into the chicken yard. So she faced a crisis of commitment and chose to tell her friend of her discomfort with their lack of boundaries.

Laurel, however, had not developed out of her rescuing, caretaking character; it still sat in the seat of power. This Demeter character sat at the head of the table in all of her primary relationships. She felt so hurt by Jane's attacking rejection of her that she could not allow the relationship to evolve into something else. She cut it off and sought to re-create the pattern elsewhere with another dependent friend.

The archetypal source of this codependent relationship pattern appears in the image of Chiron, the wounded physician who is part horse, part human. Although he is a god with curative powers, he suffers an incurable wound. When the archetype of the wounded healer is split in any relationship—that is, when one person (the identified patient) carries all of the woundedness and the other carries all of the healing powers—the power shadow emerges. In this case, Laurel is blind to her own woundedness and believes she can heal her friend, Jane. So she manipulates the relationship to get it to conform to these roles and to maintain her position of power vis-à-vis her friend. But

Jane has evoked the character of her own inner healer and now resents Laurel's projections of woundedness and helplessness. For the friendship to evolve, Laurel needs to stop denying her own vulnerability and expose her shadowy, wounded side to her friend.

In other friendships, family projections are not dominant. Instead, archetypal or divine projections are evoked, in which one friend idealizes another's appearance, wealth, competencies, or charisma. When Cheryl, thirty-eight, met Gabriella, thirty-two, she marveled at the younger woman's passion for life, her appetites for food, sex, dancing, and talking. Gabriella loved to talk endlessly about feelings, to live them deeply, and to drink of their Eros. Sometimes the new friends would talk for so many hours that they would begin to make fun of themselves, asking again and again, "How do you *really* feel? No, how do you *really* feel?" And the dramatic intensity would build until they laughed at how seriously they took themselves. And Cheryl would light up with Gabriella's rolling, booming, bodily laughter, thoroughly and deeply enjoying her friend.

When Cheryl met Gabriella, it was a close encounter between Athena and Aphrodite in the flesh, a close encounter between women so alien that each felt compelled to explore the mystery of the Other. Each felt invaded by Eros, who came on wings to bring them together and left them unable to resist, as if this friendship held some secret key to the wisdom of life.

Cheryl, an Athena-style father's daughter, used her achievements to gain male approval. Bright and independent, she had earned a doctoral degree while working as an architect. She had close male friends but few male lovers, explaining to her new friend that throughout her life men had seemed intimidated by her intellectual prowess and rejected her style of femininity. As Athena's influence had begun to wane, Cheryl longed for an intimate relationship but did not know how to attract, seduce, or nurture men. The importance of her career success paled as she felt her disappointment, then failure to find love.

Gabriella, a Raphaelite beauty, used her attractiveness to gain male attention. When she walked into a room, the men gathered around her, compelled by her voluptuous sensuality and charmed by her gift with words because, like Aphrodite, Gabriella traveled with Peitho, goddess of gentle persuasion, who woos the heart with words.

When Cheryl observed her friend at a party for the first time, she felt enraged at how easily Gabriella attracted men, and she envied her friend's charms. Then, slowly, because she also loved Gabriella, she began to become curious about her talents and suggested that they explore their Otherness with each other. Perhaps, Cheryl thought, each woman could extend herself to include more of the other's gifts.

As they talked, Gabriella slowly admitted that she, too, felt disappointment and failure, but in the arena of work rather than love. She envied her friend's talents and wished to learn how to establish a more lucrative creative life. So the women formed a learning community of two to do shadow-work, agreeing to take responsibility for their own envy and projections onto the Other and to speak from their own specialness. As a result, each felt more alive, uncovering a new direction for her energies and feeling less bound to persona. In this way, during many years of ongoing conversation, Gabriella discovered the gifts of Athena, and Cheryl discovered the secrets of Aphrodite.

In some friendships, shadow-work cannot be done in such an open exchange with the other person; therefore, it has to be done internally, perhaps through dreamwork, such as in the following example. Our client Fay brought in the following dream:

I'm working my way home in my car. I'm carrying a brown bag full of garbage for recycling. The road disappears, and the car goes up into space. I try to push it to a small road, but it blows far off. I see Rachel, a friend, on the ground below and throw her my garbage. Then I move the car to a tiny ledge and get out and crawl, hanging on to the rim. Eventually I climb down.

Fay begins by saying that the dream portrays her life at the time. She was doing a lot of driving up into the mountains and flying around curves while heading toward home. She also was "flying high" from a recent success, receiving praise for her work as a television writer. But she also felt overextended, "out on a ledge," and out of control of her time and energies, as well as cut off from her body and its pleasures. Her lover had recently withdrawn from their relationship; so, beneath the busyness of her days, she felt sad and alone. Finally, during this time, she had a number of painful communications with friends in which she felt a lot of anger and stuffed it into the "garbage bag."

Associating to the dream, Fay said she felt abandoned, alone, without shelter, on a rocky ledge. She's at risk of falling. Then she associated to her friend Rachel, who is tough, pushy, sexy, often out for herself, a single mother. She is at home in the world of mechanical things, well organized, computer literate, an excellent cook and baker, a patient mom. In the dream, Rachel is standing on the ground, while Fay is up in the air.

She associated to the garbage bag and remembered that poet Robert Bly describes the shadow as a long bag we drag behind us. "What's in my bag?" she asked with curiosity. "Why am I carrying it up in the sky? Why do I pass it down below to Rachel? What part of me does she represent?"

Clearly, Rachel represents a shadow figure who holds many opposite qualities. The moment in the dream in which Fay throws the bag down to Rachel is a snapshot of her process of projection. The garbage is the umbilical connection between that part of her that's flying up in the sky and that part of her that is down on the ground making use of what others throw away. Her dream ego needs the shadow figure down below so that she can continue to fly—that is, she needs a place to dump her garbage.

From her position up on the ledge, her dream ego has great freedom and a bird's-eye view. But she is stranded high and dry without the juicy contents of her garbage bag, in a precarious position, unable even to walk upright and forced to crawl. For her shadow sister, who has the view from below, the bag may not contain garbage at all. Instead, it holds grist for the alchemical process of recycling. The Rachel character has a firm standpoint with her feet on the ground, but she does not feel expansive and free.

Rachel, then, is a character at the table who contains Fay's pushy, seductive, selfish, sensation-oriented qualities. Perhaps, if Fay can make some of the Other's traits more conscious, she can come down out of the mountaintops and live a more embodied life. Perhaps, in this way, shadow-work with Rachel can help Fay to ground the *puella* character by finding it an appropriate place at the table.

With this goal in mind, her therapist asked Fay to return to the dream to "dream it onwards." Immediately, in her imagination, a rope appeared, connecting the two female images. With one woman holding each end, the rope was strong and stiff enough for the flying woman to descend. As she reached the ground, the shadow woman opened her arms, the other released the rope, and they hugged, disappearing into one another.

Male-male friendships also may involve personal or archetypal projections, which can lead to constructive or destructive qualities in the bond. Often less verbal than women, men tend to emphasize doing activities that offer them a joint focus outside of themselves. Even today, men, like heroes of old, band together to explore the wilderness, face dangers, and compete fiercely. At times, their activities offer an outlet for the rivalrous, comparative, envious feelings that underlie many male friendships.

Often when men bond, they unknowingly make room in the Third Body for this aggression, assuming it is not directed against one another. But when these shadowy feelings have no outlet between men, they may create passive-aggressive distancing, sarcastic backbiting, or direct aggression, which can damage the loving bond. And when they are actively directed against the friend, they may end in a wild roller-coaster ride or an unforgivable betrayal.

Jungian analyst John Beebe suggests that we learn to respect the primal forces of nature that are involved in male-male relationships rather than try to reduce them to personal psychology or change them into something else. Many men share a fidelity at the *puer* level, he says. But a tremendous aggressive force lies beneath their camaraderie, which can even lead to violence.

In the end, for men to befriend one another, they must face personal demons, as well as cultural taboos. They need to commit to time away from their top priorities of work and family to cultivate the friendship. They need to risk their vulnerability to distancing and rejection, which they may have felt from their fathers and which may cause them today to feel failure and isolation. And, finally, they need to cherish and honor their friends' authenticity as well as their own, to allow the experience of a soul-to-soul connection. In men's groups, men can experience the mysteries of male-male bonds and the healing power of love and recognition between same-sex friends.

In the end, for women to befriend one another, they must face a history of sister betraying sister, in the name of love of men. They need to face their own cattiness, envy, inferiority, and rage. They need to commit to time away from other priorities to cherish their friends. And they need to risk their authentic power, facing shadowy accusations of bitchiness or superiority. In women's groups, they can experience the mysteries of female-female bonds and the healing power of love and recognition between same-sex friends.

Where does your mother or father complex sabotage a friendship? ✭
What gods and goddesses are at play in your friends?

AN ARCHETYPAL PERSPECTIVE ON FRIENDSHIP

People who are strongly influenced by distinct archetypal patterns, which take over the seat of power at the table, also have distinct patterns of friendship. For instance, Zeus-style men who use the shield of power typically will not seek soul friends in either men or women. Unable to share power or exchange deep feeling, they will have a more utilitarian attitude toward people. Poseidon men also seek to dominate others but with emotional power rather than the power of position. They tend to compete with both male and female companions, making intimacy difficult. When a Hades character is present in a man, he, too, will find friendship difficult, but for another reason: his deep introversion. An Ares-style man, on the other hand, is a companion of men, especially in the armed forces or as a team member, where his natural aggressiveness is honored. And a Dionysus man is a companion of women, who tend to befriend and nurture him and to feel appreciated in return. When Apollo is strong in a man, he is capable of friendship with independent, competent women, especially those who share his passion for music and art; but with other men he tends to become competitive and needs to be a leader. Finally, when Hermes influences a man, he is friendly, spontaneous, and communicative, charming women and joining men in their activities. But Hermes also is a loner who comes and goes without commitment. And he may lie and cheat to win his heart's desire.

A woman who is highly influenced by Artemis tends to value friends over lovers, forming sisterly bonds with women that may include support groups and the collective spirit of sisterhood, and brotherly bonds with men, especially those like her twin Apollo, the androgynous god of music and prophecy. Athena, on the other hand, has few female friends; her rationality and competitive nature lead her to dismiss kinship with women and to side with patriarchal values. She is drawn to powerful, heroic men as friends and colleagues and may act as a hetaera, a counselor and confidante.

When Hera is at the head of the table, women also devalue

friendships with other women, putting their highest priority on marriage. As wives, they may disdain single women as failures or see them as threats to their own security. When Demeter is present in a woman, she values motherhood above everything else and therefore may value friendships with other mothers for emotional support. She may befriend a young, naive Persephone-style woman to continue her mothering pattern. Or she may befriend a young, sensitive man who needs the nurturing of a maternal woman. Finally, Aphrodite-style women have problematic friendships with both genders. Desired by men because of her erotic sensuality, she typically becomes a lover rather than a friend. Mistrusted by women for the same trait, she arouses jealousy, envy, and feelings of danger, especially in Hera women. She may establish bonds with women, but they will either feel subordinate to her powers or need to develop their own erotic self-confidence.

Another pattern of friendship holds the potential to heal a parent-child bond: *senex-puer/puella*—that is, older friend–younger friend. Because the *puer* lives in a world of ideals, he or she longs for special people who can make the grade and be called friend. When a bond is formed, the *puer* tends to fuse with the Other by melting boundaries, perhaps calling on Aphrodite and using sexuality as a means to connect, or calling on a spiritual Self-to-Self connection, which may not respect individual or worldly limits.

A person who is controlled by this pattern has no internalized parent or protector, so he or she may strive to fill this function on the outside, in the form of a parental-style friend or mentor, that is, a positive *senex*. Like the wise seer Merlin for the young King Arthur, the *senex* initially may act as a teacher or guide, who eventually becomes a soul friend. In the legend, Merlin assists the boy to cultivate his masculinity with the help of the sword Excalibur, thereby initiating him into his Kingship—that is, into the proper relationship of the ego to the Self. Those women and men who are fortunate enough to find this kind of wise friend today may experience their own felt-sense of completion if they do not continue to project their stability and wisdom outside of themselves.

★   What myths or archetypal images lie behind your friendships? How do they enrich the bonds? How do they interfere with them?

Women and Men as Friends: Dangers and Delights

Women and men can find soul friendship with one another, but the obstacles on the path to the treasure are many. For instance, if we carry our stereotyped baggage into these relationships, secretly hoping that men will be heroic, rational, and competent, or that women will be nurturing, emotionally available, and subordinate, then the full range of our authenticity cannot be expressed. Instead, our early iden-tification patterns of a man's man or a mother's daughter will be re-inforced, our emotional range reduced, and our shadow characters silenced.

Gender experts Aaron Kipnis and Liz Herron point out that many men cover up their vulnerability, using the shields of wealth and power to be accepted. Women, on the other hand, often cover up their authentic power and use a shield of vulnerability to be accepted. In these ways, members of both genders perpetuate archaic cultural myths of the hero and the princess, or the victimizer and the victim. And men's tender needs, depression, and helplessness remain in the shadow, while women's competence, authority, and capacity for vio-lence remain unseen as well.

Some opposite-sex friendships can compensate for missing ele-ments in primary partnerships. For instance, Doug enjoyed a lively intellectual exchange with his friend Celia, a father's daughter whom he had met in graduate school. In his marriage to an artist, Doug felt deeply satisfied, but after returning to school he wished for more intel-lectual stimulation. Clearly, the danger here is triangulation: His wife may feel inadequate or abandoned and forbid the friendship, or Celia may be unable to tolerate the limits of their bond. Any male-female friendship in which one partner is married will demand a solution to this potentially shadowy problem.

Sexuality complicates and sometimes endangers male-female friendships. If both know with certainty from the start that they do not wish for a romantic partnership with each other, their chances are bet-ter. But often one ends up vulnerable, Eros's arrows pierce the heart, and dangerous secret sexual desires may be aroused.

Allen, twenty-nine, who had been in therapy for several years to explore his relationships with women, finally spoke about his closest friend, Tanya, twenty-eight. Friends since childhood, they confided in one another and enjoyed dinners and movies together. Tanya even helped Allen select clothing and furniture for his home. When Allen dated other women, he gave Tanya "veto power," respecting her opinions and trusting her to hold his best interests at heart. At times, when he felt lonely and they were especially close, Allen imagined that one day he might invite her to become romantically involved. But he had not yet confided this forbidden fantasy to his best friend.

Allen had been dating June for several months when he told the therapist that he had not shared his growing feelings about her with Tanya. Instead, he communicated more openly with June, experimenting for the first time in a sexual relationship with the authenticity that he had reserved for friendship. He felt guilty, as if he were betraying the friendship with Tanya by withholding an increasingly important part of his life from her. Yet he did not feel the impulse to share these tender new feelings with Tanya. He was afraid that she would feel usurped; he was terrified that she would be critical. And he disclosed that he felt responsible for her feelings.

As he made this last point, Allen realized that he had turned his friend into his mother, projecting onto Tanya his mom's critical voice and then feeling responsible for pleasing her. If he shared this insight with her, he would need to take back the critical voice from his motherly friend and claim his independence from her. Perhaps then he might clarify the sexual feelings that he had avoided with his friend for so long. Or he might be able to deepen his relationship with June without feeling guilty for abandoning his friend, Tanya.

There are few models of male-female friendship in myth, as in life. But in early Greece, where male friendship was prized and women were seen as the property of their husbands, there was one exception: the hetaera, whose root, *heter*, means friendship in Egyptian. A hetaera woman was a companion to men, property of none. Unlike the wives, she was free to attend school, read the starry skies, set sail on rough seas, recite the great poets, and make the proper sacrifices to the proper gods. She often established salons to participate in the intellectual life of the men. She, alone among women, was their equal.

Toni Wolff, who served as Jung's hetaera, as well as his mistress, described this archetypal pattern in women: She stimulates a man's interests and inclinations, giving him the sense of personal value and leading him beyond his responsibilities to a deeper soul life. If she touches him too deeply, he may leave his work and sacrifice his security, or seek divorce because he feels that she understands him better than his wife.

Today, too, some women find themselves primarily to be intellectual or spiritual companions to men rather than mates. They may collaborate on projects, sparking the fires of creativity rather than the fires of desire. They may inspire men to achieve or to pursue an inner life; yet typically they are not chosen as mates themselves. Cheryl, the friend of Gabriella's discussed above, found that men sought her company and her guidance but did not desire her sexually. She suffered in part because she is a hetaera in a world that is blind to her beauty; she is a hetaera in a world that no longer knows her name.

Perhaps the naming of this pattern of friendship can help us to reimagine women and men together in novel ways. Perhaps hetaera men also can serve to inspire women in their creative lives, so that they free each other from the bondage of old patterns of inequality and together uncover the bonds of new friendship.

Do you have an opposite-sex soul friend? If not, what shadow character stops you?

★

SEXUAL SHADOWS:
TRIANGLES AND LOYALTY WARS

All too often, friendships and romantic relationships threaten the very survival of each other. After a loyalty struggle between a partner and a friend, the friendship is often sacrificed, at the cost of great pain to those involved. A wife, for instance, may feel endangered by her husband's female friend and attempt in some way to sabotage their bond. Or she may ask him for so much privacy that he cannot share his inner life with his friend, who ends up feeling disappointed and deserted.

Or two women friends may suffer conflict when one becomes romantically involved, leaving the other feeling envious and left out. Aligned in their singleness before the romance blossomed, the one who remains single suffers with abandonment, unable to feel happy for her friend, while the one who partners with a man cannot share her joy out of fear of heightening the friend's envy.

If two close friends discuss one's mate in a critical way, evaluating him harshly or devaluing her, the married friend, feeling forced to choose this alliance, may abandon the friendship at a later time. One man, who had listened at length to a female friend who told him not to marry another woman, danced with this friend at his wedding and never spoke to her again. Fifteen years later, breaking the silence, he told her, "You didn't respect my choice. You should have trusted that if I loved her, there was more going on than you could see."

Dennis and Gerald, soul friends for twenty years, also violated the Third Body in an irreparable way in another version of triangular betrayal. Dennis's lover told Gerald that she was unhappy in her relationship with Dennis and intended to split up with him. She recounted a series of emotionally abusive incidents, and in response Gerald expressed empathy, saying that he understood why she might want to end the relationship.

Later that day, Gerald told Dennis of the conversation, including the news that his lover intended to end their romance. Dennis became furious that Gerald had not defended him but had, instead, aligned with his girlfriend. "I don't want a friend who can do *that* to me, who is unable to give unconditional support." Dennis hung up the phone and refused calls from his friend. For a long time, Gerald tried by phone and mail to reconnect with Dennis, but to no avail.

During the first year of no contact with his friend, Gerald thought of him every day with grief and longing. In the second year, he thought of him perhaps once each week, with a sigh of sadness. Eventually, with bitter disappointment he gave up hope for reconciliation, although he continued to try to sort out why Dennis was so hurt and angry that he could not forgive him. Gerald knew that Dennis had witnessed his alcoholic father physically abuse his mother and that he had never forgiven him. And he knew that Dennis closely monitored the wrongs done to him as well, cataloging a litany of injuries by others that he could not forgive. So for Dennis to forgive Gerald's betrayal, he would have had to admit the latter's imperfection and risk being hurt by him again.

Internally, Dennis would have had to recognize his own cold resistance to Gerald as a harsh character at his table to be acknowledged. Instead, Dennis allowed scar tissue to grow over his wounds so that he would no longer feel the sensitivity. Then he could cut off Gerald without feeling anything at all.

In addition, Gerald admitted that secretly he had been angry at Dennis's lack of reciprocity in their friendship and had related to his friend's lover openly and honestly, even to the point of joining her in criticizing Dennis. In this way, Gerald realized that he had not honored the specialness of Dennis over his girlfriend. Because he rejected his own specialness, he sought to treat relationships equally, thereby dishonoring their special bond and losing the friendship.

In this story we see a psychological basis for the popular superstition: never step on a friend's shadow. In other words, do not tell a friend something difficult about himself; do not point out an unconscious flaw unless you are willing to risk the consequences, which may include destroying the relationship.

At times, the competition between male friends in a bid for a woman can be ritualized. When Lyle, thirty, and Max, thirty-two, two close friends, both felt attracted to the same woman at a conference, they argued about who saw her first and who had the right to pursue her. When Lyle walked her to the car and got her phone number, Max was furious. He felt that his friend had ignored his feelings. So the two men decided that they would have an open competition for this woman's attentions, allowing her to decide between them and putting their friendship before the romance. In the end, Lyle became her lover, Max became her friend, and the men's friendship deepened.

POWER SHADOWS: SUPERIORITY AND INFERIORITY

A soul friendship is a safe place in which to experiment with *authentic power*—that is, the power that issues from the voice of the Self. But if we use *inauthentic power*, which is tied to the ego, to relate to others, we end up creating power struggles and feelings of superiority and inferiority, which do not lead to safety but instead lead to competition, envy, and jealousy.

Lloyd, forty, tries mightily to take a stand with his friend Jay, forty-five, but often feels overpowered by the more articulate, aggressive lawyer. "I try to prove a point, but I don't feel heard. I feel impotent, as if nothing I say makes any difference. He points out that I'm not logical or that I don't get the facts right. Then I lose my words altogether. And I don't know if my opinions are legitimate anymore. In fact, I don't know if I have a right to my opinions at all."

In these conversations, which continued for about five years, Lloyd holds the inferior position and feels unseen and misunderstood by his friend. At dinner one evening with their wives, Lloyd began to make furtive, seductive glances at Jay's wife, who smiled in response. Instantly, Lloyd felt a heady sense of power, the ability to attract and perhaps lure his friend's wife into an affair. Shocked and disturbed by his own behavior, he told his therapist about the incident and discovered that the power shadow was at work, attempting to give him feelings of superiority in a relationship in which he felt so inferior.

Some people hold the superior position with an attitude of elitist self-righteousness, a kind of holy judgmentalness that keeps them on higher moral ground than others. As a result, when they meet someone with other viewpoints that they cannot tolerate, they simply write them off.

Roz, thirty-five, a white feminist diversity trainer for corporations, struggled with this pattern. She felt she needed friends who believed as she did in "political correctness," or she could not respect them and feel equality. When she went to a movie about African-American issues with a white male friend, she was stunned at his response to the film: "Blacks should give up their anger and forgive already. I wasn't a slave owner, so don't blame me for the problems today."

Roz was furious, and her self-righteous indignation flared. "If someone I know does not think about things appropriately, I can't tolerate it. I can point out where they are wrong, but I don't have the patience to teach them everything. I just can't be bothered. So, nine times out of ten, I cut them off. After all, I can't be friends with everyone."

Ironically, Roz is a diversity trainer who is ruling out diversity in her own life. Understandably, she is distressed when she sees evidence of archaic attitudes of racism or sexism in those she loves. But her politically correct ideal leaves no room for shadowy, "incorrect" feelings and attitudes. By narrowly defining what is acceptable, she creates a wide-ranging shadow and makes it more difficult to address issues with depth, complexity, and ambiguity.

As a result, people who don't fit her ideal become inferior, while she holds all of the superiority. With this kind of black and white polarization, she then finds a rationale for ending the friendship. If, instead of trying to change him, she saw her friend as a mirror reflection and looked at her own exaggerated response as a message from a rigid character seated at her table, Roz might see that she is intolerant of him just as he is intolerant of people of color. Put another way, the same racist character in him that eliminates others is living in her, eliminating him.

By refusing to collude with the dominant, power-driven institutions of society, but cutting off individual people, Roz is, in fact, colluding with the process of domination (or power shadow) in her personal life. Just as many African Americans have taken a stand in their own communities and refused to collude with the larger racist society by not participating, and just as many lesbians have created their own communities and refused to participate in a homophobic world, Roz has chosen to excommunicate people who differ from her. She does not work through her crises of commitments because the power-driven character who values being right more than cultivating empathic relationship rules at her table. So, in exasperation, she simply gives up on the Other and remains locked in the power complex.

The issue is not a simple one: Individual shadow-work on collective issues may be necessary, but it is not sufficient for solving large-scale social and political problems. In some cases, in fact, we may need to maintain our rage or even sustain a projection to feel motivated to act for change in the larger society. If therapy remains merely a place in which to reduce all issues to personal psychology, if therapists fail to see the political and economic contexts in which personal issues emerge, then therapy becomes a conservative force rather than a force for change at large.

How can you befriend someone whose attitudes are intolerable to you? How much dissonance can you accept? How much compassion can you include?

Money Shadows:
Shame, Class, and the Myth of Equality

Mark Twain once said, "The holy passion of Friendship is of so sweet and steady and loyal and enduring a nature that it will last through a whole lifetime, if not asked to lend money." Certainly, to borrow money is to evoke shadowy feelings of shame, dependency, and obligation. To loan money is to evoke dark feelings of superiority and entitlement. Perhaps this weight of money on friendship explains why so many friends carefully monitor the financial aspect of their relationship, sharing costs equally or trading things of equal value to balance their accounts. If the issue of money is not addressed in a conscious way, it quickly becomes a shadow issue.

Money also carries soul value among friends. Ken, a wealthy real estate developer, told his friend Mel that he would not loan money to many people, but he would loan it to him. Mel heard the Turkish in his friend's message: "Ken is telling me that he knows I am not his friend because of his money. I felt very valued by him even though I never took him up on his offer."

Money secrets abound among even the closest friends. It seems to represent that which we wish to keep private. To expose our money matters is, in some way, to expose our nakedness. Stephen said recently that he had earned a large sum of money when he sold his business, but he could not tell his best friends, who had less money. He feared evoking their envy and having to deal with his feelings of guilt and responsibility for them.

Envy among friends can bring on painful feelings of inferiority and inadequacy. Financial envy, in particular, may shroud deeper issues. Vicky grew up in a poor white section of Atlanta. She remembers sitting on the stoop of the family home and feeling disgraced by her older mother's white hair, her father's pawnshop, and, most of all, their dirty, ramshackle house. Vicky was the first in her family to graduate college; she had dreams of a professional life and a beautiful home. But the dreams have not come true.

Now fifty, Vicky has tried her hand at several careers but given up each one. She is married to Earl, a gifted artist who cannot work for health reasons. They live in a poor neighborhood, where she hears gunshots at night, in a ramshackle house that Vicky is ashamed to show her friends, all of whom are more successful and financially secure. "I feel as if I am branded for life with *poor white trash*, as if we live in an invisible caste system and I can't alter my fate."

Vicky describes sitting at a table of women friends who wore diamond rings. "Unlike me, they were blessed with high birth. I feel like I've done something wrong, so this is my destiny."

In particular, Vicky envies Denise, who appears to live a life of ease. "She has a career that pays well, so she can own a home in the hills and a new car. She has a closely knit family in town, so she feels loved and supported." But beneath Vicky's envious character lurks the judge: "She's like a princess with her nose in the air, no connection to the underclass, no struggle that's worth a fight, and, worst of all, no deeply held spiritual belief."

Denise senses the undercurrents of her friend's envy. She feels unseen in her struggles and unappreciated in her complexity, as if she were reduced to a stereotype. When she tries to speak to Vicky of her loneliness as a single woman or of her painful issues with her family, her friend cuts her off; Vicky feels no empathy because she cannot imagine that Denise truly suffers.

But Denise's judge character slings her arrows of projection, too. She sees Vicky as streetwise, tactless, loud, and hedonistic. She feels concerned for her friend's welfare but does not visit Vicky's home, distancing herself from the noise and chaos of the surroundings.

One night the demon shadow erupted and, bell ringing, the women began a round of shadow-boxing. At a potluck dinner party, Vicky arrived two hours late with the entree. She walked through the door and, distraught and panicky, looked at Denise, who shot a look of contempt right through her. In that moment, even unknowingly, Vicky's judge character wrote off her friend.

Cronos, father time, appeared to be a catalyst: Vicky, chronically late, offended Denise, who feels disrespected when she is kept waiting. But this difference in timing was only the latest in a series of offenses that caused the women to make hurtful comments and eventually break off communication. They had reached a crisis of commitment and found themselves unable to go on.

One year later, encouraged by their mutual friends, the two women spoke for the first time. Vicky had felt judged in her friend's eyes as loud, uncouth, unsophisticated, and out of control. Secretly, however, she held herself to be spiritually superior, closer to god. Denise had felt judged in her friend's eyes as spoiled, too nice, and lost to god. Secretly, she held herself to be intellectually superior. Realizing the pain they had caused one another and the gold they had uncovered in their Otherness, the friends continued to share their fantasies of each other more openly and honestly. Money, which had appeared as the original shadow issue, actually camouflaged much deeper issues of soul.

RACISM AND ADDICTION BETWEEN FRIENDS

Maria, seventeen, was the only Latina student in a white middle-class high school. Her father, a dentist, and her mother, a legal secretary, moved into the white neighborhood when Maria was three years old. When she came to therapy, she felt deeply confused about her direction, her social life, and her best friend.

"The truth is hard to admit: I wish I were white. I've been the only Latina kid at school for so long that I've come to feel more comfortable with whites. Yet, deep down, I know I don't belong. I suspect that no one really likes me; they just pretend to. They see me as brown, no matter what, no matter how hard I try to fit in. One day on the school bus all of these rowdy white boys from the football team got on at once. And no one would sit next to me. I mean, there were not enough seats for them, but they just stood up instead of sitting next to me. And I sat there, crying, in an empty seat.

"I guess I've felt this way forever—ugly, different, inferior. And I'm so ashamed at how much I stand out. I just want to fit in somewhere."

Maria suffered terribly as a carrier of the collective shadow projection of racism. Internalizing white hatred of her, she learned to hate and reject herself, wishing instead to become like them, to become one of them, to belong. Because she could not bear to stand out, she tried to conform, underachieving in her academic performance and underplaying her artistic talents to avoid the attention of others. But, at the same time, another part of her wanted to prove something to the white kids—she was not ignorant, lazy, or boy hungry. She was not a stereotype, but a real human being. And their racism was simply wrong.

242

One evening, Maria attended a party in another part of town with her best friend Sharon. They were surprised to find a racially mixed group dancing and eating together. Sharon remarked, unthinkingly, "Gee, I wish everyone were white. I'd be so much more comfortable." Then, terribly embarrassed, she turned toward her friend and said quickly, "Oh, I'm sorry, Maria. You know what I mean."

The heat rose up Maria's neck; the words escaped her. She felt shocked: Even her best friend was a closet racist. Even her best friend felt threatened by people of color. Even her best friend expected her to side with whites. In that moment, Maria felt lost, disoriented, betrayed. She knew that her longtime secret desire to be white was misplaced; she came to understand that her self-hatred stemmed from the racism of others, including her own father, who wished to socialize in an all-white world.

Maria faced a crisis of commitment in her friendship with Sharon: In uncovering her friend's racism, she had uncovered her own. In effect, she had seen in the Other that which she did not wish to see in herself. She faced a difficult outer task: to befriend her own racist shadow in her friend or let the relationship go. And she faced an even more difficult inner task: to heal her own self-hatred and deepen her authentic self-acceptance. In some ways, Maria's shadow-work is no different from each of ours; however, the added burden of collective shadow projection for people of color makes it particularly difficult.

Addiction also can test friendship by unraveling the threads of the Third Body. Some people find companions to act out a mutually acceptable path of action that is collectively rejected, such as getting high together. They then relate through their shadow characters, who sit at the head of the table on a drinking or drugging binge. But if one person becomes sober, realigning with the voice of the Self, and the shadow character recedes, the foundation of the friendship shifts. Then, the sober person may face a crisis of commitment, wishing to find other people who support the newfound sobriety.

Lenny, nineteen, faced this dilemma with his college roommate and longtime friend Jack, eighteen. The two young men had smoked marijuana together in high school and began to use cocaine in college. But Lenny recently found a passion for physics and decided to pursue academics more seriously, hoping to perform well enough to gain acceptance to graduate school. So he had become sober.

When Jack went on a cocaine binge that lasted for several weeks, Lenny imagined that he alone could help his dear friend by talking him down and motivating him to return to school, even though he had not succeeded in the past. "If I don't rescue him, he'll drown. I'm the only one who can make him sober," Lenny said.

This caretaker character had a familiar voice. Lenny's father had abandoned the family when the boy was twelve. In her desperation, his mother had turned him into a surrogate spouse, so Lenny knew well how to rescue others and take care of their needs. But he had never faced the pain of his father's desertion. Many people who felt abandoned as children cannot bear to abandon another; unconsciously, they do not want to repeat the betrayal. So Lenny feels that he *must* take care of his friend, as if Jack were a vulnerable child. If Lenny fails to do so, if he faces his own limits or walks away, he becomes his father, whom he despises.

When Jack overdoses and has to be hospitalized, Lenny's response is a surprise to himself: He shifts from sympathy to rage. "I'm furious at this guy. I don't deserve to be treated this way. I mean, he's choosing the coke over our friendship, over everything else. I hate his guts for that. Until today, I hated the drugs. They were the excuse, so I couldn't even get angry at him. But now I'm furious. I want to move out of our apartment. I feel used and cheated. And I'm fed up."

Like many people who love substance abusers, Lenny has to face the limits of his own efforts and the feeling of his own powerlessness as he watches his friend struggle with the demon cocaine. When this angry character emerged, he felt ashamed of himself at first. He felt disturbed that his response seemed so self-centered, rather than concerned for his friend. But the rage allowed him to separate from the rescuer character, who held him tightly in a familiar, family pattern. Lenny and his therapist cannot predict whether Jack will survive his addiction. But Lenny's shadow-work is clear: He needs to romance the caretaker character so that he does not give himself up, witness the angry character so that he does not give up on his friend, and learn to honor the friendship with limits and authenticity. In some form, every friendship requires that we face these difficult tasks. Most of us cannot stand in for a friend's fate; we can only stand by when he returns from the underworld.

Who is the racist character at your own table? How can you be an authentic, supportive friend yet know your own limits?

REDEFINING SUCCESSFUL FRIENDSHIP: A VEHICLE FOR SOUL WORK

Jung has pointed out that bitterness and wisdom form a pair of opposites. "Where there is bitterness, wisdom is lacking, and where wisdom is, there can be no bitterness." Tears, sorrow, and disappointment are bitter, he says. But wisdom is the comforter in suffering.

Clearly, our friends can be a source of countless disappointments and can evoke shadowy feelings of anger, envy, and betrayal. As these feelings accumulate in our hearts, disappointment can become the mother of bitterness, causing us to harden against our friends and turn them into foes. But disappointment can also become a strong incentive to clarify our perceptions of the Other and to modify our feelings accordingly. That is to say, disappointment can lead to shadow-work, which puts us on the path to wisdom and softens our hearts with compassion. As we develop the tools of shadow-work, we also enhance our capacities to deal with the issues of friendship: loyalty, abandonment, caretaking, addiction, racism, and betrayal.

Finally, friendship cannot be reduced to personal psychology alone; it cannot be explained away by psychodynamic patterns. Rather, friendship is a mystery, a constant source of wonder that is as near to us as our own breath. A soul friendship is a source of healing love, which can be given and taken as easily as a helping hand.

There is a story in the Talmud that illustrates the universal need for authentic friendship: When Rabbi Johanan fell ill, his friend Rabbi Hanina came to visit and asked him if he were capable of bearing willingly the punishment inflicted on him. Receiving a negative response, Hanina asked Johanan to give him his hand. When he did so, Johanan was healed.

Rabbi Hiya then fell ill. His friend Rabbi Johanan came to visit and asked him if he were capable of bearing willingly the punishment inflicted on him. Receiving a negative response, Johanan asked Hiya to give him his hand. When he did so, Hiya was healed.

With its conclusion, this teaching story illustrates the gift of the special soul friend: A prisoner cannot free him or herself. Each needs a friend, a loyal Other, to offer a healing hand. Paradoxically, the one who heals also is wounded; every friend is a wounded healer. And every friendship is an opportunity to heal and be healed.

CHAPTER 8

THE SHADOW AT WORK: THE SEARCH FOR SOUL ON THE JOB

Shake off this sadness, and recover your spirit;
sluggish you will never see the wheel of fate
that brushes your heel as it turns going by,
the man who wants to live is the man in whom life is abundant.
Now you are only giving food to that final pain
which is slowly winding you in the nets of death,
but to live is to work, and the only thing which lasts
is the work; start then, turn to the work.
Throw yourself like seed as you walk, and into your own field,
don't turn your face for that would be to turn it to death,
and do not let the past weigh down your motion.
Leave what's alive in the furrow, what's dead in yourself,
for life does not move in the same way as a group of clouds;
from your work you will be able one day to gather yourself.
                                            —MIGUEL DE UNAMUNO

A first job is a rite of passage that carries weighty meaning: a separation from the family, a step toward independence, a nascent hope for a creative, successful life. We carry our ideals, perhaps our naïvete, into the workplace like a new suit of clothes. We imagine that our company will be like a family to us, our colleagues like friends, our boss like a benign parent who holds our best interests at heart. We assume that our efforts will pay off; our loyalty will bring security; our ethics will be upheld; and our energies will be rewarded.

In effect, we long for meaningful work that is worthy of our efforts, that fills us with enthusiasm or *enthousiasmos*, which in Greek means to be inspired by the gods. Besides earning a living, many of us feel compelled by Ananke, goddess of necessity, to contribute to the lives of others and to create something larger than ourselves.

If we imagine our own creativity, we long for beauty, novelty, and originality. We dream of getting a day job that permits us enough leisure time to write or paint. Or we dream of leaving our day job to start an entrepreneurial venture that is wholly owned and operated by us, that will not require the compromises of working for others.

Unlike the tight fit of persona work, in which we identify with a one-dimensional role, soulful work feels spacious. Ideally, it permits us to express our authenticity rather than bury our feelings in the shadow, so that we feel energized rather than depleted. Ideally, it connects us to bodily and environmental rhythms, deepening our internal harmony rather than mechanizing our lives. It allows us to make a unique contribution, which is needed and valued by others. And it connects us to something greater, a nobler purpose or participation in a larger community, which fuels our efforts.

A story about three masons illustrates how much this larger purpose affects the inner experience of work: When a mason was asked what he was building, he answered gruffly, without raising his eyes from the work, "I'm laying bricks." The second mason, when asked the question, replied dryly, "I'm putting up a wall." But the third man, on hearing the question, stood up and said with pride, "I'm building a cathedral."

In a soul-centered organization, employees can risk some authenticity without fear of losing their jobs. They can also experiment with their creativity to some degree because they feel safe to learn on the job, take risks, make mistakes, and move on. Sometimes called learning organizations, these kinds of companies make room for experimentation and the creative spirit. They attempt to open communication rather than keep secrets. They attempt to honor diversity rather than homogenize workers. And they make an appropriate place for Cronos time, such as in manageable deadlines, rather than permitting this god to rule like a despot. In a soulful collaboration, agreements are honored, roles are fluid, conflict is handled through shadow-work, and the Third Body can be felt to contain the project.

There are many ways to fashion soulful work. People who work inside organizations may want to experiment with greater authenticity by expressing shadowy feelings more directly with colleagues and in this way breaking family patterns. Still others may strive to imbue the workplace with their personal or social values, such as empowering employees to innovate, respect racial or gender diversity, create energy-efficient programs, or donate corporate goods and services. Others may attempt to turn a creative passion into an entrepreneurial venture, like Mrs. Field's Cookies, The Body Shop, or Apple Computers, thereby aligning activities that pay the bills and nurture the soul. And still others may decide to accept the limits of a day job and separate their employment from more soulful work by practicing a craft or working in the service arena after hours. Finally, we may detect the archetypal theme of our lives in our work patterns. Armed with this knowledge, we may discover why what we do is deeply matched with who we are, or why we suffer a mismatch.

One archetypal image of soulful work is Kwan-yin, the Buddhist goddess who hears the cries of the world, the sounds of human and animal suffering, and permits herself to be shaped by them. In one of her forms she has a thousand arms, and in each hand she holds an instrument of work: a hammer, a trowel, a pen, a cooking pot. The goddess has developed the skills to become effective in response to the needs of the world.

This fantasy image of *soulful work*, like the archetypal image of the Beloved or of the special friend, compels us to seek it out, to yearn for it. For a fortunate few, it can become reality. Work can offer the pride of accomplishment and the self-respect of financially providing for oneself and others. A rewarding collaboration can bear the fruit of friendship, as well as an inventive product or service. A smooth-working team, like basketball players in the zone, can bring the exhilaration of group productivity. And a taste of creative intoxication can leave us hungering for more.

For many of us, however, the new suit of clothes, a symbol of our hopes and dreams, begins to wear thin before too long. If we are promoted, we may find that the weighty meaning attributed to a job quickly turns into weighty responsibility: We work long hours to solve problems under pressure. We are forced to cut back on loyal staff to meet budget requirements and to lower ethical standards to adjust to a commonplace business ethos: the bottom line. If we speak up against these efforts, we may step onto a roller-coaster ride that leads nowhere.

If we are not promoted, but passed over again and again, we may feel that our efforts go unrewarded. Heartsick with disappointment, we may disappear into the corporate grid and become depressed, resigned, or bitter. If we are fired, offered up as a sacrifice during downsizing or forced to retire early to bring in young blood, we discover that we are inessential and feel abandoned. And because our loyalty was unrequited, we feel betrayed.

In addition, the chances are great that we will have witnessed the power shadow emerge between collaborators as one steals credit for the other's work; or the sexual shadow erupt between employer and employee, when a demeaning innuendo goes unconfronted; or the money shadow first evoke faint grumblings among employees, then cries of mutiny. Inevitably, work, which once glowed brightly with promise, becomes tarnished. And it begins to feel Sisyphean.

The Loss of Soulful Work: The Myth of Sisyphus

In a well-known Greek myth, Sisyphus, the clever king of Corinth, in his arrogance fought with the gods. Twice he achieved the unspeakable: He outwitted death. The gods, to punish his hubris, devised a tortuous task for him in the underworld: to push a stone uphill, watch it roll down upon him, and push it up again. Sisyphus was sentenced to this task for eternity.

Many people experience their work as a Sisyphean task: a monotonous, repetitive chore, a thankless exertion that leads nowhere, a useless effort that is doomed to fail. Whether they are factory workers on an assembly line, inserting the same parts into the same devices day after day; or corporate executives sitting in endless meetings in golden handcuffs; or homemakers washing limitless piles of dishes and laundry; or students doing interminable homework that has no relevance to their lives, they feel as if they are living the Sisyphus myth, as if they embody dutiful but fruitless striving.

There is in this quality of life a sense of fate without mercy, effort without Eros. Like the devastating recurring problems of humanity on a global scale, like the painful recurring downward spirals in every intimate relationship, the work is never done. The tasks probably will not be completed; the worker will most likely go unrecognized; and the stone will inexorably roll downhill again. The stone, like the shadow, carries us down from the heights, forcing us to face limits, loss, and ordinariness. It will not permit us to outwit death, but it will teach us secrets if we can learn to listen.

Perhaps it is our thinking about work that needs to change; perhaps it is our fantasy of work that sets us up for the frustration, even damnation of a Sisyphus. Perhaps it is this, after all, that leads to a deeply felt enmity between life and work. The purpose of this chapter is to question archaic assumptions about work and to bring psychological insights into this arena. We hope to renew a sense of work's purpose, deepening its connection to soul life. We aim to lift work out of a workaholic culture and set it in the context of a larger life—and to help individuals make of their lives a work.

Archetypal psychologist James Hillman has pointed out that to understand individual psychology in the West we need to understand the ideas and images of business, because they provide the inescapable warp and woof on which our behavior patterns are woven. He writes:

> To set aside the profit motive, the desire to possess, the ideals of fair wage and economic justice, the bitterness over taxation, the fantasies of inflation and depression, the appeal of saving, to ignore the psychopathologies of dealing, collecting, consuming, selling, and working, and yet to pretend to grasp the interior life of persons in our society would be like analyzing the peasants, craftsmen, ladies, and nobles of medieval society all the while ignoring Christian theology.

Hillman's analogy is fitting: Like Christianity, business is the framework in which we live. Moreover, work itself has become a religion; it is pursued with religious fervor and filled with the idols of a faith. But tragically for many of us, work, like much of institutionalized religion, has lost its soul.

What do you passionately desire from work? When do you feel

most alive and inspired? What is the stone that you push uphill—that is, the burden that opposes and resists you at work?

The Promises of Shadow-Work: Nurturing Soul on the Job

While shadow-making begins at home and continues at school, it is highly refined at work, where the persona is required to fit tightly if we wish to achieve success. In fact, many workplaces institutionalize individual shadow-making by implicitly demanding adaptive, accommodating behaviors and discouraging authentic emotional exchange. They often outlaw the discussion of certain topics and may try to discourage dissent. They tend to encourage projection to scapegoat troublemakers, uphold denial through workaholism and alcoholism, and typically hoard power in a few hands. The result: a climate that increases shadow and decreases soul.

This is a commonplace context in which we work. And because it is so pervasive and so familiar, like the sea in which we swim, we typically remain unconscious of it. We simply assume that we cannot be ourselves at work. We believe, instead, that we should disappear and become who *they* want us to be. To that end, many of us follow orders, even when we don't believe they will yield the desired result. We protect our superiors, even when we don't believe they command respect. And we look away from ethical violations, colluding with others in a conspiracy of silence.

This widespread workplace ethos remains unconscious for another reason: We grow up in schools in which we learn to sit still, regardless of our bodily needs. We learn to submit to others without question, obeying outer authority and disobeying the inner voice of the Self. We learn to compete with peers as enemies, rather than as worthy opponents who inspire us toward excellence. And we learn to structure our days around Cronos time: one hour per topic. Rushed to achieve academically, at an early age we are encouraged to leave behind childish ways, including imaginary play and reverie, the deep sources of creativity. At a later age, we are encouraged to leave behind the arts and humanities, all too often banishing our unique talents into shadow.

With this preparation, we enter the workplace and find that, like individuals and families, each company has a persona or public face and a shadow, which may not shine so brightly: HMOs that purport to be client-centered restrict doctors' prescriptions to medications bought in bulk discounts; an alternative health care group fires women employees who become pregnant; a snack food company that promotes to the gay market secretly funds antigay groups; and a highly creative industry takes for granted seventy-hour workweeks, disregarding employees' health, emotional well-being, and family life.

At the individual level, each of us also lives this lie, a split between persona and shadow, a Faustian bargain in the arena of work: We give up individuality to fit into the collective mold. We trade off soul for money. We sacrifice creativity for security. We surrender emotional relatedness for a mantle of power. Turning a boss into a parent, we become childlike and mute to achieve safety and approval. Then we pick up our shields and come to believe that we *are* what we do, that our function is who we are. We become so identified with the character who sits at the head of the table in the workplace that we create *persona work*. As one client put it, "I can't allow my wife to visit me at work because she wouldn't recognize who I am there." In this way, we sacrifice our souls and create the very thing that we dread the most: soulless work.

In medieval society, despite primitive living conditions, work was imagined more soulfully. People joined guilds to apprentice with a master of a particular craft—painters, potters, weavers, masons. The guilds brought social order and offered individuals a valued sense of place in the scheme of things. Each craft had a patron saint, who linked the activity of the craft to the divine realm. The doing of the craft became both a source of identity and a way of life that was inherently worthy. In addition, viewed as the transformation of raw material into beauty, of the invisible into the visible, craft was thought to be work of the gods.

Today, with the swift pace of change, early retirement, and an epidemic lack of mentoring, the lineage of work is lost. In addition, when we think of a craft we imagine a hobby or a pastime activity that ends in the production of a handmade object, in contrast to a machine-made object that we produce at work. But for some guild members of earlier times, a craft was an initiatory process, a sacred means of self-discovery, a full-time activity that awakened the subject, as well as produced the object.

In a similar way, with shadow-work many activities in the workplace can become sacred or soulful. Despite widespread institutional impediments, they can become opportunities to deepen self-awareness, nurture the soul, and serve others. Certainly, the job needs to get done; at times, the job may seem tedious or fruitless. However, if we can learn to observe ourselves, discover the shadow characters that interfere with our self-esteem and effectiveness on the job, and obey the voice of the Self, eventually we can return the King to the head of the table and regain our equilibrium at work. For example, we may meet a shadow character that is pushy and self-promoting, or greedy and ambitious, which sabotages team spirit with others. Or we may uncover a character that is secretly lazy and indolent, which unconsciously opposes a more conscious desire to get ahead. As we romance this shadow character, we can discover its deeper need—the gold in the dark side. As a result, its influence recedes and we become more self-directive.

As we are challenged to learn new tasks and face frightening feelings of incompetence on the job, we also meet the shadow, and we may secretly feel like a fraud, as if we are faking it. Or we may secretly feel blamed, as if we are the company scapegoat. With shadow-work, the characters of the fraud and the scapegoat can slowly become more conscious. As we romance them, they have less hold over us; then we have more choices to respond differently.

In addition, when we learn to identify our emotional reactions on the job as projections from the past—"I can't *stand* that ambitious coworker, that power-hungry boss, or that demure, helpless assistant"—we can defuse negative feelings, reduce blame, slow down roller-coaster rides, and thereby decrease overall tensions in the workplace. In this way, each of us can become a more empathic, healing presence at work.

As shadow-work continues, inner freedom can grow. As a result of reconnecting with that part of us that has the capacity for soulful work, our dependency on employers and organizations may lessen. Eventually, soulful work can become, like the breath, a mast to which we are tied. As jobs come and go and relationships ebb and flow, our work can be a familiar place for productivity, contemplation, pleasure.

With shadow-work, then, we can use the job to enhance our self-knowledge, instead of permitting it to use us and eventually deplete us. Like the Roman god Janus, whose two-faced image adorned ancient homes, we can look in two directions at once: inside at the process of working and outside at the product of work. In this way, we can make of ourselves a work.

What shadow character sabotages your efforts on the job? What is being sacrificed by your Faustian bargain at work? How can you nurture your soul to make up for this sacrifice?

A PORTRAIT OF THE NEW EMPLOYEE: A SUFI TALE

Today, besides the widespread loss of soulful work, many people face the devastating loss of employment of any kind. Like the world of relationships, the world of work is undergoing tectonic shifts as job security becomes an illusion and rising unemployment becomes a global trend. As companies continue to downsize, dismembering an organization by cutting off thousands of employees, people feel bereft and betrayed. Their Faustian bargain—we became trained professionals who work hard for the company in exchange for job security—no longer holds. The new contract: The job is only as good as the next paycheck.

In the inner cities of the United States, the scenario is painted in darker colors: Chronic joblessness has stripped many potential workers of individual initiative, creating an unskilled underclass. Coupled with poor education, racism, and isolation, chronic unemployment has broken the bonds that reinforce community.

This widespread contraction—the dark side of work—also has a light side: an expansion of opportunity in other sectors. Despite the extinction of millions of jobs, there has been a net increase of 27 million jobs in the United States since 1979. Although sophisticated technology is replacing people in every sector, it also frees us from the drudgery of routine work and connects us instantaneously, via the Internet, to the global marketplace. With these systemic changes, a portrait of the new employee is emerging: resilient, self-promoting, technologically literate, capable of handling complexity and tolerating ambiguity. He or she is a lifelong learner who is willing to make lateral moves, acquire new skills, and, most important, assume responsibility for his or her own security. For those with the temperament, education, and know-how, more inventive entrepreneurial projects are available than ever before.

Together, these paradoxical trends—economic turbulence, ethical crises, and expanding opportunity—signal widespread upheaval in the world of work. Of course, the dark side of work taints the rest of life as well: If we have fewer chances to use our capacities, we will feel less acknowledged, more pressured to perform, and more endangered. If our sense of identity remains hooked to a particular job, if our self-worth is synonymous with our net worth, then our self-esteem plummets even as we work longer and longer hours. And we come home depleted, spreading a pessimistic mood to our families or repressing it into shadow with drugs, alcohol, food, or television. Typically, we blame ourselves, rather than cultural institutions and assumptions, for not being able to change our lives. As a consequence, our relationships suffer, becoming tense with resentment or deadened of feeling, which contributes to the other epidemic breakdown of marriage and family.

Just as we proposed reimagining the experience of dating, the search for the Beloved, as a mirror of the search for the authentic Self, so we can reimagine the search for soul on the job as an inner process. On the outside, it may look like the pursuit of the ideal job, the best salary, or the most creative opportunity. But beneath the boundaries of awareness, another process is taking place, as described in an ancient Sufi tale called "Fatima, the Spinner, and the Tent."

As a young girl, Fatima, daughter of a spinner, traveled with her father to sell his goods. When a storm shipwrecked the boat and left her father dead, Fatima, half-conscious, could barely recall her former life. Wandering on the sands, she was found by a family of cloth-makers, who taught her their craft. Later, she was on the seashore when a band of slave-traders landed and took her captive. Traveling to Istanbul, they sold her as a slave, and her world collapsed again.

A man who made masts for ships bought Fatima, and she worked with him and his wife in the wood yard. She worked so hard that he granted her freedom, and she became his trusted helper in her third career. When she took a cargo of ship masts to sell overseas in China, a typhoon again cast her upon a foreign shore. Weeping bitterly, she despaired of her unfortunate fate.

But there was a legend in China that a woman stranger would arrive who would be able to make a tent for the emperor. To be certain that this stranger would not be missed, the emperor sent heralds to the villages in search of foreign women. When she was brought before the emperor and asked whether she could make a tent, she agreed to try. She asked for a rope, but there was none. So she collected flax and spun it into rope. When she asked for cloth, the right kind did not exist. So she wove some strong fabric. When she asked for tent poles, there were none. So she fashioned them out of wood. When these elements were ready, she made a tent like those that she had seen in her travels. And the emperor, in his gratitude, offered her the fulfillment of any wish. She chose to settle in China, marry, and raise many children.

Like Fatima, many of us will be shipwrecked at least once in our lives. We may suffer severe losses in the world of work, forcing us to face our limitations and the greed and insensitivity of others. Like Fatima, we may appear to be victims, forced by circumstance to move from one corporation to the next or to create several careers. If we become dependent on organizations—if we allow the character of the company man or woman of past generations to sit at the head of the table—in the current climate we set ourselves up for betrayal. This character, a friend in the past, today has become an enemy.

Instead, with resilience, self-confidence, trust, and the tools of shadow-work, our lives, like Fatima's, may not be what they appear to be: For her, each unpleasant twist of fate turned out to be an essential part of her apprenticeship. Like her, we may weave together the fibers of a patchwork life that does not resemble those single, linear career tracks of past generations. Finally, like Fatima, whose name contains "fate" (*fati*), we may be surprised by the colorful fabric that is the outcome.

Where is your sense of security rooted? What shadow character stops you from seeing a challenge as an opportunity?

In the next few sections, we will describe how to use shadow-work to overcome the self-destructive habit of workaholism and to defuse negative projections between colleagues and collaborators.

Meeting the Shadow of Workaholism: Overcoming the Inner Tyrant

In some sectors of Western society, we have come to believe that work *is* life; we live to work rather than work to live. We have come to assume that all of our waking hours should be consumed with getting a job done, earning a living, or trying to attain security for the future. Therefore, the time for soul shrinks drastically and Cronos, father time, becomes a slave driver as nine-to-five jobs stretch into eight-to-six or even eight-to-eight jobs. The weekends disappear as we catch up on reading, writing, or filing for work. And deadlines loom overhead, like an ever-present guillotine about to drop.

We define this kind of workaholism as a behavior pattern that is out of relationship with soul and soul time. Instead of feeling in tune with the natural cycles of the body and the seasons, instead of experiencing periods of no-time in a creative flow state, we feel constantly that we are running out of time; it is a scarce commodity that is counted in nanoseconds. As a result, we push harder, using caffeine to stem the tides of our bodies' rhythms or, worse, cocaine. We fight against the organic cycles of rest and the natural urge toward reverie. Ultimately, we lose touch with our bodies, which grind on at work like soulless machines.

Some workaholic people develop strange symptoms: chronic fatigue, insomnia, impotence, headaches, depression, and multiple addictions. In Japan, where some companies installed beehivelike sleeping quarters so that workers did not need to go home, the government coined a term: *karoshi* refers to the results of work practices that disrupt people's life rhythms and lead to a buildup of fatigue, potentially resulting in fatal disease or suicide.

For some, workaholism is an attempt to ward off the anxiety that would arise if we faced our inner emptiness or feelings of depression. But instead of going through the anxiety into the underworld depths, we just go back to work. Like alcohol and drug addiction, which camouflage the soul's needs by covering them over with a chemical high, workaholism adds mortar to the fortress of denial; its single-minded, myopic devotion to doing an efficient job closes our eyes to what we are actually doing.

To begin to address individual workaholism as a shadow issue, we need to uncover the character at the head of the table who turns the workplace into a battlefield of enemies to be conquered. The Greek hero Hercules, revered for his strength and self-confidence, may stand behind some workaholics, urging them on to overcome opposing forces in exploit after exploit.

Others who are less heroic but equally driven may need to uncover the god behind a perfectionistic demand for efficiency or an insatiable hunger to consume material goods. When we can break our identification with this father figure or *senex*-like character who orders all work and no play, when we can separate our function at work from our larger identity as a person, we can begin to gain more internal freedom at work and, eventually, make more self-affirming decisions, as our client Pam did.

Pam, thirty-eight, had been a chief financial officer in the garment industry in New York City for many years. When she first came to therapy, she worked sixty hours each week, came home late to an empty apartment, and felt dried out and hopeless about her life. But because in her company everyone worked compulsively, the workaholic character at the head of her table felt at home there and did not understand why she suffered.

Pam had tried on several occasions to take time off, but she had not felt replenished. Instead, she returned each time to her industry because, she reported, she could not turn down the money. She would begin to panic about the future and return to the treadmill again, offering up all of her life energy in a Faustian exchange for a feeling of security. Pam's repetitive work pattern resembled an eating disorder: bingeing or fasting. She shifted between the *senex*, who demanded all work, and the *puella*, who demanded no work. Yet neither side of the equation offered her a sense of soul satisfaction or a balanced life. And Pam began to realize that she was betraying herself; her workaholic pattern had become poisonous, and she felt that a part of her was dying.

During this time Pam had the following dream: *My grandmother has lost track of a dear friend and asks me to find her. I find this strong, wise, creative old woman in a hospital. A polished, sinister, corporate-looking man tries to give me an intravenous injection, but I know that it's poisonous.*

From this dream, Pam came to realize that her creativity was sick and dying and that the corporate mentality at work had become poison to her.

Doing shadow-work, Pam discovered the *senex* tyrant, the character at the table who was driving her to do nothing but work. She found a taskmaster with her mother's voice. "She told us to be dutiful, no time to have fun. She made throwing a party seem like a chore. And when this robot would take her over, I couldn't stand being around her—I was afraid it would suck dry my life juices, too."

This tyrannical figure, which had consumed Pam's mother, was now consuming her. But she had begun to wake up, and the self-critical inner voices, which she had been able to silence earlier, were growing louder. And they held a vital message: Pam faced a crisis of commitment at work, a conflict between the call of the Self and her ego's need for safety and security. She had tried to honor the voice with short-term solutions, such as vacations. But they did not relieve the internal conflict, and her feelings of depression, resentment, and anxiety grew worse. Eventually, they became intolerable and led her into therapy.

The therapist suggested that she needed to find a way to honor the Self's demands consciously or she would continue to be unconsciously controlled by her symptoms of burnout. Pam began by shutting off the television at night and using the extra time to explore her creativity, which might result in discovering a fresh new life direction. Like many others, she found Julia Cameron's best-selling book *The Artist's Way* to have a tremendous impact. After several months of writing daily "morning pages," she uncovered a deep desire to return to school to get a teaching degree.

Pam took a part-time position at her firm in order to maintain an income without perpetuating her workaholism. In this way, she stopped swinging between the two extremes of overwork and no work. But within a few weeks she came up against a deep resistance: She felt paralyzed, unable to choose between two graduate school programs. Because of her procrastination, she missed the registration deadlines. Her heart sank with the self-sabotage and the missed opportunity.

Continuing to do shadow-work, Pam identified the voice of resistance—the saboteur—that stopped her from taking the necessary step to change her life. At a conscious level, it told her, "Graduate school is a long haul with no financial compensation. Even after I'm a teacher, it's a poor-paying profession. And where will I find a job?" At an unconscious level, Pam felt unworthy of taking her own desires seriously and fearful of giving up her dependency on the job to begin a more self-directed life.

She felt trapped: She could either challenge the voice of resistance by using her newfound impulse and direction as a catalyst for action, or she could succumb to the resistance, allowing the saboteur to take over and suffering the consequences of disappointment and depression. When she found a school that would permit her to enroll in six months, she signed up. And she reported that, although she would earn less money, the idea of working part-time for six months without school actually made her very excited; she planned to read, write, and explore her feelings about her next career.

Who is the shadow character that drives your productivity or fuels your perfectionism? What are the cues that this character has taken over the kingdom? What is the deeper need of this character that you have been unwilling to address?

MEETING THE OTHER IN A COMPANY HIERARCHY: HEALING FAMILY PATTERNS

Just as we unconsciously identify with our parents' style of intimacy, re-creating their relationship dynamics in our own, we also identify with their styles of work. If we enter a family business or join a parent's profession, we unknowingly may be living out a parent's life and risk remaining trapped in family persona, rather than doing the hard work of carving out our own fate. On the other hand, if we reject a parent's life wholesale, we unknowingly may be living out their unlived life and risk remaining trapped in family shadow. Frequently, two siblings adopt these opposite strategies: one conforms and one rebels. Either way, the legacy of family sins can be detected in our patterns of work. As a result, we have an opportunity, with shadow-work, to uncover unconscious family patterns and resolve them on the job.

Many people unconsciously project their family patterns onto their company or working group. If we project a positive experience, we may expect the group to be stable and supportive, open to communications, and able to solve conflict. When it fails us by silencing dissent or heartlessly firing a colleague, we feel betrayed. If we project family shadow issues onto the group, we may assume that there is no space for soul: Like a child, we feel that we need to behave properly, obey authority, avoid conflict, and banish our feelings into the dark.

If as an employee we project a mother or father complex, turning a boss into a parent, we may feel shamed, devalued, trapped, enraged, or terrified of being rejected. If as a boss we turn an employee into a child, we may feel overly responsible, judgmental, guilty, or rigid. If we project sibling rivalry, we may feel envious or competitive, creating an adversarial atmosphere or triangulating with one person to scapegoat another. In every case, we are blinded by projection, unable to see the Other for who she is or to act like adult individuals with a voice. This situation is a setup for shadow-boxing. However, if we can become aware of re-creating early family patterns at work and learn to witness our projection, we can return the King to the seat of power and make decisions about our work lives as adults with some knowledge of their consequences.

Terence, thirty-four, was a rising star in the men's retail shoe business in New York City who felt that he was being treated without respect by his superiors. Initially hired as a salesman, he worked his way up the ladder to become a designer for a successful chain of stores. For the first few years, Terence followed orders and was eager to please. Then, as he increasingly recognized his own abilities, he began to feel more entitled to acknowledgment from above and support from his team. But he failed to express these needs.

Terence disclosed that a year earlier a superior at the firm had stolen one of his designs and placed it in another line of shoes, thereby garnering the credit for himself. Terence had not complained because he did not want to feel petty or be seen as overly ambitious. Recently, the president offered him a year-end renegotiated contract, which included a lateral move in the organization and a small increase in income. He felt helpless to express his needs and heard a message in Turkish from his boss: You are not worthy of more. And again, he did not complain but chose to play it safe.

However, Terence soon began to feel depressed and resistant to going to work in the morning. "I dread waking up now. I'm working in my sleep, trying to solve problems instead of resting. So I wake up exhausted and just push my body through space to get ready in the morning. Then, I resent having to arrive at the office on time, to be in position like a soldier. I feel dead, lifeless. And I watch the clock. Time seems to pass so slowly. It used to fly by. Then I go home feeling empty and get up the next day to start over again."

When asked what he would like to say to the president, his body filled out and his eyes brightened. "I want to say that I'm busting my butt here, and I'm not satisfied with this nickel-and-dime response. I love my job, work hard, and want my efforts acknowledged. I would rather lie in the sun and surf than work a seventy-hour week next year at this salary."

In effect, Terence feels that the company treated him like an employee with a day job, whereas he feels as if he gave his soul to his work. As this contradiction became conscious, he began to feel more and more internal pressure. Terence faced a crisis of commitment: The authentic demands of the Self to be seen and rewarded stood in conflict with his ego's needs for job security.

Terence was unable to speak up to his boss because of a psychological law: Under stress, we regress—that is, we return to our early patterns of coping. Terence imagined that his boss, like his alcoholic dad, would lose control of his anger, intimidating and belittling him. In fact, he is treated like a child because he has been unwilling to take his place at the table as an adult. Several months later, increasingly uncomfortable, Terence decided that he had no choice: He risked his boss's rage and spoke to him about his feelings of resentment. Although he did not receive as much of a raise as he sought, he felt as if he had broken through a wall: He gained more autonomy, self-respect, and ultimately more creative freedom with his designs at work. In effect, he found the gold in his shadow: an ability to speak in his own voice and be heard without the fear of retribution.

Another example of projections coloring relationships at work: Chuck, forty-eight, head of the Chicago division of a nationwide manufacturing firm, supervised Bruce, twenty-seven, who had been hired the year before. Chuck disclosed, "Bruce is hot-tempered and demands attention by pestering me. If I don't give it, he becomes hurt and aloof. He has no regard for the rules and won't take responsibility for his mistakes. He just makes excuses. And he uses marijuana and alcohol but won't admit that he has a problem."

When asked what he would like to say to Bruce, Chuck responds quickly, "I want to take him off the premises and go man-to-man with him. I want to say, 'You have a drug problem. You're not being straight with me.' But I can't do that at work."

Chuck identifies with his function as Bruce's boss, so he believes that Bruce is behaving in this way to get at him; he takes the situation personally. He loses the perspective of the organization hierarchy and wants to go outside of it to leave his role behind because he sees no way to go inside of his role as boss and speak to his employee with soul. He cannot imagine, for instance, telling the younger man that he cares about him and sees himself in him. Instead, he gets caught in a shadow projection.

"To be Bruce's supervisor, I have to become the very thing I rebel against—the boss. I have to become an authoritarian, perfectionistic father. And I *hate* that because my dad really abused me with his power."

During the next week, Chuck's supervisor made a decision about his turf without consulting him. Chuck felt left out and took it personally. Like the powerless, abandoned child he was once, he felt alone with a door shut in his face. When he began to complain to others, forming alliances and fomenting dissent inside the company, he thought of Bruce. "You know, I was doing the same thing he does. I felt powerless, but instead of taking it on directly, I bitched and moaned about it. I mean, I did with my boss exactly what he did with me."

In that moment, Chuck felt empathy for his employee. He realized that the rebel character in Bruce is also a character at his own table, which gets overshadowed when he is the boss but erupts when he is the subordinate. In fact, even when Chuck's boss solicits his opinions, he feels that he cannot risk showing his anger or feeling his power in front of him. So he sets himself up as powerless, then rebels so that he can take power in indirect ways. He concludes: "I guess I avoid being authentic with Bruce *and* with my boss to avoid feeling my real power, even though I'm getting a green light to be more real."

To break this shadow-boxing pattern of avoiding authenticity and maintaining distance as an outsider, Chuck learned to romance the shadow characters of the rebel and the boss, allowing each to find its appropriate place at the table. As he identified the rebel as the one who emerges when he feels reactive, angry, and left out, he began to witness it and to choose more direct ways of expressing himself, instead of defaulting to indirect subterfuge. In this way, he broke his childhood pattern of powerlessness. As he identified the boss as the one who emerges when he becomes critical, superior, and rigid, withholding his approval from Bruce, he also began to witness it and to choose more caring, related ways of managing, instead of projecting and blaming. In this way, during the course of several years, he broke his father's pattern of power and learned how to use authority in a soulful way.

Finally, if we can uncover a shadow character at work that is at the root of a mother or father complex, we may discover it at play elsewhere in our lives. In this way, shadow-work at work opens a window onto life at large. For instance, one female client, who worked for ten years in a mentor relationship with an older man, reported that their collaboration was primarily friendly and supportive. However, despite her long hours and meticulous efforts, he always expressed dissatisfaction at the completion of projects. In Turkish, the woman heard that *she* was not good enough. "At some level, I continued to work for his approval—and continued to feel that I was never enough."

On saying these words, she looked up, startled. "Oh, my god. That's how I feel in my marriage. No matter how much I nurture and support my husband, it feels like it's never enough. Not enough time, not enough talk, not enough sex. And, of course, that's how I felt with my dad. I could never be good enough." So, as a result of romancing the shadow in her professional relationship, she discovered that her father complex colored her personal relationship as well. As she began to sort out the disapproving ghostly tyrant who kept her seeking approval through overworking and overgiving, she slowly found her own limits at work and at home. Eventually, her own self-acceptance deepened as well, leading her to find gold in her dark side.

What is it that you cannot *stand* in a colleague? What messages do you hear in Turkish? When did you feel this way earlier in your life? In what ways are you like this person?

Meeting the Other in a Collaboration: Taking Projections Home

Building a team of two can be as treacherous and as gratifying as building an intimate relationship. Collaborations can evoke family shadow issues, trigger projections, escalate into a confusion of French and Turkish, and end in devastating roller-coaster rides. Finally, their termination can be as excruciating as divorce. With shadow-work, a collaboration, like a soul friendship, can act like a mirror that reflects us back to ourselves, deepening our self-knowledge and enabling us to work through conflicts and disagreements so that we can remain allies.

Some collaborations begin with a romantic feeling: the two partners enter the eggshell, blind to the potential for discord. They make an agreement, blind to the Faustian bargain of each. Then, before too long, one partner begins to feel impatient: perhaps their timing to achieve their creative goals is not in harmony. Another feels disappointed: perhaps her contribution is not appreciated. Another feels resentful: perhaps their agreed-upon division of labor does not reflect the reality of the tasks. Yet another feels regret: perhaps he realizes that in the initial negotiation he gave up his power to avoid a power struggle.

Angry and anxious, the dissatisfied partner may begin to turn the collaborator into the Other, the cause of the shadowy feelings that are arising. Our client Sid, a successful entrepreneur, described this dilemma: A neighbor, Peggy, had patented a new invention with market potential but, as a teacher, she had no business expertise. So they formed a partnership: a fifty-fifty deal for both responsibility and compensation.

Six months later, however, Sid had spent full-time on the project, creating marketing materials and a strategic plan, while Peggy had basically pursued her teaching and family life. Sid's frustration built into resentment, which now bordered on rage. And these feelings began to halt the progress of the project because he avoided meetings with Peggy in an effort to escape his own anger, which for many years had been buried in shadow.

As Sid returned to the project each day, carrying its full weight on his shoulders like Atlas carrying the heavens, he began to imagine its success as his own. He began to make decisions single-handedly and to see Peggy as incompetent and inferior. When she was late with completing a task, he felt confirmed. When she blundered, he puffed up with pride. Eventually, Sid told Peggy that he wished to renegotiate their contract; he could not tolerate sharing half the profits when he was doing almost all of the work.

When Peggy refused to renegotiate, Sid felt paralyzed. He had invested nearly a year in the project and did not want to give it up; however, he felt cheated by the original agreement and did not want to go on. In our language, it was unclear to Sid whether he faced a crisis of commitment in which an authentic need of the Self went unseen in the collaboration, or whether his power shadow had erupted. He came to therapy to try to understand how to handle this dilemma.

Doing shadow-work, Sid sorted out the voice of his father as a character at the table, which criticized him relentlessly about his incompetence. He began to see that his drivenness stemmed in part from a child's need to win approval from his father, but his father was long since dead. In addition, he had projected these feelings of inferiority, internalized from his father's voice, onto Peggy: His shadowy fears of inadequacy and failure were attributed to her, freeing him to feel superior and therefore worthy of more money and credit. But at the same time, this unconscious pattern left him feeling resentful and alone, as if the collaborators were not on the same team.

During Sid's childhood, his father had perpetrated this pattern with his mother as well, forcing her to feel inferior by projecting his own anxieties. Weary of criticism and devaluing, Sid's mother had withdrawn years ago into alcohol and depression, becoming unable to defend her young son against his father's verbal onslaught. Carrying on this family sin today in the collaboration, Sid had become his father and turned Peggy into his mother.

But Peggy did not engage the pattern: As the inventor of their product, she insisted on respect for her contribution and on equal financial return. As a solution to the money issue, she proposed escalating payments to Sid after a particular income level had been reached in the future.

Sid decided to continue to invest in the project part-time, pursuing other work as well. In that way, he felt less obligated and less resentful toward Peggy, so that his insidious power shadow retreated. But he also came to see the profound difficulty of honoring agreements that end up feeling deeply unfair to him. He had entered into this agreement too quickly and too blindly and would not do so again.

An Archetypal Perspective on Work

Just as each god and goddess has a particular style of falling in love, expressing sexuality, or becoming a friend, each also has a unique way of working, which reflects differing attitudes toward change, motivation, and power. In our culture, the Greek Titan Prometheus first comes to mind because he signifies progress, the rational and technological mastery of nature, the reduction of culture to commodity. It is he who stands behind our bottom-line ethos, pressing for more growth and expansion. It is he who spurs us on to overcome obstacles, make quick decisions, cope with greater responsibility, and win the prize. Yet it is also Prometheus who risked everything to steal fire from the gods for human beings, thereby permitting us to craft things and making us who we are. As his punishment, he was nailed to a mountaintop, suspended between earth and sky in a Christ-like crucifixion. He is, then, a totem at the *axes mundi*, the center of the world, giving us our horizontal orientation to the world and our vertical orientation to the gods or Self.

Hermes appears as the god of commerce or trade. The messenger between the worlds, he can make connections where none other can; he can enhance the bartering or exchange of goods or the flow of information. So we might imagine him as the figure behind the information age, the archetypal image of the Internet. When the conscious ruling character in a businessperson is highly rigid or despotic, there is no possibility of exchange; Hermes has been banished. In addition, as guide between the conscious and unconscious realms, Hermes is alive in the psychotherapist at work. But he also has his shadows: He is tricky, a liar, and a thief. So he may be active in a businessperson whose ethics become questionable, who cuts corners just a little, or in a salesman who lies just a little to close a deal.

When the figure of Zeus is present in a businessperson, the man or woman is a natural executive who can hold the corporate vision, discipline employees, and make difficult decisions with authority. The ambition to amass power and money leads this person directly to the top of the pyramid. However, he or she may struggle with power shadows, becoming a tyrant who is emotionally isolated from others if Zeus does not move aside from time to time to allow other characters at the table a voice.

An Apollo-style man, the archetypal son, may adapt well as an organizational man, because his gifts of rationality, clarity, and strategic thinking are prized in most companies that view success as the achievement of goals. But typically he lacks the sheer will to power that is required to climb the ladder in some organizations. Too much Apollo in a man may mean that he needs law and order to the extreme, or that he sacrifices all feeling for his goal of objectivity. This character in the workplace may constellate its opposite, Dionysus, whose dark side appears in alcoholism, perhaps because of Apollo's denial of irrational states, or in an eruption of religious feeling, which leads him away from the routine of work. However, as the workplace has opened to more nontraditional ideas from science and psychology, the light side of Dionysus has found a place at work: playful creativity, intuitive decision-making, lateral thinking, and a more experimental corporate culture that honors individual talents all make room for the gifts of Dionysus.

Hephaestus has been called the god of the hard-hats, under whose banner the workers of the world unite. In myth, he is the only god who actually works, the smith at the forge whose subterranean fires draw their energy from the creativity of nature itself. In one tale, Hephaestus shapes Pandora, the first woman, who is so lifelike that art is confused with nature. Through Hephaestus, then, creativity is born: His art mimics the creative powers of nature. He is the god of *techne*, or craft, and with fire he builds the foundation of civilization. A man who is controlled by this pattern probably will not fit within a conventional company; instead, he will work as an outsider, an artist perhaps. As a mother's son, he may feel more comfortable working among women; as an introvert, he may prefer to work alone. But this man is not weak: He seeks revenge on those who betray him. And he works his craft with skill and diligence so that the drudgery of routine becomes an opportunity for worthy work.

A woman who is controlled by Hera believes that her marriage *is* her career. No matter how successful she may be in other arenas, if she does not marry, she feels like a failure. On the other hand, when

Demeter, the archetypal mother, is a ruling presence, a woman will find a way to nurture others on the job, perhaps as a doctor, nurse, therapist, or social worker. If she is not a mother of children, she may compensate by unconscious mothering in her professional relationships and risk setting up a limited pattern of relating, which keeps others in a childlike position. But if Demeter is given her proper place at the table in conjunction with other goddesses, she can bring a deep fulfillment to both people involved.

An Athena-style woman, the archetypal father's daughter, is typically ambitious, competitive, and productive. She may stride into meetings with a display of self-confidence and a sense of correctness that communicates no vulnerability to others. She can act responsibly, think strategically, thrive on deadlines, and articulate ideas to others. With these skills, she may succeed in professions that have been male-dominated in the past. However, Athena's patriarchal ego, which keeps her aligned with men, may create problems with women at work: She disdains traditional feminine values, shows little empathy for low achievers, and can become "all business" when cut off from her own feelings.

When Artemis sits at the head of the table in a woman, she will be idealistic, an advocate of a social cause or personal vision that overrides a concern with success or income. She may find it difficult to work within a conventional structure, but she can team up with her "sisters" or with male colleagues to implement a vision.

When the figure of Aphrodite is in control, a woman will want to "follow her bliss," as Joseph Campbell put it. She will seek out an emotional and an aesthetic engagement with any task. But she may have trouble working with other women, who distrust her seductiveness, or with men who are vulnerable to passions.

Finally, a hetaera-style woman and a heroic-style man may find the rewards of a successful collaboration. As platonic companions, they can stimulate each other's interests, inspire mutual creativity, and lead the way toward more soulful work.

The *puer-puella* has unique shadow issues in the world of work. For many people who are highly influenced by this pattern, the limitations of time, structure, and commitment are too difficult to accommodate. If a man has been overmothered, he may feel entitled to be supported and end up financially dependent on a partner or even on welfare. If a woman has been overfathered, spoiled and raised to feel special, she may expect to be treated like a princess. One woman who was possessed by the *puella* believed that because of her special intellectual gifts she should be paid to stay at home and think about social issues. Others maintain a future orientation, dreaming of creative possibilities or world travel; or they might imagine get-rich-quick schemes, such as multilevel marketing projects. And still others envision flying high with international fame and fortune when the world discovers their unique invention or novel idea.

In addition, if an individual who is controlled by this pattern joins a spiritual community or practices a traditional spiritual discipline with some rigor, she may one day reject material values, including money. As one Buddhist woman said, "It's all illusion anyway. If I believe that I need a lot of money, then I'll have to go to work. Then I'll become dependent on a paycheck and I won't feel spiritual, free, and unattached. So I would rather not set the wheel going at all."

In every case, an ordinary work life is disdained. The mundane, persistent efforts that are required to take action on one's own behalf, to create and market a product, or to maintain a job with periods of tedium are anathema to those who are highly influenced by this archetype. To overcome this pattern, to find an appropriate place at the table for the *puer* where it does not sabotage either employment or soulful work, we need to face the *senex*, whose ethic is all work, the other side of the *puer*'s no-work ethic. When we can romance these characters in the domain of work, we can free ourselves of deep-seated family patterns and cultural attitudes and design a unique life in which both work and play have an honored place.

POWER SHADOWS:
DENYING POWER, ABUSING POWER

As money is the currency in the marketplace, power is the currency in the workplace. And it is parceled out not only in salaries but in stock options, benefits, and square footage. Some workers, like drone bees, feel as if they have none; others rule over a small turf; still others have a bit more, although they still feel powerless in relation to their superiors. And those near the top push for access, as if power by association is the prize. Finally, those few who have the power of definition and the power of the purse in a corporate culture are believed by others to be almighty powerful.

Of course, power itself is not evil; it is power used as a shield that generates shadow issues at work. Power may be actively expressed in intimidating threats, critical comments, treating others with disrespect, and the persistent need to be right. Or it may be passively expressed in shaming, innuendo, or withholding behaviors that others understand in Turkish as power trips. Either way, it leads to feelings of superiority and inferiority, creating a perpetrator and a victim.

James Hillman points out that subordination of any sort arouses a power complex, which raises the ego above other influences. He asks: How can we exercise power without dominating? His answer: We do this by making conscious the many forms of power and their subtle nuances—control, prestige, ambition, influence, resistance, leadership, authority, charisma, tyranny.

When any kind of power remains hidden in the shadow, we feel small, helpless, dependent, and even defeated in the workplace. When we become reactive, expressing anger inappropriately or fomenting dissent among others, a rebellious character may have stolen the seat of power. When we complain and blame others for our circumstances, remaining ineffectual and expecting to be rescued, a victim character may have taken over the kingdom, as our client Olivia discovered.

A Latina attorney, Olivia, thirty, worked long hours in a criminal law firm. But when a male attorney began aggressively to encroach on her territory and to jockey for contracts, she could not compete. Instead, a passive victim character took over, telling her not to make a scene. She withdrew, disengaged, and began to feel less invested at work. When a friendly colleague suggested that she needed to assert herself, she responded, "I've felt this struggle forever. I don't want to become like one of *them*—pushy, mean, ruthless men."

Because the many kinds of power remained undifferentiated and unconscious for her, Olivia made no distinction between assertiveness and aggression. She could not risk becoming angry because she believed that it would lead to rage and destroy her career. So she held herself in check, avoiding confrontations with others, as well as with her own shadowy feelings. By projecting her aggression, she hid her self-doubt and feelings of inferiority beneath a passive, invisible persona, which she had learned from her mother. But secretly Olivia began to feel like a failure and to turn in legal briefs late for the first time. In this way, she acted out passive-aggressively rather than dealing directly with the issues. "I guess I can't be assertive and still be attractive as a minority woman," she confessed sadly.

Olivia had felt like an outsider for as long as she could remember. At her Ivy League college, she felt excluded from the privileges of the white students but did not want them to see her envy, only her contempt. So she remained isolated, worked harder, and told herself that to succeed as a Latina she needed to be the best.

As a result of continuing to silence her own voice, Olivia felt increasingly depressed and resentful at work. As she failed to challenge her colleagues, she also failed to challenge her own limits: She did not speak up in front of her peers and she did not seek out new, high-profile clients, because the voice of a shadow character told her to disappear. But in listening to it again and again, her difficult feelings did not disappear.

When Olivia separated out her function at work from her identity, she was able to speak up to a superior about the other attorney and let him handle the territorial problem. As she romanced the shadow character who kept her silent and passive, she uncovered deep cultural and family messages, which sabotaged her in her chosen career. Slowly, over the course of several years, she created her own particular style of assertiveness at work and no longer undermined her professional dreams.

Unlike Olivia and others whose power remains in the shadow, many executives in positions of authority knowingly wield the weapons of power like Hercules and other heroes of old. A few, who win headlines, permit a tyrant character to take over the inner kingdom, which renders them ruthless and cold-hearted. But many men and women who head companies struggle mightily to wield power ethically. One client, an attorney who ran a firm of twelve lawyers, described his pressing dilemma: He needed to downsize the firm by 20 percent. His law librarian, sixty, had been there for fifteen years, but had performed poorly the last two years, since her husband died. He wondered whether to hire a young, technologically literate librarian to increase efficiency. Although he did not want to have to choose between his heart and the bottom line, eventually he let her go.

Another client has run a major utility company throughout his career. To comply with affirmative action laws, he hired women and people of color until he reached a gender and racial balance. Then, with government cutbacks, he realized that he needed to downsize by 25 percent. If he follows the commonplace "last in, first out" rule, the affirmative action program will be ravaged. If he does not follow it, he will need to fire employees of fifteen to twenty years standing. In order to meet his financial needs, this man, too, is confronted with a choice between money and soul.

Eventually, many of these executives face a paradox: the shadow side of success. Although they do not feel powerful on the inside, they pay a high price for looking powerful on the outside. Rather than feeling *authentic* power, which is rooted in the Self, they feel only the power of position. As John R. O'Neil points out, this kind of power can lead to hubris, self-righteousness, and a constant need for acknowledgment. Their accomplishments may evoke the envy and resentment of others, leaving them lonely and isolated. Their one-sided competitive personalities render them incapable of vulnerability, souring their days, which should be sweet with success. They cannot slow down because they must strive to maintain their image at all costs. And they cannot promote at the top because, like devouring fathers who fear being replaced by their sons, they must maintain their powerful positions at all costs. Eventually abandoned by family and friends, some of them are left alone with the trappings of power.

Of course, the power shadow is not restricted to the top of the corporate pyramid; it also appears in the helping professions as a split archetype: doctor-patient, therapist-client, healer-sick person, privileged-underprivileged, selfless-selfish. In a way, the desire to heal, serve, or protect constellates its opposite in the Other: the need to be healed, served, or protected. And a power difference—superior-inferior—is built into these pairs.

As Jungian analyst Adolf Guggenbuhl-Craig points out, if people in the helping professions deny their own shadows and project inferiority onto patients or clients, the power shadow emerges. Eventually, with an inflated ego, the doctor or therapist begins to feel like a savior with supernatural powers. Then the risks grow large: He or she may become moralistic, imposing his values or opinions on others. He may begin to represent himself or his tools as better than they actually are. She may subtly begin to coerce the other person to submit, whether sexually, financially, or emotionally. And, eventually, the archetype is so split that he loses his humanity, identifying completely with the impostor on the throne and acting out in a destructive way.

However, those healers who continue to do their own shadow-work by examining the feelings and images that arise in them can remain connected with their own woundedness, an antidote to hubris. And if they romance the power-hungry shadow characters who seek to control or influence others' lives, these figures will take their appropriate places at the table, and the healing of both persons can continue.

What do you imagine more power at work would bring you? How ☆ do you feel inhibited from expressing yourself at work? When do you shut down the expression of others to keep them powerless?

Sexual Shadows:
Corporate Harassment and Sex in Therapy

One of the primary ways of acting out the power shadow in the workplace or in the helping professions is through unwanted sexual advances—sexist remarks, intimidation tactics, or inappropriate physical contact. For the many women who suffer the degradation of feeling objectified or used sexually, old wounds resurface, and legal action becomes a psychological rite of passage, a way to stop colluding with abuse and to reclaim their own voices. As a result, monetary rewards have skyrocketed. Also, companies lose millions of dollars annually from high turnover, absenteeism, and low productivity due to the atmosphere created by harassment. Consequently, male executives become reluctant to hire and promote qualified women, or even to eat business meals or travel with them. In a backlash to whistle-blowers, many male workers scapegoat women who report harassment as complainers or gold diggers. The result: Both genders lose the contributions and companionship of one another.

In other arenas of corporate America, where no-harassment policies are upheld, Eros has been banished altogether. In fact, one of our clients, a charismatic public speaker, said that he cannot give a compliment to a female colleague "without first thinking of my Miranda rights because anything I say *can* be used against me." As a result, he tries to avoid any friendly contact with women employees, repressing his natural sexual feelings into the shadow. When his wife mentioned that his sexual desire seemed to have decreased, he stopped in his tracks: Shutting it down consciously at work, he realized, resulted in his shutting it down unconsciously at home.

At the same time, new battlefronts emerge: The epidemic abuse of women continues in the international workplace, where the law does not yet protect them. And in the United States, evidence of discrimination against gays and lesbians at work is mounting. In a corporate culture where discrimination is the norm, homophobia remains repressed, so gays may be insulted, patronized, or harassed without recourse. But in gay-friendly companies, which embrace diversity as an ethos and promote people on merits, heterosexuals may be forced to face this shadow issue as it emerges in the larger culture. The current hot button: state recognition of gay marriages, which would permit domestic-partner benefits, including health care, sick leave, bereavement leave, and survivor benefits.

Outside of corporations, in the helping professions, where more intimate one-to-one contact prevails, the sexual shadow prevails as well. In the last two decades we have uncovered an epidemic of sexual abuse in which powerful men—therapists, doctors, teachers, and clergy—have betrayed the trust of women under their care.

Jungian analyst Peter Rutter estimates that more than one million men and women have had exploitative sexual contact in violation of a sacred boundary. He calls this phenomenon sex in the forbidden zone: Sexual behavior is prohibited because a man holds in trust the intimate, wounded, or undeveloped parts of a woman's soul. The trust derives from his role and creates an expectation in her that she will not be used to his personal advantage. His power and her dependency, then, may render a woman unable to withhold consent, so that she colludes in her own victimization, often re-creating early childhood experiences.

Recently, a psychologist friend told us that in 1985 he was part of a peer supervision group with eight other psychiatrists and psychotherapists. When he discussed his growing feelings of passion toward a female patient, the others came forward with a shocking secret: All of the men and two of the women had had sex with patients. Instead of suggesting ways for him to do shadow-work and contain his feelings, they advised him to end therapy with his client and explore the love that might emerge between them.

Today, it's highly unlikely that a young therapist would hear this disturbing advice. Although state laws differ in their approaches to the issue, most recognize that any kind of dual relationship with a client, whether social, sexual, or financial, is detrimental to therapeutic goals.

And yet . . . even with an awareness of its risky legal and ethical consequences, even with an awareness of its damaging emotional impact, some therapists, like priests, cannot contain their desires and continue to act out sexually with their clients. Perhaps, in the heat of the moment, they are compelled by Ananke, goddess of necessity, to risk everything—their careers, their marriages, and their clients' welfare. Perhaps they are swept up in the arms of Eros, and the god hidden in the sexual shadow overtakes them. Perhaps for these people, the god cannot be legislated out of the clinic. And yet . . . with their own efforts at shadow-work, perhaps they could honor the god without allowing him to take over the kingdom.

Does the sacrifice of Eros in the workplace make you feel more repressed or more rebellious? In what ways do you sacrifice your authenticity to avoid addressing sexual issues at work? If you have acted out the sexual shadow, how might you make amends?

Money Shadows: The Mistaken Grail

Of course, most people work for money. It is the medium of exchange for our labors, the mana that allows us to participate in spending and saving. It permits survival; it opens opportunity. In the end, it appears to promise security. But what is the nature of the security that we imagine money can buy?

One friend, at fifty, has earned several million dollars from a high-paying, high-profile position. He recently suffered a heart attack but returned to work the following week saying, "Gotta earn a living." To the ancient Aztecs, who practiced human sacrifice, a pulsating heart, pulled from the victim, would feed the sun and make the new corn grow. Perhaps the epidemic of heart attacks in working men is a contemporary form of sacrifice for security.

Many people long for safety, a kind of refuge from the painful vicissitudes of life. The root meaning of the word "security" is free from care. But each of us sees the falsity of this promise all around us: Money cannot save us from shadow suffering. The bottom may fall out of the stock market; we may grow ill and be forced to spend our savings on medical care; a natural disaster may destroy our home. Even social security, designed as a safety net for America's workforce, appears to be no longer secure. And with alterations to the inheritance laws, family money may be passed on less easily than ever before.

So, what is security? For most people, our fantasy of financial security leads to a longing that can never be met. One client was told blatantly by his attorney mother that he was as good as the money he earned. Reinforced by the workplace, this message keeps him in a constant panic because he lacks an internal sense of self-worth, an authentic relation to the Self. If he loses his job, he becomes worthless. He had the following dream: *I am sitting in a dark cave, looking filthy and grimy. I'm clutching some small stones for dear life. They are the only thing that is of any worth.* This man's longing for money covers over a longing for identity.

Another woman was told blatantly by her Catholic mother that money was dirty. Its cost: her soul. So, as a child, she reasoned that if she remained poor, she would not have to face this moral conflict. She could avoid the temptations of acting for money, abusing people for money, or becoming arrogant with money. She could avoid becoming "Lady Muck from Dirt Hill"—an image of her shadow as an uppity woman who looks down upon others. It's more difficult for this woman to long for money consciously because it's covered in darkness. Unable to make her business profitable, she came to therapy to try to understand how she kept herself from earning more money.

If money becomes an end instead of a means; if money becomes, in essence, the grail that we seek, then we must contemplate the question at the center of the grail myth: Whom does the grail serve? Which character at the table longs to earn more and more money? Which members of the family benefit and which lose by our focus on money? We suggest that, while we certainly need to attend to our financial stability, we also need to listen to the voice of the Self, the inner grail which, when obeyed, may lead us to soulful work.

REDEFINING SUCCESSFUL WORK AS SOULFUL WORK

Just as we long for a Beloved partner or a sustaining family life, we long for soulful work, which nourishes and sustains us. Yet work, which holds such great promise, may, like romance and family, deliver us into the very hands that betray us. In response, some people call for a return to old images of work: a nationalist cry to return to a sovereign economy before globalization; a staunch summons to return to traditional roles and values before women worked; a nostalgic yearning to return to the land before it was raped by technology.

Instead, we suggest that if, as leaders, we can embrace the challenges of a radically changing business climate and empower our employees and colleagues to do shadow-work, then our companies can become engines of transformation. And if, as individuals, we can face our fears and resistances as shadow characters with an underlying message, then we may reconnect with that part of us that has the capacity for soulful work. In addition, if we can put down our numbing anesthetics, such as alcohol, caffeine, nicotine, and television, we may reconnect with our lost creativity, which lies buried as gold in the shadow. Then our work can draw energy from soul, and our soul can gain substance from work.

In this way, we begin to make of our lives a work: We transform the stone of Sisyphus into the philosophers' stone, the alchemical image of god in matter. And we turn lead into gold, transforming our daily work into the Great Work.

CHAPTER 9

MIDLIFE AS DESCENT TO THE UNDERWORLD AND ASCENT OF THE LOST GODS

In a dark time, the eye begins to see,
I meet my shadow in the deepening shade . . .
Dark, dark my light, and darker my desire.
My soul, like some heat-maddened summer fly,
Keeps buzzing at the sill. Which I is I?
A fallen man, I climb out of my fear.
The mind enters itself, and God the mind,
And one is One, free in the tearing wind.
                                                 —THEODORE ROETHKE

At midlife, Dorian Gray's painting comes out of the closet. And, with it, all of the devils cast into darkness during the first half of life return to haunt us. Forbidden feelings of helplessness and rage; secret fears of unattractiveness and rejection; shrouded fantasies of sexual desire; private reveries of creative potency; unanswered questions of meaning and purpose, all begin to sneak up on us, pester us, then prey upon us until at last we turn to look—and face the beast.

Like Dorian's face, ours is lined with the passage of time, drawn with the pull of gravity, pinched with the pain of betrayal. Like his face, ours tells a tale: We made a bargain to survive and paid with the coin of soul. At midlife, that story no longer works. A new story demands to be lived—the descent and resurrection of the soul in the second half of life. As Jung wrote:

Our personality develops in the course of our life from germs that are hard or impossible to discern, and it is only our deeds that reveal who we are. We are like the sun, which nourishes the life of the earth and brings forth every kind of strange, wonderful, and evil thing. . . . At first we do not know what deeds or misdeeds, what destiny, what good and evil we have in us, and only the autumn can show what the spring has engendered.

During the hero's journey in the springtime of life, we leave home on a noble quest to build an identity, find love, create a family, and adopt social virtues, ultimately contributing to the greening of the larger community. During this time we identify primarily with one archetypal pattern, such as a Persephone-style mother's daughter, a Hestia woman at the hearth, a Hermes-style prankster, or a Dionysian hedonist who feasts on life. And we come to manifest primarily the behavior patterns and emotional states of this archetype, although they will be complemented by others. But at the stroke of noon, a descent begins: The midlifer's journey in the autumn can mean the browning of life.

One reason: Midlife typically involves reversals, as the trickster calls us to break old rules, ignore past customs, transgress boundaries, and laugh at the ironies of life. The trickster can be capricious, unpredictable, irrational, and playful. But typically he or she turns our lives upside down. The result: A journey of seemingly unlimited ascent begins to look like a journey of inexorable descent. Our relationship to Cronos time alters, as we shift from cramming appointments into our daily calendars to making sacred the time that remains. In effect, if we face our mortality, we move from a sense of open time to an awareness of end time.

In addition, people who turned toward the world in the first half of life may wish to turn away from it in the second, reorienting toward an inner life and reevaluating the consequences of their choices. As Jung puts its, "After having lavished its light upon the world, the sun withdraws its rays in order to illuminate itself." For some, this shift will involve adopting a more religious or spiritual orientation, as the ego and its values take a backseat. For a professional Athena woman, this transition may mean exploring a new style of femininity, including having a first child in her forties. A Zeus-style corporate executive may suffer from information overload and begin to take long retreats from work. An Artemis lover of the outdoors may turn to meditation and discover the beauty within or turn to a profession and discover her mind awakening. A highly rational Apollo man may taste the sweetness of his tender vulnerability.

On the other hand, those people who previously turned away from the world may wish to move toward it. For instance, a Demeter mother whose children are grown may return to school to begin a new career. Or a *puer*, whose early onset spirituality may have resulted in a rejection of all things worldly, may begin to build bonds of family; a *puella*, whose social and political ideals may have resulted in a sacrifice of her own gratification, may begin to uncover a secret personal ambition.

This chapter reframes the issues of the midlife transition in a broader and deeper context: Midlife crisis becomes the call of the Self to encounter the unlived life, to resurrect the lost gods lying dormant in the shadow. Midlife depression becomes the liminal time between the descent of one archetypal pattern and the ascent of another—a changing of the gods. Midlife illness becomes the way in which our shadows take on substance in our bodies and reappear as symptoms. Midlife wisdom becomes the way in which we mine precious gold from the dark side.

What have been the tasks of your hero or heroine's journey in the first half of life? What gods or goddesses have helped you on the way?

MEETING THE SHADOW AT MIDLIFE: THE PROMISE OF RENEWAL

As the shadow forces us to face the unlived life and the resulting limits of our choices, the ego is destabilized, and our sense of identity shatters. Our ideal self-image, previously reinforced by the shields of power, sex, and money, cracks like thin glass as a woman can no longer use her beauty to win approval or a man his position to command respect. And our social adaptations, once viewed as an inevitable part of growing up, come to feel like tight clothing, restricting us from the freedom we imagine to be available in the unlived life.

In each of the arenas of life that we have surveyed in this book, midlife brings new hope and the promise of renewal. But first it often ushers in breakdown: Unresolved family betrayals can no longer be tolerated, family secrets no longer kept. The many compromises made to protect a parent or to avoid family strife suddenly seem too much to ask. And in a family reversal, adult children may need to care for aging parents, evoking shadowy feelings in both.

The foundations of our intimate relationships, which appeared for years to be solid, may liquefy at midlife as shadowy feelings emerge and long-term projections rattle. If our bonds were shaped by shadow projections, which re-create childhood patterns, or formed to compensate for our own missing parts, the eggshell may crack at midlife, and these unconscious agreements break down. A crisis of commitment may ensue: The call of the Self for greater authenticity threatens the status quo. And we must choose once again to let the relationship die as it is in order to become something else. For instance, for many couples a reversal of masculine and feminine takes place with aging: A man discovers his tender feelings and a woman her keen intellect, or a man retires to introspection and a woman launches a new venture. For other couples, a man may follow Aphrodite into an extramarital affair; a woman may fall into depression with menopause, which leads her to turn within. This kind of pendulum swing may be unbearable for some, liberating for others.

Our friendships, previously a refuge for authenticity, may fall by the wayside as unresolved conflicts resurface and old resentments reappear. Or we may desert longtime friends as the shared ideals and values that were cherished in the springtime lose their color in the fall. If marriage and family have been primary, friendships may move to center stage; if friends have been primary, a midlife realignment may involve forming a family at last.

And our work, if difficult, may become intolerable. If we are identified with our function at work, if we believe that we are what we do, then when work is at risk, which inevitably it will be as we age, our very identity comes into question. We may come to feel like a fraud, a sham. We may suddenly realize that we are not indispensable. If our work was undertaken primarily as psychological unfinished business— to cover up feelings of unworthiness or fraudulence, dutifully fulfill a parent's dream, or achieve more than an older sibling—its unconscious purpose dries out. If we have striven to reach the top, we may find it empty. With retirement, but without an authentic relationship, soul friends, or soulful work, we may feel that life is over.

When our trade-offs no longer satisfy the soul, they begin to feel obligatory. We become weary with the burden of the persona, which has lived under the domination of a tyrant character for so long. We dream of throwing over the burden, tearing off the mask, walking off in another direction.

For these reasons, at midlife many people feel grief-stricken and mourn their lost youth, like Demeter mourning the lost innocence of Persephone. Some feel bewildered, as if they are wandering in a desert, dry to the bone, with no landmark in sight. Their feet are blistered, their throats unquenched, their bodies wooden from a lifetime of mechanical acts. Others, whose disillusionment becomes dissolution, drown themselves with drink. And many others, who have served a life sentence as caretakers, feel like the Greek Danaids who, at the river's edge, forever fill water jars that are full of holes. Like the water, their hope leaks out in daily tasks of self-sacrifice.

At these times, as outworn personality styles lose their charm, undeveloped traits or latent dreams may emerge with a vengeance. Like glowing coals lying dormant under piles of ash, they catch fire and light up our fantasies of another life. Henry, forty-three, married for twenty-two years and a father of two, worked as a highly successful architect. Deeply invested in his marriage and career, he felt a bit complacent and did not anticipate any drastic midlife realignment.

Henry began to spend time on the Internet having anonymous conversations in the chat rooms. He discovered to his own surprise that he enjoyed chatting with men about male sexuality. After a few sessions he began to feel compelled to turn on the computer in the evening, dreading and at the same time anticipating these chats. With alarm, Henry began to question his own sexual preference. He had no early memories of an attraction to boys and had been moderately sexually satisfied in his marriage.

But as weeks went by and Henry's curiosity grew, he began to feel a growing sexual panic: He had been visited by the god Pan, whose hot, hairy body and erect penis bring panic in his wake. Pan, an abandoned child with unknown parentage, wrapped in an animal skin, brings a nameless kind of anxiety which, like hunger and sex, connects us with our instinct and the natural world.

Henry was caught: He set up an appointment with a man for sex. Then another. He told his therapist, "I can't believe it, but I feel like I'm coming home."

Before too long, Henry's newly discovered sexuality threatened all that he had built and eventually forced him to question his entire identity. "If I'm not who I thought I was sexually, then who am I?" Emotionally overwhelmed, he opened his closet and asked, "Whose clothes are these?" He looked around his house and asked, "Whose furniture is this?" He sat still at his desk at work, staring straight ahead, and asked, "Whose life is this?" Like an adolescent awakening to sexual energies for the first time, Henry's midlife change in sexual orientation was explosive. His old life began to feel too tame, too domesticated, and eventually too inauthentic. His new life whispered of Pan's wildness, his instinctual spontaneity; it called to him.

For the first time, Henry began to be interested in non-career-oriented activities, such as playing music and gardening. The foundations of his identity as a husband and hard worker crumbled. As he began to do shadow-work, he traced some of the roots of his midlife sexual issues: His father had been cold and distant, even punishing; his mother had been helpless and weak. Henry had become "the best little boy" at an early age to protect against rejection. Eventually, he had become the best husband and provider as well; his competence protected him against his father's aggression and his mother's weakness. But it also forced him to deny his deeper feelings, permitting him to repress his own taboo sexuality.

When Henry faced his sexual shadow at midlife, he was forced to face the cold rejection of his father one last time. He had to admit, at last, that he could never win his father's approval. He also faced the helplessness of his mother in his own feelings of depression and thoughts of suicide. But as he stood for his new sexual orientation, he began to feel free of her within him. Eventually, after a turbulent struggle, Henry decided to leave his family and follow a new imperative. He felt deeply alive; however, lacking a role model for a gay man with a family, he faced the potential loss of his ties to his children. Suffering terribly, he fought hard to discover his newfound identity and to maintain authenticity with his family.

Clarisse, at forty-eight, whose singing career rocketed her to stardom in her twenties, today feels alone and bereft. Unable to sustain her creative efforts and pay her bills, she fell into despair, but soon found a new source of energy: shoplifting. When she steals discretionary items, such as cosmetics, she feels giddy with cleverness. Taken over by this irresistible self-destructive behavior, despite her awareness of its danger, she felt that she *had* to steal whenever she shopped.

As Jungian analyst Murray Stein pointed out, for some people Hermes may appear at midlife in kleptomania, when the impulse to steal is so charged with energy that the ego is rendered helpless and cannot resist the act. Stein suggests that through this unique kind of acting out, Hermes, as a messenger of an underworld complex, can lead us to discover hidden wishes that remain tainted with shadow. By romancing this character and listening to his voice, we may uncover those secret wishes and take back for ourselves lost gifts that have the power to nourish the soul.

✫   Who has come to thwart your efforts at midlife? Does this shadow character appear in the domain of your marriage, family, friendships, creativity, or work? What is its deeper, underlying message—the gold in the dark side?

Midlife as the Emergence of New Priorities: Steve's Story

On approaching fifty, I, Steve, felt physically exhausted and emotionally depleted from overwork. Although I had created my ideal therapy practice and enjoyed the work tremendously, I began to resent having to be in position hour after hour to tend to the needs of others. My work had become Sisyphean. My sleep became fitful and my marriage suffered. My wife, Paula, identified the loss of our soulful connection and paraphrased an old adage: "The shoemaker's wife gets no shoes."

Slowly, I became aware of the *senex* character at the table who continued to tell me that I needed to work harder and harder to be a dutiful husband and provider. It was he who carried the fear of reducing my income; it was he who believed that to be a man is to be a nonstop worker.

But at the same time, another voice soon could be heard: at first a whisper, then a cry from Eros told me that I needed to explore other arenas of life, such as deeper intimacy with my wife and son. As I romanced this character, listening to his voice to get a point of view that was radically different from my habitual one, I felt energized and began to realize that I was being called to another life transition.

I imagined taking drastic action, such as stopping work or changing careers, so at first I saw no way out of this situation. I longed for more time alone and for other creative outlets. I experimented with carpentry and music, spent more time with my young son, and took more vacations than usual. When Eros's longing for a different life became intolerable, I had an idea: to reduce my psychotherapy practice to three weeks per month, permitting me to spend the fourth week in any way that I chose.

When I spoke of my excitement and my fear of this new possibility in my men's group, the members fully understood, and each man recounted a unique story of this universal dilemma. Then one man noted an obvious truth: "It's unrealistic to think that you should feel no fear when you make a lifestyle change like this. Don't let the fear stop you." With their encouragement, I took the leap.

Readdressing the *senex* character at midlife, I seem to have found an appropriate place for him at the table. Unlike my youthful solution, I did not take flight to *puer* spirituality, although I may meditate during my unscheduled week. Instead, I struck a different kind of bargain, a more conscious agreement to maintain my commitment to work, as well as to the demands of soul. Soon, my passion for life and work returned.

From the point of view of ego, Henry, Clarisse, and Steve each faced a midlife crisis that looks like a terrible breakdown. But from the point of view of shadow, each crisis is a breakthrough: These threatening feelings and disruptive acts point to buried gold. They hint at a longing for something more.

At midlife, our longing typically looks in two directions at once: Standing on the mountaintop, we look backward and long for a return to an image of youthful beauty, a sensation of bountiful vitality, a vision of limitless options. We long for a carefree time before sacrifice was required, before losses were suffered. And as we look back, we buttress the walls of denial.

Without an understanding of the developmental process, some people try to make an end run around midlife: Reinforcing persona, a man may desert his wife and marry a younger woman, feeling pride once again with her on his arm, but perhaps avoiding the developmental tasks of his own life. A woman may seek multiple plastic surgeries, feeling self-esteem once again as her image is restored, but perhaps failing to come to grips with her own aging. Compelled by preverbal images, others may follow romantic fantasies in an effort to meet the shadow's need for shelter in a projection, returning to the eggshell stage of relationship for safety and security. And still others may turn to religious teachings or spiritual teachers in a regressive way, projecting the Self onto another person in an effort to gain the acceptance that they did not gain from their families. If these people lose their autonomy and maintain a childlike naïveté, they may remain caught in a *puer/puella* complex, avoiding the tasks of developing a more mature spirituality.

Yet this longing backward with nostalgia at midlife, like the longing for the disappearing nuclear family or for the romantic fantasy bond, is a yearning for the impossible: to recapture the past. Possessed by Mnemosyne, goddess of memory, filled with regret for deeds undone and remorse for roads not taken, we suffer, but we do not change. For nostalgia is *inauthentic grief*, and it cannot free us from the past or prepare us for the future. Instead, it holds us in its grip, in abeyance between worlds, like the soul passing through the Tibetan *bardo*, caught in its attachments on its way to freedom.

Only *authentic grief* carries us to the other side; only it permits rebirth. With authentic grief, we process the past and digest it, thereby assimilating a larger range of who we are as a result of our experience. On the other hand, with inauthentic grief, we deny or romanticize the past, thereby banishing into shadow an aspect of who we are. With authentic grief, we carry our losses consciously, so that they give us substance and strength. On the other hand, with inauthentic grief, we deny and bury them, carrying them unconsciously, so that they merely weigh us down. With authentic grief, we separate our black-and-white beliefs and naïve, high ideals from our newfound, more mature convictions, which contain contradictory impulses and paradoxical desires. On the other hand, with inauthentic grief, we cling to outmoded beliefs and pine for the old ways, separating the opposites as if they have nothing to do with one another.

Authentic grief, like shadow-work, is sobering. As Robert Bly puts it, "The person who has eaten his shadow spreads calmness and shows more grief than anger." Authentic grief is humbling; it causes the ego to face forces that are much greater than it can even imagine and it teaches us how to find gain in loss. With authentic grief, then, our profane wound becomes a sacred wound, permitting us to molt out of the cocoon into a wholly new life. Going through the wound like a gateway, we emerge transformed.

Still standing on the mountaintop at midlife, we recognize that in some ways we have arrived: If we have found our Beloved, the search for love is over. If we have children, they are being tended. If we have found soulful work, that longing, too, has been met. And yet, deep in the soul, there is another longing, a longing forward: We yearn for security and peace of mind. We long for freedom from the daily tasks of responsibility, freedom from Cronos time. We yearn for grandchildren, to see our line extended into the future, to play with young ones without the dutiful chores of parenting. We long for reconciliation with those we have betrayed and with those who have betrayed us.

Perhaps most of all, at midlife, we long for meaning. We pose again the questions that are scattered throughout this book like seeds. The timeless questions of meaning and purpose become suddenly more immediate, less abstract. We feel that we *must* respond to them in our own way; we no longer need to answer them, but to live more consciously in relation to them. And in this way we discover the wisdom in poet Rainer Maria Rilke's suggestion that we live into our questions.

How can your apparent breakdown be transformed into a breakthrough? What images lie buried in your longing backward? In what direction does your longing forward point?

Midlife as Descent to the Underworld: Connie's Story

When I, Connie, turned forty, the solid ground beneath my feet cracked open. I dropped through a fissure, down, down, and disappeared into a great blackness. I lived for a long while at the bottom of a dark hole looking up.

Nothing had prepared me for such an eclipse. No betrayal, no wound had shown me the way. I had not felt depressed since adolescence, when I first discovered existentialist writers Sartre and Camus. I had not felt depressed when some of my friends dog-paddled and sank beneath the surface from addiction or failed marriages. I had not felt depressed when world events turned grim and human cruelty stared back at me with hollow eyes.

Instead, I had felt some strange immunity, as if I were vaccinated against descent, as if I walked on buoyant ground filled with helium perhaps, or hope. And I saw this as a sign of grace, a sign that the gods winked at me and smiled.

Then I turned forty. And, like an unforeseen natural disaster, the earth yawned open, a long hand rose up from the depths of the underworld, grabbed me by the foot—and stopped my dancing.

The music of the underworld plays in a minor key. It hums constantly like a droning lament. The inhabitants of the underworld, shrouded in black, speak in whispers, as if they could awaken the dead. The sky in the underworld is not a blue envelope; it is a dusky tunnel that swallows every particle of light. The colors of the underworld pale and fade to gray, not an oceanic blue-gray, not a shiny silver-gray, just gray, flat and unending. Tastes—sweet, salty, bitter—turn to ash on the tongue. Life in the underworld is a still life, drawn without motion in two dimensions.

For a while, I faded into the background, monotone and colorless, part of the still life. Then, like Theseus holding on to Ariadne's golden thread, I began to follow the plumb line through my dreams. Slowly, I opened my eyes to the darkness; slowly, I opened my heart to the pregnant possibilities that gestated there. Slowly, like a blind poet, I groped my way toward images and words.

I sought an acquaintance with the journeyers who had descended before me: Inanna, Persephone, Orpheus, Dionysus, Theseus. Their strange-sounding names grew familiar to me. I recited them like a long litany . . . and slowly began to feel that I was not alone, but rather that a family of souls encircled me. Then I began to feel that I was not off the path but had stumbled onto another path, a hidden, more treacherous road that led not to enlightenment but, perhaps, to endarkenment.

The Greeks had a name for this downward path: *katabasis*, or descent. Our ancient forebears understood that we needed not only to fly above with the birds, lightly and full of grace, but also to crawl beneath with the snakes, slowly, silently, on our bellies. We do not choose this lower path; it chooses us. At midlife, we do not have depression; rather, depression has us. And if we can allow the ego to take a backseat and go along for the ride, then the real journey can begin: Depression can become descent; the refusal to go down can become the choice to go down. And the appointment with the shadow can be kept.

We propose here a symbolic approach to midlife depression. It does not preclude a psychological perspective or a biological one. In fact, we suggest that the ideal approach to depression might include all three—body, mind, and soul. But we wish to address a specific kind of depression here, the kind that typically appears at midlife. And often this garden variety does not stem from early childhood trauma or from neurochemical imbalance.

Instead, midlife depression is an archetypal event, a meeting with the daimonic. It is a symbolic turning toward the second half of life, an irreversible turning. And just this quality—its irreversibility—carries a depressive weight. For an individual to carry this weight alone, the task may be arduous, even unbearable. But if we can detect footprints on the path, we might learn the stories of those who have gone before and in this way lighten the load. We may uncover the pattern that connects us to the past and to the future. For the underworld of midlife depression is the ancestral realm and the mythical realm; it is the land of the dead and the land of the dream.

As James Hillman says, the underworld *is* the psyche. An experience of it radically alters our experience of life. For some travelers who identify with the depression, a *katabasis* leads to total despair. Jung, who saw descent as a stage in the individuation process, pointed out that "the dread and resistance which every natural human being experiences when it comes to delving too deeply into himself is, at bottom, the fear of the journey to Hades."

For this reason, Jung suggested that we need to be led downwards by another because it is not easy for us to descend from the heights alone and remain below. We fear a loss of social prestige and a loss of moral self-esteem when we have to admit our own darkness. We fear that we may never ascend again. Yet, he said, " 'below' means the bedrock of reality, which despite all self-deceptions is there right enough."

This hell-realm is bankrupt of feeling, empty of meaning. Some journeyers, unable to heed the call, refuse to walk through the door to Hell by feverishly doing more of the same: more work for more hours, more alcohol, more jogging, more sex, more gambling, even more books about the promise of immortality. For them, midlife looks like an uphill marathon race, anything so as not to stop—and hear the call to descend.

How do you deny the call to descend? What are the consequences of disobeying the voice? What do you imagine will happen if you go down into the underworld of your own soul?

The Call of the Self: Inanna's Story

For others, the descent may begin with a parent's death, an initiatory process that cannot be avoided. Or the descent may be inaugurated by a Beloved's death, which has a finality that feels impossible to accept. And the lover is suddenly thrown into bereavement like Orpheus, who follows his Beloved Eurydice into the underworld. Or the descent may come suddenly through an encounter with violence, which burns through our ideals and hopes. If the loss is shattering enough or the disillusionment deep enough, the call may be heard. If we turn toward it and listen, eventually we may obey and discover what the call asks of us.

Mythologist Joseph Campbell describes the descent as a perilous journey into the dark, crooked lanes of our own spiritual labyrinth. There we find a landscape of symbolic figures, which is frightening and marvelous. Campbell likens the mythological descent to the second stage of the classical spiritual way of mystics, which involves a purification of the senses, a humbling of the ego, and a concentration of the attention. In psychological terms, he says, the descent involves transforming the infantile images of our personal past. So, the descent to the underworld is both a psychological awakening and a spiritual initiation.

And at every stage, the encounter with the shadow is an initiatory step. This psychic movement inward and downward, toward the deep darkness, is like entering a holy place, which requires metamorphosis. We cannot bring the persona, which is adapted to the upper world, into the underworld. We shed it as a snake sheds its old skin. And this act of symbolic death brings new life, the birth of the Self.

The theme of the inner traveler's ego death and spiritual rebirth, which takes place at the bottom of the abyss, or in the world womb, is repeated over and over in human history. In traditional cultures, the shaman undergoes a rite of passage in which he descends and returns with gifts. In mythology, the Greek maiden Persephone is raped by Hades, lord of the Underworld, but makes a seasonal return to the realm above, bringing springtime with her. The Egyptian Osiris is slain, dismembered, and scattered over the sea, only to return from the dead. And Christ is hung on the cross and left to die, only to be resurrected. In the same way, each man or woman who makes the harrowing descent and suffers the required sacrifices engages in a life-renewing act.

In the oldest recorded account of the passage through the gates of metamorphosis, which comes from the land of Sumer near the Tigris and Euphrates Rivers in southern Iraq, Inanna, Queen of Heaven, made an arduous journey to the underworld. It describes many of the key psychological and spiritual aspects of the midlife journey.

First, Inanna leaves her family and all that is comfortable and familiar. Then as she approaches each gate to the underworld, she gives up a precious attribute: her role as queen, her royal power, her sexual power, each symbolized by an adornment such as a crown, a necklace, a breastplate, a gold ring, and a royal robe. In her nakedness, her powers removed, Inanna is as helpless as an infant.

At last, she meets face-to-face with her dark sister Ereshkigal, Queen of the Underworld, who eats clay, drinks dirty water, and has no props to protect her from her own instinctual nature. Ereshkigal carries primal affect—rage, greed, suffering—and, like the Hindu goddess Kali, she devours and destroys things, thereby bringing about gestation and the possibility of new life. On seeing Inanna, the fertile, beautiful goddess of love, Ereshkigal rages with jealousy and turns her sister into a corpse that is hung from a hook on the wall, as if in a crucifixion.

Inanna's mythological meeting with her shadow sister, her loathsome alter ego, inspires terror and submission. She confronts the death-dealing, rageful indifference of the one who sits on a throne within each of us in the most hidden recesses of the inner world. As a result, she turns into dead meat—lifeless, formless, hopeless—symbolic, perhaps, of how we feel in the paralysis of midlife depression.

Together, Inanna and Ereshkigal represent one goddess in her two aspects: light and dark. The meeting of these two, which often occurs in dramatic ways at midlife, is an archetypal event. As Jungian analyst Sylvia Perera says, when we connect the upperworld Self with the underworld shadow, we suffer the death of the ego-ideal. In meeting the horrific beast, we are forced to put aside pride, virtue, and beauty. We swallow up or are swallowed up by our opposite. In this alchemical process, rebirth occurs.

The lowest point of the labyrinth, where the confrontation with evil takes place, proves to be the place of reversal. Poet Kathleen Raine describes Dante's famous descent and return in this way:

> The journey had been, hitherto, always a descent into darker and worse places, the claustrophobia closing in until Hell's ruler is encountered and identified as the Shadow. . . . Now that the ruler of hell has been seen and identified, Virgil half leads, half carries the horrified Dante through a narrow passage under Satan's throne, below the hairy thighs of the half-animal, half-human figure of the Devil. What takes place is a kind of rebirth through a round opening; and, like the newborn, Dante can now for the first time see the sky and the stars. And there is literally—and how dramatically—a change of point of view. Satan on his towering throne is now seen reversed beneath the traveler's feet: his power is gone. He is no longer the ruler and the center of the psyche. What has taken place Jung described as the reintegration of the personality when we find the Self—the "other" within us—and not, as we had supposed, the ego, to be the ruler and center of the soul.

✱ If you have made a descent, who did you find at the bottom of the abyss? What was the nature of your dismemberment? What permitted your rebirth?

The Changing of the Gods:
Reimagining Midlife Depression

Like the changing of the guards at Buckingham Palace, the changing of the gods in the palace of the psyche is a symbolic shift in power— but it may have vital consequences. An unknown archetype may steal the seat of power swiftly and radically alter our self-presentation, bringing disorientation in its wake. For example, an Athena woman, who is typically independent and intellectual, may become seduced into her Aphrodite nature, turning her carefully crafted career upside down. Or a Hestia woman, who keeps order inside a closed home, may be pushed outdoors by the winds of change, such as a financial crisis, and find herself tossed about by seemingly impossible new challenges. Or a Hera woman may face the death of a spouse so that her stable identity as wife unexpectedly disappears. Or a menopausal woman, freed of the social bounds of fertility and motherly duties, may meet Baubo, the bold older woman who displays her sexuality in a statement of freedom.

A Zeus-style husband, master of his universe, may have a heart attack that leaves him dependent and out of control. Or an Apollo man may have a mystical experience that challenges his rational, well-ordered universe and sends him off on a spiritual quest. Or Hades may suddenly surface in a midlife depression and push aside Eros, our connection to life and love, making us feel low, cold, and withdrawn.

For some people, the movement between the archetypes is fluid and ever-changing. They can face the separations, grieve the losses, and cross over, letting go of old baggage and beginning anew. But for others, the crossing is difficult, painful, overwhelming. It's as if they cannot let go of one trapeze to withstand the emptiness for a moment before catching the next. They need nets, reassurances, guarantees.

Perhaps some midlife depression results when we cannot face the death of the old and get stuck in between worlds, motionless, unable to reach the other side where new life begins. Time stops; the moment seems to drag on forever. Winter, cold and relentless, does not give way to spring.

However difficult, these moments of underworld winter can open

295

out into great depth. They can bring time for incubation, for the imagination to deepen by envisioning yet greater depths. For the underworld is always with us, simultaneous and continuous with the upper world, offering us the depths in any moment. And they can bring time for gestation, an opportunity to give birth to a new life.

A midlife depression, then, with its great sacrifices and great awakenings, has the potential to help us live in those moments of depth more fully. It can show us that we were living with only one eye open—the eye of light. Now, whenever possible, we can open the eye of darkness, and our vision can embrace a deeper, wider, more paradoxical range of life.

Who is summoning you at midlife? Who is retreating from the seat of power?

Bodily Symptoms as Shadow Speaking

At midlife the shadow also speaks to us in the body's language. Insomnia, allergies, headaches, back pains, multiple drug dependencies—all tell us that the ego's illusion of control is just that, an illusion. Hot sweats, mood swings, sexual impotence, hair loss, memory loss, hearing loss—naming our afflictions begins to sound like the curses of Job, who is stripped of his attachments, one by one. Breast cancer, prostate cancer, heart attacks, degenerative diseases—all tell us that we are mortal.

In a Korean Zen tale, a prince notices two red, painful spots on his thigh one morning. Assuming they are insect bites, he has his silk sheets burned and goes about his business. But later that night he notices that the two bumps have turned into a pair of furiously darting eyes. When he wakes up, they are accompanied by a pair of flaring nostrils. Terrified, the prince binds his leg to cover his affliction and ignores the sounds of breathing that begin to arise from his thigh.

Later that night, he clamps his hand over his leg and nearly loses two fingers: The symptom has grown a mouth. With this event, he summons the court surgeon to cut away the face. For several months, life returns to normal. Then one day, while he is on his horse, a scream erupts from his leg: The symptom has returned with a vengeance. And rumors fly that the prince is possessed by demons.

When a wandering monk tells the prince of a sacred stream that is protected by Kwan-yin, goddess of compassion, whose miraculous waters heal all wounds, he eagerly journeys there. As he is about to pour the holy water onto the hated face to silence it forever, the mouth cries out: "All this time, you have never even looked at me or tried to understand a single word I have said. Do you not recognize me?"

The prince, gazing closely, suddenly recognizes a distorted likeness of his own face and begins to weep. As he does so, the eyes on his leg soften, melting into those of Kwan-yin herself. "You had no heart of compassion," she says. "No sword of self-insight. How else could I summon you to your true nature?" And the prince and the goddess speak into the night about the secret suffering that had disturbed the prince's sleep long before the face appeared. When the sun comes up, the prince is healed.

Perhaps our secret sufferings make us sick. Our private shames and silenced sorrows may descend into our bodies, lodging in our muscles and nerves, our blood and bones, perhaps even trapped in our tiny cells, the building blocks of our physical world. There they rest in deadly silence, banished into darkness, only to erupt decades later as a pernicious cancer, a blocked artery, a tidal wave of anxiety, or a mysterious, undiagnosed chronic pain. In our symptoms our shadows take on substance.

Today it's common knowledge that the mind cannot be separated from the body, distilled out like salt from seawater. Each mental event, whether sorrow or ecstasy, has physical and chemical correlates. Each bodily event, whether a pregnancy or a common cold, has its corresponding state of consciousness in the brain. In effect, the mind is in the body, or so say psychoneuroimmunologists, who scramble to discover the proper set of attitudes to extend a cancer patient's chances for survival. And the body is in the mind, or so say psychiatrists, who scramble to discover the proper set of chemicals to ease our mental suffering.

In other words, emotional shadows—pessimism, cynicism, depression, aggression—have physical correlates. While one does not cause the other in a simple, linear way, it is clear that they are coterminous, sharing one boundary. Therefore, to some extent, shadow-work can be done via the mind or via the body. For example, Jungian analyst Marion Woodman uses images, movement, breath, and sounds to approach the shadow through the body, a road less traveled than the mind's symbolic route. And Arnie Mindell, founder of process work, uses a shamanic approach to amplify the symptom, advising patients to focus intently on their pain until something new emerges—a voice, a movement, a sound, a story. In this way, a creative, perhaps healing process may be initiated when the archetypal image and the buried emotion are linked more consciously. Once again, the goal is not a cure, but an encounter with the mystery.

James Hillman suggests that instead of dreading or despising our symptoms, whether psychological or physiological, we owe them a great debt: They tell us that we can never take back into our ownership the events caused by our complexes. Our symptoms refuse to submit to our ego's view of ourselves as a unified person. Instead, in their stubborn autonomy, they insist on voices of their own. By suffering our symptoms, Hillman proposes, by moving through our pathologies to find depth and meaning, we descend to soul.

In this way, we come to our own understanding of Jung's famous statement: "The gods have become diseases." That is, we imagine in our heightened rationality that we have left behind the archaic gods; however, we are as much possessed by the archetypes today as ever. Like Kwan-yin, they simply go by different names.

✮   Which midlife symptoms speak to you of shadow? If you were to do shadow-work via the body, what gold might you find?

Reclaiming the Unlived Life:
The Resurrection of Lost Gods

At the end, we return to the beginning. The cry of the banished soul, hidden in the cellar of childhood, can no longer be silenced. Taboo traits and forbidden feelings resurface as fully formed shadow characters who pound their fists on the table, demanding to be heard. If we turn our backs on them and deny their needs, the kingdom falls into the hands of a tyrant or a victim, or it disintegrates into chaos. Either way, the precious gold in the dark side remains concealed.

If instead we heed the call of the Self rather than deny it, obey the Self rather than debate it, then midlife crisis becomes an opportunity: We can begin to reclaim the unlived life. We can unearth the gold long buried in the depths of our souls.

And with ongoing shadow-work we can halt the transmission of intergenerational family sins. We can learn to risk expressing our feelings with authenticity, shadow-dance with our partners, work shorter hours to spend time with family or on spiritual or creative pursuits, and respect the autonomy of our children's souls. In these ways, we give our children a new legacy of hope.

At forty-three, our client Andrew, a father's son with few friends or creative passions, faced his worst demon: dependency. At midlife, soon after he married Annette, who worked as a designer, he received a job offer out of town, which they decided to accept. So they suddenly shifted from a two-income to a one-income family, with Annette becoming financially dependent on Andrew for the first time. His terror of her powerlessness and dependency on him brought up the following story.

As a young boy, Andrew adored his dad, a career military man who overpowered him, saying, "I'm bigger than you, so do what I say," and shamed him for having any needs, including financial support. Having identified early with his father's heroic ways, the boy dreamed of becoming a policeman or a soldier. His persona became brusque and aloof and his passions competitive, as his father urged him to stay focused, perform well, and beat others at any cost. This performance pressure became so much a part of his personality that he did not know it was a shadow character; however, every success became a success for this *senex*-tyrant, who protected the parent and made certain that the dependent child, so small in the face of the giant, had no room to breathe.

But when Andrew was nine, his father deserted the family, telling his young son, "You're on your own. Take care of yourself now." Like his dad, Andrew made a necessary Faustian bargain: He developed a hostile kind of autonomy, denying his own feelings of dependency and powerlessness and denying his playfulness as well. Since then, he needed no one, and no one needed him.

So, when his independent wife, who also hid her own neediness, suddenly depended on him, this intolerable shadow quality evoked panic. He began to tell her that she should find a job—and do it now. He began to treat her as his father had treated him—with dogmatic impatience for her own needs and rhythms. He could not tolerate her dependency because he could not tolerate his own.

When the therapist suggested to him that with the process of aging, he, too, would one day become dependent, he found this idea insufferable. He could not imagine physically or mentally deteriorating to the point of needing to be cared for. "I would rather lose an arm than become incontinent, needy, and old. If I had to depend on people, they would take advantage of me." Unconsciously, Andrew believed that if he needed others, they would betray him as his father had done.

With shadow-work, Andrew slowly began to see the family patterns emerging in his marriage during this time of transition. If Annette were to become dependent like a child upon him, he could not rely on her and would feel abandoned as if by a parent. In effect, he would have to become the adult with enough money to support them both. As Andrew thought through his dilemma, he displaced his anxiety about dependency onto money and unknowingly tied together power and money shadows. He calculated that to support them both he would be forced into debt after six months. And to go into debt would mean to disavow his father within, which made him feel terribly anxious.

Therefore, in order to relocate with his wife, Andrew must surpass his father by assuming responsibility, rather than evading it, and by allowing his vulnerable shadow character to be heard. In this way, the crisis situation becomes a doorway to his own development: He can discover a new kind of masculinity that is beyond the father's son pattern because it includes responsibility without the overbearing *senex* complex. This pattern of archetypal masculinity, which is postheroic, vulnerable, and connected to soul, has no representation among the prepatriarchal Greek gods. Perhaps Andrew and men like him today, who struggle with these issues, are writing a new story for the rest of us.

Lisa, forty-one, an attractive brunette with a thick, unruly head of hair, nearly sagged from a standing position onto the therapy couch, reporting: "I feel depressed, but I don't have the faintest idea why." Although she is a mother's daughter, Lisa has also lived this archetypal pattern: as a highly independent, overly responsible wife and mother, she is a female *senex*. Her mother, now seventy and a Holocaust survivor, encouraged her to work incessantly in order to survive and not to waste time with *kinderspiel*, or child's play.

Asked when she last played like a child, Lisa began to recall how much she enjoyed drawing and dressing up as a young girl. When she suddenly burst into tears with these memories, she quickly recovered her composure, saying, "I can't believe how sad I feel about those times. After all, they happened so long ago." Encouraged to do shadow-work with her lost inner child, Lisa spent time drawing her, visualizing her, and imagining carrying her through the day.

Then, one evening, while Lisa washed dinner dishes, her young daughter tried to win her attention. "She wanted to show me her art-work from day care. But I just cut her off saying, 'I don't have time for that.' Suddenly, I realized that I was banishing my own daughter in the same way that my childhood had been banished. I stopped doing the dishes and had some fun with Laurie, who was thrilled. But afterwards I felt frightened. If I let this playfulness in, it may take over my life. I may never want to work again."

Identifying with her tyrant mother, who understandably was obsessed with survival and material goods, Lisa did not know how to value emotional goods. Feeling desperately threatened by these newly emerging feelings, she reasoned that she could take another job to earn more money and fend off this playful inner child, who seeks to throw her off course. Or she could begin to relate to her negative inner mother differently, lifting her curse by honoring the emerging child. And in this way, by romancing the shadow character, she might uncover the gold that the child offers—her own lost innocence, playfulness, and creativity. In addition, she would not transmit the family sin to her own daughter, whose innocence and playfulness had not yet been stolen from her.

Eileen, tall and thin in a tailored suit and loafers, arrived for her first session and announced that she suffered from a "failure syndrome": Unmarried at fifty, she had failed to bond with a man. And she had failed to have a child. She reported that, like Virginia Woolf, she preferred to birth books, not children. Her books, however, remained unpublished, so she had also failed to bring her work out into the world. In short, she had failed to make a contribution to the larger society.

Grieving her failures, she railed against herself. "I should have specialized; I'm not an expert in anything. I should have married Jeff; I just didn't love him enough. I should have left Los Angeles a long time ago; I thought this was the place to make it." And as she looked at her losses and the consequences of her choices, suffering her authentic grief, the deeper story emerged.

A father's daughter, Eileen grew up in the Deep South, where "nothing unpleasant was ever said or done." Her mother, a proper southern belle, discouraged her natural rowdiness and curbed her aliveness, especially her budding sensuality. She remembers feeling that she wanted to grow up to be nothing like her mother, whose rigid persona masked a chaotic emotional world. With this rejection, Eileen also buried her desire to bond and her maternal instincts in the shadow, becoming a self-reliant woman whose creative life did not resemble her mother's dependent, family-oriented one.

With this choice to live an unconventional life, Eileen suffered as an outsider among her married friends. They envied her freedom, but she envied their ties.

After moving to California, Eileen discovered yoga and mysticism. "I felt that I was finding out the secret meaning and purpose of life." She dedicated herself to meditation and yoga classes, read avidly in Eastern philosophy, and slowly began to believe that, although she was not a high achiever in a worldly way, she was superior to others who were more worldly. In effect, she had identified unconsciously with the *puella* character, who kept her on high moral ground, separated from ordinary men whom she might love and from ordinary work that she might accomplish. Eventually, the *puella* character even convinced her that, unlike the rest of humanity, with enough yoga she would not die.

As Jungian analyst Jeffrey Satinover points out, the person who is controlled by the *puer-puella* archetype experiences midlife differently from others: It becomes a demand to give up something that may not yet have been achieved—an ego identity. Therefore, this transition may involve a unique reversal: If a *puer* has lived out a premature and grandiose identification with the Self, in which spirituality alone holds meaning, humility sets in. As Eileen's midlife grief broke through, she was forced to face her buried feelings of vulnerability and dependency, which had been hidden by a spiritual power shield. And she was forced to face her limits, which the *puella* disavowed.

At first, Eileen felt enraged and terrified. She refused to give up her spiritual beliefs, with which she deeply identified. "I don't have a family or a successful career. My spirituality *is* who I am," she lamented. But Eileen did not yet understand that she is not the *puella*; the *puella* is simply a part of her, a character at the table. If she can break her identification and begin to witness the *puella*, it will return to its proper place in the kingdom, where it can point Eileen in a spiritual direction but no longer sabotage her in relationships and work, which require her to live out her human limitations. For Eileen, the gold in the dark side is the sacred value in ordinary life. Her ascent to spirit needs to be linked to a descent to soul, which can be achieved through shadow-work.

Jerry, forty-two, mined the shadow slowly for several years until, at last, the gold began to shine. When he was a child, his mother had been emotionally intrusive and physically inappropriate with him. Helpless to speak up for himself, he had become a dutiful child. But the price for this bargain was high—he felt disgusted with his mother and eventually acted out in passive-aggressive ways, such as withholding his affection to feel his own power, which he now does with his wife.

Jerry's dad betrayed him in other ways. Distant and aloof from his son and his wife, he stayed away from home for long periods and had numerous sexual affairs.

A mother's son with boyish good looks, even at midlife Jerry continues to feel angry at his mom's neediness and her dependency on him. "She calls me at all hours and hugs me constantly. I understand that she felt abandoned when I was young, but as an adult I no longer want to be treated like this." Although Jerry often has the old familiar feelings of being intruded upon and coerced by his mother, with shadow-work he has found a way to establish boundaries with her, responding as an adult rather than a child. Using the emergence of the good-boy character as a warning that he is stepping into dangerous territory, he is more able to resist her demands and less willing to take care of her neediness in an obligatory way. Instead, he sets his own limits and has found that, in a strange twist, he can be more loving to his mother than ever before because he is no longer caught in resisting her, and he is no longer stuck in his mother complex.

In addition, by taking responsibility for his own father complex, which he recognizes as his legacy, he can at times relate to his father differently. "I'm less angry with him for letting me down. And I'm more aware of that character in me who expects him to be the father I wanted as a boy. When I remember that he's not going to change for me after all this time, then I can relate to him as he is." With the end of blame, Jerry and his dad feel less distant and share the hope for a more authentic relationship.

Recently, the older man apologized for his affairs and their effects on the family. At first, Jerry did not want to accept the apology. But with a growing sense of his own masculinity, he can recognize his father's shadow side and his father's gifts. Their reconciliation is not the end of the story, but it may promise a new beginning.

This midlife reconciliation with elderly parents may bring a reconfiguration of the larger family pattern. As we accept ourselves more deeply for who we are, we can also accept our parents' dark sides with greater compassion. As we uncover and forgive our own sins, we can forgive our parents theirs, stepping out of the child's reactive role into our own emotional adulthood.

Having obeyed the call of the Self, survived a midlife descent, encountered the monstrous shadow, and paid tribute to the lost gods, we are prepared to move into the late-life transition, where we may meet the wise old woman, or crone, and the wise old man, or sage. For this changing of the gods, we cannot cling to the ego's inauthentic secular power. With shadow-work, once again the ego recedes and the Self takes the front seat, bringing with it authentic sacred power. As Jung says, "There can be no doubt that the realization of the opposite hidden in the unconscious—the process of reversal—signifies reunion with the unconscious laws of our being, and the purpose of this reunion is the attainment of conscious life."

EPILOGUE

This being human is a guest-house.
Every morning a new arrival.
A joy, a depression, a meanness,
some momentary awareness comes
as an unexpected visitor.
Welcome and entertain them all!
Even if they're a crowd of sorrows,
who violently sweep your house
empty of its furniture,
still, treat each guest honorably.
He may be clearing you out
for some new delight.
The dark thought, the shame, the malice,
meet them at the door laughing,
and invite them in.
Be grateful for whoever comes,
because each has been sent
as a guide from beyond.
                                    —JELALUDDIN RUMI

As children, we are taught to fear the dark if our parents turn on the light when we are afraid. We are afraid of the darkness still, of the demons lying in wait inside our minds. This book has been an invitation to light candles in the dark.

At first, a single candle may light up a corner of the cave, but the rest will remain in shadow. In a short time our eyes will grow used to the little light, and we will want to see more of the darkness, more of that which is hidden there. So we'll light another candle, and another part of the cave will take shape. Slowly, patiently, over the course of a lifetime, the cave will become filled with lights, like the night sky filled with constellations. And just as the early astronomers detected patterns among the stars, we can begin to recognize images among the lights in the dark skies of our minds.

This short parable, which describes the process of making the unconscious conscious, is not merely a story; it's the subjective experience of doing shadow-work—of reclaiming lost images, feelings, and abilities from the dark cavern of the unconscious.

With shadow-work, we can begin to acknowledge the divine characters lying dormant deep within our souls. Slowly, gently, we can begin to recognize them, speak their names, and hear their messages. Instead of obeying them unconsciously, we can begin to live in relation to them more consciously. Instead of burying them, we can begin to carry them. Paradoxically, our burden becomes lighter.

And the knights at the round table of the psyche become united in purpose for moments at a time. Instead of listening to the cacophonous voices of a committee, we can hear the ringing voice of the Self.

Therefore, we have written a work in defense of shadow—all that we defend against—the one in us who thwarts our efforts, opposes our intentions, tricks and sabotages our aspirations. We have written in defense of shadow, the one who takes us to the abyss—and with shadow-work guides us back again.

We have tried to show that the shadow is not an error, a failure, a flaw. It is a part of our nature, a portion of the natural order of who we are. And it is not a problem to be solved; it is a mystery to be faced. The shadow connects us to our own imaginal depths. Shadow-work fuels our creativity, which in turn frees us from the grips of an archetype. And shadow-work links us with the ancestors and the unborn, with the commons and with other species.

Romancing the shadow is not a way to slay the shadow; it's not a heroic gesture, a killing off of a monstrous part of ourselves. And romancing the shadow is not a way to harness the beast to do the ego's work. Instead, it's a way of being with a part of ourselves that is repulsive or grotesque. It's a way to witness it, be present for it, and understand it; but, more deeply, it's a way to honor it. As Christ could not complete his destiny without the betrayal of Judas; as Faust could not complete himself without the encounter with Mephistopheles, so we become who we are through romancing the shadow. That is why we say that shadow-work is soul work.

Finally, in this book, we have seen how our longing awakens an ache, a hunger, a yearning for more. We long to be seen and accepted for all that we are. We yearn for family soul, a sense that we are deeply at home with family members. We long for healing and forgiveness of parent-child betrayals. We yearn for the Beloved and the Third Body, the soul of relationship that nourishes and sustains us. We hope for the soul friend, who brings an end to loneliness, and for soulful work, which fills us with enthusiasm. And we long for meaning, which gives us direction and connects us to a larger pattern.

Our longing points the way to a fantasy image, which is hidden at the center of an archetype and compels us to follow it. It speaks to us of an unspoken need, an untold feeling, an unlived life. And in each case we can follow the golden thread down into the underworld, down to the realm of shadow, where we can uncover a lost god.

With shadow-work, we can follow the golden thread back to the upper world. We can build a bridge between the depths of the soul and the heights of the Self. As we learn to listen to and obey the voice of the Self, we can set our star upon it like a sextant. And in this way we uncover yet another longing: a spiritual craving, a longing for the light. But that's another story. . . .

A Shadow-Work
Handbook

O nce you understand why the shadow is formed in early life and how each character is shaped by a rich mix of personal, family, and cultural forces, you can begin to do shadow-work, an imaginal approach to the Other within that enables you to honor and romance it. You can learn to identify when the shadow appears in your life and how it sabotages your conscious intention in recurring ways. Then you can begin to imagine it as a character at King Arthur's table. Eventually, you can offer each character an appropriate seat at the table, so that it no longer steals the seat of power and throws you into turmoil.

The Greeks had a unique perspective on the encounter with a shadow figure, the common feeling of losing oneself for a moment and acting irrationally, then feeling so ashamed that one cannot admit the act. They believed that a spiritual force of divine temptation, known as *até*, can take over our volition, bringing unwise and unexplainable conduct in its wake. Sent by the goddess Até, this force can spread folly and bring ruin to those under its power. For example, Aphrodite, jealous of the beautiful Helen of Troy, sent wild *até* into the latter's heart so that she left her husband, child, and native land and fled with her lover Paris. The result of her impulsive act: the Trojan War. Later, Helen lamented the blindness that led to her behavior.

So *até* is a state of mind, a temporary clouding of normal consciousness. Whereas the Greeks ascribed it to a daimonic agency, we know today that, like Mephisto, the daimons are within us. We suggest that shadow-work is a prescription for dealing with *até*.

CENTERING TO DO SHADOW-WORK: THE MYTH OF ODYSSEUS

When we begin to teach shadow-work to our clients, we start with a portion of the Greek myth of Odysseus, which offers a hint about what to do when you feel blown about by the strong winds of emotion or caught in repetitive thought patterns or trapped in compulsive behaviors. It provides an image of how to prepare to do the difficult job of shadow-work, specifically how to cultivate a state of mind that can withstand the storms and provide safe harbor by breaking your unconscious identification with the shadow character.

Sailing the seas in the Trojan War era of Odysseus, many mariners perished when they passed the island of the Sirens, seductive and powerful female warriors who enticed their victims by singing evocative songs. As the sailors sought their female counterparts, unable to resist approaching the island, their ships cracked up on the rocks nearby, and the Sirens attacked and destroyed them all.

Odysseus knew ahead of time of these dangers, so when he needed to sail by the island, he devised a plan: His oarsmen wore earplugs so that they could not hear the seductive music and become seduced, thereby endangering the ship. And he tied himself to the mast of the ship, so that he could hear the temptations without cracking up on the rocks. In our view, the mast of the ship is like the Self; the experience of being tied to the mast is the sense of being rooted or grounded within the center of yourself, so that alien forces of *até*—disturbing thoughts, powerful feelings, or painful sensations—cannot throw you off course. Cracking up on the rocks represents the fall into alien forces, the loss of connection to the Self.

When you are tied to the mast, you can hear the voices and feel the feelings without cracking up on the rocks. In this way, you can develop the capacity for self-observation, which is also known as witnessing. When you can witness your thoughts, feelings, and sensations with some detachment, you can experience them fully without allowing them to take over.

Before you learn to witness, the psyche is splashed with the emotions of the moment, and your identity is colored by them, even stained. A partial, temporary experience feels as if it becomes the whole person. You might say "I am depressed," rather than "I feel depression." Or "I am no good," rather than "I am no good at doing that task."

After you learn to witness, you watch the emotions of the moment, and your identity remains clear, uncolored by the passing phenomenon. You might say "I feel sad with this loss, but I know it will pass." Or "I'm not skilled at this task, but it doesn't detract from my overall value." Witnessing provides a sense of spaciousness in the mind, so that you are more able to live with the onslaught of emotions. When you can witness them, they will control you less and, in this way, your relationship to them changes. To put it differently, with witnessing shadow characters speak to us rather than through us.

To tie yourself to the mast, you need a rope—that is, a practice that provides a connection to the Self. We suggest using the breath like a rope, as explained in the following meditation exercise. Ideally, you can practice this belly breathing meditation three times a day, cultivating a relaxed, alert state in the nervous system until it is stabilized and present even during the Sirens' songs.

For now, take fifteen to twenty minutes to sit quietly and comfortably. Please read the entire directions first, then follow them step by step.

BELLY BREATHING

Close your eyes. Place your hands on your abdomen with the tips of your thumbs resting lightly just below your navel. Place your tongue on the roof of your mouth. Imagine that a tube extends down from your throat directly to the center of your abdomen, ending several inches below your navel.

As you inhale through your nostrils, with your mouth closed, imagine that the breath extends down the tube and into your abdomen like a balloon filling with air. Feel the breath press your hands forward against your pubic bone and expand backward so that you feel the pressure against the inside of your spine and below the kidneys. As you exhale, imagine that the breath returns through the tube, relaxing your abdomen and lower back like a balloon deflating. (First, you may want to use your muscles to experience the abdomen expanding and contracting in this way. But don't use them during the meditation; simply allow the breath to move your abdomen gently. Ideally, your ribs do not expand and contract outward but move up and down.)

We suggest that you make belly breathing a part of your daily routine, as regular as brushing your teeth. As the breath ties you to the mast in meditation, it will do so more and more outside of meditation, so that eventually you can feel centered even when strong winds try to blow you off course. You can quiet your mind, settle your emotions, relax your body, and witness the Sirens. In this way, the meditation practice prepares you to meet the shadow with awareness and a capacity to respond more effectively.

Beginning Shadow-Work:
Identifying Shadow Characters

Next, you need to identify the presence of a shadow character. Odysseus's story teaches us to recognize early warning signals that indicate that the Sirens' seduction is about to begin. These signals typically appear as mechanical, repetitive thoughts ("I'll never succeed; I'm too dumb; I'm too fat; I need to get high; I can do it tomorrow"), or intractable feelings (fear, guilt, sadness, anger), or specific bodily sensations (tightening in the abdomen, chest, or throat; a feeling of emptiness; a craving). When you begin to recognize these signals as sounds of the Siren, you have an opportunity to avoid being swept away by practicing witnessing.

The next task: You need to recognize that this thought, feeling, or sensation is not who you are; this is not your identity, your Self. Rather, a character at the table has taken over. And it has a set of specific traits that can be identified as a specific shadow figure.

As you personify the internal character in an effort to make it more conscious, you can create a distance between it and the King/Queen, who personifies the Self. Then, you can begin to grow

311

more familiar with the specific thoughts, particular feelings, and bodily sensations that belong to this character.

To personify the character visually, you might ask, Who is there in this moment? Is it a male or female character? Young or old? What does it feel like? What does it need? You ask these questions to evoke an unexpected image. You do not ask them to evoke an old, well-worn answer, but to invite an unknown stranger to come out of the darkness, to make itself available for conscious relationship.

Then you might ask, What is the voice of the character saying? Some of these characters' inner voices are only partially conscious and require acute attention to track. Shadow characters typically lack compassion and are highly critical. In other words, they may say "You can't do it right" or "Who do you think you are?" and in this way reinforce feelings of failure, worthlessness, and unlovability, which create a self-fulfilling prophecy. For instance, our client Lou had published three books and just sold a fourth when he said to the therapist, "I really don't know how to write." Or the shadow characters may be overly praiseworthy, reinforcing a false, inflated identity, saying, for example: "You're so much smarter than everyone else and deserve to be recognized. They're losers," thereby setting you up for an impossible standard, which ultimately results in constant attempts to prove yourself. And, of course, this message results in inevitable attacks by the critical inner voice, which bring feelings of failure and separation from others.

Then you might try to detect the feeling or sensation that precedes the voice inside your mind by asking, What parts of the body feel tight and constricted, numb or empty, tingling and alive when this voice appears? Most people feel these sensations in the chest, middle, and abdominal areas.

Next, you can trace the roots of this shadow character by recalling a recent time when you fell into the same self-sabotaging pattern. Perhaps you disregarded your own needs or boundaries by making a commitment that you did not want to keep. Or perhaps you had sex although you really did not feel erotic. Maybe you remained silent with a friend or colleague and avoided expressing your authentic feelings or opinions.

What thoughts, feelings, or sensations stopped you? Which character told you not to express yourself? Perhaps you listened to a voice.

312

What did it say? Each character has a few standard phrases that it uses to usurp power, such as: "You're stupid." "He'll attack me." "You're unworthy." "It doesn't matter." Or perhaps you had a feeling. Specify it. Where did you feel it in the body? What qualities did it have?

To go farther back and trace the history of this pattern, close your eyes and recall an earlier time in your life when you experienced the same inner messages, emotions, or bodily sensations. Once you uncover the history of this pattern and trace its roots, you will see that your reaction in the present moment is really a reaction from the past, a shadow character's attempt to protect you from reexperiencing an old emotional wound, which instead sabotages you in the present.

As these patterns recur repeatedly and you identify the image, thoughts, and feelings as a character at the table, they can take on a shape, a personality, even a name. In this way, they become what Jung called shadow figures, differentiated out from the general mass of unconscious material. A few of our clients' examples: the General, Trixie the Vamp, the Failure, Helga, Meany, Kali, Baby Laura, the Terrorist, the Nazi, the Loser, the Dutiful Daughter, Maude the Fraud. By naming them, locating them in the body, and eventually hearing their messages, you can loosen their hypnotic grip over your life and uncover new choices for yourself. If you use the breath and self-observation to slow down and identify the pattern the next time it occurs, you may have a nanosecond in which you can choose not to respond automatically and potentially express yourself more authentically.

Furthermore, you can benefit from discovering the consequences of continuing to obey or disobey a certain character. If you begin to observe yourself falling into a maladaptive pattern in daily life as you automatically obey the message of a shadow character, you can see that the results are predictable: The character repeatedly creates its own suffering.

In the beginning, we suggest that your goal is not to change rapidly. You have probably been responding in this way for decades. So while you may seek immediate results, we suggest that it may be valuable to observe the pattern for a few more weeks or months. Your goal is to learn to witness the character's patterns through self-observation and awareness, to be with the shadow rather than to slay it. You can use the belly breathing meditation to center yourself and witness the character, thereby breaking your identification with it.

At some point down the road, you will meet the shadow character and feel a greater choice; you will not feel compelled to obey. You will be able to wrestle with it, reject its message, and contain the feeling, rather than act it out. For that moment, you are freed of the clutches of the complex and the grasp of Ananke, and you are romancing the shadow. And the character, which had been an enemy, becomes an ally.

As you continue to bring this shadow character into the light of awareness, the Self can regain the seat of power, so that you can make more self-affirming decisions more consciously for the benefit of the whole kingdom. The character, then, returns to its proper seat at the table, where it can be heard and honored in an appropriate way, such as in a safe relationship or therapeutic setting or creative expression.

Finally, after identifying a character, tracing its roots, and observing it act out, you may discover its archetypal origins. In this way, you can detect your own *mythos*, as I, Connie, uncovered the story of Athena and I, Steve, the story of Parsifal. If the central god or goddess in your story is sabotaging your soul's desires, it may have become a shadow character. For example, if Ares stands behind the fighting spirit of a man who wishes more peace of mind; if Aphrodite lurks behind a seductive wife who wishes to remain monogamous; if Athena, a virgin warrior, controls a woman who wishes to marry and have children; if Dionysus influences a man who is struggling to give up his nightly bottle of wine, then you can learn to honor these gods without identifying with them. When you read their stories and feel more connected to their universal qualities, you also will feel more connected to the story of humanity as a whole. And you will have recovered a piece of your own soul.

Unconscious of your story, you are in its grasp; but with consciousness, an alchemical process begins: The solidity of the complex dissolves and you can open up to the arrival of a new archetype, the birth of a new cycle of life. In the shadow, then, lies our myth and our fate.

Tuning to the Voice of the Self

After you have learned to identify the voice of a Siren—that is, to know when a shadow character at the table has taken over the seat of power—you can begin to listen for the voice of the Self, the ruler of the kingdom. At first, this voice speaks in an almost inaudible whisper. It may feel like a soft, gentle nudge, or it can be seen in the mind's eye as a fleeting image.

We like to think of it as a radio station that plays celestial music, a higher frequency that's accessible but difficult to find. You will know, however, when you reach it because it sounds so right. At first, fiddling with the dial, you may catch the voice of the Self for only a few seconds. It can be difficult to hear it above the din; a shadow character may say that you do not deserve something, or you will be punished, or no one will listen. The Self, on the other hand, may speak with authority, but it is not denigrating to you or to others. It offers guidance and an intuitive sense of right action.

The consequences of not listening to the Self are high: You may feel anxious, unworthy, diminished, moody, or out of balance as you continue to obey a shadow character. Using the defenses and the shields, you may try to anesthetize the pain. Instead, we prescribe a little shadow-work:

- Meet the shadow: Identify a self-sabotaging behavior and the nanosecond in which the character takes over, silencing the voice of the Self.
- Try to detect the early warning signs: an image of the character, as well as the bodily sensations and repetitive thoughts that accompany it.
- Romance the shadow: Tie yourself to the mast and witness the difficult feelings rather than obey them.
- Trace the roots of the shadow character in your personal history and family patterns.
- Trace the archetypal sources of the character, including the underlying story it is trying to tell.
- Explore your choices: Ask yourself which options are available and how can you respond with more authenticity, as well as more compassion for the other person.
- Observe your resistances: if you choose not to respond differently, be aware of both the internal and external consequences of your choice.

- If you choose to respond in a new way, realign with the voice of the Self and feel revitalized as the shadow character recedes.

As you practice listening to the shadow characters and tying yourself to the mast, you may focus in on the voice of the Self and begin to hear it more frequently. You get it, then lose it, perhaps projecting it onto a lover or spiritual teacher. Then you can reclaim it again, until you finally lock on. Gradually, you can distinguish the signal from the noise, the voice of the Self whispering below the clatter of the knights. And as you realign with it and the shadow character moves backstage, you become more self-directed and self-accepting. As you begin to trust the wisdom of the Self, you will have the compass you need to sail north on stormy seas.

WHO'S WHO IN
GREEK MYTH: FROM
APHRODITE TO ZEUS

Aphrodite (Roman: Venus). Born in the ocean foam, she is the daughter of the Titan Uranus, the wife of Hephaestus, and the lover of Ares and Adonis. She is the goddess of love who stirs sexual passions for the sake of pleasure itself, while she remains self-sufficient and ultimately unavailable. She is the goddess of beauty, whose skill at the female arts bewitches others and lures them into deep connection. She is an archetypal image of the Beloved and the Lover.

Apollo. The son of Zeus and Leto, the twin brother of Artemis, the father of Orpheus. He is the god of healing, music, and poetry whose shrine at Delphi reveals the future to mortals. Apollo embodies rationality, linearity, order, predictability, and the day world as against irrationality, disorder, and the night world. He stands for civilization and the words on his temple say: Know thyself.

Ares (Roman: Mars). Son of Zeus and Hera, father of Romulus and Remus and perhaps of Eros, he is the god of war whose lust for battle, helmet, sword, and spear signify virility. His style of masculinity involves impulsive physical action, but he also protects communities.

Artemis (Roman: Diana). Daughter of Zeus and Leto, twin of Apollo, she is the goddess of hunting and of the moon. She is also priestess of women's mysteries: menstruation, childbirth, abortion, and menopause. As a virgin goddess, she is self-contained and loves soli-

tude. Her domain is the virgin forest, which is untouched and uncivilized. And she is linked to the wild beasts: lion, wolf, boar, deer,
and bear.

Athena (Roman: Minerva). The daughter of Zeus and Metis, she
sprang forth in full armor from Zeus's head and continues to identify with men and the masculine ever since. She is the virginal father's daughter, goddess of wisdom and weaving, and aide to
heroes. As the goddess of civilization, she is the namesake of
Athens, who brings the plow and the olive tree. After she helped
Perseus kill the Gorgon Medusa, she wore the snake-haired head
on her shield.

Cronos. Son of Ouranos and father of Zeus, he is also known as father
time. He is one archetypal image of the *senex*.

Demeter (Roman: Ceres). She is the corn goddess and archetypal
mother of Persephone, who is snatched away by Hades to the underworld. Demeter then wanders in grief for nine days and nights,
causing the earth to go barren with winter. When Zeus arranges
for the return of her daughter, the seasons return as well. She embodies the experience of motherhood as loss.

Dionysus (Roman: Bacchus). He is the son of Zeus and Semele, who
insisted on seeing Zeus's godlike nature and, as a result, was struck
dead by lightning. Zeus rescued the unborn Dionysus and carried
him in his thigh. He is the god of wine and ecstasy, an archetypal
image of appetite and excess, known as the Loosener. He is present when we celebrate, dance, drum, and wail, telling us that
there is no sanity without a taste of madness.

Eros (Roman: Cupid). Son of Aphrodite, god of love and relatedness,
he carries a quiver of arrows and those he strikes fall in love. He in
turn fell in love with Psyche, who did not know his divine origins.
When she broke a vow by observing him by candlelight, he abandoned her. And his mother, Aphrodite, assigned the girl impossible tasks to atone. Eros is an archetypal image of connection
or relatedness. He brings together any two people in a bond of
intimacy.

Hades. Son of Cronus and Rhea, brother of Zeus, abductor of Persephone, he is god of the underworld, which is also called
Hades. Mythologically, he embodies the deep darkness, the realm
of souls. Known as the Invisible One, he is hidden from view. Psy-

chologically, he represents the unconscious realm. Known as the Rich One, he oversees the gold in the dark side.

Hephaestus (Roman: Vulcan). He was born to Hera to spite Zeus for bearing Athena. When the parents quarrel, Zeus flings Hephaestus from Olympus and he becomes lame. The only Olympian who works, he is god of the forge, where he creates Pandora. As the husband of Aphrodite, he crafts ornaments of great beauty.

Hera. Wife and sister of Zeus, she is the archetypal wife, patron of wedded love, as seen by the patriarchy. They rule the kingdom as a pair, but Zeus's many escapades with other goddesses and women stir her jealous rage. She plots revenge against his lovers and their children. In this way, she discovers that she cannot gain her own fulfillment through her husband.

Hermes (Roman: Mercury). The son of Zeus and Maia, he is messenger of the gods. He wears winged sandals and a hat that makes him invisible. He is patron of merchants and thieves and escorts souls to Hades. As a Trickster god, he is always moving and changing, like liquid mercury. He is one archetypal image of the *puer aeternus*.

Hestia (Roman: Vesta). The goddess of the hearth, she embodies stability and order inside the home. She upholds tradition and offers hospitality. She does not come to us; we must go to her.

Mnemosyne. She is the goddess of memory, mother of the Muses. She uses rhyme, rhythm, image, and myth, the tools of oral culture, to preserve remembrance.

Pan. Son of Hermes, he is the half-goat, half-man god of wild places who plays reed pipes and brings panic in his wake. He became an archetypal image of the Christian devil.

Pandora. Fashioned by Hephaestus at his forge, she is given breath by Athena, beauty by Aphrodite, and deceit by Hermes. Then she is offered to Epimetheus as wife and told not to open a secret box. When she does, the sorrows of humanity are released. At the bottom of the box lies hope.

Persephone (Roman: Proserpina). Daughter of Demeter, she is Kore, the maiden; then she is kidnapped by Hades and becomes his consort, queen of the underworld. In her ascent each year, she embodies the beauty of spring. In her intimate link with her mother, the two hold the key to the Eleusinian mysteries.

Poseidon (Roman: Neptune). Brother of Zeus and Hera, he is god of the sea, signifying authority from below. Known as the Earth Shaker, he generates earthquakes and tidal waves. He is present when a man is overwhelmed by waves of feeling or trembles with rage.

Prometheus. His name means forethought. He gave fire to humans in violation of Zeus's command and, in punishment, was forcibly chained to a mountain, where an eagle ate his liver. He also brought the gifts of craft and navigation by the stars.

Psyche. A beautiful mortal who arouses Aphrodite's jealousy. The goddess sentences her to death. But Eros falls in love and rescues her, asking only that she live in his castle without seeing his true nature. When she spies his divinity, she is cast out and Aphrodite sets her four seemingly impossible tasks. With the completion of each task, Psyche develops an aspect of her own soul. She embodies the lover, the wife, and the pregnant mother, as well as the developing soul. In the end, she is reunited with her beloved Eros.

Zeus (Roman: Jupiter). He overthrew his father, Cronos, with the help of his mother, Rhea, and became the most powerful Olympian or sky god. He married his sister, Hera, and had many love affairs with goddesses and mortals, making him the father of dynasties. He is an archetypal image of the king or ruler whose power, vision, and decisiveness bring obedience by others.

NOTES

INTRODUCTION

p. 3   **Perhaps all the dragons**   Rainer Maria Rilke, *Letters to a Young Poet* (New York: W.W. Norton & Co., 1934), p. 69.

p. 7   **serious psychological problems**   For psychopaths or sociopaths, who live out the shadow rather than repress it, more ego building is needed rather than more shadow awareness. For those people with difficult personality disorders, more ego strengthening is also advised before shadow-work.

p. 8   **The individual who wishes**   C. G. Jung, *Memories, Dreams, Reflections* (New York: Pantheon Books, 1973), p. 330.

p. 8   **"There is no doubt**   William James, *The Varieties of Religious Experience* (New York: Modern Library, 1902).

p. 8   **"If only there were evil people**   Aleksandr Solzhenitsyn, *The Gulag Archipelago* (New York: HarperCollins, 1978).

p. 11   **This view does not honor the gods**   See James Hillman, *Re-Visioning Psychology* (New York: Harper, 1975).

p. 16   **two-million-year-old man**   Cited in *C.G. Jung Speaking: Interviews and Encounters*, edited by William McGuire and R. F. C. Hull (Princeton, N.J.: Princeton University Press, 1993), pp. 88–93.

p. 19   **"the experience of the Self**   C.G. Jung, *Collected Works*, translated by R. F. C. Hull and edited by H. Read (Princeton, N.J.: Princeton University Press, 1953–90), vol. 14, p. 546.

p. 19   **soul offers an approach**   Hillman, *Re-Visioning Psychology*.

NOTES

OUR STORIES

p. 27   **another kind of femininity**   The first stage of this quest led to my anthology, *To Be a Woman: The Birth of the Conscious Feminine* (New York: Tarcher/Putnam, 1990).

p. 27   **Greek story of Medusa**   From Catherine Keller, *From a Broken Web* (Boston: Beacon Press, 1988).

p. 28   **Just as Athena**   From Edward Edinger, *The Eternal Drama: The Inner Meaning of Greek Mythology* (Boston: Shambhala Publications, 1994).

p. 30   **the legend of the Holy Grail**   We used three sources for the legend: Emma Jung and Marie-Louise von Franz, *The Grail Legend* (New York: Putnam, 1970); Linda Sussman, *Speech of the Grail* (Hudson, N.Y.: Lindisfarne Press, 1995); and Robert A. Johnson, *The Fisher King and the Handless Maiden* (San Francisco: HarperSanFrancisco, 1993).

CHAPTER 1

ME AND MY SHADOW

p. 36   **One need not be a chamber**   Emily Dickinson "One need not be a chamber," in *The Complete Poems of Emily Dickinson* (Boston: Little, Brown, 1960), p. 333.

p. 37   **"Faust is face to face**   C. G. Jung, *Collected Works,* translated by R. F. C. Hull and edited by H. Read (Princeton, N.J.: Princeton University Press, 1953–90), vol. 10, p. 215.

p. 38   **The meeting with oneself**   C. G. Jung, *Collected Works,* translated by R. F. C. Hull and edited by H. Read (Princeton, N.J.: Princeton University Press, 1953–90), vol. 91, p. 22.

p. 45   **Archetypal psychologist James Hillman**   James Hillman, "On the Necessity of Abnormal Psychology," in *Facing the Gods* (Dallas: Spring Publications, 1980), pp. 1–38.

p. 45   **in the circle of Ananke**   Ibid., p. 10.

p. 50   **The word "money"**   From Tad Crawford, *The Secret Life of Money* (New York: Tarcher/Putnam, 1994).

p. 53   **Cultural differences**   These ideas appeared in Tyler Marshall, "Still the Untied States of Europe," *Los Angeles Times,* May 20, 1996.

p. 54   **James Hillman has pointed out**   James Hillman, "Notes on White Supremacy," *Spring* 1986, pp. 29–58.

p. 55   **Jung studied Goethe's work**   Gratitude to Jungian analyst Naomi Lowinsky for the ideas in this paragraph.

CHAPTER 2

THE FAMILY SHADOW: CRADLE OF THE BEST AND THE WORST

p. 57 **Sometimes a man** Rainer Maria Rilke, "Sometimes a Man Stands Up," in *Selected Poems of Rainer Maria Rilke*, translated by Robert Bly (New York: HarperCollins, 1981), p. 49.

p. 58 **In fact, many families** As evidence of this tragic fact, in the United States every fourteen hours a child under five is murdered. And homicide has replaced auto accidents as the leading cause of death of children under age one. Cited in Terence Real, *I Don't Want to Talk About It: Overcoming the Secret Legacy of Male Depression* (New York: Scribner, 1997), p. 113.

In addition, as of 1993 one out of six crimes in the United States occurs inside the home. In the same year, nearly half a million cases of child neglect were reported; more than a quarter of a million cases of physical abuse were reported; and 139,000 cases of sexual abuse were reported. About 50 percent of all sexual abuse is perpetrated by a family member on children age twelve or under. Cited in *Child Abuse: Betraying a Trust* (Wylie, Tex.: Information Plus, 1995).

p. 61 **When the family soul** From John Sanford, *Fate, Love, and Ecstasy* (Wilmette, Ill.: Chiron Publications, 1995), p. 7.

p. 63 **Once upon a time** From Carl Kerenyi, *The Gods of the Greeks* (New York: Thames and Hudson, 1951).

p. 64 **"When an inner situation** C. G. Jung, *Collected Works*, translated by R. F. C. Hull and edited by H. Read (Princeton, N.J.: Princeton University Press, 1953–90), vol. 9ii, p. 71.

p. 65 **a shame complex** Jungian analyst Connie Crosby presented some of these ideas on shame at the Los Angeles C. G. Jung Institute, March 17, 1996.

p. 65 **The shadowy feeling of envy** Betty Smith presented some of these ideas on envy at the Los Angeles C. G. Jung Institute, November 1, 1995.

p. 66 **Family therapist Terence Real** Real, *I Don't Want to Talk About It*.

p. 67 **"We either face it** Ibid., p. 229.

p. 67 **witness to violence** For an excellent review of the effects of trauma, see Judith Herman, *Trauma and Recovery* (New York: Basic Books, 1992).

p. 76 **experts estimate** According to the National Incident Study of Child Abuse and Neglect, the number of abused and neglected children doubled from 1.4 million to 2.8 million from 1986 through 1993. Children were at risk from age three, and girls were the target more often than boys.

CHAPTER 3

A PARENT'S BETRAYAL AS INITIATION INTO SHADOW

p. 88 **I am not a mechanism** D. H. Lawrence, "Healing," in *The Complete Poems of D. H. Lawrence* (New York: Viking Press, 1971).

p. 88   **In her tale**   Ursula K. Le Guin, "The Ones Who Walk Away from Omelas," in *The Wind's Twelve Quarters: Short Stories* (New York: HarperCollins, 1975).

p. 90   **Marion Woodman points out**   Marion Woodman, *The Pregnant Virgin* (Toronto: Inner City Books, 1985).

p. 91   **Archetypal psychologist James Hillman**   James Hillman, "Betrayal," in *Loose Ends* (Dallas: Spring Publications, 1975), pp. 63–81.

p. 91   **If, as adults**   Ibid.

p. 93   **In a story from the oral tradition**   From *The Book of Legends: Legends from the Talmud and Midrash*, edited by Hayim Bialik and Yehoshua Ravnitzky (New York: Schocken Books, 1992), p. 32.

p. 98   **the *puer* archetype**   Whereas the discussion here focuses on male psychology, Jungian analyst Linda Leonard has written in *The Wounded Woman* (Boston: Shambhala Publications, 1982) about the *puella*, or female carrier of this archetype, which she sees as the wounded daughter trying to free herself of the father complex. For the woman who has an absent, weak, or addicted father, there is no *senex* energy in the household, no sense of law and order, responsibility, or discipline. As a result, she feels no inner sense of authority.

As Hillman suggests for *puer* men, Leonard suggests that *puella* women need to work consciously with this split archetype, linking pleasure to work and innocence to responsibility. She is aware of the risks: The *puella* may identify with her father and remain undeveloped or become an addict; she may rebel and make a *senex* adaptation, losing her connection to spirit; or she may marry a *senex*, projecting her authority onto him. But if the woman is to move her development forward, she will need, finally, to face her own and her father's limitations, and her own and her father's gifts. She will need to face the shadow to discover her deeper identity.

p. 98   **focuses on the dark side**   Marie-Louise von Franz, *Puer Aeternus*, 2d ed. (Boston: Sigo Press, 1981).

p. 99   **"the spirit of youth"**   James Hillman, *Puer Papers* (Dallas: Spring Publications, 1979).

p. 99   **the *puer* needs to pair up**   Ibid.

p. 99   **the "naive male"**   Robert Bly, *Iron John* (New York: Addison-Wesley, 1990).

p. 108   **"The Tell-Tale Heart"**   Edgar Allan Poe, *Tales* (New York: Dodd, Mead & Co., 1952), pp. 363–367.

CHAPTER 4

LOOKING FOR THE BELOVED: DATING AS SHADOW-WORK

p. 110   **The minute I heard**   Jelaluddin Rumi, "The minute I heard," in *The Essential Rumi*, translated by Coleman Barks and John Moyne (San Francisco: HarperSanFrancisco, 1995), p. 106.

NOTES

p. 110   **When Cupid struck Apollo**   From *Bulfinch's Mythology*, edited by Richard Martin (New York: HarperCollins, 1991), pp. 22–23.

p. 121   **feeling of being gay**   John Beebe, lecture on Male-Male Partnership at the Lexus Conference, sponsored by the C. G. Jung Institute of Los Angeles, October 9, 1987.

p. 121   **Zeus seduces the innocent**   Christine Downing, *Myths and Mysteries of Same-Sex Love* (New York: Continuum Publishing Company, 1989), p. 147.

p. 121   **The life of Apollo**   Ibid.

p. 137   **the powerful, invulnerable hero**   Thanks to Tanya Wilkinson for her discussion of these issues is *Persephone Returns* (Berkeley, Calif.: Pagemill Press, 1996), pp. 2–10.

CHAPTER 5

SHADOW-BOXING: WRESTLING WITH ROMANTIC PARTNERS

p. 144   **How do I Love**   Elizabeth Barrett Browning, "How Do I Love Thee?" in *101 Classic Love Poems* (Chicago: Contemporary Books, 1988), p. 47.

p. 145   **Eros the bittersweet**   Anne Carson, *Eros the Bittersweet* (Princeton, N.J.: Princeton University Press, 1986).

p. 145   **"The soul cannot exist**   C. G. Jung, *Collected Works*, translated by R. F. C. Hull and edited by H. Read (Princeton, N.J.: Princeton University Press), vol. 16, pp. 164–201.

p. 147   **When we were very young**   Robert Bly, *A Little Book on the Human Shadow*, edited by William Booth (San Francisco: Harper & Row, 1988).

p 148   **a kind of fusion**   For an excellent discussion of the fusion stage of relationship, see Robert W. Firestone, *The Fantasy Bond* (New York: Human Sciences Press, 1987).

p. 159   **archetypal aspect to the image**   Robert Bly, *A Little Book on the Human Shadow*.

p. 161   **it's a difficult but necessary task**   Robert A. Johnson, *Lying with the Heavenly Woman* (San Francisco: HarperSanFrancisco, 1994).

p. 161   **In those fits of rage**   For an excellent discussion of Lilith, see Barbara Koltuv, *The Book of Lilith* (York Beach, Me.: Nicholas Hays, 1987).

p. 166   **projection**   It's not our intention to imply that relationships are nothing but projection, that there is no foundation for connecting deeply with another human being beyond the shadow's needs—that is, beyond individual psychology. Some people believe in metaphysical explanations for their relationships: karma, past lives, astrological fits, soul mates. They may meet someone and feel such an instantaneous recognition that they spend no time getting to know one another on a persona level. Instead, it's as if they have known each other all along. However, at some point, whether after three months, six months, or a year, the shadow emerges and conflict erupts. Then

325

the lovers discover that their spiritual connection cannot save them from shadow suffering. Because of the inevitability of this process, this book focuses on illuminating the psychology of the shadow in an effort to help people return to the love and the soul connection more readily.

CHAPTER 6

SHADOW-DANCING TILL DEATH DO US PART

p. 177   **A man and a woman**   Robert Bly, "A Man and a Woman," in *Selected Poems of Robert Bly* (New York: HarperCollins, 1986).

p. 178   **relationship today**   Murray Stein, "Relationship: A Myth for Our Time." Lecture at the C.G. Jung Institute in Los Angeles, January 25, 1990.

p. 179   **reports from men in power**   Aaron R. Kipnis, *Knights Without Armor: A Practical Guide for Men in Quest of Masculine Soul* (New York: Tarcher/Putnam, 1991).

p. 179   **In millions of single-parent families**   In late 1996, 18 percent of white children, 28 percent of Hispanic children, and 53 percent of African-American children were raised in single-parent households, primarily with mothers. One in five had not seen their fathers for five years. Cited in the American Psychological Association *Monitor*, August 1996, p. 8

p. 181   **the uniform of adulthood**   Murray Stein, "Marriage Alchemy," audiocassette from Chiron Publishing, 400 Linden Avenue, Willmette, IL 60091, 1984.

p. 184   **Tarot deck**   We refer here to Juliet Sharman-Burke and Liz Greene, *The Mythic Tarot* (New York: Simon & Schuster, 1986).

p. 194   **"The Lizard in the Fire"**   From Michael Meade, *Men and the Water of Life* (San Francisco: HarperSanFrancisco, 1993), pp. 111–20.

CHAPTER 7

SHADOWS AMONG FRIENDS: ENVY, ANGER, AND BETRAYAL

p. 215   **I am as a spirit**   Percy Bysshe Shelley, "The Poet's Lover," in *Complete Poetical Works of Percy Bysshe Shelley* (Cambridge, Mass.: Houghton-Mifflin, 1901), p. 487.

p. 217   **philia, meant love of soul**   From Eileen Gregory, *Summoning the Familiar* (Dallas: Dallas Institute of Humanities and Culture, 1983).

p. 217   **The ideal of male friendship**   From Christine Downing, *Psyche's Sisters* (San Francisco: HarperSanFrancisco, 1988), p. 58.

p. 218   **a tale of the Trojan War**   Christine Downing, *Myths and Mysteries of Same-Sex Love* (New York: Continuum Publishing, 1989), pp. 176–79.

p. 218   **identify their best friend**   Lillian Rubin, *Just Friends* (New York: HarperCollins, 1985), pp. 6–7.

p. 221   **Members of other cultures**   Robert A. Johnson, "Homoerotic and Homosexual Relationships." Lecture at the Nexus Conference, sponsored by the C. G. Jung Institute of Los Angeles, October 10, 1987.

p. 221   **In Germany**   From Lillian Rubin, *Just Friends*, p. 4.

p. 222   **Mnemosyne, goddess of memory**   Ginette Paris, *Pagan Grace* (Dallas: Spring Publications, 1990), p. 121.

p. 223   **They embody the mystery**   Eileen Gregory, *Summoning the Familiar*, pp. 69–70.

p. 224   **James Hillman has pointed out**   James Hillman, "Friends and Enemies," *Harvest* 8 (1962):1–22.

p. 229   **a long bag we drag behind us**   Robert Bly, *A Little Book on the Human Shadow*, edited by William Booth (San Francisco: HarperSanFrancisco, 1988).

p. 230   **male-male relationships**   John Beebe, Lecture on Male-Male Partnership at the Lexus Conference, sponsored by the C.G. Jung Institute of Los Angeles, October 9, 1987.

p. 231   **People who are strongly influenced**   Some of these points were made by Jean Shinoda Bolen in *Gods in Every Man* (San Francisco: HarperSanFrancisco, 1989).

p. 231   **A woman who is highly influenced by Artemis**   Some of these points were made by Jean Shinoda Bolen in *Goddesses in Every Woman* (San Francisco: HarperSanFrancisco, 1984).

p. 233   **men cover up their vulnerability**   Aaron Kipnis and Elizabeth Herron, *What Men and Women Really Want* (Novato, Calif.: Nataraj, 1995).

p. 234   **There are a few models**   From Barbara G. Walker, *The Woman's Encyclopedia of Myths and Mysteries* (San Francisco: HarperSanFrancisco, 1983), p. 400.

p. 235   **She stimulates a man's interests**   Toni Wolff, "Structural Forms of the Feminine Psyche," *Psychological Perspectives* 31 (Spring/Summer 1995):77–90.

p. 240   **"The holy passion of Friendship**   Mark Twain, *Pudd'nhead Wilson* (New York: New American Library, 1964).

p. 245   **"Where there is bitterness**   C. G. Jung, "The Mysterium Coniunctionis: The Personification of Opposites," *The Collected Works*, translated by R. F. C. Hull and edited by H. Read (Princeton, N.J.: Princeton University Press, 1953–90), vol. 14, p. 246.

CHAPTER 8

THE SHADOW AT WORK: THE SEARCH FOR SOUL ON THE JOB

p. 247   **Shake off this sadness**   Miguel de Unamuno, "Throw Yourself Like Seed," in *The Rag and Bone Shop of the Heart*, translated by Robert Bly and edited by Robert Bly, James Hillman, and Michael Meade (New York: HarperCollins, 1992).

p. 251   **To set aside the profit motive**   James Hillman, *Kinds of Power* (New York: Doubleday, 1995), p. 5.

p. 253   **In medieval society**   See D. M. Dooling, ed., *A Way of Working* (New York: Parabola Books, 1979).

p. 255   **work is undergoing tectonic shifts**   More than 43 million jobs have been erased in the United States since 1979. Whereas twenty-five years ago, the vast majority of people laid off found jobs that paid as well as the old ones, today only 35 percent find equal pay. From *The Downsizing of America: Special Report to* The New York Times (New York: Times Books, 1996).

p. 255   **Despite the extinction**   Ibid.

p. 256   **our relationships suffer**   Ibid. The divorce rate is as much as 50 percent higher than the national average in families in which one earner, usually the man, has lost a job and cannot find an equivalent one.

p. 256   **"Fatima, the Spinner, and the Tent"**   From Idries Shah, *Tales of the Dervishes* (New York: Dutton, 1967), pp. 72–74.

p. 258   **In some sectors of Western society**   Although productivity has more than doubled in the last fifty years, those with jobs work longer hours today than before the onset of the information age. In fact, overall work time has increased by one month a year, while leisure time has decreased by more than one-third. From Jeremy Rifkin, *The End of Work* (New York: Tarcher/Putnam, 1995), p. 223.

p. 268   **the Greek Titan Prometheus**   See Eileen Gregory, "Human Making and the Fires of Earth," in *Summoning the Familiar* (Dallas: Dallas Institute of Humanities and Culture, 1983).

p. 268   **Hermes appears**   For a lengthy discussion of Hermes, see Rafael Lopez-Pedraza, *Hermes and His Children* (Dallas: Spring Publications, 1977).

p. 269   **Hephaestus has been called**   Murray Stein, "Hephaistos: A Pattern of Introversion," *Spring* 73, pp. 35–51.

p. 272   **a power complex**   James Hillman, *Kinds of Power*.

p. 274   **this kind of power**   John R. O'Neil, *The Paradox of Success* (New York: Tarcher/Putnam, 1993).

p. 274   **if people in the helping professions**   This is explained at length by Adolf Guggenbuhl-Craig in *Power in the Helping Professions* (Dallas: Spring Publications, 1978).

p. 275   **One of the primary ways**   One recent study reported that one out of two women will be harassed during her working life. From L. F. Fitzgerald, "Sexual Harassment: Violence Against Women in the Workplace," *American Psychologist* 48, pp. 1070–76.

p. 275   **For the many women**   In 1986 the U.S. Supreme Court first considered sexual harassment as a violation of civil rights, determining that it must create an abusive working environment and result in psychological damage for it to be legally penalized. Since then, charges have more than doubled: in 1990, 6,127 charges were filed with the Equal Employment Opportunity Commission; in 1995, 15,549 were filed. From a report, "U.S. Companies Move to Curb Sex Harassment on Job," in the *Christian Science Monitor*, May 30, 1996.

p. 275   **monetary rewards have skyrocketed**   Ibid. In 1990, $7.7 million were awarded to plaintiffs; in 1995, $24.3 million were awarded.

p. 276   **discrimination against gays and lesbians**   As of 1993, only nine states had laws prohibiting discrimination based on sexual orientation. Many gay employees continue to live with a fear of being found out. They report that when they form support groups as part of a corporate culture, they are swamped with hate mail. From Ed Mickens, *The 100 Best Companies for Gay Men and Lesbians* (New York: Pocket Books, 1994).

p. 276   **in the helping professions**   One study of physicians reports that 25 percent violate their female patients. From R. Pearlman, "Doctors Tell of Sex with Patients," *San Francisco Chronicle*, August 7, 1992. In a questionnaire of 1,057 psychiatrists, 7.1 percent reported sexual contact with patients. From N. Gartrell, J. Herman, S. Olarte, M. Feldstein, and R. Localio, "Psychiatrist-Patient Sexual Contact: Results of a National Survey." Among psychotherapists, one expert estimates that as many as 30 percent have sexual contact with clients. From Peter Rutter, personal communication. The above findings were cited in Nancy Novack, *Gender Roles and Sexual Exploitation in Professional Relationships of Trust*, doctoral dissertation, February 1996.

A study of sexual harassment on college campuses revealed that 30 percent of undergraduate women felt harassed by a professor. From M. A. Paludi, ed.; *Ivory Power: Sexual Harassment on Campus* (Albany, N.Y.: SUNY Press, 1990).

A recent television report on the clergy disclosed that out of some fifty thousand Catholic priests, at least three thousand or 6 percent actively sexually abuse children, including engaging in oral sex, mutual masturbation, and paddling. Some use the fear of excommunication and the threat of damnation to maintain silence. More than six hundred reports have been filed in the past ten years. And the Catholic church has spent many hundreds of thousands of dollars in damage control, often taking an adversarial role with law enforcement. The members of the church hierarchy, unable to face the sexual shadow, maintain the rule of celibacy but protect its violators. Even today, with full knowledge of the devastating long-term consequences of the spiritual betrayal of children, church leaders turn the other way. A few who have tried to speak out have been silenced. As a result, the public image of the priesthood has been tainted with shadow, and those members who are innocent carry a terrible burden. From "Priestly Sins," an original HBO-BBC production, which aired in Los Angeles in May 1996.

p. 276   **more than one million men and women**   Peter Rutter, *Sex in the Forbidden Zone* (New York: Fawcett Books, 1990).

p. 276   **His power and her dependency**   The effects on the women involved can be life-changing. In a study of eight such women, seven suffered from the symptoms of post-traumatic stress, including flashbacks of the experience, depression, psychosomatic illnesses, and poor intimate relationships even five years later. In addition, none of the women had had children. Cited in Novack, *Gender Roles and Sexual Exploitation in Professional Relationships of Trust.*

p. 277   **Although state laws differ**   In fifteen states, sex between therapists and clients has become illegal, as the law attempts to compensate with outer constraints for the individual's absence of inner constraints.

p. 277   **Some therapists, like priests, cannot contain**   In California between 1992 and 1995, nineteen psychologists and four psychiatrists lost their professional licenses for sexual misconduct. From the American Psychological Association's *Monitor*, June 1996, p. 3.

CHAPTER 9

MIDLIFE AS DESCENT TO THE UNDERWORLD AND ASCENT OF THE LOST GODS

p. 280   **In a dark time**   Theodore Roethke, "In a Dark Time," in *The Collected Poems of Theodore Roethke* (New York: Doubleday, 1960).

p. 281   **Our personality develops**   C. G. Jung, "The Development of Personality," in *The Collected Works*, translated by R. F. C. Hull and edited by H. Read (Princeton, N.J.: Princeton University Press, 1953–90), vol. 17, p. 172.

p. 281   **"After having lavished its light**   C. G. Jung, "The Stages of Life," *The Collected Works*, translated by R. F. C. Hull and edited by H. Read (Princeton, N.J.: Princeton University Press, 1953–90), vol. 8, p. 399.

p. 282   **early onset spirituality**   Gratitude for this phrase to Jeffrey Satinover, "Aching in the Places Where We Used to Play," *Quadrant* 25, no. 1, p. 24.

p. 284   **the god Pan**   See James Hillman, *Pan and the Nightmare* (Dallas: Spring Publications, 1988) for an extended discussion of this theme.

p. 286   **Hermes may appear**   Murray Stein, *In Midlife* (Dallas: Spring Publications, 1983).

p. 289   **"The person who has eaten his shadow**   Robert Bly, *A Little Book on the Human Shadow* (San Francisco: HarperSanFrancisco, 1988), p. 42.

p. 291   **the underworld**   James Hillman, *The Dream and the Underworld* (New York: HarperCollins, 1979).

p. 291   **"the dread and resistance**   C. G. Jung, "Religious Ideas in Alchemy: The Prima Materia," *The Collected Works*, translated by R. F. C. Hull and edited by H. Read (Princeton, N.J.: Princeton University Press, 1953–90), vol. 12, p. 336.

p. 291   **we need to be led downwards**   C. G. Jung, "Flying Saucers: A Modern Myth of Things Seen in the Skies," *The Collected Works*, translated by R. F. C. Hull and edited by H. Read (Princeton, N.J.: Princeton University Press, 1953–90), vol. 10, pp. 355–56.

p. 292   **Joseph Campbell describes the descent**   Joseph Campbell, *The Hero with a Thousand Faces* (Princeton, N.J.: Princeton University Press, 1949).

p. 293   **Inanna, Queen of Heaven**   Born of the gods, she descended to earth as Inanna and was later called Ishtar, Astarte, and Asherah, goddess of the groves. Her life story, told in pictographs by an anonymous Sumerian poet on tablets found by archaeologists, includes her youth, her reign as queen, her love affair with a shepherd-king, and her descent to the underworld. From Diane Wolkstein and Samuel Noah Kramer, *Inanna: Queen of Heaven and Earth* (New York: HarperCollins, 1983).

p. 294   **when we connect the upperworld Self**   Sylvia Perera, *Descent to the Goddess* (Toronto: Inner City Books, 1981).

p. 294   **The journey had been**   Kathleen Raine, "The Inner Journey of the Poet," in Molly Tuby, ed., *In the Wake of Jung* (London: Coventure, 1983).

p. 296   **In a Korean Zen tale**   As told in Marc Barasch, *The Healing Path* (New York: Tarcher/Putnam, 1993).

p. 298   **instead of dreading or despising our symptoms**   James Hillman, *Re-Visioning Psychology* (New York: HarperCollins, 1975).

p. 298   **"The gods have become diseases."**   C. G. Jung, *The Collected Works*, translated by R. F. C. Hull and edited by H. Read (Princeton, N.J.: Princeton University Press, 1953–90), vol. 13, p. 37.

p. 302   **the *puer-puella* archetype**   Jeffrey Satinover, "Aching in the Places Where We Used to Play."

p. 304   **"There can be no doubt**   C. G. Jung, "Alchemical Studies: Commentary on the Secret of the Golden Flower," *The Collected Works*, translated by R. F. C. Hull and edited by H. Read (Princeton, N.J.: Princeton University Press, 1953–90), vol. 13, p. 21.

EPILOGUE

p. 305   **This being human is a guest-house**   Jelaluddin Rumi, "The Guest-House," in *Say I Am You*, translated by John Moyne and Coleman Barks (Athens, Ga.: Maypop Press, 1994), p. 41.

A SHADOW-WORK HANDBOOK

p. 308   **divine temptation, known as *até***   John A. Sanford, *Fate, Love, and Ecstasy* (Wilmette, Ill.: Chiron Publications, 1995), p. 56.

p. 308   **Whereas the Greeks**   E. R. Dodds, *The Greeks and the Irrational* (Berkeley: University of California Press, 1951), p. 5.

p. 309   **We suggest that shadow-work**   The Greeks also had a prescription for dealing with *até* that parallels our more contemporary approach. They suggested that we can become aware of the influence of a god upon us through developing *suneidesis*, a capacity for consciousness and higher perception through "the spiritual eye." *Suneidesis* means both self-awareness and conscience—that is, knowing the activity of our mind and heart—as well as knowing what is morally correct. From Sanford, *Fate, Love, and Ecstasy*, p. 64.

BIBLIOGRAPHY

The following list includes our sources and other related titles.

Andersen, Hans Christian. "The Shadow," *Eighty Fairy Tales*. New York: Pantheon Books, 1976.

Barasch, Marc Ian. *The Healing Path: A Soul Approach to Illness*. New York: Tarcher/Putnam, 1993.

Bauer, Jan. *Alcoholism & Women*. Toronto: Inner City Books, 1982.

Becker, Ernest. *Escape from Evil*. New York: Free Press, 1975.

———. *The Denial of Death*. New York: The Free Press, 1973.

Bernstein, Jerome S. *Power & Politics: The Psychology of Soviet-American Partnership*. Boston: Shambhala, 1989.

Berry, Patricia. *Echo's Subtle Body*. Dallas: Spring Publications, 1982.

Bly, Robert. *A Little Book on the Human Shadow*. New York: Harper & Row, 1988.

———. *Iron John*. New York: Addison-Wesley, 1990.

———. *The Sibling Society*. New York: Addison-Wesley, 1996.

Boer, Charles. "In the Shadow of the Gods: Greek Tragedy." *Spring*, 1982.

Bolen, Jean Shinoda. *Goddesses in Everywoman*. San Francisco: Harper & Row, 1984.

———. *Gods in Everyman*. San Francisco: Harper & Row, 1989.

Borysenko, Joan. *Guilt Is the Teacher, Love Is the Lesson*. New York: Warner Books, 1990.

Bradshaw, John. *Healing the Shame That Binds You*. Deerfield Beach, Fla.: Health Communications, 1988.

———. *Family Secrets*. New York: Bantam, 1995.

Branden, Nathaniel. *The Disowned Self*. New York: Bantam Books, 1978.

Brewi, Janice, and Anne Brennan. *Celebrate Mid-Life: Jungian Archetypes and Mid-Life Spirituality.* New York: Crossroad, 1989.

Bulfinch, Thomas. *Myths of Greece and Rome.* New York: Penguin, 1981.

———. *Bulfinch's Mythology,* edited by Richard Martin. New York: Harper-Collins, 1991.

Butler, Katy. "Encountering the Shadow in Buddhist America." *Common Boundary,* May/June 1990.

Campbell, Joseph. *The Hero with a Thousand Faces.* Princeton, N.J.: Princeton University Press, Bollingen Series, 1973.

Carotenuto, Aldo. *To Love, to Betray: Life as Betrayal.* Wilmette, Ill.: Chiron Publications, 1996.

Carson, Anne. *Eros the Bittersweet.* Princeton, N.J.: Princeton University Press, 1986.

Chinen, Allan. *Once Upon a Midlife: Classic Stories and Mythic Tales to Illuminate the Middle Years.* New York: Tarcher/Putnam, 1992.

Conger, John P. *Jung & Reich: The Body as Shadow.* Berkeley, Calif.: North Atlantic Books, 1985.

Crawford, Tad. *The Secret Life of Money: Teaching Tales of Spending, Receiving, Saving, and Owing.* New York: Tarcher/Putnam, 1994.

Dallett, Janet. *Saturday's Child.* Toronto: Inner City Books, 1991.

D'Aulaire, Ingri, and Edgar D'Aulaire. *Book of Greek Myths.* Garden City, N.Y.: Doubleday, 1962.

Diamond, Stephen A., *Anger, Madness, and the Daimonic.* New York: State University of New York Press, 1996.

Dodds, E. R. *The Greeks and the Irrational.* Berkeley: University of California Press, 1951.

Downing, Christine. *Psyche's Sisters.* New York: Harper & Row, 1988.

———, ed. *Mirrors of the Self.* New York: Tarcher/Putnam, 1991.

———. *Myths and Mysteries of Same-Sex Love.* New York: Continuum, 1989.

———. *The Goddess: Mythological Images of the Feminine.* New York: Crossroad Publishing, 1981.

———. *Gods in Our Midst: Mythological Images of the Masculine: A Woman's View.* New York: Crossroad Publishing, 1993.

Edinger, Edward F. *The Anatomy of the Psyche.* La Salle, Ill.: Open Court, 1986.

Eichman, William Carl. "Meeting Darkness on the Path." *Gnosis* 14 (Winter 1990).

Estés, Clarissa Pinkola. *Women Who Run With the Wolves: Myths and Stories of the Wild Woman Archetype.* New York: Ballantine Books, 1992.

Fassel, Diane. *Working Ourselves to Death: The High Cost of Workaholism and the Rewards of Recovery.* San Francisco: HarperSanFrancisco, 1990.

Feinstein, David, and Stanley Krippner. *Personal Mythology: The Psychology of Your Evolving Self.* New York: Tarcher/Putnam, 1988.

Firestone, Robert W. *The Fantasy Bond.* New York: Human Sciences Press, 1987.

Frey-Rohn, Liliane. "Evil from the Psychological Point of View." *Spring*, 1965, pp. 5–47.

Fromm, Erich. *Anatomy of Human Destructiveness*. New York: Henry Holt, 1973.

Galland, China. *Longing for Darkness: Tara and the Black Madonna*. New York: Penguin Books, 1990.

Gallard, Martine Drahon. "Black Shadow/White Shadow." *The Archetype of the Shadow in a Split World*, edited by Mary Ann Mattoon. Zurich: Daimon, 1987.

Gerzon, Mark. *Listening to Midlife: Turning Your Crisis into a Quest*. Boston: Shambhala Publications, 1992.

Glendinning, Chellis. *When Technology Wounds: The Human Consequences of Progress*. New York: Morrow, 1990.

Goldberg, Jane. *The Dark Side of Love*. New York: Tarcher/Putnam, 1991.

Greene, Liz, and Stephen Arroyo. *The Jupiter/Saturn Conference Lectures*. Sebastapol, Calif.: CRCS Publications, 1984.

Gregory, Eileen. *Summoning the Familiar*. Dallas: Dallas Institute of the Humanities and Culture, 1983.

Grof, Christina, and Stanislav Grof. *The Stormy Search for the Self*. New York: Tarcher/Putnam, 1990.

Guggenbuhl-Craig, Adolf. *Eros on Crutches*. Dallas: Spring Publications, 1980.

———. *Marriage Dead or Alive*. Dallas: Spring Publications, 1977.

———. *Power in the Helping Professions*. Dallas: Spring Publications, 1978.

———. "Quacks, Charlatans, and False Prophets." *The Reality of the Psyche*, edited by Joseph Wheelright. New York: G. P. Putnam's Sons, 1972.

Hannah, Barbara. "Ego & Shadow," Guild of Pastoral Psychology, lecture 85, March 1955.

———. *Encounters with the Soul: Active Imagination*. Boston: Sigo Press, 1981.

Harding, Esther M. *The I and the Not I*. Princeton, N.J.: Princeton University Press, Bollingen Series, 1965.

———. "The Shadow." *Spring*, 1945.

Henderson, Joseph L. *Shadow & Self: Selected Papers in Analytical Psychology*. Wilmette, Ill.: Chiron Publications, 1989.

Hendrix, Harville. *Getting the Love You Want*. New York: Harper & Row, 1988.

Herman, Judith Lewis. *Trauma and Recovery*. New York: Basic Books, 1992.

Hillman, James. *The Dream & the Underworld*. New York: Harper & Row, 1979.

———. "Friends and Enemies: The Dark Side of Relationship." *Harvest* 8 (1962): p. 1–22.

———. *Loose Ends*. Dallas: Spring Publications, 1975.

———. *Insearch: Psychology and Religion*. New York: Charles Scribner's Sons, 1967.

———, ed. *Soul and Money*. Dallas: Spring Publications, 1982.

———. "Notes on White Supremacy." *Spring*, 1986, pp. 29–59.

———, ed. *Puer Papers*. Dallas: Spring Publications, 1979.

————. *Re-Visioning Psychology*. New York: Harper & Row, 1975.

————. *Kinds of Power: A Guide to Its Intelligent Uses*. New York: Doubleday, 1995.

Hollis, James. *Swamplands of the Soul: New Life in Dismal Places*. Toronto: Inner City Books, 1996.

Houston, Jean. *The Search for the Beloved*. New York: Tarcher/Putnam, 1987.

————. *A Mythic Life*. San Francisco: HarperSanFrancisco, 1996.

Jacoby, Mario, Verena Kast, and Ingrid Riedel. *Witches, Ogres, and the Devil's Daughter: Encounters with Evil in Fairy Tales*. Boston: Shambhala Publications, 1992.

Jaffe, Aniela, ed. *C. G. Jung: Word and Image*. Princeton, N.J.: Princeton University Press, Bollingen Series XCVII: 2, 1979.

Johnson, Robert A. *Owning Your Own Shadow*. New York: Harper & Row, 1991.

————. *The Fisher King and the Handless Maiden*. San Francisco: HarperSanFrancisco, 1993.

Jones, Alan. *The Soul's Journey*. San Francisco: HarperSanFrancisco, 1995.

Joy, W. Brugh. *Avalanche: Heretical Reflections on the Dark and the Light*. New York: Ballantine Books, 1990.

Jung, Carl Gustav. *Answer to Job*. London: Routledge & Kegan Paul, 1952.

————. *Collected Works*, vols. 1–20, translated by R. F. C. Hull and edited by H. Read, M. Fordham, G. Adler, and William McGuire. Princeton, N.J.: Princeton University Press, Bollingen Series XX, 1953–90.

————. "The Fight with the Shadow." *Listener*, November 7, 1946.

————. *Memories, Dreams, Reflections*. New York: Pantheon Books, 1973.

Jung, Carl Gustav, Marie-Louise von Franz, Joseph Henderson, Jolande Jacobi, and Aniela Jaffe. *Man and His Symbols*. Garden City, N.Y.: Doubleday, 1964.

Jung, Emma, and Marie-Louise von Franz. *The Grail Legend*. New York: Putnam, 1970.

Keen, Sam. *Faces of the Enemy*. New York: Harper & Row, 1986.

Kelsey, Morton. *Discernment: A Study in Ecstasy & Evil*. New York: Paulist Press, 1978.

Kerenyi, Carl. *Gods of the Greeks*. New York: Thames and Hudson, 1951.

Kipnis, Aaron. *Knights Without Armor: A Practical Guide for Men in Quest of Masculine Soul*. New York: Tarcher/Putnam, 1991.

Kipnis, Aaron, and Elizabeth Herron. *What Women and Men Really Want*. Novato, Calif.: Nataraj, 1995.

Koestler, Arthur. *Janus: A Summing Up*. New York: Vintage Books, 1978.

Kramer, Samuel Noah, and Diane Wolkstein. *Inanna: Queen of Heaven and Earth*. New York: Harper & Row, 1983.

Le Guin, Ursula K. *The Wizard of Earthsea*. New York: Parnassus Press, 1975.

————. *The Wind's Twelve Quarters: Short Stories*. New York: HarperCollins, 1975.

Leonard, Linda Schierse. *The Wounded Woman*. Boston: Shambhala Publications, 1982.

————. *Witness to the Fire*. Boston: Shambhala Publications, 1989.

————. *Meeting the Madwoman*. New York: Bantam. 1993.

Lifton, Robert, J. *The Nazi Doctors: Medical Killing and the Psychology of Genocide*. New York: Basic Books, 1986.

Lorde, Audre. *Sister Outsider*. New York: Crossing Press, 1984.

Lowinsky, Naomi. *The Motherline*. New York: Tarcher/Putnam, 1991.

May, Rollo. *Power & Innocence*. New York: W. W. Norton, 1972.

Meade, Michael. *Men and the Water of Life: Initiation and the Tempering of Men*. San Francisco: HarperSanFrancisco, 1993.

Metzger, Deena. "Personal Disarmament: Negotiating with the Inner Government." *Revision* 12, no. 4 (Spring 1990).

Mickens, Ed. *The 100 Best Companies for Gay Men and Lesbians*. New York: Pocket Books, 1994.

Miller, Alice. *Banished Knowledge: Facing Childhood Injuries*. New York: Doubleday, 1990.

————. *For Your Own Good: Hidden Cruelty in Child-Rearing and the Roots of Violence*. New York: Farrar, Straus, Giroux, 1983.

Miller, Patrick D. "What the Shadow Knows: An Interview with John A. Sanford." *Sun*, issue 137, 1990.

Miller, William A. *Your Golden Shadow*. New York: Harper & Row, 1989.

Mindell, Arnold. "The Golem." *Quadrant* 8, no. 2 (Winter 1975), pp. 107–114.

————. *City Shadows: Psychological Interventions in Psychiatry*. London: Routledge, 1989.

Mofitt, Phillip. "The Dark Side of Excellence." *Esquire*, December 1985.

Moore, Thomas. *Care of the Soul*. New York: HarperCollins, 1992.

————. *Soul Mates*. New York: HarperCollins, 1994.

Morrish, Ivor. *The Dark Twin: A Study of Evil & Good*. Essex, England: L.N. Fowler, 1980.

Murdock, Maureen. *The Heroine's Journey*. Boston: Shambhala Publications, 1990.

————. *The Hero's Daughter: An Exploration of the Shadow Side of Father Love*. New York: Ballantine, 1994.

Nebel, Cecile. *The Dark Side of Creativity*. Troy, N.Y.: Whitston Publishing, 1988.

Nelson, John, and Andrea Nelson, eds. *Sacred Sorrows: Embracing and Transforming Depression*. New York: Tarcher/Putnam, 1996.

New York Times Special Report: The Downsizing of America. New York: Times Books, 1996.

Nichols, Sallie. *Jung & Tarot*. York Beach, Maine: Samuel Weiser, 1980.

O'Neil, John. *The Paradox of Success*. New York: Tarcher/Putnam, 1993.

Pagels, Elaine. *The Origin of Satan*. New York: Vintage Books, 1995.

Paris, Ginette. *Pagan Grace*. Dallas: Spring Publications, 1990.

Peavy, Fran. "Us & Them." *Whole Earth Review* 49 (Winter 1985).

Peck, M. Scott. *People of the Lie*. New York: Simon & Schuster, 1983.

Pedersen, Loren E. *Dark Hearts: The Unconscious Forces That Shape Men's Lives*. Boston: Shambhala Publications, 1991.

Perera, Sylvia Brinton. *The Scapegoat Complex: Toward a Mythology of Shadow and Guilt*. Toronto: Inner City Books, 1986.

———. *Descent to the Goddess: A Way of Initiation for Women*. Toronto: Inner City Books, 1981.

Raine, Kathleen. "The Inner Journey of the Poet." In *the Wake of Jung*, edited by Molly Tuby. London: Coventure, 1986.

Rank, Otto. *The Double*, translated and edited by Harry Tucker, Jr. New York: New American Library, 1977.

Rifkin, Jeremy. *The End of Work: The Decline of the Global Labor Force and the Dawn of the Post-Market Era*. New York: Tarcher/Putnam, 1995.

Rilke, Rainer Maria. *The Sonnets to Orpheus*, translated by Stephen Mitchell. New York: Simon & Schuster, 1985.

———. *The Selected Poetry of Rainer Maria Rilke*, translated by Stephen Mitchell. New York: Vintage Books, 1982.

———. *Selected Poems of Rainer Maria Rilke*, translated by Robert Bly. New York: HarperCollins, 1981.

Rosen, David. *Transforming Depression*. New York: Tarcher/Putnam, 1991.

Rubin, Lillian B. *Just Friends: The Role of Friendship in Our Lives*. New York: Harper & Row, 1985.

Rushing, Janice Hocker, and Thomas S. Frentz. *Projecting the Shadow: The Cyborg Hero in American Film*. Chicago: University of Chicago Press, 1995.

Rutter, Peter. *Sex in the Forbidden Zone*. New York: Tarcher/Putnam, 1989.

Sandner, Donald F. "The Split Shadow and the Father-Son Relationship." *Betwixt & Between*, edited by Louise Mahdi et al., La Salle, Ill.: Open Court, 1988.

Sanford, John A. *Evil: The Shadow Side of Reality*. New York: Crossroad, 1984.

———. *The Strange Trial of Mr. Hyde*. New York: HarperCollins, 1987.

———. *Fate, Love, and Ecstasy: Wisdom from the Lesser-Known Goddesses of the Greeks*. Wilmette, Ill.: Chiron Publications, 1995.

Satinover, Jeffrey, and Lenore Thomson Bentz, "Aching in the Places Where We Used to Play." *Quadrant* 25, no. 1, 1992, pp. 21–57.

Scarf, Maggie. *Intimate Partners: Patterns in Love & Marriage*. New York: Random House, 1982.

Schachter-Shalomi, Zalman, and Ronald S. Miller. *From Age-ing to Sage-ing*. New York: Time-Warner, 1995.

Sharman-Burke, Juliet, and Liz Green. *The Mythic Tarot*. New York: Simon & Schuster, 1986.

Sharp, Daryl. *The Survival Papers: Anatomy of a Mid-Life Crisis*. Toronto: Inner City Books, 1988.

Sidoli, Mara. "The Shadow Between Parents & Children." *The Archetype of the Shadow in a Split World*, edited by Mary Ann Mattoon. Zurich: Daimon, 1987.

———. "Shame & Shadow." *Journal of Analytical Psychology* 33, no. 2, pp. 127–42.

Solzhenitsyn, Aleksander. *The Gulag Archipelago*. New York: Harper & Row, 1978.

Stark, Marcia, and Gynne Stern. *The Dark Goddess: Dancing with the Shadow*. Freedom, Calif.: Crossing Press, 1993.

Stein, Murray. *In Midlife: A Jungian Perspective*. Dallas: Spring Publications, 1983.

———, ed. *Encountering Jung on Evil*. Princeton, N.J.: Princeton University Press, 1995.

Stillings, Dennis. "Invasion of the Archetypes." *Gnosis*, no. 10 (Winter 1989).

Stone, Hal, and Sidra Winkelman. *Embracing Ourselves*. San Rafael, Calif.: New World Library, 1989.

Sussman, Linda. *Speech of the Grail*. Hudson, N.Y.: Lindisfarne Press, 1995.

Taub, Gary. "The Usefulness of the Useless." *Psychological Perspectives* 18, no. 2 (Fall 1987).

Tuby, Molly. "The Shadow." The Guild of Pastoral Psychology, Guild Lecture 216, London, 1963.

Ventura, Michael. *Shadow Dancing in the USA*. New York: Tarcher/Putnam, 1985.

von Franz, Marie-Louise. *C.G. Jung: His Myth in Our Time*. New York: G.P. Putnam's Sons (for the C.G. Jung Foundation, N.Y.), 1975.

———. *Projection & Re-collection in Jungian Psychology*. La Salle, Ill.: Open Court Publishing, 1980.

———. *Shadow & Evil in Fairy Tales*. Dallas: Spring Publications, 1974.

———. *Puer Aeternus*, 2nd ed. Boston: Sigo Press, 1981.

von Franz, Marie-Louise, and James Hillman. *Jung's Typology*. Dallas: Spring Publications, 1971.

Walker, Barbara G. *The Crone*. San Francisco: HarperSanFrancisco, 1985.

———. *The Woman's Encyclopedia of Myths and Mysteries*. San Francisco: HarperSanFrancisco, 1983.

Watson, Lyall. *Dark Nature*. New York: HarperCollins, 1995.

Welwood, John. *Love and Awakening*. New York: HarperCollins, 1996.

Whitmyer, Claude, ed. *Mindfulness and Meaningful Work: Explorations in Right Livelihood*. Berkeley, Calif.: Parallax Press, 1994.

Wilber, Ken. *The Spectrum of Consciousness*. Wheaton, Ill.: Theosophical Publishing House, 1982.

———. *Sex, Ecology, Spirituality*. Boston: Shambhala Publications, 1994.

Wilkinson, Tanya. *Persephone Returns: Victims, Heroes, and the Journey from the Underworld*. Berkeley, Calif.: Pagemill Press, 1996.

Wolff, Toni. "Structural Forms of the Feminine Psyche." *Psychological Perspectives* 31 (Spring/Summer 1995).

Woodman, Marion. *Addiction to Perfection*. Toronto: Inner City Books, 1982.

———. *The Pregnant Virgin*. Toronto: Inner City Books, 1985.

————. *The Ravaged Bridegroom*. Toronto: Inner City Books, 1990.

————. *Dancing in the Flames: The Dark Goddess in the Transformation of Consciousness*. Boston: Shambhala, 1996.

Woodruff, Paul, and Harry Wilmer, eds. *Facing Evil at the Core of Darkness*. La Salle, Ill.: Open Court, 1989.

Yandell, James. "Devils on the Freeway." *San Francisco Chronicle*, "This World," July 26, 1987.

Ziegler, Alfred J. *Archetypal Medicine*. Dallas: Spring Publications, 1983.

Zweig, Connie, ed. *To Be a Woman: The Birth of the Conscious Feminine*. New York: Tarcher/Putnam, 1990.

————, ed. *Meeting the Shadow: The Hidden Power of the Dark Side of Human Nature* (with Jeremiah Abrams). New York: Tarcher/Putnam, 1991.

INDEX

Abandoners, 39, 42
Abandonment, fear of, 131, 134, 151, 152, 155, 156
Abraham, 89, 93, 95
Abusers, 39, 42
Achilles, 218
Adam, 160
Adams, John, 86
Adaptation, strategies of, 10
Addiction, 4, 11–12, 18, 39, 40, 48
  camouflages, 51
  friendship and, 243–244
Adonis, 149, 317
Adultery, 59
Agamemnon, 89
Agapé (spiritual love), 61
Agave, 89
Aggression, 4, 13, 158, 272–273
Ahriman, 160
Ahura Mazda, 160
Aidos, 169
AIDS epidemic, 54, 141, 163
Alcohol, 12, 52–53, 59, 67
Alcoholics Anonymous, 11
Ananke, 45, 47, 248, 277, 314
Anti-Semitism, 68
Anxiety, 48, 66

Anxiety disorders, 4
Aphrodite, 14, 16, 49, 52, 120, 122, 123, 132, 142, 149, 169, 206, 210, 227, 228, 231, 270, 295, 308, 314, 318–320
  description of, 317
Apollo, 15, 110, 111, 121, 143, 151, 231, 269, 282, 295
  description of, 317
Appearance, 114–115
Apple Computers, 249
Archetypal perspective
  on dating, 121–124
  on friendship, 231–232
  on romance, 172–173
  on work, 268–271
Archetypes, 10, 11, 13, 14, 16
  of love, 150–164
Ares, 14, 49, 52, 231, 314
  description of, 317
Ariadne, 172, 290
Arica, 33
Aristotle, 217
Artemis, 13, 92, 104, 122, 123, 150, 206–208, 210, 231, 270, 282, 317
  description of, 317–318

Arthur, King, 44, 72, 232
Artist's Way, The (Cameron), 260
Até, 308
Athena, 15, 24–29, 63, 92, 104, 123, 151, 152, 210, 227, 228, 231, 270, 281, 295, 314, 319
  description of, 318
Authentic grief, 288–289
Authentic guilt, 171
Authenticity, sacrifice of, 69–72
Authentic power, 49, 237
Authentic shame, 169
Aztecs, 277–278

Bast, 160
Baubo, 295
Beatrice, 163
Beebe, John, 121, 230
Behaviorism, 31
Belly breathing, 310–311
Betrayal (*see* Parent's betrayal)
Bhagavad Gita, 16
Biological shadow, 54
Blaming, 4, 8, 114, 125, 188–189, 254
Blended stepfamilies, 58
Bly, Robert, 99, 147, 159, 177, 181, 183, 229, 289
Body Shop, The, 249
Bosnia-Herzegovina, 54
Breathing exercise, 15, 81, 189, 310–311
Browning, Elizabeth Barrett, 144
Buddhism, 53, 249

Caffeine, 11, 258
Camelot, 44, 45
Cameron, Julia, 260
Campbell, Joseph, 270, 292
Cassandra, 69
Castor, 217, 223
Catholicism, 53
Celibacy, role of, 7
Centering, 15, 39, 300–311
Change of attitude (*metanoia*), 8

Childhood abuse, 10, 58, 67
  sexual, 75–82, 158, 161
Childhood memories, 11
Childlessness, 105–106
Chiron, 226
Clergy, 7, 163, 277
Cocaine, 11, 51, 258
Codependency, 131
Collaborations, 266–268
Collective morality, 16
Commitment, crises of, 139–142, 148, 191–196, 198–200
Compensation period, 149–154
Competition, 4
Condoms, 134
Conscious communication, 187–191
Consciousness, evolution of, 10
Contemplation, 5
Coping strategies, 46–48 (*see also* Projection)
  denial, 5–7, 14, 21, 43, 46, 48, 65, 69, 77, 80, 258
  dissociation, 77
  identification, 46–48, 76, 90, 93, 107
  regression, 48
  repression, 46, 77, 107
  somaticization, 46
  suppression, 46
Counterdependency, 83, 131
Covert depression, 66, 67
Creativity, 12, 41–42, 269
Crises of commitment, 139–142, 148, 191–196, 198–200
Critics, 39
Cronos (Father Time), 63, 94, 96, 241, 248, 252, 258, 281, 289, 320
  description of, 318
Cultural shadow, 52–55
Cupid, 110

Daedelus, 99
Danaids, 284
Dante Alighieri, 163, 294

Daphne, 110, 111, 143, 151
Darth Vader, 37
Dating, 21, 110–143, 181 (*see also*
    Marriage; Romance)
    archetypal perspective on, 121–124
    crises of commitment, 139–142
    inner process, 124–131
    money shadows and, 131,
        135–136
    power shadows and, 131, 137–139
    sexual shadows and, 131–135
    shame and, 119–121
    single men and, 119–121
    single women and, 116–119
David, King, 163
Daydreaming, 148
Defense styles (*see* Coping strategies)
Demeter, 15, 28, 29, 94, 101, 105, 122,
    123, 173, 179, 226, 232, 270, 282,
    284, 319
    description of, 318
Demonic forces, 7
Denial, 5–7, 14, 21, 43, 46, 48, 65, 69,
    77, 80, 258
Dependency, 4
Depression, 4, 9, 18, 47, 66–67, 148,
    201–202
    midlife, 291, 295–296
Depth psychology, 10
Despair, 47
Dickinson, Emily, 36
Dionysus, 132, 152, 153, 172, 206,
    210, 231, 269, 290, 314
    description of, 318
Dioscuri, 217
Dissociation, 77
Dissociative disorders, 48
Divorce rate, 173
Dreams, 41, 98, 138, 228–229,
    259–260, 278
Drugs, 11, 33, 52, 58, 68, 102,
    243–244
Dumuzi, 172
Durga, 160

Eating disorders, 4, 65
Einstein, Albert, 180
Embarrassment, 40
Engagement, 191–195
Envy, 4, 18, 65–66, 84, 240
Epimetheus, 319
Ereshkigal, 293–294
Eros, 49, 52, 144, 145, 159, 168, 172,
    176, 206, 216, 217, 275, 277, 286,
    287, 295, 317, 320
    description of, 318
Eros (erotic love), 61
Ethnic cleansing, 54
Eurydice, 173, 292
Eve, 73, 160, 176
Evolution of consciousness, 10
Ex-spouse complex, 196–198
Extramarital affairs, 4, 203–210

False memory syndrome, 77
Family shadow, 11, 21, 57–87,
    180–181 (*see also* Parent's
    betrayal)
    family secrets, 69–72
    family soul, 61–63
    incest, 75–82
    intergenerational sins, 63–69
    money shadows, 82–86
    siblings, 72–75
    work styles, 261–265
Family soul, 61–63
Fantasies, 205–206, 209
Father's daughter, 24–29, 92, 102–106,
    196, 211
Father's son, 66, 92, 93–96, 202
"Fatima, the Spinner, and the Tent,"
    256–257
Faust, 38, 55–56, 307
Faustian bargains, 37–38, 45, 55, 76,
    78, 142, 207, 209, 253, 259
Fear, 48, 66
    of abandonment, 131, 134, 151,
        152, 155, 156
    of rejection, 115, 204–205

Fisher King, 32–34, 77
Fool, 40
Frankenstein, 37
French and Turkish language,
    187–192, 201, 202, 213
Freud, Sigmund, 10, 16
Friendship, 21–22, 215–246
    addiction and, 243–244
    archetypal perspective on, 231–232
    family projections and, 225–227
    friends as gods, 227–231
    loss of loyal, 217–221
    money shadows and, 240–242
    opposite-sex, 233–235
    power shadows and, 237–239
    racism and, 221, 238, 239, 241–243
    redefining successful, 245–246
    sexual shadows and, 235–237
    soul friends/shadow friends,
        221–225
Fundamentalism, 6

Gaia, 63
Gang violence, 58
Ganymede, 121, 172
Gays, 54, 120–121
    marriages, 58, 276
    relationships, 163, 164
    work issues, 276
Genocide, 54
Gifted child, 73–74
Glass Menagerie, The (Williams), 101
Goethe, Johann Wolfgang von, 36–37,
    55
Gorgon, 28
Gothic horror, 7
Great Mother archetype, 16, 18
Greed, 4, 59, 84
Guggenbuhl-Craig, Adolf, 274
Guilt, 4, 51, 78, 127–129, 171, 183

Hades, 63, 76, 78, 101, 102, 180, 231,
    293, 295
    description of, 318–319

Hate crimes, 7
Healing model, 10–11
Helen of Troy, 308
Helplessness, 66, 118
Hephaestus, 89, 92, 120, 269, 317
    description of, 319
Hera, 14, 122–123, 172, 179, 204, 231,
    232, 269, 295, 317, 320
    description of, 319
Hercules, 259, 273
Hermes, 15, 85, 86, 92, 210, 231, 268,
    286
    description of, 319
Herron, Liz, 233
Hestia, 61, 295
    description of, 319
Hetaera, 234–235
Hillman, James, 19, 45, 54, 91, 99,
    224, 251, 272, 291, 298
Hinduism, 53, 160
Holocaust, 54, 68
Holy Grail, 30–34, 77
Homelessness, 54
Homophobia, 68, 216, 276
Homosexuality (see Gays)
Hopelessness, 47, 66, 118
Humor, 40–41
Hyacinthus, 121

Icarus, 99, 100
Ichazo, Oscar, 33
Identification, 46–48, 76, 90, 93, 107
Immigrants, illegal, 54
Impulsivity, 12
Inanna, 172, 290, 293–294
Inauthentic grief, 288
Inauthentic guilt, 171
Inauthentic power, 49, 237
Inauthentic shame, 169
Incest, 75–82, 158
Individuation, 16, 75
Inferiority, 237–239
Inheritance, 83
Intergenerational sins, 63–69

Internet, 53, 255
Iphigenia, 89
Isaac, 89
Isis, 172

James, William, 8
Janus, 255
Jason, 89
Jealousy, 4, 12, 59, 148, 193
Jesus, 6, 89, 293, 307
Jobs (see Work)
Johnson, Robert A., 160–161
Journal-keeping, 14–15
Judas, 307
Jung, Carl, 7–8, 10, 16, 18, 23, 31,
    178, 234
  and Goethe's "Faust," 55–56
  quoted, 38, 64, 145, 281, 291, 298
Juno, 50

Kali, 12, 52, 76, 159, 160, 293
Kipnis, Aaron, 233
Kleptomania, 286
Knights of the Round Table, 44, 72
Kore, 319
Kwan-yin, 249, 297, 298

Language, 54, 187–192, 201, 202, 213
Lawrence, D. H., 88
Laziness, 4, 12, 59
Learning organizations, 248–249
Leda, 217
Le Guin, Ursula, 88, 90, 92
Leto, 317
Lilith, 73, 160, 161
"Lizard in the Fire, The" (Meade),
    194–195
Love
  archetypes of, 159–164
  psychology of, 154–159
Loyal friendship, loss of, 217–221

Madonna/Whore syndrome, 152
Maia, 319

Marriage, 112, 177–214
  conscious communication in,
    187–191
  crisis of commitment and, 139–142,
    148, 191–196, 198–200
  ex-spouse complex, 196–198
  French and Turkish language
    language in, 187–192, 201, 202,
    213
  money shadows and, 210–212
  parenthood, 212–214
  power shadows and, 200–203
  sexual shadows and, 203–210
  shadow, 21, 198–200
  Third Body, 21, 181–186, 188, 190,
    197, 203
Masculine/feminine, 21, 24–28
  father's daughter, 24–29, 92,
    102–106, 196, 211
  father's son, 66, 92, 93–96, 202
  mother's daughter, 28–30, 92,
    100–102
  mother's son, 92, 96–100, 212
Meade, Michael, 194
Medea, 89
Medical model, 11
Medication, 11, 121 (see also Drugs)
Meditation, 310–311
Medusa, 27–29, 76, 318
Memories, Dreams,
    Reflections (Jung), 55
Menopause, 283
Mephistopheles, 37, 55–56, 307
Merlin, 172, 232
Metis, 24, 63, 318
Midlife, 13, 22, 41, 42, 46–47, 115,
    117, 280–307
  bodily symptoms, 296–298
  as descent into underworld,
    289–294
  as emergence of new priorities,
    286–289
  as promise of renewal, 282–286
  reclaiming the unlived life, 298–304

Mindell, Arnie, 297
Misstatements, 40
Mnemosyne, 81, 222, 288
  description of, 319
Moneta, 50
Money shadows, 48, 50–51,
    210–212
  dating and, 131, 135–136
  family shadow and, 82–86
  friendship and, 240–242
  work and, 277–279
Moral behavior, cultural attitudes
    toward, 53
Mother's daughter, 28–30, 65, 92,
    100–102
Mother's son, 92, 96–100, 212
Mrs. Field's Cookies, 249
Multicultural relationships, 58
Multiple personality disorder, 48

Native Americans, 54
Nazis, 54
Negative traits, 12, 46, 59
Nicotine, 11

Odysseus, 24, 184, 309, 311
O'Neil, John R., 274
"Ones Who Walk Away from Omelas,
    The" (Le Guin), 88–90, 92
Opposites, attraction of, 149
Orgasm, 132
Orpheus, 173, 290, 292, 317
Orual, 73
Osiris, 108, 160, 172, 293
Ouranos, 63, 318
Overt depression, 66

Pan, 284, 285
  description of, 319
Pandora, 120, 269
  description of, 319
Pandora's box, 169
Parent's betrayal, 88–109, 181
  father's daughter, 92, 102–106
  father's son, 92, 93–96

mother's daughter, 92, 100–102
mother's son, 92, 96–100
Paris of Troy, 89, 90, 308
Parsifal, 30, 31, 33, 34, 314
Patroclus, 218
Penelope of Ithaca, Queen, 184, 214
Pentheus, 89
Perera, Sylvia, 294
Perfectionism, 115, 186, 200
Persephone, 12, 76, 78, 101, 102, 180,
    231, 284, 290, 293, 318
  description of, 319
Perseus, 24, 28, 318
Philemon, 55
Phone sex, 203–205
Physical symptoms, 41, 296–297
Picture of Dorian Gray, The
    (Wilde), 3
Plato, 217
Poe, Edgar Allan, 108
Pollux, 217, 223
Pornography, 203–205
Poseidon, 63, 94, 96, 231
  description of, 320
Positive traits, 12, 46
Power shadows, 48, 49
  dating and, 131, 137–139
  friendship and, 240–242
  marriage and, 200–203
  romance and, 166–168
  work and, 271–275
Premature ejaculation, 132
Primal trust, 91
Procrustes, 117
Projection, 40, 46, 48, 65, 146–149,
    160–163
  breakdown of, 164–166
  splitting, 207–208
Projective identification, 153, 201
Prometheus, 268
  description of, 320
Promise Keepers, 179
Psyche, 73, 144, 145, 172, 176, 318
  description of, 320

Psychiatrists, 11
Psychosomatic disorders, 4
Psychotherapy, 10, 44
  current trends in, 12
Puer-puella aeternus (eternal youth),
  16, 33, 34, 96–100, 123, 155, 232,
  270–271, 282, 302–303, 319

Racism, 7, 68
  friendship and, 221, 238, 239,
  241–243
Rage, 4, 18, 47, 59, 118
Raine, Kathleen, 294
Real, Terence, 66, 67
Regression, 48
Rejection, fear of, 115, 204–205
Relationships (*see* Dating; Marriage;
  Romance)
Remus, 317
Repression, 46, 77, 107
Retirement, 284
Rhea, 63, 318, 320
Rilke, Rainer Maria, 3, 57, 86, 289
Roethke, Theodore, 280
Roller-coaster ride, 158–159, 185, 187,
  190, 203, 213, 216, 254
Romance, 111–112, 144–176, 181
  archetypal perspective on,
  172–173
  breakdown of projection,
  164–166
  compensation period, 149–154
  end of relationship, 173–175
  partners as gods, 159–164
  partners as parents, 154–159
  power shadows and, 166–168
  projection and, 146–149
  redefining successful relationship,
  175–176
  sexual shadows and, 168–172
Romulus, 317
Rubin, Lillian, 218
Rumi, Jelaluddin, 110, 305
Rutter, Peter, 276

Sadness, 47, 80
Salem witch-hunts, 54
Satinover, Jeffrey, 302
Security, 278
Sekhmet, 160
Self-blame, 76, 114
Self-centeredness, 12
Self-esteem, 3, 73, 75, 83, 84, 201
Self-hatred, 21, 46, 68, 77, 82, 114,
  204
Self-medication, 48
Self-reflective attitude, 14, 15
Semele, 318
Senex (rigid old man), 33, 34, 94–96,
  99, 232, 259, 260, 286, 287, 318
Seth, 160
Seven Deadly Sins, 53
Sex, addiction to, 11
Sex in therapy, 276–277
Sexism, 64, 221, 238
Sexual desire, 132
Sexual harassment, 275–276
Sexual shadows, 48–50
  childhood sexual abuse and, 75–82
  dating and, 131–135
  friendship and, 235–237
  marriage and, 203–210
  at midlife, 284–285
  romance and, 168–172
  work and, 275–277
Shadow-boxing (*see* Romance)
Shadow characters, identification of,
  311–314
Shadow-dancing (*see* Marriage)
Shadow marriage, 21, 198–200
Shadow-work, defined, 18
"Shadow-Work Handbook, A," 15, 39,
  308–316
Shakti, 172
Shame, 3, 4, 30–40, 46, 51, 64–65, 80,
  84, 169, 171
  and single person, 113–115
Shelley, Percy Bysshe, 215
Shiva, 172

Short-term treatment, 12
Siblings, 72–75
Single-parent households, 58, 179
Sirens, 309, 311
Sisyphus, 250–251, 279
Slavery, 54
Solzhenitsyn, Aleksandr, 8
Somaticization, 46
Soul friendship, 222
Soulful work, 248–249
  loss of, 250–252
Stealing, 4, 39, 85, 86
Stein, Murray, 178, 181, 286
Storgé, 61
Strategies of adaptation, 10
Sufi tales, 8, 18, 112, 256–257
Suicide, teen, 58
Superego, 16
Superiority, 237–239
Suppression, 46

Teen pregnancy, 58
"Tell-Tale Heart, The" (Poe), 108
Terminator, 37
Terminology, 15
Themis, 72
Theseus, 290
Thieves, 39, 85, 86
Third Body, 21, 181–186, 188, 190,
  197, 203, 222, 223
Titans, 63
Triangles, family, 60
Twain, Mark, 240

Unamuno, Miguel de, 247
Unconscious, Freud and Jung on, 10
Unemployment, 255

Virgin, 142
Vivianne, 172
Von Franz, Marie-Louise, 98

Wife battering, 58, 67,
  192–194
Wilde, Oscar, 3
Williams, Tennessee, 101
Witch, 202–203
Withdrawal, 158
Withholding behavior,
  202–203
Wolff, Toni, 234–235
Women's movement, 122, 137
Woodman, Marion, 28, 90, 297
Woolf, Virginia, 301
Work, 22, 247–279
  archetypal perspective on,
    268–271
  collaborations and, 266–268
  family patterns and, 261–265
  midlife and, 283–284
  money shadows and, 277–279
  nuturing soul, 252–255
  power shadows and, 271–275
  redefining successful, 279
  sexual shadows and, 275–277
  workaholism, 5, 47, 258–261
Workaholism, 5, 47, 258–261

Yahweh, 160

Zeus, 16, 24, 63, 104, 121, 141,
  172, 179, 210, 217, 231,
  268–269, 282, 295,
  317–319
  description of, 320

About the Authors

CONNIE ZWEIG, Ph.D., is a Jungian psychotherapist who specializes in shadow-work, as well as creative and spiritual issues. The former executive editor of J. P. Tarcher, Inc., she has written for *Esquire*, *Omni*, the *Los Angeles Times*, the *Christian Science Monitor*, *Psychology Today*, and *Spring: A Journal of Archetype and Culture*. She is coeditor of the bestselling collected volume *Meeting the Shadow: The Hidden Power of the Dark Side of Human Nature* and founder of The Institute for Shadow-work and Spiritual Psychology in the Los Angeles area.

STEVE WOLF, Ph.D., a clinical psychologist, developed shadow-work as an integration of twenty-five years of experience with psychology, mysticism, martial arts, and storytelling. He has held trainings in corporations, schools, and prisons and offers ongoing workshops and individual and couples psychotherapy. He lives with his wife and son and maintains his therapy practice in Los Angeles.

An Invitation

We would like to extend an invitation to our readers to do individual, couple, or group shadow-work. We can envision a network of leaderless groups of partners and friends who join together to form a local learning community, to care for one another with authenticity and soul. If you're interested in shadow-work seminars, professional training, or psychotherapy, please call us at our toll-free number.

Call Connie at 1-800-484-9962 (hear tone, then press 3104).
Call Steve at 1-888-myshadow (or 888-697-4236).

Or see our Web site
http://www.myshadow.com

Or e-mail us at:
swolf@myshadow.com
czweig@myshadow.com